KV-637-976

CUSTOM, IMPROVEMENT AND THE LANDSCAPE IN EARLY MODERN BRITAIN

Custom, Improvement and the Landscape in Early Modern Britain

Edited by
RICHARD W. HOYLE
University of Reading, UK

ASHGATE

Published by

Ashgate Publishing Limited
Wey Court East
Union Road
Farnham
Surrey, GU9 7PT
England

Ashgate Publishing Company
Suite 420
101 Cherry Street
Burlington
VT 05401-4405
USA

www.ashgate.com

British Library Cataloguing in Publication Data

Custom, improvement and the landscape in early modern Britain.
1. Agriculture – Great Britain – History – 16th century. 2. Agriculture – Great Britain – History – 17th century. 3. Agriculture – Great Britain – History – 18th century. 4. Land use, Rural – Great Britain – History – 16th century. 5. Land use, Rural – Great Britain – History – 17th century. 6. Land use, Rural – Great Britain – History – 18th century. 7. Sociology, Rural – Great Britain – History – 16th century. 8. Sociology, Rural – Great Britain – History – 17th century. 9. Sociology, Rural – Great Britain – History – 18th century. 10. Landscape changes – Great Britain – History. I. Hoyle, R. W. (Richard W.)
333.7'615'0941-dc22

Library of Congress Cataloging-in-Publication Data

Custom, improvement, and the landscape in early modern Britain / [edited by] Richard W. Hoyle.
p. cm. ISBN 978-1-4094-0052-3 (hardcover) 1. Land use, Rural—England—History. 2. Landscapes—England—History. 3. Landscape changes—England—History. 4. Landlord and tenant—England—History. 5. Agriculture—England—History. 6. Country life—England—History. 7. Human ecology—England—History. 8. England—Rural conditions. 9. England--Economic conditions. 10. England—Environmental conditions.
I. Hoyle, R. W. (Richard W.)
HD604.C87 2010
307.1'41209410903—dc22

2010045028

ISBN 9781409400523 (hbk)

Printed and bound in Great Britain by the MPG Books Group, UK

Contents

List of Figures and Tables

Figures

Tables

Notes on Contributors

Julie Bowring is a PhD candidate in History at Yale University.

Heather Falvey is the post-doctoral research assistant on the project 'The Social Topography of a Rural Community: Chilvers Coton, Warwickshire, *c.*1650–1700' and is editorial assistant for the *Economic History Review.*

Henry R. French is Professor of Social History at the University of Exeter, and reviews editor of *Agricultural History Review.* He is author of *The Middle Sort of People in Provincial England, 1600–1750* (2007).

Elizabeth Griffiths has written extensively on the agrarian history of seventeenth- and eighteenth-century Norfolk. She is an honorary Research Fellow at the University of Exeter and co-author, with Professor Mark Overton, of *Farming to Halves: The Hidden History of Sharefarming in England from Medieval to Modern Times* (2009).

Richard W. Hoyle is Professor of Rural History at the University of Reading, and editor of *Agricultural History Review.*

Briony McDonagh is currently a Leverhulme early career fellow in the School of Geography, University of Nottingham. She was previously a Research Fellow on the Arts and Humanities Research Council (AHRC)-sponsored Landscape and Enclosure project at the University of Hertfordshire.

Alasdair Ross is Director of the Centre for Environmental History and Policy at the University of Stirling.

Bill Shannon is an honorary Research Fellow at Lancaster University, and is currently researching the extensive corpus of pre-1650 large-scale manuscript maps of Lancashire from the perspective of landscape and agrarian history.

Paul Warde is Reader in Early Modern History at the University of East Anglia, and the author of *Ecology, Economy and State Formation in Early Modern Germany* (2005).

Nicola Whyte is a Lecturer in History at the University of Exeter (Cornwall campus), and author of *Inhabiting the Landscape: Place, Custom and Memory, 1500–1800* (2009). Her research and teaching interests focus on the landscape and the environmental and social history of Britain in the post-medieval period.

Introduction: Custom, Improvement and Anti-Improvement

*R. W. Hoyle**

Custom and improvement are linked together like chalk and cheese, sweet and sour, gin and tonic. They are not bipolar opposites and yet in a strange way one is the antithesis of the other. Custom is perceived as anti-modern, indeed, backward-looking. Improvement is seen to be a process of modernization. It is the desirable sweeping away of the irrational and inefficient practice of the past. To improve attracted applause, for improvement was seen to be a public benefit: it might even have been a responsibility placed on man by biblical injunction.[1] Not to improve was reprehensible, a denial of this duty, a wasting of God-given possibilities. Both might be characterized as casts of mind: the one believing past practice to be a guide to present observance, the other believing in the promise of future achievement. The idea of improvement was never subjected at the time to the critique it deserved, but many people expressed reservations about improvement as it affected them, and sometimes it attracted resistance, occasionally violent opposition. Hence we can talk of a streak of anti-improvement sentiment within society, even a fear of improvement.

Seen from a British and Irish perspective, the historiography of custom and improvement in the early modern period is curiously uneven. Custom has been the subject of much scholarly endeavour in England[2] but has not been a significant factor in history writing in either Scotland or Ireland. As Houston shows, custom was alien to Scottish legal thought, the exact reverse to its place

---

* I am grateful to Liz Griffiths, Alasdair Ross and Paul Warde for reading the introduction, but especially to Heather Falvey for an acute reading and providing additional references.

1 See, for instance, Sir Keith Thomas, *Man and the Natural World: Changing Attitudes in England, 1500–1800* (London, 1984), pp. 14–15.

2 Recent interest in custom may be said to have started with E. P. Thompson's *Customs in Common* (London, 1991), esp. his ch. 3, 'Custom, Law and Common Right'. Recent work includes A. Fox, *Oral and Literate Culture in England, 1500–1700* (Oxford, 2000); A. Wood, 'Custom and the social organisation of writing in early modern England', *Trans. Royal Historical Society*, 6th ser., 9 (1999); and A. Wood, 'The place of custom in plebeian political culture: England 1550–1800', *Social Hist.* 22 (1997), pp. 46–60.

in English jurisprudence.[3] Both countries lacked customary forms of land tenure until the emergence of tenant right in early nineteenth-century Ireland. Custom was therefore unable to act as a counterweight to the landlord interest within the Scottish and Irish village in the way it did in England. But both Scotland and Ireland saw movements of reform which looked to 'improve' rural society and economy, and the word 'improvement' has been used by historians of both nations in ways which the English have largely eschewed.[4] Conversely, England had its enclosure movements and its agricultural revolution(s), but these phrases have little currency in those countries which underwent 'improvement'. Indeed, within England, improvement as a historical phenomenon has often been located after our period, in the late eighteenth or early nineteenth centuries.[5]

We might usefully divide improvement into four different forms of behaviour, all of which might coincide and be elements in a campaign 'of improvement'. As Warde shows, the usages tend to develop sequentially.

The first is institutional change to enable a lord or landlord to recover his proper dues. Obviously what a landlord regards as a fair return for the lease of his land might be seen by his tenant as an oppressive burden. Improvement in this sense might involve the change of tenancy arrangements, the eviction of tenants, the enclosure of ground, the revival of lost rents. This is the sense in which improvement is understood in the sixteenth century.

Second, improvement can be the ambition to change the landscape by transforming land which seemed to be little used (lowland or highland common, woodland and freshwater or salt marsh) into land suitable for intensive (normally arable) farming regimes. In this sense, improvement continues to the present day,

---

3 R. A. Houston, 'Custom in context: medieval and early modern Scotland and England', *Past and Present* 211 (2011), pp. 35–76. I am grateful to Professor Houston for answering my enquiry about custom in Scotland with a copy of his paper.

4 For instance, N. T. Phillipson and R. Mitchison (eds), *Scotland in the Age of Improvement: Essays in Scottish History in the Eighteenth Century* (Edinburgh, 1970) or T. M. Devine, 'A Conservative People? Scottish Gaeldom in the Age of Improvement', in T. M. Devine and J. R. Young (eds), *Eighteenth-Century Scotland* (East Linton, 1999), pp. 225–36. For an up-to-date overview, C. McKean, 'Improvement and Modernisation in Everyday Enlightenment Scotland', in Elizabeth Foyster and Christopher A. Whatley (eds), *A History of Everyday Life in Scotland, 1600–1800* (Edinburgh, 2010), pp. 51–82. For Ireland, see most recently Toby Barnard, *Improving Ireland? Projects, Prophets and Profiteers, 1641–1786* (Dublin, 2008) but also works such as D. Dickson, *Old World Colony: Cork and South Munster, 1630–1830* (Cork, 2005), ch. 6. Improvement is a contemporary coinage, as, for instance, in The Honourable the Society of Improvers in the Knowledge of Agriculture in Scotland, founded in 1723, or Allan Ramsey's poem, 'The Pleasures of Improvements in Agriculture' of the same year.

5 Asa Briggs, *The Age of Improvement, 1783–1867* (London, 1959); Sarah Tarlow, *The Archaeology of Improvement in Britain, 1750–1850* (Cambridge, 2007).

often in ways which we deplore. Seventeenth-century English improvers would surely have applauded the progressive felling of the Amazon rainforest and yet we are well aware that the act is damaging and the rewards trivial by comparison. Improvement, in this and many historical senses, is despite the rhetoric to the contrary, driven not by the needs of the commonwealth but by the opportunities for private gain which it allowed. Improvement in this second sense of the word is undertaken for private profit and advantage even if it often has the rhetoric of public benefit associated with it: we have an instinctive sympathy with those who have been displaced by the juggernaut of improvement.

In a third sense improvement can be the intensification of farming practice by new techniques, new crops and rotations. In this sense improvement is something that can be approved of: it was, in the words of a tract we shall mention later, 'bread for the poor'. Past agricultural innovation and improvement is what sustains the world today – and in this sense it is 'a good'. But improvement brings its own problems: of rural depopulation, environmental degradation and even ecological disaster. And there is a thin line between production for an adequate sufficiency and overproduction. Improvement offers a challenge to customary agricultural regimes, established rotations, set quotas of animals and the principle of levancy and couchancy.

Fourth, and this is not an area discussed in this book, improvement in Scotland and Ireland could also include the establishment of towns, markets and infrastructure such as harbours; and the provision of work for the inhabitants of an estate, notably, in the eighteenth century, linen weaving.[6] Elsewhere though, improvement could take the form of a marked – and welcome – rural depopulation.[7]

I

Custom is an understood set of rules which govern some aspect of behaviour. As we noted, its key feature is that it draws on past practice to guide current practice. Custom is therefore based on precedent and a belief that the tried and tested ways of the past are a guide to the ways of the future. It could regulate any aspect

---

6 For flax growing and linen weaving projects, see Barnard, *Improving Ireland?*, pp. 151–2, 172–3; Dickson, *Old World Colony*, pp. 203–9; H. Hamilton (ed.), *Life and Labour on an Aberdeenshire Estate* (Aberdeen, 1946), pp. xxxiv–xl.

7 As, for instance, in the Highland and Lowland clearances, but there is accumulating evidence that early modern English enclosures were depopulating, even in the eighteenth century: see Stephen Thompson, 'Parliamentary enclosure, property, population and the decline of classical Republicanism in eighteenth-century Britain', *Historical J.* 51 (2008), pp. 621–42.

of social organization, not merely the relationship between lord and tenant or the conduct of farming, but also the rating of a parish, the selection of its officers and the conduct of weddings and funerals. Custom could permeate the family. The treatment of widows and children could be in accordance with customary rules.[8] Access to mineral rights could be governed by custom in mining areas.[9] The customs which concern us here – those relating to tenancy and farming – are but a part of a much wider range of forms of customary behaviour which governed the medieval and early modern village. Because of their economic value, and the ways in which they were placed under pressure, it is customs relating to property which are most contested and most fully recorded.

What was at stake can be quickly explained. Custom served to limit a lord's income from his tenants. In its fullest form, a customary estate allowed the tenants to buy and sell their tenements, bequeath and inherit them, and sublet them. It involved a progressive loss of control by the lord over his land so that, over time, the use-rights of the tenants came to be more important than his ownership of the land. As the customary tenant's outgoings to his lord were relatively fixed, increased agricultural profit remained in his hands. If the tenant sublet, then it was he – and not his lord – who received a market rent from the occupiers of the land.

In a static agricultural society, in which prices were fixed and outputs broadly unchanging, this might not matter. In these circumstances it might also be a matter of small importance if rents were paid in labour or tenancies took the form of sharecropping. But in a society which was rapidly changing and undergoing price inflation, custom brought substantial financial penalties to the landlord. We must remember that rents had often fallen in the fifteenth century, but as the demand for land increased with renewed population growth, there was every hope – as lords might see it – that rents would increase once more. Any expectation that lords would quickly claw back some or all of their lost income was dashed by Henry VIII's inflation of the 1540s when the currency was debased to generate revenue to finance his wars in Scotland and France. As customary rents were fixed, real income was catastrophically undermined. Lords therefore had a double incentive to try to increase their income: they needed to claw back their historic losses as well as those of the 1540s whilst accessing the increased value of land and the evident prosperity of their tenants

[8] For instance, the testamentary custom of the province of York: G. G. Alexander, 'The custom of the Province of York: a chapter in the history of wills and intestacies', *Thoresby Soc.* 28 (1928), pp. 417–30.

[9] See here A. Wood, *The Politics of Social Conflict: The Peak Country, 1520–1770* (Cambridge, 1999); also J. A. Buckley, *The Bailiff of Blackmoor by Thomas Beare* (Camborne, 1994).

(as famously described by William Harrison).[10] If they were locked into customary relationships, there was nothing they could do about the annual rent; but they could try to increase their income by charging higher fines on the change of tenant. But custom might, at an extreme, hold that only notional fines were liable to be paid, or that fines were fixed in a devaluing currency. Lords therefore had every reason to want to escape from these customary relationships into market relationships, marked by the lease, in which the tenant had a finite term in his land and paid rents and fines determined by negotiation in the light of market conditions.

It is important to understand how custom came to be recorded. Custom was, in effect, an oral medium. It was memory. Custom was what people had experienced for themselves or understood to have been the case in the past. The adage was that a custom was good when it had existed from before the memory of man – that it had started before the recollection of anyone living. For this reason the testimony of the old was especially valuable in proving a custom. But custom could also be chronologically shallow. Peasant thinking on this can be seen in the Mousehold articles of 1549 and the Norfolk petition tentatively dated to 1553. The former sought rents to be returned to the levels of 1485, in one sense perhaps an arbitrary date sufficiently far beyond memory to be a safe datum.[11] (The government conceded that rents should be fixed at the level of 1509 in a letter to the Norfolk commons.) The Norfolk petition complains of the practice of expelling tenants from lands which had been held as demesne copyholds for 30 or 40 years, the implication being that this was a sufficient period of time for a customary estate to have developed.[12] It is noticeable that in

---

10 William Harrison, *The Description of England: The Classic Contemporary Account of Tudor Social Life*, ed. G. Edelen (Washington DC, 1968), pp. 200–204. This section summarizes an area I have treated at greater length in my 'Rural Economies under Stress: "a world so altered"', in S. Doran and N. Jones (eds), *The Elizabethan World* (Abingdon, 2010), pp. 439–57. For an example of a landlord shifting from customary to leasehold tenancies, R. W. Hoyle, 'The management of the estates of the earls of Derby, 1575–1640: some new sources', *Northern Hist.* 29 (2002), pp. 25–36.

11 Fletcher and MacCulloch suggest that the commons looked 'back to the 1480s as a golden age before inflation and rack-renting began'. A. Fletcher and D. MacCulloch, *Tudor Rebellions* (Harlow, 5th edn, 2008), p. 85. What is less clear is the extent to which 1485 was also chosen as marking a change of dynasty, i.e. the date was an implicit criticism of the Tudors. I owe this point to Heather Falvey.

12 Fletcher and MacCulloch, *Tudor Rebellions* p. 157; E. H. Shagan, 'Protector Somerset and the 1549 rebellions: new sources and new perspectives', *English Historical Rev.* 114 (1999), p. 55; R. W. Hoyle, 'Agrarian agitation in mid-sixteenth century Norfolk: a petition of 1553', *Historical J.* 44 (2001), pp. 226–7, 230, 234 and 237.

the aftermath of Kett's revolt, the justices resolved that 60 years' usage made a good copyhold.[13]

The telescoped view of custom can be seen in my chapter on Taverner in North Elmham in which what the tenants of the manor (or at least some of them) held to be custom was defeated by witnesses with a longer recollection. They were able to show that a permissive custom in the 1560s had replaced a much more restrictive one which had applied the 1520s and 1530s. This, in turn, leads to two further points. The first is that where manorial supervision grew lax, the tenants quickly moved to claim advantageous customs. It seems likely that this is a characteristic feature of manors which passed out of the control of well-managed monastic or episcopal estates into the hands of the Crown or absentee landlords in the 1530s and 1540s. The second, which the case of North Elmham well illustrates, is the essential flexibility of custom: that custom could mutate very quickly in new circumstances when it favoured the tenants. Custom was therefore dynamic, perhaps changing in line with the consensus within the tenant community of what was most equitable at any given moment. Lords could play the same game. French and Hoyle showed how the Harlakendens, lords of the manors of Earls Colne and Colne Priory (Essex), attempted to create a custom of timber rights which favoured the lord and denied the tenants' rights.[14]

This all argues for a view of custom as an amorphous set of rules that might twist and change over time and which therefore contained within it its own uncertainties. This may be to go too far, but there is certainly a tension within custom between the patina of antiquity, the 'beyond the memory of man' element (the legal criteria which underpinned custom), and the adoption of recent practice as custom. That said, custom was not left to chance. In her chapter, Nicola Whyte shows how people could be deliberately told about customary uses of the landscape. It was also possible for custom to be encapsulated in rhymes, as Heather Falvey shows, some of which came to be recorded in writing. And this brings us to a key question about custom: its difficult relationship with the written text.[15] Tenants who saw their custom as being under pressure might see the creation of custumals as being a way to protect what they had

13 In 1552: Sir John Baker (ed.), *The Reports of William Dalison, 1552–58* (Selden Soc. 124, 2007), p. 7. This decision left copyholders vulnerable to disputes over the rate of fines in which much older precedents might continue to be employed (as we will see subsequently).

14 H. R. French and R. W. Hoyle, *The Character of English Rural Society: Earls Colne, 1550–1750* (Manchester, 2007), pp. 147–53.

15 This is unconsciously encapsulated in a memorandum issued by a former vice chancellor of the University of Reading on 19 May 1994. Headed 'Relationships between staff and students', the vice chancellor 'confirmed for Heads of Department and other staff the University's *long-standing but unwritten* [my italics] attitude to relationships between staff and students'. Three

by freezing it in its most advantageous form. The difficulty, as the account of Taverner shows all too clearly, was that custumals were ultimately in the lord's gift. A custumal which was the tenants' alone lacked any strength or standing. Exactly the same problem arose with the voluminous writings of Falvey's man Bradshaw. There is something highly irregular about the deputy steward of the manor duplicating the manorial court rolls as an independent record of the court's business which would be accessible to the tenants. It is far from clear what force this second record would have in law although, as Falvey shows, Bradshaw's writings were still being cited before the courts as a record of the custom of the manor even most of 200 years after his death. Of course, where the tenants did have documents in their hands that supported their customs, they could be alleged to be the lord's records which had been pilfered from his archive. Both Hoyle's and Falvey's chapters raise questions of the possession of documents by tenants. They relate to a larger struggle to control the court rolls of the manor which, in some manors, seem to have been in the possession of the tenants – as at Bosham (Sussex), where they were in a chest in the manor house which could only be opened with two keys, one in the hands of the steward and the other held on behalf of the tenants.[16] As Whittle has pointed out, in a reverse of late fourteenth-century attitudes, by the mid-sixteenth century the manorial court's records were seen as the guarantee of tenant customs rather than the lord's weapon against the tenants.[17]

Lords were well advised to eschew custumals as they served to tie their hands in the future. But lords' distaste for the written record could also be turned to their fiscal advantage as a custumal could be sold to the tenants for a price. This might be a win-win situation for the lord. Custumals of this sort are negotiated, so the level of fines established in them might be larger than that previously claimed by the tenants, and the tenants might also have paid a composition to the lord for his agreement.[18] As an example of this, take the so-called 'Bosham Bible'. In 1564–65 the tenants of Henry Lord Berkeley's manor of Bosham, fearing

---

clauses followed which codified in writing the previously unwritten attitude. I am grateful to Stephen Taylor for letting me have his copy as he cleared out his office.

16 A. Fox, 'Custom, Memory and the Authority of Writing', in P. Griffiths, A. Fox and S. Hindle, *The Experience of Authority in Early Modern England* (Basingstoke, 1996), pp. 101–2; and for Bosham, The National Archives (TNA), C 78/320, no. 4.

17 Jane Whittle, 'Peasant Politics and Class Consciousness: The Norfolk Rebellions of 1381 and 1549 Compared', in C. Dyer, P. Coss and C. Wickham (eds), *Rodney Hilton's Middle Ages: An Exploration of Historical Themes* (*Past and Present* Supp., 2, 2007), pp. 243–4.

18 Jane Whittle, *The Development of Agrarian Capitalism: Land and Labour in Norfolk, 1440–1580* (Oxford, 2000), p. 81, discussing the rate of fines at Hevingham Bishops, confirmed in 1543 at 6*d*. an acre, although 4*d*. an acre had been the more usual rate over the previous century.

that Berkeley was looking to undermine their customs, bought a confirmation from him. This gave 50 years of peace in the manor (whilst the Berkeleys' control of the manor slowly ebbed away) until Elizabeth Lady Berkeley challenged the confirmation in Chancery in 1617 and managed to overturn some of its terms on the grounds that the confirmation did not describe the practice of the manor at the time it was made. But one might say that it was never meant to.[19]

Where lords felt that the recording of custom may have given the tenants some advantage, then they might quite consciously leave them to wither unrecorded. It is not too hard to find surveys which make no mention at all of manorial custom. Lords did however have a further source at their disposal on which they could draw to prove or disprove aspects of custom: the manorial court rolls. Court rolls do not explicitly set out the custom of a manor, but some aspects of custom can be deduced from them. Take the rate of entry fines. Tenants preferred to believe that fines were fixed and in the short term this might be so, but over the longer term fines had reflected the demand for land and so had ebbed and flowed with economic conditions. It was not too hard to use extended runs of court rolls to show that there had been no fixed custom of fines. In a prime example of this, in 1607 Lord Chancellor Ellesmere disproved the claim of the tenants of Great Gaddesden to fixed fines by having the court rolls from Edward II onwards read to their representatives in their counsel's office at Gray's Inn.[20] In another early seventeenth-century case, Ellesmere, sitting as Lord Chancellor rather than as plaintiff, reviewed evidence from the court rolls of a Staffordshire manor running back to Henry III and preferred this evidence – which pointed to an uncertain rate of fines – over the tenants' claim that 'the customs of the said manor do lie and rest in the breast of the copyholders'.[21]

---

19 Sir John Maclean (ed.), *The Berkeley Manuscripts: Lives of the Berkeleys ... by John Smyth of Nibley* (3 vols, Gloucester, 1883), vol. 2, pp. 373, 432–3; TNA, C 78/320, no. 4. As with his comments on Taverner (below, p. 40), Kerridge describes this in the worst possible light, seeing the confirmation not as an agreement between lord and tenant but as a fraud perpetrated by the tenants. 'About 1563 the Bosham copyholders corrupted Lord Berkeley's stewards in order to obtain the confirmation of spurious customs ... Over half a century later Chancery found that the copyholders had not obtained this alleged ascertainment of fines from Lord Berkeley on good composition, for he had been wronged by his officers therein ...'. E. Kerridge, *Agrarian Problems in the Sixteenth Century and After* (London, 1969), p. 57. As with Taverner, there is little sign that Kerridge probed beyond the most immediate sources. I hope to describe events here in greater detail in the future.

20 Fox, 'Custom, memory and the authority of writing', p. 100. Again, I hope to write further about Great Gaddesden.

21 TNA, C 78/175 no. 4, discussed in R. B. Manning, *Village Revolts: Social Protest and Popular Disturbances in England, 1509–1640* (Oxford, 1988), p. 140.

Court rolls could also shed light on such matters as the tenants' right to timber by showing them either buying or being granted licences to take timber, or being prosecuted for it. At Petworth the claims of the tenants to use underwood and windfalls – which they illustrated with examples of them exercising those rights – were compared with examples from the fifteenth-century court rolls of tenants being fined for using the same rights. Likewise the right to sublet tenancies paying only a notional fine was disproved from the court rolls, again by showing that fines on subleases had been demanded in the fifteenth century but also earlier in Elizabeth's reign.[22] One might go so far as to say that a competent lawyer with a good long run of court rolls at his disposal could disprove any claim made by the tenants.

This all serves to make custom more complicated than is sometimes allowed and begs the question of how custom – in the broadest sense – was enforced by the tenant community themselves when its terms might be uncertain. The first, and certainly the way hardest to identify in practice, was through the operation of the solidarity of the community itself. We have to envisage that those who did not accept the mind of the community suffered from ostracism and other informal penalties. Where those who refused to toe the line were the bigger tenants of the village, then one imagines that custom itself was imperilled. Some of the individuals described by Nicola Whyte in her chapter were plainly placing their own economic interests before the more general interest of the community. It may be that custom can only really exist where communities are homogenous and egalitarian: bigger tenants, and entrepreneurial tenants only interested in their own advancement, disrupted custom. We tend to take it for granted that most English villages over the later sixteenth century saw a polarization in wealth and landholding. If, as some have suggested, the larger tenants increasingly eschewed an oppositional policy and came to see landowners as their natural allies in the management of the poor and their work force ('incorporation' in the sense meant by Professors Wrightson and Hindle), then custom could well have withered, being neither supported nor enforceable. When Dr Whyte shows us the Elizabethan inhabitants of Norfolk villages attempting to use the court of the Exchequer to enforce the customary use of land, we must recognize that the cause of custom was lost because the consensus within the village which underpinned it had collapsed – a reflection of changing balances of power.

The second way in which custom might be enforced is through the making of by-laws in the manorial court. This plainly implies the conversion of custom to text. In this sense, by-laws stand in the place of statute law to the larger common

---

22 P. Jerrome, *Cloakbag and Common Purse: Enclosure and Copyhold in Sixteenth-Century Petworth* (Petworth, 1979), ch. 6.

law: they amend but also establish penalties for deviations. Manorial by-laws contain a mixture of statements of the general and the highly specific aimed at named individuals. So, in the Giggleswick (Yorkshire) by-laws of 1564, a penalty of 3*s*. 4*d*. was laid on those who did not make their outdykes (the boundary walls between Giggleswick fields and the common) 1½ yards high – this plainly being the customary responsibility of tenants.[23] A fine of twice this rate was levied on anyone who dug pits or holes on the moor and failed to fill them in, and on alehouse keepers who served during the time of divine service. On the other hand, one Richard Burton was ordered to make a path from the kiln to the garth 'in the open time of the year' on pain of 10*s*. The implications of this are largely lost on us, but what we surely have here is a customary rule that there should be such a path at a certain time of the year, and the by-law serves to reinforce it, perhaps making the point that Burton was not meeting customary expectations. In a way by-laws can be read as a sign of a community whose values are in decay: so in the by-laws gathered together in 1602, the Giggleswick court held that anyone who allowed stones to fall off his walls and into the highway to the 'annoyance of passengers' should be fined 3*s*. 4*d*. But by-laws could neither make stones stay on walls nor ensure that they were picked up and the walls rebuilt, unless the community, or at least its politically influential figures, wished them to do so. The permutations of language in the Earls Colne manorial court show how hard it increasingly came to root by-laws in some form of public consent.[24] Nor could they operate without a forum in which transgressors could be prosecuted, and this, in most communities, had to be the manorial court. Without, on the one hand, the support of the manorial lord and his steward, and on the other the subscription of the wealthier tenants of the village, it is hard to see the manorial court working. There is a strong suspicion that some manorial lords saw the manorial court as a rival focus of political authority and were happy to see it wither.[25] In other locations its authority passed to the vestry which might, to a greater or lesser extent, be a closed taxpayers' meeting – but not necessarily one which concerned itself with ditches, or stones in roads.

The third way, of course, was to apply to a higher jurisdiction – Chancery, Requests, one of the regional councils – for injunctions to compel people to adhere to custom.[26] The subject of these injunctions might be manorial lords,

---

23 Printed in Thomas Brayshaw and Ralph M. Robinson, *A History of the Ancient Parish of Giggleswick* (Gloucester, 1932), pp. 83–7.

24 French and Hoyle, *Character of English Rural Society*, pp. 170–71.

25 John Broad, *Transforming English Rural Society: The Verneys and the Claydons, 1660–1820* (Cambridge, 2004), pp. 50–52.

26 For this being done in a very different context, see P. Warde, 'Law, the "commune" and the distribution of resources in early modern German state formation', *Continuity and Change* 17

or other tenants. To embark down this road is almost to admit the declining purchase of custom.

One might say that custom – certainly in its tenurial dimensions – only worked when both sides subscribed to it. There are instances where lords seem to have accepted custom and allowed it to guide their relationships with their tenants. But others rejected it and in this event custom might become the sole possession of the tenants. They might articulate their belief in customary rights in bills to Chancery and Requests when they believed that their custom was being infringed by their lords; but, as we saw, custom could only have credibility when backed by tenant solidarity, and increasingly this could not be guaranteed. If the tenants themselves were split over the character of custom – or even its desirability as a way of regulating relationships – then it had, to all purposes, lost whatever force it might have possessed. Hence one might suggest that sixteenth-century communities generally accepted custom as a guide to behaviour – both internally, but also in their outward-facing relationships with lords – but it progressively atrophied except where it still regulated relationships between lord and tenant. Over time manorial by-laws disappeared together with the courts themselves as functioning instruments of government. Doubtless stones continued to fall off walls, but a system of thought which provided penalties for not putting them back had disappeared.

One further point might be made about custom. There were no clear-cut lines of demarcation between customary tenants and manorial lords: disputes over the terms of customary tenancy were also arguments within the landowning class. By the middle of the sixteenth century (and perhaps some decades earlier) copyhold was considered to be a sufficiently secure form of tenancy for it to be a perfectly satisfactory investment, not so very much different to freehold land. Once a manorial lord had conceded that a copyhold bought by a non-resident could be sublet, then he had lost control of his property. The lord no longer had any direct relationship with the man who tilled the land; nor did he receive rent from him.[27] A copyholding customary tenant in one manor might be the manorial lord of another: in the first manor he might resist the lord's demands as unprecedented and unreasonable; in the other he might be as oppressive as any lord one might meet. Taverner needs to be seen in this context: the leader of resistance to a manorial lord in North Elmham, but as Dr Whyte shows, an unpleasant manorial lord himself in Wighton. Bradshaw has a not dissimilar ambivalence about him: not only a lawyer and deputy steward but also a landowner (it is regrettably not clear on what scale) in Duffield and, one

(2002), pp. 183–211.

27 See here the comments of Mavis Mate, *Trade and Economic Developments, 1450–1550: The Experience of Kent, Surrey and Sussex* (Woodbridge, 2006), pp. 212–13, 231.

assumes, a tenant of the manor of which he was an officer. As with Taverner, his commitment to custom and customary tenure could well be seen as essentially self-serving. And yet my chapter on Taverner does contain suggestions that, in the 1560s at least, the estate officers of a manorial lord should not simply be seen as his hired lackeys, determined to force through a seigneurial agenda to secure greater profits for their employer. There is certainly an appearance that Bradshaw went native, became a renegade and was ultimately removed from his post because his loyalty was to Duffield rather than the Earl of Shrewsbury or even the Duchy of Lancaster. A more nuanced account of change in the countryside would pay greater attention to figures such as Bradshaw and the surveyors and estate officers employed by Henry Lord Cromwell, whose behaviour is described in the chapter on Taverner. It should not be assumed that they were all proto-Nordens.

II

In his contribution to this book discussing the multiple and shifting meanings of the word 'improvement', Paul Warde shows how the phrase was little used in the sixteenth century but how widespread and ultimately debased its usage became in the seventeenth. There is some additional evidence for this in the use of 'improvement' in the titles of printed books as analysed by Tarlow: there are few or none before 1650; fewer than five a decade before 1750; but by the end of the eighteenth century there are two or more a year.[28]

Even if the word itself was little used in the sixteenth century, the implementation of improvement proceeded at some speed. There is growing evidence of enclosure before mid-century and of a tendency to increase rents and fines although the ferocity of the 1549 disturbances may have delayed the raising of rents and fines by a generation. Certainly there was view which saw the disturbances of that year as being stimulated by the greed of landowners and there is some evidence that the generation who lived through 1549 remained aware of the dangers of inflaming the commons.[29] It was only in the next generation – in the second half of Elizabeth's reign – that landowners began to explore the potential of their estates in earnest and to commence an overdue process of modernization – or improvement.[30]

---

[28] Tarlow, *Archaeology of Improvement*, Fig. 1.1 (p. 15). Note that the caption to this figure does not match the figure itself.

[29] See the comments of Philip Gerrard cited in Hoyle, 'Agrarian Agitation', p. 228 and Harrison, *Description of England*, p. 257.

[30] I have discussed this at greater length in my 'Rural economies under stress'.

This took several forms. One of them was the crushing – where possible – of those institutional restraints on landlord income in the form of tenancy relationships which could not yield something akin to market rents. There was therefore a great deal of probing of customary tenancies in the later part of Elizabeth's reign and this in turn generated litigation in Chancery, the Court of Requests and the northern and Welsh councils. As I propose to write about this at length elsewhere, I will say less rather than more about it here, except to note that late Elizabethan landowners had the aid of a new professional, the surveyor. He employed what had originally been a military technology – surveying – to produce measured surveys and, as an added extra, maps, the latter having attracted a disproportionate amount of interest amongst historians to the disadvantage of the former.[31] The landowner now had an independent way of seeing his estates (rather than relying on the self-description of his tenants) which gave him measures of both acreage and value. The whole process of mapping also disclosed land for which no rent was paid and identified possibilities for improvement by the consolidation of land, the extinction of common rights over arable and the enclosure of commons. The surveyor was therefore a company doctor who could be sent to review and audit an asset and make recommendations of how additional revenue could be squeezed from it. The two who wrote most about their work – Robert Johnson and the much better-known John Norden – were both of an improving cast of mind even if they made little use of the word. Johnson's tracts on the reform of the Crown estates[32] and Norden's *Surveyor's Dialogue* show a distinctively modern cast of mind, with the surveyor the purveyor of a professional service which would repay the landowner's investment. It is in this sense that Thomas Wilson wrote in 1600 that gentlemen had 'become good husbands and know well how to improve their lands to the uttermost'.[33]

Other than the reform of tenure, the other process of improvement was a land grab by lords. H. R. French shows how urban commons were progressively whittled away and how in some cases the urban populace were convinced that town councils did this to feather-bed their own members. We, perhaps

31 P. D. A. Harvey, 'Estate Surveyors and the Spread of the Scale-Map in England, 1550–1580', *Landscape Hist.* 15 (1993), pp. 37–49; A. McRae, *God Speed the Plough: The Representation of Agrarian England, 1500–1660* (Cambridge, 1996), ch. 6.

32 I planned an edition of Johnson's writings a long time ago and might yet see it through to fruition. The most convenient text of his letters is Bodleian Library, Oxford, Perrot Ms 7, fos. 49r–86v.

33 F. J. Fisher (ed.), 'The State of England, Anno Domini 1600, by Thomas Wilson', *Camden Miscellany* XVI (Camden, 3rd ser., 52, 1936), p. 19; J. Norden, *The Surveyor's Dialogue* (1618 edn, repr. 1979).

appreciating better the financial pressures under which councils operated, might be more forgiving of the abolition of customary use rights. Custom, even when backed by weight of numbers, proved to be an inadequate protection for the poor commoners' rights.

If the extent of urban commons perhaps comes as a surprise, it seems likely that we have also understated the degree of rural waste enclosure in the sixteenth century. In his chapter, Bill Shannon shows the extent of the enclosure of the low-lying mosses of Lancashire, suggesting that this proceeded at some pace until the limits on what could be achieved without sophisticated drainage were reached in the early seventeenth century. In law, the process of drainage and enclosure was authorized by the law of approvement by which a lord could exercise his right to enclose wasteland provided that sufficient was left to meet his tenants' needs. Approvement was grounded in the Statute of Merton (1236), but its importance was such that it was confirmed by statute in 1549. While Shannon has now alerted us to the importance of approvement in a lowland context, it remains to be established whether it was also important in the improvement of wastes either as the legal underpinning to seigneurial initiatives which the commoners had to accept or for more consensual enclosures in which some of the land was allocated to the commoners themselves. In this context it is helpful to consider briefly a Lancashire Star Chamber case from the very first years of the seventeenth century concerning an upland enclosure in the manor of Upper or Nether Wyresdale undertaken by Sir Thomas Gerard.[34] Exactly what happened here is not material, except to say that the enclosure was delayed by repeated riots by some of the commoners of the manor. The whole matter descended into acrimony and a Star Chamber suit. In his bill to Star Chamber, Gerard based his right to enclose very firmly on the law of approvement. Having said that there were 8,000 acres of unenclosed commons in the manor, he continued:

> the which said common or waste grounds being much more than was or is sufficient for the tenants of the said manor and the commoners therein, your subject by the laws and statutes of England may improve and enclose so much of the said common or waste grounds as [he] pleaseth without the consent of any of the tenants or commoners of the said manor (leaving sufficient of the said common or waste grounds to lie in common for the tenants and commoners together) with convenient ways and passages unto their freeholds.

This was approvement even if the word was never mentioned. In fact Gerard chose to proceed consensually (as we shall see).

[34] This is discussed in Manning, *Village revolts*, pp. 115–16.

It is Shannon's first achievement to have alerted us both to the importance of this word, which can all too easily be overlooked or even misread, and so to the legal authority which underpinned much early modern enclosing activity. His second is to make us appreciate that enclosure could take place on a large scale without leaving much trace in the public records. This has important consequences for future research. A generation ago, Wordie argued that sixteenth-century enclosure was unimportant because it prompted little protest or comment.[35] Shannon shows that the absence of noise does not mean that nothing of note happened, and both he and French give us reason to reconsider the extent and chronology of sixteenth-century enclosure. But we should not see urban and rural enclosure as distinct processes. An interesting rhyme circulating in Cambridge in 1549 even thought that the enclosure of urban commons might be an encouragement to rural landowners to try the same:

> For Cambridge baliffs truly
> Give ill example to the country
> Their commons likewise to engross
> And from poor men it to enclose.[36]

Why there should have been so little objection to approvement remains slightly mysterious. Perhaps we need to accept that sixteenth-century enclosure generally generated little comment except in the special circumstances of depopulating enclosure, when arable open fields were enclosed and converted to pasture – with a corresponding loss of employment and, inevitably, depopulation. One might go further and say that our mistake with enclosure is to see it as inevitably landlord-driven, and imposed on the commoners. To refer again to Nether Wyresdale, Gerard claimed in his Star Chamber bill that some of the tenants approached him with a request that some of the wastes be improved:

> being such as by manurance and good husbandry might be made much more profitable to the commonwealth than at that time they were, and that many people by that means be set to work and that divers of such tenants who had not in their occupations ground sufficient to set one plough on work should by these means be much enabled in their estates.

---

35 J. R. Wordie, 'The chronology of English enclosure: a reply', *Economic History Rev.* 37 (1984), p. 560.

36 Cited in A. Wood, *The 1549 Rebellion and the Making of Early Modern England* (Cambridge, 2007), p. 60 (the spelling is modernized here).

This coupled the current preoccupations of shortage of arable and provision for the poor. Enclosure was further justified because it enabled more people to do their (military) service to the queen. As it was to everyone's benefit, Gerard was only too happy to agree that 'a convenient part of the said large and spacious commons or waste grounds should be improved and converted into tillage for the good of the commonwealth and for the good of the tenants'. Whether any of this happened in the way Gerard suggested might be doubted; but if not wholly right, the story he spun, of the tenants taking the initiative and using the language of improvement, was plausible enough to pass in Star Chamber.[37]

III

The speech Gerard places in the mouths of his tenants shows how improvement had ceased to be a matter of the expropriation of communal resources for private profit and was now valued for its public benefits as well. From here it was a small leap to asking why unimproved land should be allowed to remain in that state when the public advantage in improvement was so obvious and so great. The survival of unimproved land increasingly came to be seen as an affront to civilized behaviour and one which needed to be condemned. Norden, in his *Surveyor's Dialogue*, reprimanded his foil, the bailiff, for tolerating a piece of ground:

> to lie idle and waste and foster nothing but bogs, sedges, flags, rushes and such superfluous and noysome weeds, where, if it were duly drained and carefully husbanded, it would make good meadow in short time.[38]

The view that commons and wastes were a resource requiring improvement can be traced from *A Dialogue between Pole and Lupset* of *c.*1530, through Alderman Box writing in *c.*1576, through Norden, Manwood and the other Jacobean commentators on the Crown lands, through Blith and other members of the Hartlib circle in the 1650s, to Defoe in the early years of the eighteenth century.[39]

---

37 The previous quotations are all from Gerard's bill in TNA, STAC 8/153/3. Gerard had already shown himself to be an aggressive landlord and it is far from inconceivable that enclosure was his agenda. Manning, *Village Revolts*, p. 115 attributes the tenants' speech to Gerard.

38 Norden, *Surveyor's Dialogue*, p. 146.

39 The references not otherwise considered in this chapter are Thomas Starkey, *A Dialogue between Pole and Lupset*, ed. T. F. Mayer (Camden, 4th ser., 37, 1989), pp. 99–100; for Alderman Box's proposal to divide and sow common wastes, *c.*1576, R. H. Tawney and E. Power (eds), *Tudor Economic Documents* (3 vols, London, 1924), vol. 2, pp. 72–7; and for the commentators on the

For all of them the landscape was to be exploited, and to fail to do so was to commit an offence. Exactly the same logic could justify the coerced 'civilizing' of the Irish or the expansion into 'vacant' land occupied by Amerindians. As Alasdair Ross shows, a variety of this logic survived as a rhetorical form in Scotland as late as the 1760s.

The reasoning behind this might be based on pragmatic considerations such as providing employment or enhancing the supply of grain to domestic markets, a logic which shades into mercantilism. It might also be associated with the notion that the inhabitants of waste places such as woodlands, fens or levels were themselves idle and uncivilized. On one occasion Norden characterized the inhabitants of forests as suffering from 'idleness, beggary, atheism and consequently all disobedience to God and King' and described the forests as:

> desert forests, chases and wastes, wherein infinite poor yet idle inhabitants have thrust themselves, living covertly, without law or religion, *rudes et refractarii* by nature, among whom are nourished and bred infinite idle fry, that coming ripe grow [into] vagabonds and infect the commonwealth with most dangerous leprosies.[40]

Adam Moore, in *Bread for the poor*, tried to vocalize the attitude of the borderers of commons to explain their idleness and reluctance to work in terms which we would probably describe as a culture of low expectations.[41]

The reform of wastes could therefore not be distinguished from the reform of the civil society which inhabited that landscape and so was a social mission as well. It was also buttressed by theological injunctions which stressed man's duty to tame nature and feed himself. This could come to be an objective of the state. A projector of 1608 asked 'whether it were not fit that the superior power should compel where it is wilful and careless refusal?'.[42] It was reported that it was a matter of national honour for James I that the fens be improved.[43] In the case of King's Sedgemoor, enclosure and drainage was said to be for the good of the commonwealth, the relief of the borders (the inhabitants of the neighbouring villages) as well as the king's revenues. It would also improve the food supply for all of the king's subjects who were reliant on imported foodstuffs.[44] Ultimately

Crown lands, R. W. Hoyle, 'Disafforestation and Drainage', in Hoyle (ed.), *The Estates of the English Crown, 1558–1640* (Cambridge, 1992), pp. 358–63.

40 John St John, *Observations on the land revenue of the crown* (1792), p. 290.

41 Adam Moore, *Bread for the poor and advancement of the English nation promised by the enclosure of wastes and common grounds of England* (1653), pp. 6–8.

42 St John, *Observations on the land revenue*, p. 313.

43 H. C. Darby, *The Draining of the Fens* (2nd edn, Cambridge, 1956), p. 38.

44 TNA, E 112/119/385.

any improvement could be justified in terms of the benefits it provided for the commonwealth. This was almost a matter of definition but it also made it possible for private entrepreneurs interested primarily in their own profit to give their projects a veneer of public utility.

The problem with much of the literature advocating improvement is that it ignores two elementary points. The first is the character and quality of the land which was identified as requiring improvement. Much of it was unimproved for a reason, that is to say, that the prevailing agricultural use of the land was a compromise between what might have been ideal and what was practical. Manwood's proposal for establishing farms in the king's forests (and perhaps more specifically the New Forest) of 1608 makes perfect sense if one ignores the quality of the ground there. It is far from clear that Defoe's proposal of 1709 to establish a new town of Palatine settlers in the New Forest could ever have delivered its promise given the physical environment which he proposed to colonize.[45] The drainage of the fens was made to work, but as Julie Bowring shows in her chapter in this volume, the resulting landscape was far from perfect and those who tried to make a living from it had to cope with persistent winter flooding. In short, seventeenth-century fen drainage operated at the limits of what was technically possible. What emerged was a high-cost, high-maintenance landscape, the problems of which were never resolved until steam-powered drainage became available. Norden dismissed the bailiff when he asked whether the cost of digging fishponds was worth the expenditure,[46] but there is a real sense in which many projects for improvement were paper exercises built on a foundation of unreality, both environmental and fiscal.

The second point which was never given the weight it deserved by the projectors was that the landscapes which seemed empty were in fact owned, and they supported economies which were not by any means backward.[47] Existing property rights therefore had to be ignored or strategies developed to circumvent them. In the case of King's Sedgemoor, the assumption seems to have

45 'Manwood's project for improving the land revenue by improving wastes' [1609], pr. in John St John, *Observations on the land revenue of the crown* (1787), pp. 285–8; for the projected new town in the New Forest, below, pp. 26–7.

46 Norden, *Surveyor's Dialogue*, p. 180.

47 The same approach to land used extensively rather than intensively is still found in the third world. The London newspaper, *The Observer*, carried a story describing the contemporary neo-colonial seizure of land in Africa and quoted at length an Ethiopian exile in London: 'All the land in the Gambella region is utilised. Each community has and looks after its own territory and the rivers and farmlands within it. It is a myth propagated by the government and investors to say that there is wasteland or land that is not utilised in Gambella. The foreign companies are arriving in large numbers, depriving people of land they have used for centuries. There is no consultation with the indigenous population. The deals are done secretly.' *The Observer*, 7 Mar. 2010, p. 28.

been in Elizabeth's reign that the moor belonged to the Crown and the lords of the neighbouring manors had merely encroached on it. The same assumption was made when plans for the drainage of the moor began in earnest in *c.*1618, although this may have been something of a device to force the neighbouring lords to a composition with the Crown's agents.[48] The king's agents in the endeavour to drain Sedgemoor – John Shotbolt, William Bernard and Adam Moore – held that the king 'expected a general concurrence for effect of the service, then a disputation whose it is, or to whom it belongeth', showing the strength of the royal assumption of ownership. Later the same writers moved beyond conventional legal rights to maintain that:

> in this supreme office, of such force are his commands, that he is justly the master also of every his subjects and servants estates, to rule, dispose and order them, for their own and the public weal, where they shall be either negligent or unable to doe that which by his princely care and providence he conceiveth and findeth fit to be done .... he solititeth, endevoureth and comandeth, the effect and accomplishment thereof, for the general weal of them all, and especially of the poorer sort, whose necessities he desireth by all means to see better relieved.

He was like the 'wise master of an household, [who] compell[ed] his servants to cohere and labour [for] the good of the whole family. He sought to take no man's profits but sought to enrich them by his grace and profit'.[49] This claimed a major extension of the king's prerogative powers, conferring a right to improve what no man had improved before. Following this, before the Civil War, projectors argued that their opponents were guilty of *lèse-majesté*: to oppose projectors was to oppose the king himself.[50]

The drainage of the fens posed similar problems to those familiar from Sedgemoor, but on a much larger scale. Here the constellation of property rights within the fenland were overturned first by a sleight of hand which allowed a general project to go ahead, and then the rights and interest of the Bedford consortium were abrogated by the Crown, which established itself as its own undertaker.[51] In all of these instances there is something doubtful about the

---

48 SP 12/276 no. 76 (perhaps connected to SP 12/368, no. 102, *c.*1598); E 112/119/385.

49 British Library (BL), Royal Ms 17A XXXVII, fos. 14r–v. I hope to publish an edition of this tract in the future.

50 C. Holmes, 'Drainers and fenmen: the problem of popular political consciousness in the seventeenth century', in A. Fletcher and J. Stevenson (eds), *Order and Disorder in Early Modern England* (Cambridge, 1985), p. 168.

51 M. A. Knittl, 'The design for the initial drainage of the Great Level of the fens: a historical whodunit in three parts', *Agricultural History Rev.* 55 (2007), pp. 23–50.

Crown's behaviour – a willingness to ignore existing property rights, if not actually to go outside the law in order to advance their agenda. Whilst this was overtly one of improvement, the Crown's fiscal advantage was never far removed from consideration. We can view aspects of this in a number of ways: through the company the Crown kept; through Charles I's own views so far as they can be discovered; and through the Crown's demonstrable actions.

First, we can consider the patent granted to Robert Chivers, gent, in 1637 and renewed in 1639.[52] In early 1637 he petitioned for a grant of the exclusive right for 14 years of his invention for the improving of land and growing hops, and he offered a half of all profits made from the improvement of other men's lands to the Crown for the concession. This was granted in May 1637. Two years later he submitted a new petition citing delays in getting started and asking for a new 14-year patent 'for the manuring and improvement of lands' dated from that moment. In addition, he asked that the patent should confer the right to use 'waters, rivers, water-courses, highways, wastes, moors, marshes, fens, lands, soil and grounds covered or not covered with water of His Majesty's or any of His Majesty's subjects meet for improvement', that is that it should empower Chivers to enter, improve and profit from the land of any individual, paying the Crown a rent for the privilege.[53]

The grant of the patent was backed by an elaborate justificatory case. This began by drawing attention to the growth of population, and then recommended improvement to avoid scarcity and to ensure that prices did not become too high. In order to implement this, Chivers needed 'free liberty without interruption of the owners of the lands to improve what lands he finds meet for improvement'. The unknown author then posed two questions: first, whether Chivers could be authorized by common law, statute law, the prerogative or any act of state to enter the lands of any man and improve them, allocating a third part of the profits to the landowner for their permission; and second, whether the king could take a third part of the profits, and Chivers the final third in recompense of his 'industry, great pains and invention'. These questions were then examined at length using a mixture of scriptural and classical authority to prove the case. The paper's inevitable conclusion was that the king had the right to compel his subjects to use their lands to the greatest advantage of the kingdom, and be remunerated for it. Moreover, statute was unnecessary: the prerogative was sufficient authority to undertake this 'public improvement'. A further tract by one John Cusacke offered additional reasons as to why improvement should

52 Exactly who Chivers was is uncertain. One Robert Chivers of Quemerford in the parish of Calne, Wiltshire, made his will in 1646, probate Aug. 1647. TNA, PROB 11/201, fos. 261v–63r.

53 Bodleian Library, Oxford, Banks Mss, 11/36, 50/36; also TNA, E 214/526.

be undertaken using the authority of the prerogative and concluded with the assertion that to oppose improvement authorized by the prerogative was an act of treason against the king.[54]

The surprising thing is not that such ideas circulated, but that the Crown treated them seriously and were prepared to offer petitioners the sanction of a patent to implement their ideas. The patent amounted to a right to invade private property and improve it for private profit; or, alternatively, it fined the landowner for not undertaking the improvement himself. Whilst the profits would be split three ways (and a process was instituted by which the local Justices of the Peace (JPs) could arbitrate over the improved value of the land), the improved land would at least remain the property of the original owner. Exactly what panacea Chivers had up his sleeve for the improvement of land is not clear: like other patents of this period, the technical processes involved remained confidential to the patentee and the patent never specified them with any clarity. Unfortunately, or perhaps fortunately, it would seem unlikely that Chivers was able to make much use of his patent before the breakdown of order in 1640–41, otherwise we might envisage that the arrival of Chivers and his workmen on some unimproved property, whether owned in severalty or held as common, would have drawn mountains of litigation down on his head. The implication of these writings however is that the monarch had not only the *right* to authorize improvement on private land, but also the *duty* to advance improvement – a duty which stands comparison with and perhaps even parallels the responsibility placed on the prince in Protestant thought to reform religion.

This seems to have been a responsibility which the king accepted. It was expressed in what appears to be a statement of the king's personal attitude to improvement found in a printed broadsheet entitled *Sir John Banks his report to King Charles concerning employing all the poor and idle persons of the nation and concerning the commons, [made in] Anno 1637 when he was Attorney General.*[55] This purports to be the response of Banks to four heads arising out of a discussion between the king and the Earl of Holland. The first of these was:

[54] Bodleian Library, Banks Mss, 48/22, 48/13. For Cusacke see Linda Levy Peck, 'Beyond the pale: John Cusacke and the language of absolutism in early Stuart Britain', *Historical Journal*, 41 (1998), pp. 121–49.

[55] Sheffield University Library, Hartlib Papers, 26/66. This may be a unique copy as it seems not to be noticed in the standard bibliographies or to be included in Early English Books Online (EEBO). Bill Shannon's thesis drew it to my attention and I am grateful to him for supplying a copy from the Hartlib Papers CD-Rom. I am grateful also to Richard Cust for his opinion of the document. I have altered some of the paragraphing in the quotations.

> your majesty taking it for a maxim that idle men and waste lands were the canker of all states and considering how prejudicial they were to this of yours was graciously pleased to propound the finding out of the proper and sovereign remedy thereof in the first place.

To which Banks replied:

> touching the first, whether a full power of administering justice being granted until all parts of your majesty's kingdoms, that the subject might be enabled to follow his proper calling without distraction, might not prove a sovereign remedy for the better employment both of land and men.

He then went on to discuss the treatment of idle men before continuing:

> And touching wastes not employed to the best use, it was humbly conceived that the greatest part of the kingdom consists of commons, fields, moors, wastes and fens producing for the most part a brood of the most idle people of the kingdom, and by consequence the most beggarly, the worst sort of horses cows, and sheep, and in these places you will find no manufactures at all. Nor any child put down to any other trade than fishing or fowling, or following of a sorry horse or cow up and down a common field or a waste.
>
> Now if some one or more men living in such a town and perceiving what benefit improvement would be to the said town, and should desire to effect the same after a proportionable manner for the good of all, yet meeting with some persons refractory, as the best things seldom please the most; what journeys should he be forced to make to London, what moneys and time to expend before he could effect so public a good ...

So Banks proposed the establishment of courts within each county with 'such judges as should be always at leisure to resent [sic] and promote things of this nature'.

The third head asked whether the king had 'the power to ordain such a remedy', to which Banks replied that 'For your Majesties power there is no question, you may do it by commission or by erecting new courts either in parliament or out of parliament.'

This is a perplexing document which appears to have escaped previous attention and deserves a fuller discussion than is possible here. But some points may be made. First, it offers us a view of Charles as being personally concerned to bring about the improvement of his nation. He shared the stereotypical characterization of wastes and fens as being the resort of idle people, and was presumably persuaded of the benefits of improvement. Banks claimed that improved countries were three times more valuable to the country than 'open countries'.

Second, perhaps because the problem was passed to a lawyer, the paper envisages the creation of a system of county courts which would have been empowered to act against people who were seen to be impeding improvement, and so, by implication, courts which would act to drive improvement forwards. In effect, these would have been courts for the reformation of people as well as landscapes.

Third, we can identify a tension, a piece of double thinking within the document so characteristic of improvement: that everyman should be entitled to use his lands as he wished, but only if they were improved; a man whose lands were not improved and who was disinclined to improve them could, in effect, be coerced into improvement by a judicial process. This reflects a subordination of private property rights to the god of improvement, with the court forcing improvement on the reluctant. This tension, moreover, extended into other areas. The Caroline government was also outwardly hostile to the enclosure of arable which it regarded as deleterious because it depopulated the countryside; hence it was not an improvement. The disruption of communities by fen drainage or upland enclosure, however, was an improvement, and the disruption that it brought to them was hardly a matter of regret as they had been, by definition, idle and unproductive. Of course, nothing came of Banks's proposals, and yet they form a fascinating might-have-been from which government retreated, perhaps because of another concern in his paper: whether the remedy might provoke 'some sudden alteration in your state', a fear which Banks dismissed but to which more prudent figures might have attached more weight.

Finally we have the king's actions. We have already referred to the drainage of the fens, a project to which Charles seems to have been personally committed and where he envisaged the creation of a town to be named Charlemont.[56] The royal projects to disafforest and improve forests have been described to a degree, although primarily as adjuncts to discussions of the disorder they provoked.[57] A further example of the cavalier treatment of property rights has been recently been described by Beaver in his account of how, in 1640, the Crown simply denied the commoners their common rights in Windsor Great Park.[58] So there can be little doubt that two successive English monarchs favoured improvement,

---

56 Darby, *Draining of the Fens*, p. 60.

57 Hoyle, 'Disafforestation and drainage'; Buchanan Sharp, *In contempt of All Authority: Rural Artisans and Riot in the West of England, 1586–1660* (Berkeley, 1980), chs 4–8.

58 D. C. Beaver, *Hunting and the Politics of Violence before the English Civil War* (Cambridge, 2008), pp. 114, 117.

not only for its capacity to improve land and people and potential contribution to Crown finance, but also because they espoused, perhaps even encouraged, a fashionable culture of improvement.

There was a rush of publications on improvement in the years immediately after 1649 but following Hindle's identification of 1648–49 as notably hard years,[59] this can probably be attributed as much to renewed concerns over food supply as regime change. The general condemnation of the abuse of prerogative powers in the first months of the Long Parliament and then the Civil War made it impossible for the prerogative to be used as an instrument to force through future improvement. Whilst the Commonwealth government placed fen drainage on a new (statutory) footing and pursued it to a conclusion, the heroic age of the improvement of landscape had drawn to a close. The post-war generation looked to parliament to legislate for improvement. Blith's *English improver* (1649) was dedicated to parliament with a prefatory request that they should remove laws which hindered improvement and establish laws which encouraged it: in the extended version, *English improver improved* (1652), the dedication was to Cromwell and he was enjoined in the same words to be a supporter of improvement, but their hopes were never answered.[60] The idea that the king should lead improvement was by no means dead after the Restoration: as Warde notices, John Evelyn was of this mind.[61]

The early 1650s also saw the publication of a number of tracts which advocated the improvement of commons. There was, for instance, Sylvanus Taylor's *Common Good: or the improvement of commons, forrests and chases by inclosure* (1652). Taylor held that these landscapes could house far more people and advocated dividing the commons four ways: a quarter into smallholdings of 20–40 acres each; a quarter into land for the lord, and the remaining half allocated to the freeholding and copyholding commoners who, once given this land, would improve it and create new farms. As Thirsk remarks, this scheme paid no attention to the suitability of the soil for the arable cultivation which Taylor envisaged.[62] Then there was Adam Moore's *Bread for the poor* of 1653, a more problematical pamphlet than at first sight appears. Moore had been active in the enclosure and drainage of King's Sedgemoor at the end of the 1610s and it quotes in a small way from the tracts circulated at that time. How far it was

59 S. Hindle, 'Dearth and the English Revolution: The Harvest Crisis of 1647–50', in S. Hindle and J. Humphries (eds), *Feeding the Masses: Plenty, Want and the Distribution of Food and Drink in Historical Perspectives* (*Economic History Rev*. Supp. 1, 2008), pp. 64–98.

60 W. Blith, *The English improver improved* (1652), preface.

61 See below p. 145.

62 J. Thirsk, 'Agricultural Policy: Public Debate and Legislation', in J. Thirsk (ed.), *The Agrarian History of England and Wales*, V (2 vols, Cambridge, 1984), vol. 2, pp. 318–19.

a work of the second decade of the century and how much of mid-century is not immediately clear, but whilst the title reflects the preoccupations of the 1650s, the text reflected earlier concerns. Moore offered separate accounts of the inadequacies of upland and marshland wastes. The advantages of upland enclosure were the increase of feeding for animals, the increase of corn and the increase of fuel through the provision of more hedgerow timber. The advantages of draining marsh were proved by the example of Aldermoor in Somerset, which in a single year now produced 'more good to the owners and commonwealth than to his lain in its old lethargy it could have done to the world's end'.[63] The other advantages of drainage and enclosure were the improved supply of fuel, the spread of tillage and the increase of employment. Moore offered some speculative calculations for the number of people who could be relieved by enclosure: 1.5 million. All of this improvement was to be overseen by county grand committees. It was, as with all projects, an obvious thing to do with immediate benefits. Doubts could be readily countered (the rights of manorial lords in their commons could be quickly disposed of) and the nation led to new heights of prosperity.

What brought this type of improvement to an end was the success of the other forms of improvement advocated by figures like Blith and Sir Richard Weston – the improvement of arable regimes by the use of artificial grasses. From the late 1660s the country entered into a prolonged agricultural depression marked by low farmgate prices which pulled rents down behind them. In 1685 Sir William Petty drafted a note to himself expounding the desirability of enclosing commons. He thought that in England there were about 30 million acres of land which would feed about 10 million people. But the population was only (on his computation) about 6 million, 'and consequently there is already too much land'. Population was falling. The draining of the fens, the planting of clover and the Irish cattle trade had all been 'equivalent to increasing land in England'. There was no prospect of carrying forwards a scheme to enclose commons until population increased. Indeed, there is evidence of a lull in enclosure after the 1670s.[64]

The notion that wastes and commons were simply empty spaces which were available to be improved never entirely disappeared. Forests in particular continued to be seen as contributing less to the national economy than they were capable of doing, and became caught up in concerns about the supply of timber for the navy. Thirsk has noticed a parliamentary bill of 1674 which, if

---

63 Moore, *Bread for the poor*, p. 27.

64 Marquis of Lansdowne (ed.), *The Petty Papers: Some Unpublished Papers of Sir William Petty* (2 vols, London, 1927), vol. 2, pp. 129–30. I look at the chronology of enclosure in a chapter in my forthcoming *Idleness, Improvement and Industry*.

passed, would have given the owners of forests the right to enclose portions of their forests and hold them free of common rights. If their commoners failed to agree, then a commission of JPs could be convened to enforce a division.[65] Similar proposals for a statute were canvassed by Petty in James II's reign. His proposal began by outlining three contentions: that there was an imminent shortage of timber for ships, that England was underpopulated and could spare land for timber and hemp, and that there were too many royal forests in the nation. Drawing these together, Petty proposed a disafforestation whereby the king would receive half the land area of the forests and the commoners the remainder, and that the king's share be devoted to flax growing and timber production.[66]

A disregard of commoners' rights was marked in proposals of 1709 by one Thomas Smith to create a new town in the New Forest to house the refugee German Lutherans, the 'Palatines', most of whom were finally shipped to North America.[67] For a period of weeks the project seems to have been taken seriously enough, but when in May the Attorney General and Solicitor General were asked whether the queen had the right to grant parcels of land in her forests on which cottages could be built, they could surely only have answered in the negative. Smith answered criticisms by saying that he had assumed that the queen's property was hers to dispose of as she wished, thus revealing a complete misunderstanding of the situation within the forests; but, undeterred, he argued that if allotments of the forest were also made to neighbouring farmers then the commoners would be satisfied, thus further displaying his ignorance.[68]

When he undertook his tour of England a decade later, Defoe still regretted the failure to build a town in the New Forest to house the Palatines. Indeed, he even revealed where the settlement was to be located. This brings us to Ross's chapter in which he demonstrates the influence of Defoe's *Plan of the English commerce* (1728) on William Lorimer and Sir James Grant in the 1760s. Defoe's *Plan* described a proposal he had seen for the establishment of a town in southern England on vacant land at the point where three manors joined.[69] It is unclear whether this is a further reference to the New Forest scheme – the

---

65 Thirsk, 'Agricultural Policy', p. 375.

66 Lansdowne (ed.), *Petty Papers*, vol. 2, pp. 127–9, and a mass of unpublished material, including draft bills, in BL, Add. Ms 72,893, fos. 42–67.

67 For the Palatine migration, see Philip Otterness, *Becoming German: The 1709 Palatine Migration to New York* (Ithaca, 2004).

68 BL, Add. Ms 61649, fos. 76–82; *Journal of the Commissioners for Trade and Plantations, Feb. 1708–09–Mar. 1714–15*, p. 39; TNA, CRES 6/24, pp. 271–2.

69 Daniel Defoe, *A tour through the whole island of Great Britain* (Everyman edn [1928], 2 vols), vol. 1, pp. 200–206; Defoe, *A plan of the English commerce: being a compleat prospect of*

few details Defoe provides implies that it was not – but Defoe describes how the settlement might have developed, with the establishment of 50 pioneer farmers resulting in the development of a town of 1,000 people to service and victual them. Plainly this seized the imagination of the Scots and the fulfilment of Defoe's pipe-dream town in the New Forest may perhaps be found in the multiple new towns founded in Scotland (although in all fairness the Scots were establishing new settlements long before Defoe wrote and it is equally possible that Defoe was thinking of the Scottish, Irish or New World experiences when he saw opportunities in the New Forest).

IV

Three papers – Elizabeth Griffiths on Hunstanton, Briony McDonagh on Mrs Prowse of Wicken and Alasdair Ross on the Grants of Strathspey – all consider aspects of the improvement of gentry estates, in the case of the Le Stranges of Hunstanton in the decades before the Civil War, and the other two in in very different conditions and circumstances in the eighteenth century. All three show us activist gentry, resident on their estates for a large part of the year, for whom improvement was plainly a dimension of their view of what it was to be a gentleman (or gentlewoman) and a landowner. Improvement was undertaken with regard for the tenantry in the English cases, where the abrupt and rough treatment of the tenants on the Grant estate seems nothing less than the sort of shock treatment one might imagine the World Bank recommending to a modern third world economy, made all the worse by the estate giving the tenants no opportunity to prepare for the new regime. It amounted to Grant and Lorimer making war on the tenants. The tenantry seem to have been less the victims of circumstances in Grant and Lorimer's eyes than the problem themselves.

In all three locations improvement here also had its aesthetic dimension: it included the development of the house but also the creation of landscapes of pleasure, whether for wildfowling or woodland walks, and the creation of a landscape which screened its less attractive elements by the planting of trees.

Both Griffths's and McDonagh's chapters describe hands-on landowners, closely engaged in the development of their estates, intellectually interested in developments in agriculture, willing to invest current income in improvements – the full benefits of which would be felt long after their own lifetimes. In the case of Mrs Elizabeth Prowse, this is perhaps all the stranger given that she was

the trade of this nation, as well the home trade as the foreign (London, 1728; Oxford, 1927 edn), pp. 15–21.

only life tenant of her late husband's estate and the eventual inheritor of her endeavours would be a relation of his and not hers. For both the Le Stranges and Mrs Prowse, the improvement of the estate was almost a mission.

Other examples of the same mindset can be found. One of particular interest is Sir John Lowther of Lowther in north Westmorland (d. 1675) who maintained for most of his adult life a journal of his improvements at Lowther and on the estates – his 'memorable observations of the house and grounds at Lowther'.[70] This began with an account of the house at Lowther and the family's other houses, recording what was then known of their building history. The development of Lowther itself is recorded in the journal, but most of it consists of an account of land purchased to be added to the estates, walls and hedges rebuilt, land cleared of stone and gorse, barns built, trees planted and woods felled. Lowther describes the making of water meadows; he enumerates the crops from lands he had cleared, ploughed, limed and cultivated for the first time. Apart from the occasional setback (for example, his new bridge into Yanwith Wood was swept away in a flood within a matter of months of its erection), it is a relentless account of achievement, of investment of time, money and energy. Lowther was a lawyer and it was doubtless the earnings of his practice which paid for his endeavours. Indeed, they were not entirely rational in strict economic terms:

> But my profession in the law hindered my endeavours, and took my care of it, though I naturally loved the improvement and meliorating of grounds, holding it no less good husbandry to improve the waste and barren grounds as to purchase new ... yet in corn [growing] I never found much profit, only it was a pleasure to see things mended, the poor set on work and the ground thereby amended, which was the principal thing I still aimed at in ploughing any more than was necessary for my house.[71]

And later he added that whereas his grandfather had grown corn for sale, he had no need to 'but for pleasure and diversion'.[72]

Lowther's journal was in part autobiographical, in part a record of achievement for posterity, in part a letter of advice to his son and successors (as when he discusses the problems of managing woods to maintain an adequate supply of fuel in a county short of both wood and coal). It is permeated with a sense of the enjoyment and rewards of improvement. The difficulty posed by the chapters by Griffiths and McDonagh, as well as by Lowther's journal,

---

[70] C. B. Phillips (ed.), *Lowther Family Estate Books, 1617–1675* (Surtees Soc., 1979), pp. 233–55.

[71] Ibid., pp. 236–7.

[72] Ibid., p. 253.

is one of establishing just how typical they are of the English landowning experience. Well-documented estates draw historians to them. The Le Strange family were certainly obsessive about keeping accounts and writing about themselves, but this seems to be more concerned with current management than recording for posterity, which was plainly Lowther's intention. Mrs Prowse left an autobiography. One has to suspect that the personal commitment of these people to the improvement of their estates does mark them out as being at an extreme.

At the other pole are those landowners who saw their estates as a source of rental income alone and who were reluctant to invest in their estates or deal personally with their tenants. As an extreme example of this we might note Sir Marmaduke Constable, the running of whose East Riding estates is graphically described in the surviving correspondence between him and his steward. Constable – a Catholic – went abroad in 1730 and did not return until 1744, maintaining a postal relationship with his steward, John Bede Potts, a Catholic priest. Constable was not uninterested in the estates when younger. But after he left England, the estates were primarily a source of income to finance his continental travels. Communications with Potts through these years were by letter except for a single meeting in 1741, but the letters were intermittent to the point that Potts frequently feared that his employer was dead. With little guidance from Constable, Potts was disinclined to take initiatives on the estate and consequently it started to go to rack and ruin. Arrears accumulated; the fabric of the buildings on the estate markedly deteriorated to the point that some collapsed.[73]

Yet absenteeism did not have to end like this. Rollison has described a peculiar incident at Westonbirt, on the Gloucestershire estate of the Master in Chancery, Sir Richard Holford (d. 1719) in 1716.[74] Broadly, this involved an alleged homosexual act between Holford's bailiff, one George Andrews, and an itinerant farm worker, the details of which do not concern us here. What this episode does show us is Holford's determination to micromanage his estate by post and occasional visits. (He came down to Westonbirt to hold the annual manorial court, and then entertained his tenants with a dinner. He called this his 'annual ramble in the country'.) He encouraged his tenants to write to him directly. In an agricultural sense he was an improver, but he was also, in Rollison's

---

[73] P. Roebuck, *Yorkshire Baronets, 1640–1760: Families, Estates and Fortunes* (Oxford, 1980), pp. 186–94 summarizes the correspondence between Constable and Potts printed by Roebuck in *Constable of Everingham State Correspondence, 1726–43* (Yorkshire Archaeological Society Record Ser., 136, 1974).

[74] D. Rollison, 'Property, Ideology and Popular Culture in a Gloucestershire Village, 1660–1740', *Past and Present* 93 (1981), pp. 70–97.

phrase, attempting to 'civilize' the estate and its people. Rollison viewed this as a form of colonialism (we do not follow him) but there was a conflict of cultures, and the groaning which followed Andrews' conduct was seen by Holford as a challenge to his authority. In fact the solution to tenant incivility was not education but their removal from the landscape. By 1798 all that remained of the village community were two farms and the great house of Westonbirt.

The intermediate position between Constable and Holford was, of course, the management of estates through a steward. In his manual for estate officers, it is striking just how much delegation Edward Laurence supposed the steward would have.[75] Estates could be owned by absentees but still be well run.

There were then those landowners who devoted their lives to politics and even more rakish activities, and those for whom the beautification of the house and its grounds, and the improvement of its estates in all the ways that the word implies, were a major part of their life's purpose. The necessity for personal commitment and supervision was probably greater in Scotland and Ireland than in England. It is not wholly unreasonable to see both nations as trying to emulate English practice in much the same way as some mid-seventeenth century English improvers saw their purpose as being to introduce Flemish practices into England. As an example of this, we can cite Randall MacDonnell, latterly first Marquis of Antrim (1609–39), an Irishman educated in England, writing in 1637 after a visit to re-lease his Antrim estates:

> I have compounded my affairs here with my tenants wherein I was not so inward to my [own] profit as to the general good and settlement by binding them to plant [trees] and husband their holdings so near as may be to the manner of England.[76]

He also encouraged his tenants to enclose and build stone houses, all emblematic of an improved estate.

The establishment of English conditions was something to which landowners in Scotland and Ireland aspired. The methods used to achieve this often involved *imposing* English models – as Ross shows – rather than allowing the organic development of a new regime. Improvement was an attempt to accelerate economic and social changes which it had taken centuries to bring

---

75 Edward Laurence, *The duty of a steward to his lord* (1st edn, 1727); for stewards, see Christopher Clay, 'Landlords and Estate Management in England', in Thirsk (ed.), *Agrarian history* V, vol. 2, pp. 119–251 and John Beckett, 'Estate Management in Eighteenth-Century England: The Lowther–Spedding Relationship in Cumberland', in J. Chartres and D. Hey (eds), *English Rural Society, 1500–1800: Essays in Honour of Joan Thirsk* (Cambridge,1990), pp. 55–72.

76 Jane H. Ohlmeyer, *Civil War and Restoration in the Three Stuart Kingdoms: The Career of Randal MacDonnell, Marquis of Antrim, 1609–1683* (Cambridge, 1993), pp. 40–41.

about in England but which improvers hoped could be achieved in a generation. The need for the investment of major sums in infrastructure was much more obvious in Ireland and Scotland than in England, where the provision of bridges and adequate roads could be left to the county authorities or, from the second quarter of the eighteenth century, trusts established for the improvement of selected sections of road through turnpiking. It is perhaps for reasons like this that there was a much greater interest in both Scotland and Ireland in the establishment of markets and the building of market halls, the foundation of new towns and the provision of bridges and harbours. In Scotland the need for landowners to invest in infrastructure was all the greater because of the high proportion of rent received in produce before the mid-eighteenth century. So, George MacKenzie of Tarbat, first Earl of Cromarty (1630–1714), was selling rent grain into the lowland market and built a harbour and grain store at his port of Portmahomack. He also employed Dutch engineers to reclaim land and took an early interest in turnips. He was also a leading advocate of the Scottish fishing industry.[77]

As Ross suggests, Grant and Lorimer plainly saw the switching of populations as a sure road to success in improvement. The lack of education of the native population, their commitment to old ways and alleged idleness are reflected in the demand for Scots or English tenants throughout seventeenth-century Ireland. But such people were in short supply and, being footloose, often had more promising options open to them.[78] It was perhaps the greater attractions of America which made the flow of English into Restoration Ireland so disappointing, and led Sir William Petty to dream of the wholesale exchange of populations between England and Ireland – the English to exploit Ireland and the Irish to be civilized in England.[79] In reality, there was little alternative but to make do with the existing tenants and hope that over time they might absorb some of the new thinking. This meant that improvement required constant landlord pressure. Sir William Petty who, at different times, was both optimistic and pessimistic about the improvement of his estates in county Kerry and the fortunes of Ireland generally, came to understand this: 'our estates here [Ireland] are mere visions and delusions and require more attendance than a

---

77 Eric Richards and Monica Clough, *Cromartie: Highland Life, 1650–1914* (Aberdeen, 1989), pp. 41–5.

78 For a comment that importing experienced farmers from the south onto the Monymusk estate in Aberdeenshire had not been successful, J. H. Smith, *The Gordon's Mill Farming Club, 1758–64* (Aberdeen, 1962), pp. 41–2.

79 Barnard, *Improving Ireland?*, p. 46; Ted McCormick, *William Petty and the Ambitions of Political Arithmetic* (Oxford, 2009), ch. 5.

retail shop'. An Irish estate 'cannot subsist without the owner's daily presence and inspection'.[80]

This was not simply an Irish problem. It is in this respect that we can understand a Le Strange, a Lowther or even a Prowse personally superintending improvement to make sure that it was done, and done well. The hands-on approach of a figure like Sir John Lowther is not so very different from that of Sir Archibald Grant of Monymusk in Aberdeenshire (1696–1778), who devoted much of his life to the improvement of the Monymusk estate.[81] Although an absentee for the first 15 or so years of his possession of the estate (until his parliamentary career was brought to an abrupt end in 1732), he was thereafter a hands-on manager of the estate. Even in his periods of absence 'he never abrogated his duties as an enlightened landowner. His factors, gardeners and other leading estate employees sent him detailed weekly accounts of their work, and by a shower of letters and memoranda he inspired and directed them.'[82] He thought it best to keep his distance from his tenants ('Don't allow tenants to be so familiar, it looses authority') but:

> It was evidently his habit to ride round the estate 'to prompt people to industry and improvements'. 'In conversations with tenants', he writes in his own memorandum book, 'endeavour to convince them of the great benefit and ease of watering land and sowing clover and turnip and get them to try a little each'.[83]

Watering land, clover and turnips, and in addition the consolidation and enclosure of tenements, the planting of trees (allegedly some two million at Monymusk), was in a real sense an English agenda. Grant, having for a period sat in the Westminster parliament, was doubtless familiar with English agricultural practice. He bought at least some English agricultural literature, including Jethro Tull's *Horse-hoeing husbandry* in 1736. He urged his tenants to send their children to England. He employed an English farmer called Thomas Winter at Monymusk from 1726 to introduce 'the best of English methods': one of his first steps was to send for an English horse harness. Whilst Winter had found an English plough, he wanted a Gloucestershire wheel plough sent him.[84] Later

80 Barnard, *Improving Ireland?*, p. 68.

81 See *ODNB*, Sir Archibald Grant (1696–1778), which is notably weak on his interests as an improver; H. Hamilton (ed.), *Selections from the Monymusk Papers (1713–55)* (Scottish History Soc., 3rd ser., 39, Edinburgh, 1945); Hamilton (ed.), *Life and Labour*. The following account is based on the introductions to Hamilton's two volumes.

82 Hamilton (ed.), *Life and Labour*, p. x.

83 Hamilton (ed.), *Monymusk Papers*, pp. lxix–lxx, 179, 182.

84 Winter's letters are printed in Hamilton (ed.), *Monymusk Papers*, pp. 100–19.

in the year, the implements having arrived, Winter told Grant that peas would be a good improvement but the tenants were reluctant to adopt them: 'but I hope by often repeated conversation to bring them to see their errors in that and several other points of husbandry'. Winter apparently remained at Monymusk into the 1740s.[85] English practice, and in particular the benefits of the Norfolk rotation, remained potent for Scots improvers. Ross shows us Lorimer and Grant looking at it for themselves: the Gordon's Mill Farming Club (an early agricultural society in Aberdeenshire) also received extensive reports on the Norfolk rotation.[86] What worked in England though could not be guaranteed to work much further north.

V

Schemes of improvement naturally attracted opposition. Where improvement involved the wholesale transformation of the landscape, the destruction of existing economies and the displacement – one way or another – of the inhabitants, it might be violently opposed. Where improvement took more modest forms – the introduction of new technologies of farming for instance – then it might be viewed sceptically by those who the improvers wished to adopt the new ideas. It was easiest to blame the failure of improvement on those who were faced with having to make it work, dismissing them as conservative and backward-looking. As the opponents of improvement rarely expounded their reasons for resisting,[87] we tend to get a sense of their doubts only through the writings of frustrated and disappointed improvers, all too often somewhat messianic and obsessive figures.

If we are talking about improvement in the sense of introducing technical changes bit by bit within existing property rights, then the advocates of improvement found farmers disappointing in their lack of enthusiasm. A figure like Drayner Massingberd of South Ormsby (Lincolnshire) (d. 1689) pioneered the use of sainfoin, but seems to have only slowly found an echo in the practice of

85 Ibid., pp. 117, lxix.

86 Smith, *Gordon's Mill Farming Club*, pp. 136–50.

87 At an extreme, alleged rioters rarely even admitted their involvement let alone gave reasons for that involvement. See, for example, H. Falvey, 'Crown policy and local economic context in the Berkhamsted Common enclosure dispute, 1618–42', *Rural History* 12 (2001), pp. 134–5; rioters from Berkhamsted who were questioned in Star Chamber simply affirmed their rights in the enclosed land and denied any involvement in the riots.

his tenants.[88] Indeed, the evidence from inventories seems to be that new crops were often slow to be adopted, their potential perhaps not being obvious outside the narrow circle of zealots and proselytizers. A Yorkshire landlord who was advocating that his tenants should turn to dairying in the depressed years of the late 1720s was told by his agent that were like 'old cart horses, one can't thrust 'em out of their beaten tracks; they'l not be persuaded to try experiments'.[89] This is far from a comment on farmers as whole. Farming communities could also embark on full-scale enclosure if it seemed appropriate. They were also capable of radical reorganizations of their open fields to boost productivity. Landlords and their stewards did not have a monopoly on wisdom.[90] Where farmers rejected or were merely tepid about improvement, we should perhaps see weak incentives to change, or insurmountable institutional rigidities, rather than a predisposition to reject the possibility of change out of hand.

It is in this light that we need to consider a tract by Sir Archibald Grant which he prepared for the Gordon's Mill Farming Club in 1760, entitled *A dissertation of the chief obstacles to the improvement of land*. It would be easy to suppose that Grant would use this as a vehicle for expressing his disillusionment with his tenants in particular and the Scottish farmer in general. In fact he concentrates on structural problems within the Scottish rural economy: the severe out-migration and shortage of people produced by a lack of local opportunity; the inattentiveness of the Scottish gentry to their land; the size of the farms in Scotland, too large to be profitably employed; the poverty of the farmers themselves. Then, reviewing lesser problems in his final chapter, he identified a lack of personal industry (a direct criticism of the farmer); the short length of leases which discouraged improvement and the high entry fines demanded when longer leases were offered; the work services placed on tenants and the openness of the countryside which allowed cattle and sheep to graze on open fields throughout the winter months. It is only in the very last pages of his pamphlet that he comes to 'the obstinacy of common farmers in persisting in improper methods of agriculture when proper ways are in many instances practicable even in their present situation'. Even then he attributes much of this to ignorance rather than obstinacy:

---

88 B. A. Holderness, 'The Agricultural Activities of the Massingberds of South Ormsby, Lincolnshire, 1638–c.1750', *Midland Hist.* 1 (1972), pp. 15–25.

89 Clay, 'Landlords and Estate Management', p. 234; and see that and the following page for other examples.

90 For tenant-inspired alterations in open-field practice, Robert C. Allen, *The British Industrial Revolution in Global Perspective* (Cambridge, 2009), pp. 68–73; Dan Byford, 'Open Field Farming in Fishlake and Hatfield: The Evidence of the Court Books, 1592–1808', in B. Elliott (ed.), *Aspects of Doncaster* (Barnsley, 1997), pp. 86–110.

> Common farmers do not read, and if they did, characters wrote with *pen and ink* are not what they can understand in a subject so interesting that the bread of their family might be in hazard if they made the necessary trials and failed of success. The characters intelligible to them must be wrote with the *plough and the spade*. They must see the event with others before they can judge, for they themselves have nothing to risk in doubtful tho' feasible experiments. Hence the usefulness of heritors and of other gentlemen undertaking farms, besides what Pliny alludes to so elegantly, 'sive honestis manibus omnia laetius proveniunt, quoniam et curiosus fiunt'. They can afford to loose on a trial either if what has been proposed by others, or of what occurs to themselves, and the poor farmer reads their farms as they read books, profits at their expense and tries a new method with certainty of success. The farmer indeed is oft struck with a further doubt; lest the expense should exceed the return, which would make it unprofitable tho' above the common.[91]

Much therefore depended on education and the opportunities that young members of the profession had to see the new techniques in use on the farms of gentlemen. So, if agriculture in Scotland was backward, it was not because the farmers had rejected the idea of progress but because they laboured under multiple disadvantages, of which their ignorance was only one. In the same year, a member of the Gordon's Mill Farming Club prepared for its consideration a 15-item list of 'Errors and neglects of the common farmers', some of which were indeed faults of farmers but most of which were again structural problems, some matters of knowledge, some questions of attitude. In a letter of 1777 reviewing the problems faced by the improving farmers, Grant's factor wrote with sympathy of their difficulties, ending by saying that improvement 'should be what an industrious man can easily perform and execute rightly so as to benefit himself and bring the matter to repute'.[92] There seems to be much wisdom in this gradualist approach, and little sense in the shock treatment that Alasdair Ross shows Sir James Grant employing on his Strathspey estates.

If, on the other hand, we mean improvement in the sense of landscape change and the rearrangement of property rights, then those concerned could often pass beyond grumbling and foot-dragging and the legal defence of their rights into active hostility, finally resulting in violent opposition.[93]

---

91 Sir Archibald Grant, *A dissertation of the chief obstacles to the improvement of land* (Aberdeen, 1760), pp. 91–2.

92 Smith, *Gordon's Mill Farming Club*, pp. 72–3, 41–2.

93 At Duffield, Derbyshire, opponents of the improvement of the royal forest exercised various forms of resistance prior to actually rioting. See H. Falvey, 'Custom, resistance and politics: local experiences of improvement in early modern England' (unpublished PhD thesis, University of Warwick, 2007), pp. 178–93. For passive resistance such as grumbling, see J. Walter,

The Jacobean promoters of the Sedgemoor drainage knew their opponents so well they divided them into seven categories. First, there were the 'rich oppressors' who overgrazed the moor for their own advantage and were satisfied with current arrangements; second, the 'simply ignorant', whose opinions vacillated 'pro et con upon every motion', but who could be managed into agreement; third, the 'wilfully obstinate' who held that 'an old (evil) custom is better than any (worthy) new invention'; fourth, those who held that a service intended for the common good was really for the advantage of the king alone; fifth, 'the whisperers' who spread opposition and even sedition; sixth, 'the popular persons' who were creating a monster (the crowd) which might rival the king; and seventh, the 'impugners of their sovereign's just benefit' who could not see that their own advantage was tied to that of the monarch. Unfortunately the pen portraits of these seven forms of opponents do not extend to identifying the types of people who formed them.[94]

We may speculate that there is a division between those property owners whose opposition was largely conducted through legal avenues but who finally had some incentive to compromise, and the poor commoners, whose common rights may have been judged to have been invalid or who were compensated with only a share in a poor man's allotment. Precisely because they had nothing to lose, the latter may have been all the readier to oppose the tangible signs of improvement by destroying new fences, filling in ditches and dykes and intimidating the workmen employed to bring about change. It is becoming clear though that the support of the middling sort was vital to the success of opposition to improvement.[95] Walter's work on the abortive Oxfordshire Rising of 1596 demonstrates that the participation of the middling farmers was vital for the successful launch of the movement: no one would follow the lesser sort.[96] Whilst rioters might be an independent force, they could also form an

'Public Transcripts, Popular Agency and the Politics of Subsistence in Early Modern England', in M. J. Braddick and J. Walter (eds), *Negotiating Power in Early Modern Society: Order, Hierarchy and Subordination in Britain and Ireland* (Cambridge, 2001), pp. 123–48. Jeanette Neeson discusses grumbling as a form of resistance to (parliamentary) enclosure and the various forms that it could take in J. M. Neeson, *Commoners: Common Right, Enclosure and Social Change in England, 1700–1820* (Cambridge, 1993), ch. 9, esp. p. 270. Other forms of resistance are discussed in detail in Manning, *Village Revolts*, ch. 5.

94 BL, Royal Ms 17A XXXVII, fos. 3r–5v.

95 See, for example, Falvey, 'Crown Policy and Local Economic Context', pp. 123–58; S. Hindle, 'Persuasion and Protest in the Caddington Common Enclosure Dispute, 1635–1639', *Past and Present* 158 (1998), pp. 37–78; S. Hipkin, '"Sitting on his Penny Rent": Conflict and Right of Common in Faversham Blean, 1595–1610', *Rural History* 11 (2000), pp. 1–35.

96 J. Walter, 'A "Rising of the People"? The Oxfordshire Rising of 1596', *Past and Present* 107 (1985), pp. 90–143.

element in a larger strategy which could be disowned. Their identity may well have varied from area to area, but there is nothing incompatible with Buchanan Sharp's finding (itself challenged) that the opponents of disafforestation and enclosure in the Western Forests were tradesmen and artisans and Clive Holme's view that the equivalent opponents in the fenlands were yeomen farmers and their households. This merely reflects the different character of the societies involved.[97] Those accused of rioting at Duffield in Derbyshire in 1642 (215 men and two women) were identified by the absentee landlord's counsel as being entirely manorial tenants who had either consented to the enclosures or who were the successors of those who had.[98]

We should not allow ourselves to conclude that this sort of opposition to improvement entirely ceased after 1660. Bowring shows us the fens as a landscape in which farmers and tenants often continued to oppose the Bedford Level Corporation for its failure to manage the fens properly, and she lists multiple failings which impinged on the fenland communities. But as Holmes shows, the Bedford Level was the only area placed within a legislative framework after 1663. This provided severe penalties for those found guilty of damaging or sabotaging the works, but also provided for a tribunal to resolve disputes. The petitions which Bowring exploits reflect the articulation of grievances in an established process rather than being left to be argued out in the courts or on the ground.[99]

Violent demonstrations against drainage continued intermittently throughout the late seventeenth century in the fens, not in any random way but as an element within a larger strategy to draw attention to mismanagement.[100] We may speculate that the key change after the Restoration was that a diminished demand for land no longer made reclamation attractive; investors were unwilling to become involved in projects once the Crown's backing diminished; and the fear grew that improvement might provoke litigation and disorder and so runaway costs.

---

97 Holmes, 'Drainers and Fenmen', pp. 172–86. Underdown has shown that Sharp's analysis is severely flawed – many of the *known* rioters in the western forests were manorial tenants, i.e. those with legal and landed interest in the forest commons. D. Underdown, *Revel, Riot and Rebellion: Popular Politics and Culture in England, 1603–1660* (Oxford, 1985), p. 109.

98 Falvey, 'Custom, Resistance and Politics', passim; H. Falvey, 'Voices and faces in the rioting crowd: identifying seventeenth-century enclosure rioters', *Local Historian* 39 (2009), pp. 137–51; and her 'Searching for the population in an early-modern forest', *Local Population Stud.*, 81 (2008), esp. pp. 40–41.

99 Holmes, 'Drainers and Fenmen', pp. 176–7.

100 But see the riots in the fens under the guise of football matches, both planned and carried out, in 1699: Falvey, 'Voices and faces in the rioting crowd', pp. 148–9.

What did not develop in this period is a counter argument against improvement. There were indeed those who argued that fenland communities were viable and, in their own way, both prosperous and industrious,[101] but few argued that this was a way of life worth keeping. The idea that communities – whether in the fens or Strathspey – had actually optimized their productivity given the limitations of environment, technology and market demand is one that is little heard, if heard at all. Opposition to improvement concentrated on its disregard of property rights. Good husbandry implied the exploitation of resources to their full: as with so many words, its meaning has almost come full circle. The covenant with God was to exploit the world, not preserve it. That they held it in trust for the future is not an idea that the improver acknowledged: it was as redundant as custom itself.

---

[101] See, in the context of fen drainage, accounts of the economy of the fens like that of *The Anti-projector* (1606, repr. 1646), cited by Darby, *Draining of the Fens*, p. 52.

Chapter 1

Cromwell v. Taverner: Landlords, Copyholders and the Struggle to Control Memory in Mid-Sixteenth Century Norfolk

*R. W. Hoyle**

James Taverner of Wighton in Norfolk is not unknown to historians: indeed, his notoriety has lasted from his day to ours. His offence at the beginning of Elizabeth's reign was to forge a manorial custumal of the manor of North Elmham, for which he was sued and punished in Star Chamber. The legal points which his prosecution provoked were of sufficient interest to contemporaries for Taverner's case to be recorded in the law reports, and a brief reference to it appeared as late as 1641 in a collection of leading Star Chamber cases.[1] A further aspect of his case was raised in the House of Lords as a question of privilege by Taverner's protagonist, Henry Lord Cromwell, and it became a leading case in the definition of the privileges of a peer. Amongst more recent historians, Eric Kerridge mentioned Taverner's case, citing the account in Sir James Dyer's reports, but felt no need to establish either the details of the case or Taverner's motivation.[2] In fact there is no single case, but a whole succession of cases in Chancery and Star Chamber (as well as those alluded to in Common Pleas)

* Much of the material for this chapter was gathered by Dr Danae Tankard when she was my research assistant on the ESRC-funded 'Custom, Chancery and institutional restraints on landlord income, 1540–1640' project (R 000223641) in 2002–03, the full results of which will achieve publication in *Tenure in Tawney's Century* (forthcoming). I am grateful to her for her assiduous work in the archives. Jane Whittle very kindly read a draft and made valuable suggestions, not all of which I have been able to incorporate. All MSS cited are in The National Archives (TNA) unless otherwise indicated: and extracts from the MSS appear in modernized spelling.

1 [Richard Crompton], *Star Chamber cases showing what causes properly belong to the cognizance of that court* (1641), pp. 35 [printed 25]–37.

2 E. Kerridge, *Agrarian Problems in the Sixteenth Century and After* (London, 1969), p. 57.

between Taverner and successive lords of the manor of North Elmham which ran from the mid-1560s to the first years of the seventeenth century.

The story is an odd one, and for that reason alone is worth the telling. It is in part an account of self-help by a body of tenants; in part a study of the victimization of a tenant by a particularly ruthless manorial lord. It casts light on the continuing tensions and bitterness between landlords and tenants in Norfolk society in the generation after Kett's revolt. It also shows how custom was contested, and memory annexed by landowners.

I

In the pedigree they recorded at the 1613 visitation of Norfolk, the Taverner family claimed to have been resident in North Elmham since the reign of Henry II.[3] Our Taverner was one of the younger sons by a second marriage of John Taverner of North Elmham (d. 1545). James was a late son, born *c.*1540. His father entailed land on him in 1546, which he was to enter at age 28; he was admitted to this land in 1558. There was an even younger brother, Thomas. The four (much) older sons by their father's first marriage made careers outside Norfolk. The eldest brother, Richard, is included in the *Oxford Dictionary of National Biography* (*ODNB*), which calls him a translator (of Erasmus amongst others) and evangelical reformer, but he was also clerk of the signet and by the end of his life owned a landed estate near Oxford. Another brother was Roger Taverner, surveyor of the Court of Augmentations and later surveyor of woods in the Exchequer, a post which passed to his son John.

Taverner is normally given the title of gentleman and on one occasion is described as being of the Inner Temple. (I have, however, not been able to find him in the Inner Temple's own records.) The lands his father entailed on him in North Elmham extended to 130 acres and, in the following decade, he bought a further 49 acres.[4] In 1567 he married Grace, the daughter and heiress of John Russell of Wighton, the widow of a younger son of the Norfolk gentry, Edmund Bedingfield.[5] It seems likely that he lived on his wife's estates, but within North

---

3 For the family see W. Rye (ed.), *Visitations of Norfolk, 1563, 1589 and 1613* (Harleian Soc., 32, London, 1891), p. 280.

4 G. A. Carthew, *History of the Hundred of Launditch and Deanery of Brisley* (3 vols, Norwich, 1879–79), vol. 2, pp. 577. This contains a mass of materials on the Taverner family, including extracts from the pleadings in the successive cases, pp. 576–86. Taverner is referred to as of the Inner Temple in STAC3/35/9 (1591), but the context is of the early 1560s.

5 Norfolk RO, 926/27 372x8 is a surrender of Grace Bedingfield's lands, 1565, with a copy of her husband's will.

Elmham he owned a sizeable acreage of land, both freehold and copyhold. In about 1567 the estate officers of the lord of the manor, Henry Lord Cromwell, updated a survey of 1454, from which it has been calculated that Taverner was then the largest tenant in the manor, with a holding of 298½ measured acres and some additional land as well. Another list of lands held by him gives about 230 acres, whilst a survey of his lands in North Elmham – made in 1599 in a dispute over the rating of the fifteenth and tenth – itemizes 320 acres.[6] Grace Taverner died in 1601 and was buried at Wighton, but whilst the visitation says that James Taverner died in 1604, neither will, nor grant of administration nor inquisition post mortem has been discovered.

In these respects Taverner comes over as a transitional figure in much the same way as Robert Kett. His family had been in North Elmham for generations as peasant tenants of the Bishop of Norwich, and had acquired a considerable acreage of copyhold. This was not randomly distributed, for the family were plainly moving towards establishing a consolidated, enclosed holding.[7] There are signs that Taverner had some legal education: he could call on half-brothers who had used their education to advance in government posts. He married into the lower ranks of the Norfolk gentry. If he was not unambiguously a gentleman, Taverner was no peasant either. Like Kett, his wealth was not so large as to prevent him acting as a communal leader in opposition to the lord. But, as a landowner, Taverner was as ruthless an expropriator of his neighbours as any man. Again, this is no different from Kett, the encloser who would sit in judgement on other enclosing gentry.[8] It was dog-eat-dog in mid-sixteenth century Norfolk. There were no clear demarcations between oppressor and oppressed.

Whilst Taverner was probably too young to have seen Mousehold, he must have grown up in a countryside in which the memory of Kett and the summer of 1549 was still raw. North Elmham contributed men and money to the Mousehold camp and we may guess that in common with many other Norwich villages, some of its tenants and young men died in the pitched battles between the Earl of Warwick and Kett's irregular forces in and around Norwich, or were

---

6 D. Yaxley, 'The Manors and the Agrarian Economy', in P. Wade-Martins (ed.), *Excavations in North Elmham Park* (2 vols, East Anglian Archaeology, 9, 1980), vol. 2, p. 567; Norfolk RO, NNAS 52/42; BRA 1751.

7 Yaxley, 'Manors and the Agrarian Economy', p. 569.

8 The picture that Nicola Whyte draws of Taverner in Wighton is deeply unattractive: this volume, pp. 109–10. Andy Wood calls Kett a 'yeoman in late middle age with extensive landholdings and a tanning business whose wealth placed him on the edge of the lesser gentry' and stresses how unlikely a leader he was: A. Wood, *The 1549 Rebellions and the Making of Early Modern England* (Cambridge, 2007), p. 61; and for details of his wealth, Julian Cornwall, *Revolt of the Peasantry, 1549* (London, 1977), p. 139.

summarily hanged in the repression which followed.[9] How far the lessons of that summer weighed on Taverner and his fellow tenants is impossible to know. What we see in his behaviour, however, is an attempt to carry forwards one of the ambitions of 1549 – to curb seigneurial exploitation – by legal means.

His opponent would have none of this, perhaps knowing all too well what the stakes were. Henry Lord Cromwell (d. 1592) was the grandson of Henry VIII's minister Thomas Cromwell, Earl of Essex (executed 1540). North Elmham was one of the manors of the Bishopric of Norwich which were ceded to Henry VIII by Bishop Rugge in exchange for monastic manors in 1536. It was then granted to Cromwell.[10] Whilst Cromwell had amassed a considerable estate by the time of his attainder and execution, it was mostly forfeited, and Henry Cromwell was one of those poorly endowed Elizabethan peers who had difficulty maintaining the dignity of his title. In so far as anything is known of him – there are no personal or estate papers and he played no role in Norfolk local government that can readily be discovered – he comes over, by turns, as litigious and violent. His son Edward liquidated the family's English estates and, having participated in Essex's revolt, moved to Ireland to restore his fortunes, where he died in 1607. Taverner's lands in North Elmham were plainly a juicy morsel for Cromwell to add to his own limited estates in the manor.[11] In an interesting flanking manoeuvre, Cromwell's title to North Elmham was challenged by Roger Taverner on behalf of the Crown. He tried to show that an indenture of 30 March 1539 settling the estates on Cromwell and his wife, with the remainder to Cromwell's son Gregory and his heirs, had not been properly executed and that the manors should therefore have been forfeited to the Crown on Cromwell's attainder in 1540. This suit finally failed, but it plainly contributed to the bitterness between Cromwell and Taverner.[12]

---

9 A. G. Legge (ed.), *Ancient Churchwardens' Accounts in the Parish of North Elmham* (Norwich, 1891), pp. 55–9; Jane Whittle, 'Peasant politics and class consciousness: the Norfolk rebellions of 1381 and 1549 compared', in C. Dyer, P. Coss and C. Wickham (eds), *Rodney Hilton's Middle Ages: An Exploration of Historical Themes* (*Past and Present* Supp. Ser., 2, 2007), p. 237.

10 For the circumstances of the exchange, F. Heal, *Of Prelates and Princes: A Study of the Social and Economic Position of the Tudor Episcopate* (Cambridge, 1980), pp. 110–12; for the subsequent grants, *Letters and Papers of the Reign of Henry VIII*, X, no. 1256 (26); XIII (i) no. 1519 (5).

11 Cromwell seems to have been resident in North Elmham at some periods but A. G. Legge, *The Ecclesiastical and Civil History of North Elmham* (East Dereham, [1894]) p. 31 reports that both he and his wife died at Elmham but were buried at Launde Abbey in Leicestershire.

12 See here the papers in Norfolk RO, NNAS 52/40 and the summary of the case in BL, Lansdowne Ms 106, no. 33.

II

What Taverner did can be quickly outlined from his answer to the Chancery bill of Sir John Paulet – Lord St John, later Marquis of Winchester – who held the manor in the right of his wife, the widow of Gregory Lord Cromwell.[13] Taverner, in September 1559, together with a number of other tenants

> doubting lest the customs of the manor might go out of remembrance to the disinherison and great hindrance of the defendants and the rest of the tenants and by occasion of the death of some of the old tenants who had knowledge and best understanding of the customs and also the ignorance and negligence which might ensue by reason of the change and alterations of the stewards of the manor

took the initiative and drew up a custumal of the manor, which they sealed with their own seals. Taverner then held that he had presented this to St John's officers with the request that it should be reviewed by the jury of the manorial court: in short, that he wanted it approved by them, even if this involved having the document 'reformed'.[14] The reading placed on this by Paulet shows all too plainly how it was not a neutral act of recording, but a highly political act. As in other East Anglian manors in the later sixteenth century, there was no agreement over the custom of the manor. To St John, Taverner was intending:

> by ungodly practices and incontinent slights [to devise] how to alter the old ancient customs of the manor and to bring in and wrongfully set up and create new devices and customs in the stead of the true and ancient customs.

Paulet, or rather his lawyers, offered a rival narrative replete with incriminating detail when they petitioned Chancery in 1567. Taverner had first approached two other tenants of the manor, William Batche and Simon Shittell the elder, who both agreed to support his initiative. Taverner, Batche and Shittell then called the tenants together for a meeting at Batche's house where Taverner addressed them, showing how he had looked in Domesday Book and other ancient records and had discovered customs and privileges which had been hidden from the tenants. If the tenants would back him, then he would 'find the means to bring them in use again and revive the old and ancient customs'. He would record them in a parchment book which all the tenants would sign

[13] Gregory Cromwell died in 1550 and his widow remarried Sir John Paulet, Lord St John. Elizabeth died on 17 March 1568 and Henry Lord Cromwell entered. For these details, see the account of the descent of the manor in STAC 5/C35/9.

[14] This and the next paragraph are based on C 3/144/5 and the decree, C 78/36 no. 38.

and to which they would affix their seals.[15] He had also discovered a seal of great antiquity belonging to the manor which they would also set to the book. The finished book would then be locked away until the time was right to produce it and use it to challenge the surmised customs. Taverner had gone on to produce his parchment 'wherein ... is contained divers sundry, unreasonable, unlawful and new-fangled customs and by laws'. To it he attached a great brass seal bearing the words 'sigillium ville de northelman'. Taverner, Batche and Shittell were joined in signing the book by the majority of the tenants of the manor and, as agreed, it was lodged in a chest. More recently some of the tenants had begun to claim some of the bogus customs claimed in the book to the disinherison of the lord. St John had therefore commenced suit in Star Chamber claiming that the document was a forgery, but Taverner had escaped with a pardon at the last parliament. But as Taverner retained the custumal in his own hands, St John's request to Chancery was that Taverner should surrender it to be cancelled. Taverner was indeed instructed to bring the document into Chancery although, when he did so, it had already been defaced and cut. Later it seems that it was either retrieved from the court by persons unknown or somehow lost, and Taverner was questioned about its whereabouts in 1572.[16]

This narrative contained a good number of smears and half-truths designed to attract the attention of the court, some of which Taverner attempted to answer when examined in 1572.[17] He denied that he had tried to conceal the parchment. On the contrary, he had tried to get the lord's officers to accept it as a true statement of manorial customs. And rather than he, Taverner, trying to create new customs, he was consciously engaged in an act of rescue. It was Paulet and his servants who were establishing new customs for the felling of timber and the rate of copyhold fines.

Thus began a sequence of litigation between St John and his stepson Henry Lord Cromwell, and Taverner, that was to last for the remainder of the century. The facts of the creation of the custumal were raked over several times; and as a result, we can establish in some detail the format it took and what it contained.

---

15 A book does not necessarily imply a bound volume with pages.

16 STAC 5/C73/17, qq. 14–16.

17 For instance, he denied that he had mentioned Domesday Book when addressing the tenants.

III

First, the custumal was written on parchment.[18] It had tags and was sealed: it may therefore have been a single sheet of parchment similar in format to the 1553 petition now in the National Archives.[19] Taverner signed it with a seal about the size of a groat or teston. Taverner had also had a hollow seal made with the words 'North Elmham' running around its circumference which fitted around his own seal. The allegation in the initial pleadings – that this was a seal of great antiquity bearing the words 'sigillum ville de northelman' – was denied by Taverner: on the contrary, he had it made by a seal-maker at Ivy Bridge out of either pewter or tin (he was not certain which).

Taverner had the document engrossed in Latin ('because he supposed that such kind of writings are in Latin rather than English'). The title of the document claimed it was:

> the customary of divers customs, prescriptions and uses of the manor of North Elmham ... which time out of memory of man living have been used and executed ... also approved, allowed and suffered by the lord of the said manor ... which ... free and customary tenants now at this present gathered together with their common assent and consent, the customs, prescriptions and uses ... have caused to be renewed, inferred and entered ... .[20]

It therefore made the contestable claim that the rights detailed had been used beyond the memory of man. And whilst the custumal claimed to have been made by the assent of the tenants, making it their property, what was more questionable was whether it had been made with the *approval* of the lord: it was certain the custumal was not made with the *assent* of the lord. As Taverner freely acknowledged, it was a freelance effort and his problem was to get the lord to accept the tenants' own view of what their customs were – or should be.

The question of how many tenants showed their consent by signing and sealing the custumal is far from easy to resolve. Taverner acknowledged that he signed it, as did all the other tenants present – with the exception of Henry Heyward and Thomas Heyward, who had something of a reputation of being the

18 The fullest accounts are in the interrogatories put to Taverner in 1572 and his answers, STAC 5/C73/17, and the arguments to prove Taverner guilty of forgery, E 36/194, pp. 458–66.

19 Described in R. W. Hoyle, 'Agrarian agitation in mid-sixteenth-century Norfolk: a petition of 1553', *Historical J.* 44 (2001), pp. 223–38.

20 E 36/194, p. 458, translated from the Latin; also quoted in part in the interrogatory to STAC 5/C73/17.

lord's narks in the manor.[21] A legal brief of the late 1560s or early 1570s suggests that only 10 tenants out of a 100 consented; and a much later a hostile account in a Star Chamber bill of 1591 claims that Taverner and Batche assembled only the most favourably inclined tenants, not all of whom would agree to sign.[22]

There is, however, some evidence suggesting the popularity of Taverner's actions. Taverner's co-conspirator William Batche was the fifth largest tenant in the mid-1560s and persistently served as churchwarden. Although a smaller copyholder, Simon Shittell was churchwarden from 1557 to 1560.[23] Much more than Taverner, these people seem likely to be the natural leaders of the village community. In an interrogatory made on behalf of Cromwell in 1569, the vicar of North Elmham, Edmund Denny, was accused of being a supporter of Taverner, and deponents were asked to confirm that they had heard him, in the company of diverse of the manor's tenants, say 'that if he had been a tenant himself, he would likewise had subscribed and sealed the same [the custumal]'. Unfortunately no witnesses deposed in response to this so it remains unconfirmed.[24] A further question in the same interrogatory asked whether witnesses had heard it 'published abroad and by whom that the country is bent against the lord and that some copyholders of the country would make a purse or spend £5 or £1000 or other great sums of money to bear out James Taverner and the petty jury in the attaint', the last referring to a further stage in the proceedings against Taverner – our account of which will show the distaste and reluctance with which Cromwell's prosecution of Taverner was viewed. Again, regrettably, no one answered this question.[25]

The legal brief and the Star Chamber bill outline the claims made by the custumal in greater detail (although, as this is a hostile account, the possibility of exaggeration may be noted).[26] The first claim which was so offensive to the lord was that every customary tenant had the right to fell all the timber on their

21 Taverner alleged that Henry Heyward had been put on a manorial jury despite not being a tenant 'as the especial and lewd instrument to bring his evil practice to pass', and suggested that his role was to steer the jury to the outcome Cromwell sought; conversely, Thomas Cromwell was alleged to have referred to Heywood as his lordship's only 'honest man in the town' for the jurors would not do as he urged. C 21/T2/17, plaintiff's interrogatory, qq. 8–9.

22 E 36/194, p. 460; STAC 5/C35/9.

23 Legge (ed.), *Ancient Churchwardens' Accounts*, pp. 73, 76, 83; Yaxley, 'Manors and the Agrarian Economy', p. 567.

24 C 21/T2/17, defendant's interrogatory, q. 44. At a later date, Cromwell sued Denny for defamation after a dispute over preachers in North Elmham, Legge, *Ecclesiastical and Civil History*, pp. 14–15.

25 C 21/T2/17, q. 56.

26 The following is based on STAC 5/C35/9. The customs are also noticed in C 21/T2/17, defendant's interrogatory q. 9.

copyholds to their greatest profit, i.e. with the right either to use the timber on the copyhold or sell it for profit: 'By which custom the inheritance in the said woods is claimed to be in the copyholder where as the same is and of right ought to be in the lords of the said manor.' The second claimed a right of fixed fines when tenants took their copyholds by either surrender or inheritance of *4d.* an acre, to be paid within a year of entry, 'whereas in truth the fines in such cases have always time out of memory of any man living within the manor been uncertain and arbitrable at the will and pleasure of the lords'. The third pretended custom was the right to take from the lord's wood, called Burgrave, rods of the underwood called 'prickwood' and 'bindings' to be used to roof buildings within the manor. Instead, it was claimed that the wood was the 'several' (i.e. enclosed) wood of the lord and that the tenants had been punished for taking wood from it. A fourth custom was a denial that any general fine or tallage was due on the entry of a new lord where in fact the lord claimed a fine of 10 marks as an acknowledgement on his first entry. Finally the custumal claimed that the tenants had the right to enclose their copyhold lands into closes for their best profit and advantage, but the lord claimed unlicensed enclosure as a forfeiture. The third and fourth clauses bore on essentially local issues. The fifth may well have been a creative piece of custom-making by the lord. Enclosure had certainly been proceeding in the manor and, if the claim that unlicensed enclosure was forfeiture, it left some tenants, including Taverner, vulnerable to the loss of their lands or the payment of penal fines. The enclosure of lands may have made it impossible for the lord to exercise his rights to the foldcourse, this giving him reason for being hostile to developments which the tenants seem to have sought.[27]

The real meat of the tenants' claims lies in the first and second articles. Complaints about rising rents are found in the articles compiled at Mousehold in 1549. The Mousehold articles sought notional fines, either 'an easy fine as a capon [hen] or a reasonable sum ... of money for a remembrance' where the custumal conceded fines of *4d.* an acre, perhaps in a bid to hold them at that level.[28] The inclusion of this clause may indicate that the lords of North Elmham were in the vanguard of attempts to raise the level of fines; but it might also reflect no more than an awareness that other manorial lords saw increasing fines as a way to raise their incomes. (The lack of any manorial archive makes it hard

27 Cromwell's interrogatories in Chancery in 1569 sought information on the extent of the Lord's foldcourse, C 21/T2/17, qq. 22–25, and the answers showed that areas of the manor included within it has been progressively enclosed by the tenants.

28 E. Shagan, 'Protector Somerset and the 1549 Rebellions: New Sources and New Perspectives', *English Historical Rev.* 114 (1999), pp. 44, 55; article 14 of Kett's demands, most conveniently printed in A. Fletcher and D. MacCulloch, *Tudor Rebellions* (5th revised edn, Harlow, 2008), p. 157.

to be certain.) Whittle thought that fines in Norfolk generally remained much the same between the 1440s and 1570s and only started to rise after that date; but she also observed that the lord of Hevingham Bishops tried to raise the rate (which had been at about the *4d.* an acre which Taverner held to be custom in North Elmham) at the beginning of the 1540s but entered into a composition with his tenants in 1543 in which he conceded fixed fines at a rate of *6d.* an acre.[29] The second article, about the ownership of timber, may seem esoteric, but disputes over the right of copyholders to timber on their copyhold rattled around East Anglia from the case of the tenants of Abbots Ripton in the 1540s to at least the early 1620s, when the disputes between the lords of the manor of Earls Colne and his tenants were resolved.[30] Manorial tenants typically claimed the timber and could often show that they had cut it without the lord's licence; but the notion that the timber belonged to the tenants was anathema to manorial lords, who argued that unlicensed felling was a forfeiture of the copyhold. Where lords tried to claim, or re-establish, a right to timber, the reaction of the tenants was often one of great bitterness. Thomas Taverner, James's brother, was quoted as saying: 'If it fall out that we may not be permitted to fell such woods as do grow upon our copyholds, for my part, I will not suffer any spring to come up of the bigness of my finger but I will pluck the same up by the roots.'[31]

These grievances, especially timber rights, appear in other contemporary complaints – notably the petition sent from Norfolk in 1553.[32] Here, in an extensive and polished text, the grievances are reduced to five but expanded in detail and made the subject of cogent argument. The first article complains about the expulsion of tenants from demesne copyholds, i.e. copyholds fairly recently established. The article argues, in effect, that the occupation of lands for 30 or 40 years should create a customary right. This makes custom into a set of rights with chronologically shallow roots, an attitude which the North Elmham tenants seem to have shared. The second article bears directly on the dispute at North Elmham with a request that the ownership of timber on a copyhold should be vested in the copyholder and not the lord. The third article complained of the exploitation of the foldcourse (which may also bear on circumstances here); the fourth the competition between lords and tenants. The fifth is something of a ragbag of grievances: the buying up of lands by the

29 Jane Whittle, *The Development of Agrarian Capitalism: Land and Labour in Norfolk, 1440–1580* (Oxford, 2000), p. 81.

30 R. W. Hoyle, 'Redefining Copyhold in the Sixteenth Century: The Case of Timber Rights', in B. J. P. Bavel and P. Hoppenbrouwers (eds), *Landholding and Land Transfer in the North Sea Area (Late Middle Ages–19th Century)* (Turnhout, 2004), pp. 250–64.

31 C 21/T2/17, defendant's depositions, John Brown jun., q. 45.

32 Hoyle, 'Agrarian agitation'.

landlords and the engrossment of tenements; the high rents they demanded; the inclusion of common land in parks. The authors of the petition saw themselves as being engaged in an unequal struggle with the landlords and sought legislative help to restrain them; otherwise they believed that they would be better off in Scotland than living in penury and misery in Norfolk.

The petition draws a picture of lords and tenants competing to control resources – timber, grazing rights on commons – and tenants trying to limit aggressive seigneurial expansion into tenant space.[33] The areas of conflict where custom needed to be recorded at North Elmham concerned the control of resources within the manor, notably wood and timber. Progressive enclosure may additionally indicate a rejection of the lord's right of foldcourse.

John Taverner seems to have recognized that custom was under pressure, and that without the act of recording it was likely to be lost. No court rolls are extant for the decades around mid-century and the scanty surviving materials fail to tell us how great the pressure on the tenants was before Taverner compiled his custumal. We cannot determine whether he was reacting to existing tensions within the manor or merely acknowledging a more generalized anxiety over the direction of change in the decade after the failure of Kett's revolt. The depositions do give us some clear evidence of how Cromwell's estate managers operated in the mid-1560s, and this may be seen, in part at least, as justifying Taverner's anxieties.

IV

Cromwell's officers and in particular his brother Thomas, who seems to have acted as his lawyer and agent, were determined to limit the tenants' claims to timber and were willing to resort to intimidation to get the results they sought.[34] The tenants maintained in their depositions a right to fell and carry away timber growing on their copyholds and offered examples of tenants (including Taverner) who, in the recent past, had taken advantage of that right. John Lusher of North Elmham recalled how John Taverner, James's father, had felled timber in Fulfordhaugh about 50 years previously and how James Taverner had felled further trees 19 years before. John Skoggone, who had been a servant of the Bishop of Norfolk's in the early 1520s, deposed that he was often at North

33 There is an echo of this in North Elmham with a dispute over the right of the lord to graze the Great Heath and have shack in Burgrave Field and West Field. C 21/T2/17, plaintiff's interrogatory, q. 14 and answers.

34 The following section draws on the depositions in C 21/T2/17 (taken on 15–16 August 1569). Individual references generally are not given.

Elmham and had never heard anything except that the tenants might fell timber for their own uses.

Cromwell sought to prove that the older practice had been to restrict the use of timber to repairs. William Rudde of Swanton Morley testified that 50 years previously it had been usual for the tenants to be charged in the manorial court to enquire for wilful waste in cutting down timber. He was quite emphatic that the tenants had no right to sell timber: it might only be deployed in repairs on their copyholds. On one occasion the Bishop of Norwich had cut wood and employed it in building a prison at King's Lynn. Rudde pointed to the case of one William Wakefield who was punished for waste in cutting down trees some 40 years earlier and had his lands seized. (Other deponents said that Wakefield had been forced to compound with the bishop for his copyhold.) Rudde also admitted to have colluded with the tenants over one Henry Rushton who escaped presentment for felling timber because 'diverse of the tenants required this deponent to do nothing therein for if he did, it would undo all the copyholders'. Other deponents gave evidence that the homage had enquired into the waste of trees. The example of the Town Close in Beetley was also brought forwards: after timber had been felled by the town, the bishop had forced the town to take it by a new copy as a punishment. Hence, on the spectrum of timber rights, the claim of the tenants was that the lord had no claim to the timber on copyholds: the current lord, Cromwell, claimed on the basis of older practice the ownership of the timber and so denied the tenants' right of sale. Hence he sought to revive an older custom which had perhaps lapsed in the first generation of lay ownership.

It is therefore a neat question to ask who was guiltier of creating new customs. Cromwell's estate officers were not satisfied to demonstrate the recent origins of the tenants' claims to timber but to secure what was – in effect – their submission and punishment. Taverner was eager to secure evidence of Cromwell's officer's conduct at a manorial court held in the spring of 1566.[35] The court met on the Monday before Whitsunday before William Yelverton as steward and John Brown as understeward. It would appear that the outcome of this court did not satisfy Cromwell's officers. According to Taverner, the officers kept the court going for three or four days, 'long seeking and devising by all means possible to have established their devices and new alterations'. The jurors were then called by two of the lord's officers, Edward Ireland and Thomas Hardy, to a meeting to view wastes made in Burgrave Wood. According to Taverner, this reconvened court met at 4am on the Monday after Whitsun; unfortunately, this is not confirmed by other witnesses.[36] It met in the absence of both Yelverton

35 C 3/155/5; Taverner's replication, but this account again draws heavily on C 21/T2/17.

36 This claim is made by Taverner in the replication in *Paulet v. Taverner*, C 3/155/5 from which the quotation is taken. In his sur-rejoinder, Paulet says that the verdict was given at 'nine

and Brown (although Brown deposed that he had engrossed the presentments arising from this extraordinary court session). Once at the wood, the tenants were confronted with a demand that they should find William Batche, James Taverner, Simon Shittell sen. and Richard Lackford guilty of cutting trees on their copyhold tenements, contrary to custom. It seems that the jury either twice or thrice refused to find the tenants guilty of the misdemeanour: 'They could not find any waste committed for the like was never used in their days'. On each occasion the presentment was rejected 'with stout words' by the officers present, and the tenants threatened. Finally, the tenants were intimidated into making the presentment that the officers sought.

This was not the limit of the intimidation to which individual tenants were subjected. Taverner, in his interrogatory, alleged that Thomas Cromwell had threatened a number of tenants who had approached him at Swaffenham on Taverner's behalf, leading them to fear that they would forfeit their copyholds if they deposed for him. It was alleged by Taverner that he had insinuated Henry Hayward onto the jury 'as his especial and lewd instrument to bring his evil practice to pass'. And it was claimed that Cromwell had rejected the tenants' verdict when it had not matched his or Heyward's 'fantasy', and had threatened the tenants 'with foul and indecent speech, calling them knaves, slaves and such like dishonest terms, affirming that "my lord has not an honest man in the town but only Henry Heyward"'.[37] None of the deponents testified in support of these claims, so there must be an element of doubt as to how true they were, but they may have found it prudent not to offer comment on the behaviour of the lord of the manor's brother. The interrogatories for Cromwell asked whether it was true that Thomas Cromwell had admonished the jury to be beware of perjury, and here perhaps lies the heart of the matter: what for the tenants was an honest account of their custom was, for the lord, their perjury.[38]

V

If Cromwell's officers were prepared to bully the tenants to get the outcome they sought, their treatment of Taverner bordered on the vindictive and far exceeded what was required to have the custumal abrogated.

It is not clear when or how the custumal came to the notice of Sir John Paulet and his officials. As we saw, Taverner was adamant that he had not tried to conceal

---

or ten o'clock in the forenoon'. Unfortunately the time at which the court was convened was not put to witnesses.

37 C 21/T2/17, plaintiff's interrogatory, qq. 7–9.

38 C 21/T2/17, defendant's interrogatory, q 17.

it but had sought to have the custumal accepted by the lord.[39] Paulet responded to Taverner with a suit in Star Chamber against him with Simon Shittell as co-defendant, alleging that the custumal was a forgery within the definitions of the 1563 act against forgery; but it seems that Taverner escaped by arguing that the custumal had been made before the queen's pardon issued at the end of the 1563 parliament and that it was not amongst the exceptions to the pardon.[40] Taverner therefore appears to have got off lightly at this point, and it was perhaps with some frustration that Paulet launched a suit in Chancery asking the court to order him to surrender the custumal to be defaced or destroyed. This was ordered by the court by its decree of February 1568.[41]

Paulet's interest in the manor ended with the death of his wife the following month. It then seems likely that Cromwell launched an ejectment (*ejectio firmae*) against Taverner and the other tenants, alleging that the making of the custumal was a forfeiture of their tenements and claiming forfeitures for unlicensed timber felling. Taverner responded with a defensive action in Chancery, the pleadings for which have not been found, but Chancery held in April and May 1570 that the alleged forfeiture should be tried at the common law. It also held that Cromwell's further claim – that forfeiture for felling timber on one copyhold entailed forfeiture of all of a tenant's copyholds within the manor – should not be accepted until further proof was shown.[42]

The litigation then moved to the theatre of the common law. Cromwell launched the first of a series of suits against Taverner, the first being (it would seem) an action of ejectment which came to be tried at Norwich assizes in 1568–69. The outcome of this was bills in both Chancery and Star Chamber. The nature of the ejectment was that a lease was made by the plaintiff, in this case one Cuthbert Fawcett, and the suit was brought in Fawcett's name against Taverner for the possession of the land. Notionally the suit was about Fawcett's ejectment from the land by Taverner, and so the trial was, in effect, one of who had the best title to the land – the lord's lessee, Fawcett, or the copyholder, Taverner. As the suit was tried before a jury, both parties could argue their title in a public forum. It was also possible for the trial to be, in effect, about issues

---

39 One wonders whether it was actually drafted with the consent of the elderly Paulet, who then found that his son-in-law would not accept it. Paulet was, of course, tenant by courtesy of England only, so his interest in the manor and capacity to bind his successors as lord was very limited indeed. I am grateful to Simon Healy for suggesting this line of thought.

40 This is claimed in the pleadings in the following Chancery suit and seemingly accepted by Paulet.

41 C 78/36 no. 38.

42 C 33/39, fos. 333r (27 April 1570), C 33/40, fo. 379r (8 May 1570). The depositions for this suit are C 21/T2/17.

other than the strict ownership of the land, and this was the case here. It is not immediately clear whether Cromwell wished to maintain that the custumal or the felling of timber was the justification for the forfeiture of Taverner's lands. But as Taverner says that the cause of the forfeiture was only worth 16*s*., it is likely that the case was conducted on a specimen charge of timber felling only.[43]

The trial of the lands was heard at Norwich assizes before Sir Robert Gatlyn, Lord Chief Justice, and Gilbert Gerrard, the queen's attorney general, and a jury of Norfolk gentlemen. In Taverner's account, the gentlemen were reluctant to hear the case 'for they understood the matter to be of great difficulty and also for that they were almost all of them utterly unacquainted with such business'.[44] He continues:

> The jury being very honest and substantial gentlemen did appear and being charged at the bar did move and persuade the defendant [Taverner] upon such promises as they said the Lord Cromwell ... had made unto them ... that he sought but the honour of the cause and not the thing in question, to submit himself to the same Lord Cromwell in giving him the honour by confessing the action, and they having such great trust to the promise of the said Lord Cromwell ... did warrant the defendant if he lost one foot of land ... they would give him as much of their own lands.

Taverner took the advice of his counsel and did not defend the case, saying that his confession should be neither prejudicial to his freehold lands nor to any copyhold he had purchased since the supposed forfeiture. Cromwell accepted this submission, and 'in open court before the jury then sworn, the worshipful of the shire and in the hearing of the people then assembled'[45] told the court that he would set down such an order with Taverner at the beginning of Michaelmas term as James and his friends would find very acceptable. Should Taverner not like what Cromwell proposed, then he would stand to the arbitration of the assize judges. In this way the trial was sidestepped. The jury, together with Taverner, then went and ate supper in Cromwell's lodgings. Cromwell showed Taverner great courtesy there and reiterated his promises to him; and also requested that Taverner should let him have the field book and other records Taverner had brought with him for the trial.[46]

---

43 For the process, A. W. B. Smith, *A History of the Land Law* (2nd edn, Oxford, 1986), ch. 7. For the reference to 16*s*., C 3/180/48, bill.

44 The following account is based on Taverner's bill in C 3/180/48 and his answer in STAC 5/C35/9 (first answer in the file).

45 C 3/180/48, bill.

46 Exactly what this book was remains slightly mysterious. Cromwell claimed it as 'an old ancient terrier or field book made in the time of King Henry VI' which Taverner had mutilated,

Afterwards (and here we must assume the following day), a number of gentlemen[47] attended on Cromwell to hear the final end which he had promised, but Cromwell made his excuses and deferred giving his award. Then Taverner, riding from Norwich after the assizes in the company of the vicar of North Elmham, was waylaid whilst on the queen's highway at Drayton Heath by several unknown men in Lord Cromwell's company. Taverner was able to outride his assailants, but the vicar was chased and beaten up. Then, at the next term (meaning, one must assume, at the next assizes), Cromwell did nothing regarding his former promise but secured a judgement against Taverner.

In fact, Taverner found that he had merely been manoeuvred into a position of vulnerability by Cromwell who, on his account, had the postea of the trial brought into Chancery for execution. Henry Lord Cromwell, on the other hand, insisted that a verdict had been given for Fawcett after three hours of debate between the counsels for both parties, and also alleged that Taverner had moved a writ of oyer in Queen's Bench for the reversal of the judgement.

Taverner then petitioned the Lord Chancellor, Sir Nicholas Bacon, a Suffolk landowner who had had his own problems with copyhold tenants and who must have been familiar with the issues of which Taverner complained.[48] Bacon spent some time with both parties trying to broker a settlement and offered to continue to do so, but Cromwell refused his invitation. The gentlemen of the county, evidently scandalized by Cromwell's conduct, wrote to Bacon complaining of him, and in Chancery Cromwell again refused to fulfil the promises he had made. He was therefore instructed that neither he nor anyone acting for him should execute any verdicts made against Taverner at the common law. By this time he was also bound to the court by recognizances.

At a later date Cromwell appeared in Chancery asking that the injunction against him should be dissolved and that he should be released from the recognizances. On 30 June 1571 Chancery gave Cromwell three options: to compromit the dispute to be settled by persons named by the court; to go for a new trial at common law, without taking advantage of the submission which the court clearly believed Taverner had been tricked into making, or to nominate

cutting out some leaves and gluing others in their place (STAC 5/C35/9). Taverner said that the book had been his father's, written for him by his brother-in-law Richard Silvester, vicar of North Elmham, 'for his own memory and knowledge of his own freehold and copyhold as by the hand of the said Richard appears' (STAC 5/C35/9, first answer).

47 Named as Mr Drew Drury, Thomas Payne, Nicholas Mynne and Bassingbourne Gawdy.

48 It is not clear whether Taverner petitioned Bacon privately or whether he petitioned Chancery. See Alan Simpson, *The Wealth of the Gentry, 1540–1660* (Cambridge, 1961), pp. 79–82 for Bacon's dealings with the tenants of Walsham-le-Willows. As Bacon negotiated fines of 2*s*. an acre here, it is unlikely that he was sympathetic to a claim of fines of 4*d*. an acre.

representatives to take part in a new arbitration. Thomas Cromwell, appearing for his brother, asked for time to confer with him and, appearing again a few days later, accepted the third option. Cromwell then appeared in person and named his arbitrators as the Chief Justice of King's Bench and one Adrian Stokes, and Taverner chose the Solicitor-General and a Mr Bell, both of whom were Cromwell's counsel. When Cromwell was asked to agree to this panel of four arbitrators he refused to accept any of them and would only compromit the hearing of the dispute with Taverner to his father-in-law Paulet and Thomas Cromwell, or to himself alone. This was unacceptable to Chancery, which responded by insisting that the injunctions against Cromwell should remain in force, whilst releasing Taverner from an injunction restraining him from pursuing a common law suit against Cromwell.

At the beginning of the following term, Chancery was informed of Cromwell's flouting of its rulings and injunctions. He had sued out and then persuaded the sheriff of Norfolk to serve a writ of execution on Taverner, and, with a party of servants, Cromwell had entered Taverner's lands and carried away his hay and corn. On 16 October the court, having considered its options, issued an attachment against Cromwell and, on 28 November, he appeared in person seeking to be released from it. When the court sought to question him about his contempt, he simply left the court and Westminster. He was finally arrested in January 1572 and ordered to attend the court daily until licensed to the contrary. Within a matter of days he pleaded that his wife was ill and was permitted to leave.[49]

The attachment of a peer took the court into uncharted waters. Cromwell protested about his treatment in the next session of parliament, and it was this which led to the House of Lords' ruling that Cromwell's treatment had been 'derogatory and prejudicial to the ancient precedent claimed to belong to the said lords of this realm'. This decision was against the advice of Bacon, who had doubtless had his fill of Cromwell, and with him in mind, argued that:

> [T]o leave all copyholders of noblemen without remedy, if they be removed from their copyholds by their lords, and all other men against noblemen in matters of equity, seems a great inconvenience and much prejudicial to the commonwealth considering how great the number of these besides ... [W]hat an inconvenient thing it is to have a

[49] The account in STAC 5/C35/9 continues as far as Cromwell's first withdrawal from Chancery. The orders of June 1571–Jan. 1572 are printed in C. Monro (ed.), *Acta Cancellariae, or selections from the records of the court of Chancery* (London, 1847), pp. 386–92 and are discussed in M. A. R. Graves, 'Freedom of peers from arrest: the case of Henry second Lord Cromwell, 1571–72', *American J. Legal History* 21 (1977), pp. 5–13.

> noblemen bring a matter in the Chancery and the court shall have power to do justice for him, but not against him. This is not *Jus equabile*.

The Lords ignored these arguments from principle and relieved Cromwell of the attachment against him.[50]

This seems shabby behaviour – and there are indications that it was deplored by some amongst the Norfolk gentry – which worked against Cromwell's own interests. Where he had greater success was in persuading Star Chamber that Taverner's custumal was an act of perjury and forgery which fell within the compass of the statute of 5 Elizabeth.[51] It seems that an early attempt to prove this failed, and Taverner managed to give Paulet the slip both by claiming that the statute did not encompass the particular circumstances and by citing a previous general pardon. There survives a set of proofs to show that Taverner's act was indeed forgery under the terms of the act.[52] This may date from the legal arguments which accompanied Cromwell's new Star Chamber suit, although the issue remained so opaque that a conference of judges was called to determine whether Taverner's actions fell within the terms of the act. Once they had found against him on the point of law, there was no question of Taverner's guilt and the records describe how he fell to his knees in court begging the queen's pardon, which was granted. He managed to escape the penalty of the forfeiture of his lands for life and the corporal punishment the act provided for malefactors. He was, though, liable to pay double the plaintiff's costs and damages. The costs were set at £21 16*s*. and the damages at £50, so Taverner found himself liable to pay what was in effect a fine of £142 2*s*. 8*d*. It was claimed by Cromwell in 1583 that he had recovered Taverner's lands as a forfeiture (although exactly how is not clear) and that as a result of this, Taverner had petitioned Star Chamber to be allowed to pay a reduced fine.[53]

VI

It would seem that Taverner had lost at least some of his lands to Cromwell. In 1582 he launched an attempt to recover them by bringing an action of trespass

---

50 Ibid. The case is also described in Sir John Baker (ed.), *Reports from the Lost Notebooks of Sir James Dyer* (2 vols, Selden Soc., 109–10, London, 1993–94), vol. 1, pp. 247–9.

51 The Star Chamber pleadings for this suit seem not to survive except for Taverner's examination made in February 1571/2, STAC5/C73/17. Extracts from the lost Star Chamber registers are printed by Baker (ed.), *Dyer's Reports* vol. 1, pp. 295–6.

52 E 36/194, pp. 458–66.

53 STAC 5/C42/9.

against Cromwell's lessee, no longer Fawcett but one James Cromwell. This was then sent for trial at Norwich assizes and, whilst the outcome of this trial is unknown, Cromwell launched a further Star Chamber suit alleging partiality in the selection of the jury to hear the suit. This finally came to be decreed in Star Chamber in Trinity Term 1587. The case provides an excellent insight into just how charged the treatment of copyholders had become in Norfolk by this time; it also suggests the continued unpopularity of Cromwell's treatment of Taverner.

The accusation was one of maintenance.[54] In the words of the *Oxford English Dictionary*, maintenance is 'the action of wrongfully aiding and abetting litigation; *specifically*, [the] support of a suit or suitor at law by a party who has no legally recognized interest in the proceedings'. Cromwell's claim was that Taverner had calculated that his action could succeed if it was heard by a jury of 'mean copyholders' who would disregard the earlier Star Chamber decrees and the evidence of the manor's court rolls. Taverner thus entered into a conspiracy with Roger Townsend esq., John Ferror and Thomas Feaverier for the return of a favourable jury. They ordered one Thomas Steward, gent, who was responsible to the Earl of Arundel for the return of juries in Launditch hundred, to return a jury of either people who had shown support for Taverner or who had been nominated by him. The panel he gathered consisted of persons:

> of very mean calling and such whose estate of living consists in substance depends upon copyhold lands, diverse of the persons so being of kindred, alliance or otherwise great friends or greatly beholden to [Taverner, Townsend, Farror and Feaverier].[55]

The allegation of suborning a jury was apparently made *before* the hearing, which suggests strongly that Cromwell was convinced that a jury of this character would find against him.

The key evidence in the suit was presented by Thomas Steward. It suggests that if anyone was behaving improperly, it was Cromwell. When Taverner launched his suit, Steward was summoned to Cromwell's house, where Cromwell offered him 'many favours' which Steward declined, asking Cromwell not to try to corrupt him. But Cromwell 'thrust £5 into [his] bosom'. Subsequently Cromwell sent to Steward's deputy, a man called Bastard, the names of a jury he wanted returned, and gave Bastard 10*s*. In Easter Term 1583 Steward was again requested to meet Cromwell and was again subjected to Cromwell's persuasions. Thomas Cromwell read him the names of a preferred jury from a roll, then told him that he would not give him the roll himself but would leave it in a window

---

54 The following account is based on STAC 5/42/9 and STAC 3/9/142, depositions in STAC 5/C58/5 and STAC 5/C78/14.

55 STAC 5/42/9, bill.

in Lord Cromwell's dining chamber, where Steward was to pick it up. Then in Trinity Term Steward was called to Cromwell a third time, entertained richly, given a deer pasty and promised all Cromwell's future favour.

The same term, Taverner delivered to Steward the writ to call a jury, the *venire facias*, and urged Steward to empanel an honest and indifferent jury. Steward told Taverner that he would not know their names until they were returned. Steward later jotted down a list of 30 names which he showed to Taverner to see if any of them were Cromwell's tenants. Taverner noted that the list contained Sir Roger Woodhouse, Sir Arthur Hevingham, John Peyton, John Drury and Anthony Brown, and diverse others 'of good worship and credit', and said that 'they would never appear and that if they were returned he [Taverner], "would not have his trial" or the like words in effect'.[56] Steward was also placed under pressure by both Townsend and Arundel to return an indifferent jury.

Steward then had some contact with Feaverier. Finding him uncertain as to how to approach the selection of the jury, Feaverier advised him to call 50 or 60 names out of which 24 indifferent men could be chosen. But Feaverier also suggested the names of people who were missing from the freeholders' book, and Feaverier, knowing the hundred better than Steward, supplied Steward with a list of additional names. In the end Arundel asked Steward for a list of freeholder's names. He then called Thomas Cromwell and Taverner to a meeting at his house to show them the names and invite them to choose an indifferent panel. But Cromwell would not cooperate, even when a second list of names was produced, insisting on a jury of knights and esquires. In the end an impartial panel of 24 men was made up on the earl's instructions by Townsend and two others. On Cromwell's complaint, it seems that the whole question was referred to the two chief justices, who held that the jury had been lawfully selected without any partial practice.[57] Cromwell's suit against Townsend dragged on until 1587 when he was acquitted of maintenance.[58]

For all the parties' attempts to secure a jury favourable to their cause, it seems likely that the jury which was finally empanelled was never asked to decide the case.[59] In the pleadings initiating the next round of litigation between Cromwell

56 STAC 5/C42/9, answer of Steward, Taverner and Feaverier.

57 STAC 3/9/142.

58 4 Leonard 203, repr. in *English Reports* 74, pp. 822–3 reports the Star Chamber hearing and Townsend's acquittal. The account it gives of the case is extremely selective and makes no reference to Cromwell's attempts to secure a favourable jury.

59 For what follows, see STAC 5/C17/9, bill, and depositions taken at Walsingham on 15 Sept. 1586; and STAC 5/C30/21, examination of Taverner and others, 26 Oct. 1586. It is not clear whether the trial took place in Trinity Term 1585 or the following year; both dates are implied but 1585 seems most likely.

and Taverner, Cromwell described how at the previous trial he had shown how the cause of the forfeiture was the forgery of the custumal. Cromwell proved the erroneous nature of its claims in three respects – the payment of knowledge money, the right to take timber and the custom of fixed fines – and further had read to the court the earlier judgements of Star Chamber which had found against Taverner. The presiding judges ruled that the evidence against Taverner was so clear-cut that he had no case. Nonetheless he was allowed to give evidence for the fixity of the rate of fines, and this led to a new claim of forgery in a further Star Chamber suit of 1585–86.

Cromwell's accusation was that Taverner had given in evidence to the court a survey which claimed, *inter alia*, that the fine due on surrenders of copyhold should be 4*d*. an acre and no more. This, in Cromwell's view, was another false and forged document which Taverner had conspired to make with one John Brown of Marsham. Taverner pleaded not guilty to the allegation and described not only what the book was, but also how it came into his possession, and his claims were verified by successive deponents. The book had been made by Lord St John's estate officers, Edward Ireland and Thomas Hardy, in 1566. The surveyors had invited the tenants who could write to enter into it an abstract of their copies and leases, to which were added further abstracts by Brown who was then steward of the manor. The book came into Taverner's hands through his brother Roger when he was bringing the action of intrusion into the manor in the Queen's name against Cromwell. On inspection, Taverner found that the majority of entries contained a statement on the lines of 'et dat de fine secundum ratum cuiuslibet acre iiijd secundum consuetudine manerii', which he took to be evidence of a fixed rate of fines. When the book was exhibited in Queen's Bench, Brown had been present and was asked directly by the presiding judges whether the entries were in his hand, and he confirmed that they were. Brown was named as co-defendant in the Star Chamber suit: his answer was evasive in the extreme, claiming that he had written out a copy of some notes concerning the fine of copyhold lands at Taverner's request. Taverner rejected the notion that he would have used Brown as a scrivener and pointed out that after the hearing of Taverner's case, Brown had been deprived from the stewardship and then reinstated. Indeed, Taverner suggested that Brown recorded the fines of the manor as being fixed at 4*d*. an acre because, until that time, there had never been any suggestion to the contrary.

The depositions therefore concentrated on the circumstances in which the survey was made in 1566. A number of tenants, including some of the lord's officers, gave evidence for Taverner. Simon Gogney of Brisley, gent – who at the time was Cromwell's bailiff in North Elmham and Beetley – described how Ireland and Hardy had stayed at Brown's house in Brisley at Whitsuntide when making the survey. Hardy, at the end of the previous year, had commanded the tenants to come in and show him their copies and leases. Gogney, on Hardy's instructions and with the help of others, entered copies of these documents into the book in contention. He confirmed that some of the entries referring to the fixed rate of fines were in the hand of John Brown, Cromwell's steward. This collection of documents had been a preliminary to the making of a field book by the surveyors in the company of the tenants of the manor. Other tenants confirmed the broad outlines. Thomas Heyward of North Elmham, and his brother Henry of Thetford, gent., both identified by Taverner as Cromwell loyalists, and William Batche, one of the individuals sued by St John in the late 1560s, confirmed both the circumstances in which the book was made and the hands that it contained. There is therefore no credible support for the claim of forgery: the book was made by St John's own officers as a preparatory to the surveying of the manor. It seems that it was sufficiently incautious to record evidence of a fixed rate of fines, but the depositions suggest that the surveyors themselves did not see it as any of their purpose to raise fines, nor did they see themselves as being the means by which fines could be raised. William Batche, who was amongst those who were anxious about Cromwell's intentions and had supported Taverner's drafting of a custumal, recounted how he and Thomas Heyward had dined with Hardy at Simon Gogney's house. In this company Hardy had said:

> What is a wretch is this Taverner to report and give out that the lord of the manor or we for him do go about to change and alter the accustomed fine of 4*d*. the acre of copyhold lands of the manor.

Other deponents gave evidence that before Cromwell's entry into the manor, the rate of fines had indeed been 4*d*. an acre. In this light, Cromwell's charge of forgery is not an attempt to suppress *manufactured* evidence so much as it is an overt attempt to suppress *inconvenient* evidence. The book of copies had been made by Cromwell's own employees. It contained what they knew – or at least believed – to be true at the time. It represented a memory – a knowledge – which was unacceptable to Cromwell and which he sought to suppress.

VII

This did not conclude the problems which Taverner had with Cromwell, or Cromwell with Taverner. Taverner brought a further Star Chamber suit against Cromwell for the possession of his land in 1590, the *casus belli* for which seems to have been a survey of the manor instituted by Cromwell and an attempt to distinguish Cromwell's land from Taverner's.[60] The difficulty of distinguishing the lands of the parties continued after Cromwell's death in 1592 and it seems that his son, Edward Lord Cromwell, was willing to come to a composition with Taverner for the return of his copyholds and the settlement of other disputes, on payment of a fine of £400. This was passed to the arbitration of the attorney-general, Sir Edward Coke, who then agreed to buy the manor from Cromwell, and the arbitration was assigned to Robert Houghton. Taverner was reluctant to accept Houghton's award, but it was finally decreed by Chancery in 1602.[61]

VIII

Two years after Taverner's death, the tenants of Methwold in Suffolk explained how 'For our fines, they were certain: but now, by what means we know not, our custom is so broken that they are arbitrable.'[62] In a great many manors, this erosion of tenants' rights was incremental and largely unrecorded. *Cromwell v. Taverner* shows just how sharp the conflicts between custom and improvement could be – and it describes them in some detail. Read in one way, this is a story of a maverick copyholder, determined to protect his rights and conscious of the way in which the safeguards inherent in custom were evaporating.[63] He therefore set about establishing those customary claims by making an attested record of them. He was not without the support of his fellow tenants in this endeavour. His difficulty though was that the tenants' recollection outside a manorial or curial forum carried little weight, and his attempt not only to preserve memory but also to secure seigneurial sanction for it drew down on him a lifetime of litigation. It was, in one sense, an act of forgery, but it is not as though Taverner was tampering with existing documents: he was creating one from first principles.

---

60 STAC 5/T11/3.

61 For letters concerning this arbitration, Carthew, *Launditch Hundred*, vol. 2, pp. 567–68. The decree is C 78/103 no. 14. Coke plainly found Taverner a difficult and truculent customer and wrote him an aggressive letter telling him not to cross him.

62 Simpson, *Wealth of the Gentry*, p. 80.

63 For another maverick figure, Hoyle, 'Redefining Copyhold', pp. 259–61.

It is also an account of an unusually vindictive manorial lord, who perhaps saw the opportunity to seize the lands of a prosperous copyholder as a means of securing his own windfall profit. Cromwell might best be understood as an example of a phenomenon discussed elsewhere: the lord who entered into a manor which had been laxly administered over the previous generation, and who tried to overturn settled arrangements for his own profit.[64] Cromwell can be seen trying to shift the balance of power in the manor from the tenants to himself, to recover lost rights (for instance the foldcourse) but also to prick tenant pretensions. On the way we get insights into the more general state of landlord–tenant relations in Norfolk in the third quarter of the sixteenth century, not least the conviction, apparently shared by both Cromwell and Taverner, that copyholder jurors would vote in solidarity with another copyholder.

Read in another way, this is an account of rival attempts to control memory. Taverner expressed a fear that the customs of the manor would be lost with the death of the older tenants and through the ignorance and negligence which might arise through changes of steward. Hence, for Taverner, the custom of the manor lay first and foremost in the memory of the tenants. In another example, after the old custumal of Great Bentley in Essex was lost, it was the tenants who were asked, in 1583–84, to depose as to their customs.[65] Likewise, in suits over custom, the process of writing pleadings and then having individual tenants depose was all a process of discovering the custom of the manor from the tenants. Notoriously, Samuel Sandys at Ombersley waited until the older tenants were dead and their recollection of custom lost before he started to challenge custom, understanding that the memory of younger tenants carried less weight in the courts.[66] This introduces us to two paradoxes: first that the answer to the fragility but flexibility of memory was the permanence of parchment; and the second that Taverner seems to have been trying to record the middle-distance recollection of the tenants, their experience since the acquisition of the manor by Henry's minister, Thomas Cromwell. But the most compelling evidence against them seems to have come from deponents who recalled conditions on the manor during the administration of the Bishops of Norwich in the generation before. Fines may well have remained at around *4d.* an acre throughout the middle decades of the sixteenth century; but the permissive timber custom seems to

---

64 H. R. French and R. W. Hoyle, *The Character of English Rural Society: Earls Colne, 1550–1750* (Manchester, 2007), pp. 32–4, 145–7, 171–2.

65 F. G. Emmison, *Elizabethan Life: Home, Work and Land from Essex Wills and Sessions and Manorial Records* (Chelmsford, 1976, repr. 1991), p. 320.

66 P. Large, 'Rural Society and Agricultural Change: Ombersley, 1580–1700', in J. Chartres and D. Hey (eds), *English Rural Society, 1500–1800: Essays in Honour of Joan Thirsk* (Cambridge, 1990), p. 116.

have been something new and an aspect of the lax administration of the manor by Gregory Lord Cromwell, his widow and perhaps her second husband, Paulet. What lay at the heart of the dispute were rival memories, both self-serving.

The evidence points towards the rate of fines on the manor being *4d.* an acre in the years before Henry Lord Cromwell entered. Taverner therefore stood in the way of the modernization of the income from the manor, but in a real sense his formulation of the custumal gave Cromwell the stick with which to beat him. The custumal made claims and recorded practices which the lord would have preferred to be forgotten. For Cromwell though, the competition was not only about the control of memory but also the control of the documentary representation of memory. He demanded to know of Taverner whether he had ever perused the court rolls. He recovered from him manorial estreats which were probably of little value and legitimately in tenant hands.[67] He insisted on Taverner surrendering the 'forged' custumal. He persuaded Taverner to give him his father's book of records which Cromwell plainly viewed with suspicion. Cromwell claimed that a document made by his own estate officers, some of whom he still employed, was a further forgery. For Cromwell, the memory of the tenants was a thing best lost. Where memory was perishable and wasted with time, the documents posed a continuous threat. Hence documents which offered evidence to counter Cromwell's preferred narrative had to be denounced as forgeries: confiscated and perhaps destroyed. Whilst Cromwell could not control the memory of the tenants, he could count on its effacement through time; but he was determined, it seems, to establish a manorial monopoly over the documentary evidence of memory.

---

[67] STAC 5/C73/17, qq. 12–13 and Taverner's answers.

Chapter 2

The Articulation, Transmission and Preservation of Custom in the Forest Community of Duffield (Derbyshire)

*Heather Falvey**

In February 1641, during a lawsuit concerning the nature of entry fines brought before the court of the Duchy of Lancaster by the leading tenants of Duffield against the lord of the manor, deponents on behalf of the tenants were asked whether one Anthony Bradshaw was 'well acquaynted with the customes and usages of the said mannour? And was hee not industrious and carefull in wryteing and keepeing books of the sayd customes and usages? And was not the booke nowe shewed unto you the sayd Anthony Bradshawes booke?'.[1] Some four decades later, in 1683 during the commission relating to a Chancery suit between John Heynes *et al.* and Henry Mellor *et al.*, another of Anthony Bradshaw's books, entitled 'Notes of Duffeld Frythe customes', was shown to Vicesimus and George Bradshaw, two of his descendants, when examined on various interrogatories for the complainants.[2] During that commission, the two men were also required to answer interrogatories relating to a third volume written by Bradshaw, which comprised a dialogue on the customs of

---

* I began researching the subject of this chapter in 1999. Thanks are due to three people who were there at the beginning: Andy Wood, who signposted Duffield and has frequently discussed with me the preservation of custom; Evelyn Lord, who provided a copy of a vital article in *The Reliquary*; and, above all, Steve Hindle, who from the outset has been a constant source of guidance and encouragement. Thanks also to Richard Hoyle for asking me to contribute to this volume, enabling me to fix my ideas in the written record.

1 The National Archives (TNA), DL 4/98/29, Attorney General on behalf of Thomas Chaloner *et al. v.* Sir Edward Leech, interrogatory number 2 for the defendant. The document shown to deponents was entitled 'These concern Coppyholders specially and concordat *cum le Cowcher* etc. and *Libertates et Consuetudines* etc.' It does not seem to be in the collection of Bradshaw's writings now held in the Derbyshire Record Office (DRO). In this chapter extracts from MSS are printed with their original spelling, but with capitalization and punctuation according to modern practice.

2 DRO, D2402 A/PZ 2/1, fo. 15v.

Duffield between him and an old friend.[3] Furthermore, as late as 1792, during the commission relating to the Exchequer suit between William Lygon *et al.* and Jedediah Strutt *et al.*, this latter volume was shown to one Charles Upton, gentleman, when being examined on one of the defendants' interrogatories.[4]

Anthony Bradshaw's writings evidently proved crucial to the defence of custom in this particular community. This chapter investigates who Bradshaw was and why it was that his records of Duffield's customary practices continued to be so important in local usage nearly 200 years after his death. Having first discussed the changing nature and form of custom in early modern England, it will then examine in detail the Crown's attempts to implement improvement policies at Duffield, and the community's reactions to them, principally through Bradshaw's tripartite role as champion, recorder and transmitter of its many and varied customs. Whether he adopted this role because he believed in the superiority of custom over contractual tenancy *per se* or because he wished to advance his own interests as a copyholder is unclear – perhaps a combination of the two. What is clear is that his private role clashed with his official role as deputy steward of the manor, since he actively aligned himself with the tenants against the landlord. Whatever his motivation, by defending and protecting local customs in court and recording them for posterity, his career and writings embody the various strategies that might be mobilized in defence of custom. In rendering Duffield's customs into verse, moreover, Bradshaw was transmitting them in a form that was both traditional, by rhyming memories for future generations, and yet at the same time innovative, by mirroring or even anticipating the work of the newly formed Society of Antiquaries. Before considering his activities, we should meet the man.

I

Born in February 1545/6, Anthony was the fourth and youngest son of William Bradshaw of Bradshaw, near Buxton.[5] He graduated BA at Oxford in 1566 and in 1573 was admitted to the Inner Temple, where he was to practise for more than

---

3 Ibid., p. 68.

4 Ibid., note on front cover.

5 Sheffield Archives (SA), BD 97, 'register' of the births of the children of William Bradshaw of Bradshaw; SA, BD 121, the pedigree of Anthony Bradshaw of Duffield. Transcripts of these two manuscripts have been published in C. E. B. Bowles, 'Bradshaw and the Bradshawes', in J. C. Cox (ed.), *Memorials of Old Derbyshire* (London and Derby, 1907), p. 175 and insertion between pp. 180–81.

30 years.[6] He was also an attorney in the Court of Common Pleas at Westminster for over 20 years but few details of his legal practice have survived.[7] As early as 1576, various commoners in Duffield Frith retained him as their solicitor in a suit against Charles Pagett, esquire, who was preventing them exercising their common rights. Bradshaw's appointment on this occasion probably owed much to local connections, for although he himself was not then resident there, members of the extended Bradshaw family were already living in the Duffield area.[8] By 1593, however, Bradshaw had been living in Duffield for several years, although he apparently still considered himself a 'stranger in effect there, And yette not throughlie acquynted with the true customes of the same mannour'.[9] This claim was either falsely modest or disingenuous since in 1588, together with several leading tenants, he had attended a meeting with the Crown's agent, Sir Edward Stanhope, concerning Duffield's manorial customs.[10] In 1594 he was noted as being a suitable man to serve as coroner and steward of nearby Belper.[11] By the 1590s he had made his home at Farleys Hall, on the opposite side of the River Derwent from Duffield's parish church of St Alkmund, but little is known of the house and its estate.[12] In addition to this large house, he held arable, meadow and pasture in the manor, together with various cottages and lands that he let to 'certen other poore men his undertenants'.[13] From his testament, dated September 1613, it is clear that some of his lands were copyhold or customary holdings, and others were freehold; however, the precise details of his landed wealth are impossible to reconstruct due to the absence not only of manorial surveys and rentals but also of his will, by which, according to his testament, he had disposed of his freeholdings and to which he had surrendered the use of

---

6 J. Foster, *Alumni Oxonienses: The Members of the University of Oxford, 1500–1714* (4 vols, Oxford, 1891), vol. I, p. 168.

7 DRO, D2402 A/PZ 6/1, p. 60.

8 T. L. Tudor, *New Light on Duffield Church and Its Ancient Parish* (Derby, 1939), p. 52. One of the homage jurors for Duffield Frith in 1542 was named Thomas Bradshaw (DRO, D6230/2/20). Bradshaw's defence of the tenants had been successful but he subsequently brought a suit against them for non-payment of his fees, TNA, DL 1/124/B15.

9 TNA, DL 1/160/B5, *Bradshaw v. Johnson*, 35 Elizabeth.

10 TNA, DL 44/305, fo. 1. This meeting is discussed in detail below.

11 C. Jamison (ed.), *A Calendar of the Shrewsbury and Talbot Papers in Lambeth Palace Library and the College of Arms*, I, *Shrewsbury MSS in Lambeth Palace Library (MSS 694–710)* (Derbyshire Record Ser., 1, 1966), MS 701, fo. 159.

12 Nothing remains of the house today but its site is indicated on early Ordnance Survey maps by two areas of woodland called 'The Farleys' and 'Little Farleys', east of the Derwent.

13 TNA, DL 1/160/B5, Bradshaw *v.* Johnson.

his customary holdings.[14] He was farmer of the queen's two mills at Duffield, a supposedly lucrative holding that nevertheless proved costly in lawsuits.[15] From at least 1606 to 1609 he also held the prestigious office of steward to the sheriff's tourn.[16]

Married twice, he fathered no fewer than 23 children, 15 of whom were living when he drew up his pedigree in 1610.[17] His funeral monument, constructed in 1600, 14 years before his death, depicts him, his wives Griselda and Elizabeth and his 20 then-born children.[18] Most of his children's names were unusual for the period and are indicative not only of erudition but also of a sense of humour: several were classical in origin, for example, Jacinth (as a boy's name), Cassandra and Felix (as a girl's name). Others were ancient saints' names, for example, Quintin, Petronilla, Isodora, Athanasia and Mildred; and yet others were 'new', in that he appears to have invented them, for example, Exuperius (possibly from *exuperate*, 'to overtop, surpass, excel; to overcome'), Brandona (origin unknown), Vicesimus (the twentieth child) and Penultima (the twenty-second).[19] Under normal circumstances providing for such a large brood would have been expensive, but Bradshaw's testament also reveals an extraordinary strain on his finances: Exuperius, his eldest surviving son, had mishandled his expenses whilst holding county office, so Anthony had had to stand surety for him and had borrowed heavily to settle his son's accounts.[20]

Apart from making provision for his younger children, Bradshaw's main testamentary concerns were the perpetuation of the almshouse that he had recently established in Duffield, and the preservation and future use of his numerous records of local customs. In terms of its size, the almshouse was a modest foundation for 'two aged or ympotent men and two like women, widows

---

14 Lichfield RO, B/C/11, testament of Anthony Bradshaw, gentleman, dated 16 Sept. 1613; probate granted 3 May 1614.

15 TNA, DL 1/171/A15; 180/B33; DL 4/38/45; DL 5/19, fos. 209v–13r; DL 42/98, fos. 279r–v.

16 DRO, D6386/1, minutes of the sheriff's tourn, Morleston and Litchurch hundred, 1606–09. Bradshaw kept the minutes of the eight twice-yearly courts recorded in this document. It appears that sheriff's records were not kept systematically and no similar records have been traced for any other county. For the sheriff's tourn, see J. H. Baker, *An Introduction to English Legal History* (3rd edn, London, 1990), pp. 29, 30.

17 SA, BD 121.

18 The monument, recently restored, stands in a small chapel off the north aisle of St Alkmund's church, Duffield.

19 The definition of *exuperate* is from the *Oxford English Dictionary* (*OED*). At least one local family, the Fletchers, imitated Bradshaw and named a son 'Exuperius' (TNA, SP17/E14, m. 23, Hundred of Appletree (1639): Exuperius Fletcher of Belper, private man armed with a pike.)

20 Lichfield RO, B/C/11, testament of Anthony Bradshaw, gentleman.

or others of honest behaviour', established in a cottage that he owned in Duffield and funded by the rent from a freehold property in Derby.[21] The purposes of the foundation were less modest: every Christmas the residents were to be given russet coats 'to have thereupon sowed on the brest this lettre .AB. in red cloth';[22] every week the youngest was to 'dresse, make cleane, and dust downe my pew, formes, and monument in the church of Duffeld';[23] and the eldest was to keep the key to his 'register' (of which more below). Regarding his records of local customs, he bequeathed Jacinth, his eldest son by his second wife, all his 'bookes of the lawe and written bookes of Customes and notes touching the manours in Duffeild Frith and copyhoulds, to keepe and peruse them some times for his owne experience and to ayd his neighbors withal, as occacion may serve'.[24] Whereas his almshouse foundation encapsulates Anthony Bradshaw's view of his own self-importance, his bequest to Jacinth encapsulates the importance that he placed on the perpetuation of Duffield's customs.

II

'Custom' is a multi-faceted concept. Here the focus is on its particular legal sense: custom that governed the local organization of access to property in terms of land tenure and inheritance arrangements, or of agricultural routines and the apportionment of common rights. In this context, custom was the articulation of the usages of any community, but usually those of a manor. Indeed, custom had no existence outside a community for, as Susan Reynolds has pointed out, 'it is the nature of custom that it presupposes a group or community within which it is practised'.[25] Richard Gough, writing early in the eighteenth century, described it thus: 'Custome is a law or right, not written, which being established by long use and the consent of our ancestors, hath been and is dayly practised'.[26] As the expression of communal practice, custom might be both respected by most (though not invariably all) inhabitants and contested by outsiders.

21 For the endowment of the almshouse and the regulations governing the inmates, see DRO, D2402 A/PZ 6/1, pp. 65–8; these have been published in C. Kerry, 'Anthony Bradshaw, of Duffield, and the alms houses founded by him at that place', *The Reliquary* 23 (1882–83), pp. 137–40. Quotation here from DRO, D2402 A/PZ 6/1, p. 65.

22 Ibid., p. 66. The 'AB' is written as a ligature in the original.

23 Ibid., p. 67.

24 Lichfield RO, B/C/11, testament of Anthony Bradshaw, gentleman.

25 S. Reynolds, *Kingdoms and Communities in Western Europe, 900–1300* (Oxford, 1984), p. 21.

26 R. Gough, *The History of Myddle*, ed. D. Hey (Harmondsworth, 1981), p. 64.

Custom had the force of law in the manor: it was *lex loci*, that is, the law of the place; indeed, E. P. Thompson called it the interface between law and common practice.[27] Provided that it fulfilled three important criteria, custom was also accepted as legitimate by the central courts of common law and equity.[28] Firstly, it had to be 'reasonable, and of benefit to the person(s) exercising the claim'; secondly, it had to originate 'beyond the memory of man' (Gough: 'consent of our ancestors'), legally prior to 1189 but effectively within the memory of the oldest inhabitants; thirdly, it had to be exercised continuously (Gough: 'hath been and is dayly practised').

Since custom was transmitted from the past, many historians have described it as 'conservative'. Both Buchanan Sharp and Keith Lindley have concluded that by defending 'ancient customs' opponents of improvement in forests and fens were trying to restore the former *status quo* rather than better their lot or transform the social order, and that they were aiming to preserve the existing fabric of local society from the onslaught of progress.[29] However, as John Walter has argued, 'there is a danger of conflating custom with conservatism'.[30] Although those invoking custom were harking back to the traditions of the past, they did not necessarily intend or desire to return to past circumstances. Rather they anticipated the consequences of proposed changes and concluded that they would benefit the encloser, rather than the majority of commoners; the new lessees, rather than those excluded from the disputed land; the drainers, rather than local inhabitants; and those controlling the land allotted to the poor, rather than the poor themselves. Walter suggests therefore that whilst there was clearly what we might term 'a politics of nostalgia', historians should not confuse 'traditional' with 'conservative'.[31] Defenders of custom sought to confer on it the authority of the past in order to preserve the inheritance of their posterity.[32] Janus-like, they were simultaneously looking backwards and forwards.

27 E. P. Thompson, *Customs in Common: Studies in Traditional Popular Culture* (London, 1991), p. 98.

28 A. Wood, 'Custom and the Social Organisation of Writing in Early Modern England', *Trans. Royal Historical Society,* 6th ser., 9 (1999), p. 259.

29 B. Sharp, *In Contempt of All Authority: Rural Artisans and Riot in the West of England, 1586–1660* (London, 1980), p. 86; K. Lindley, *Fenland Riots and the English Revolution* (London, 1982), p. 57.

30 J. Walter, *Understanding Popular Violence in the English Revolution: The Colchester Plunderers* (Cambridge, 1999), p. 4.

31 J. Walter, 'The English people and the English Revolution revisited', *History Workshop J.* 61 (2006), p. 175.

32 A. Wood, *The Politics of Social Conflict: The Peak Country, 1520–1770* (Cambridge, 1999), p. 325; A. Wood, 'The place of custom in plebeian political culture: England 1550–1800', *Social Hist.* 22 (1997), pp. 52–3.

Although their origins are impossible to trace, many customary systems appear to have their roots in the late Saxon period.[33] Local custom was passed down orally, and was preserved by and in living memory.[34] The elders of a community were, accordingly, 'the repositories of local precedent and the custodians of communal memory'.[35] As Fentress and Wickham have noted, however, social memory was 'not a passive receptacle but instead a process of active restructuring in which elements may be retained, reordered or suppressed'.[36] What was being remembered might transmute over time; consequently although custom was a source of definition, giving form to local practices, this form could be highly flexible. Thus custom was frequently a source of contention, both creating and resulting from differing interpretations and recollections: there was scope for change over time, and even for invention.[37] But there was always the risk that memories might be lost altogether. In another chapter in this volume, Richard Hoyle shows how the awareness of John Taverner of North Elmham to the dangers of loss led him to compile a custumal without seigneurial sanction. At Ombersley (Worcestershire), the lord of the manor, Samuel Sandys, waited until most of the oldest inhabitants – 'the embodiment of the local customary heritage' – were dead before attempting to make entry fines arbitrary by virtue of a suit in the Exchequer.[38]

Debates over the effects of literacy on the nature and significance of custom have focused on the issue of codification. Did the 'fixing' of custom in the written record weaken the power of its oral articulation or did it strengthen, perhaps even jog, local memory?[39] David Rollison has suggested that writing might have resulted in 'the delegitimisation of the oral and aural cultures' because literacy

---

33 Personal communication from Andy Wood.

34 J. Fentress and C. Wickham, *Social Memory* (Oxford, 1992), ch. 1, 'Remembering'.

35 A. Fox, *Oral and Literate Culture in England, 1500–1700* (Oxford, 2000), p. 261.

36 Fentress and Wickham, *Social Memory*, p. 40.

37 K. Wrightson, 'The Politics of the Parish in Early Modern England', in P. Griffiths, A. Fox and S. Hindle (eds), *The Experience of Authority in Early Modern England* (Basingstoke, 1996), p. 23.

38 R. W. Hoyle, '*Cromwell v. Taverner*: Landlords, Copyholders and the Struggle to Control Memory in Mid-Sixteenth Century Norfolk', above pp. 39–63; P. Large, 'Rural Society and Agricultural Change: Ombersley 1580–1700', in J. Chartres and D. Hey (eds), *English Rural Society, 1500–1800: Essays in Honour of Joan Thirsk* (Cambridge, 1990), p. 116, quotation from p. 113.

39 A. Fox, 'Custom, Memory and the Authority of Writing', in Griffiths, Fox and Hindle (eds), *Experience of Authority*, pp. 89–116; Fox, *Oral and literate culture*, especially ch. 5; D. Rollison, *The Local Origins of Modern Society: Gloucestershire 1500–1800* (London, 1992), pp. 12–15 and ch. 3; Wood, 'Custom'.

was the tool of the 'ruling classes'.[40] Rather than being a prompt, he insists, literacy 'dis-located memory': that is, because writing located memory in a document which could be archived anywhere rather than in the remembrances of the local community, literacy 'removed the junction between collective memory and local identity'.[41] As Sandys had hoped at Ombersley, however, oral memories might themselves be permanently entombed in the parish churchyard, dying with those who remembered them. Despite Rollison's pessimism, therefore, writing might actually perpetuate customs which were otherwise at risk of attrition. Hence Isaac Gilpin of Egremont (Cumberland) was persuaded by his neighbours to record local customs so that 'what I had learn[e]d from my old father or by my own experience, I would committ to writing that it might remaine to posterity and not be buried with me in my grave'.[42] Accordingly Adam Fox has considered the role played by writing in the preservation and articulation of custom. When charting the rise of literacy, he has been careful to demonstrate that there was 'no simple or linear substitution' of memory by writing.[43] Indeed, in the past many envisioned writing as an adjunct to memory. This is certainly the implication of a scribal formula used in twelfth-century Burgundy which observed that writing was 'invented for the preservation of the memory of things ... [so that] things that we are unable to hold in our weak and fragile memories, are conserved by writing, and by the means of letters which last forever'.[44] As Fox and Woolf have demonstrated, moreover, the spheres of oral and written culture were overlapping rather than 'mutually exclusive and opposed processes for representing and communicating information'.[45] There were, nonetheless, some arenas in which oral and written culture did clash, the most significant conflict being that between custom and the law.

From the mid-sixteenth century onwards, an increasingly active market for land meant that the legitimacy and form of customs passed down by word of mouth began to be challenged. Many incoming landlords were new to the locality, others were non-resident; few of them, therefore, either knew or

---

40 Rollison, *Local Origins*, p. 13.

41 Ibid., p. 71. The definition of 'dislocation' is from Wood's critique of Rollison in Wood, 'Custom and the social organisation of writing', p. 259.

42 A. Bagot, 'Mr Gilpin and manorial customs', *Trans. Cumberland and Westmorland Antiquarian and Archaeological Society*, new ser., 62 (1962), p. 226.

43 Fox, *Oral and Literate Culture*, p. 297.

44 J. Le Goff, *Historie et mémorie* (Paris, 1988), p. 140, quoted in Fentress and Wickham, *Social Memory*, p. 8.

45 A. Fox and D. Woolf, 'Introduction', in Fox and Woolf (eds), *The Spoken Word: Oral Culture and Britain, 1500–1850* (Manchester, 2002), p. 8.

understood the *lex loci*.[46] In such manors, the local laws and regulations recalled by juries were often written down as an *aide-memoire* for the new landlord. It might be assumed that such written agreements would only benefit the landlord, since tenants' memories were now codified and could no longer be selective or transmuted, but where charges such as entry fines and heriots were fixed in these agreements, the landlord was prevented from making arbitrary charges in future. Thus, even in manors where customs were transliterated, it does not necessarily follow that the landlord exercised unlimited authority over the wording of custumals. These documents frequently resulted from negotiation, following an elaboration of the customs alleged to obtain. In such circumstances, the rendering of oral custom into writing was 'a formal, ideal statement of the balance of power at one given moment'.[47] Having examined many such documents, drawn up following manorial surveys or inquisitions, Fox has concluded that in 'attempting to transmute oral or ill-defined customs into written and codified documents, people of all sorts attempted to provide themselves with what they believed to be the best means of defending and advancing their rights and interests'.[48] Such written records were not, however, wholly trusted, especially as they were produced for and kept by the lord of the manor – whose interests might be diametrically opposed to those of his tenants. Written records relating to a community compiled, maintained and retained by an astute local resident might, accordingly, be viewed in a different light by his neighbours. The more significant issue, therefore, is not whether writing was preferable to oral memory, but the locus of possession of the written record once it had been produced. During disputes between the Cotton family and the tenants of Glatton and Holme (Huntingdonshire), for example, both sides took possession of various old manorial records in order to substantiate their case or to prevent their opponents from so doing.[49] Thus the ownership of the archive in which memory was inscribed might be a significant variable wherever custom was mobilized or contested, and this certainly proved to be the case at Duffield.

46 Fox, *Oral and Literate Culture*, p. 289.

47 Wood, 'Custom', p. 265.

48 Fox, 'Custom', p. 110.

49 R. B. Manning, 'Antiquarianism and the seigneurial reaction: Sir Robert and Sir Thomas Cotton and their tenants', *Historical Res.* 63 (1990), pp. 277–88, *passim*. Again, this is also an aspect of the conflict between Cromwell and Taverner.

III

Duffield was a classic example of a 'custom-driven' community, and its inhabitants not only frequently exercised their rights but also carefully preserved them in local memories and in written records. During the late sixteenth and early seventeenth centuries the Crown and its officers proposed numerous schemes for increasing revenue from royal estates like Duffield, many of which would directly undermine or even abolish ancient customs and customary rights. Even though they were allegedly for the benefit of the 'commonwealth', projects such as the drainage of the fens, the exploitation of woodland and mineral resources, the enfranchisement of copyholders, the sale of manors and the disafforestation and enclosure of forests all rode roughshod over local considerations and practices.[50] Between the 1580s and 1630s the manor of Duffield and the ancient royal forest known as Duffield Frith, both of which were part of the Duchy of Lancaster, appeared to be ripe for such pickings.[51] The Crown's fiscal harvest at Duffield was, however, paltry. As the following discussion suggests, royal policies failed there principally because they underestimated the strength of local opposition: most tenants considered their ancient customs and rights more beneficial than any inducements that might be on offer from Crown surveyors or projectors.

Situated in the east of Appletree Hundred, on the cusp of fertile south Derbyshire and the barren Peak Country, the parish of Duffield covered approximately 16,000 acres. Lying within and astride the boundaries of the parish were several manors, the most extensive being that of Duffield *cum membris* – the 'members' being the sub-manors of Belper, Biggin, Hazelwood, Heage, Holbrook, Hulland, Idridgehay, Makeney, Southwood, Turnditch and Windley. As part of the Duchy of Lancaster, a steward administered the manors on behalf of the Crown, reporting initially to Duchy officials at Tutbury Castle (Staffordshire), about 12 miles away. The villages and dispersed settlements that comprised the manors all bordered on or lay within Duffield Frith, which was managed separately from the manors and was regulated by a well-established body of forest law.[52] The early modern Frith comprised three wards: Chevin

50 See, for example, R. W. Hoyle, '"Shearing the Hog": The Reform Of The Estates, *c*.1598–1640', and Hoyle, 'Disafforestation and Drainage: The Crown As Entrepreneur?', both in R. W. Hoyle (ed.), *The Estates of the English Crown, 1558–1640* (Cambridge, 1992).

51 H. Falvey, 'Custom, Resistance and Politics: Local Experiences of Improvement in Early-Modern England' (unpublished PhD thesis, University of Warwick, 2007), chs 2 and 4.

52 For accounts of the history and management of Duffield Frith, see *VCH Derbyshire*, vol. 1, pp. 413–21; G. Turbutt, *A History of Derbyshire* (3 vols, Cardiff, 1999), vol. 2, pp. 585–95; J. C. Cox and F. Strutt, 'Duffield Forest in the sixteenth century', *Derbyshire Archaeological J.* (*DAJ*), 25 (June 1903), pp. 181–216.

(or Duffield), Belper and Hulland; Chevin and Belper Wards were wholly in Duffield parish whereas much of Hulland Ward lay in Mugginton.[53] In 1633 the areas of the three wards totalled some 5,000 acres.[54] Although manorial land (arable, pasture and meadow) was theoretically distinguished and distinguishable from forest land, the boundaries were in practice ill-defined, with the result that manorial tenants and other inhabitants exercised customary common rights within the woodlands and wastes of the Frith. Just below the surface of Duffield's hills and valleys, moreover, lay various mineral deposits – including iron, stone, slate, coal and lead. Compared with elsewhere in England, the scale of mineral extraction and production in Duffield was modest; nevertheless it was long to remain an important source of supply for industries in the area.[55] Most pertinent to this study is the iron-works at Hopping Mill, north of Makeney, owned by Gilbert Talbot, Earl of Shrewsbury.[56] Fuel for the forge there, in the form of charcoal, was produced from trees felled in the Frith.[57] Although some inhabitants were wholly or partly employed in mining, smelting, quarrying or manufacturing in the neighbourhood, such industries brought little benefit to the whole community, not only because they put great pressure on timber resources in the Frith but also because owners of the mineral rights were reluctant to reinvest their profits locally. In contrast, the customary benefits derived from that royal forest were numerous and widely enjoyed by the local population.

---

53 The medieval Frith had included a fourth ward, Colebrook, nearly all of which lay in Wirksworth parish. During the reign of Henry VIII it was granted to the Lowe family; thereafter it was a separate entity (*VCH Derbyshire*, vol. 1, p. 418). For a detailed study of the medieval Frith, see M. Wiltshire, S. Woore, B. Crisp and B. Rich, *Duffield Frith: History and Evolution of the Landscape of a Medieval Derbyshire Forest* (Ashbourne, 2005).

54 TNA, DL 44/1127, Sept. 1633: Belper 1,846 acres, Chevin 1,248 acres and Hulland 1,911 acres.

55 A summary of surveys made by commissioners appointed by the Commonwealth during the 1650s shows that 'the mines, delfes or pitts of coal' in the manor of Duffield were by far the most valuable in the county at that time (*VCH Derbyshire*, vol. 2, p. 352). The original surveys of the Duffield mines are TNA, E 317/Derb/16 and Derb/18. In the eighteenth century the Derwent valley was at the forefront of the Industrial Revolution.

56 TNA, DL 1/319 (unnumbered piece), bill of William Cavendish, Earl of Newcastle *v.* Robert Treswell and Thomas Jaye, 23 June 1629; TNA, DL 4/79/14, examination of Andrew Clayton, 24 Sept. 1629.

57 On the relationship between the iron industry, charcoal and woodland, see G. F. Hammersley, 'The charcoal iron industry and its fuel', *Economic History Rev.*, 2nd ser., 26 (1973), pp. 593–613.

IV

As a Duffield inhabitant with legal expertise, Anthony Bradshaw became actively and regularly involved in defending and preserving local customary practices, advising fellow tenants and commoners whenever the Duchy sought to stifle or attack their customs. In 1581, for instance, Edward Stanhope, surveyor of the Duchy's possessions in the north, was commissioned to survey and report upon the condition of the Frith and its potential for increasing the Crown's revenue.[58] Responses by the Duffield jurors summoned by Stanhope indicate some of the rights and customs that were exercised in the Frith. Tenants claimed unstinted common of pasture in all three wards all year round. In addition, during winter months in order to feed the queen's game, commoners used to 'cropp, browse or top of[f]' some of the underwoods; they also fed their own animals on these loppings, for which they were amerced in the forest court.[59] Since the cropping and browsing were still being practised in the absence of the game which had once provided its justification, the fines so raised were effectively fees charged by the Duchy for this privilege. This *laissez-faire* attitude seems all the more generous because although sheep were explicitly deemed 'not commonable' animals, not only tenants but also inhabitants were pasturing and feeding unlimited numbers of sheep as well as cattle in the Frith.[60] Following the 1581 investigation Stanhope and his fellow commissioners concluded that there was insufficient timber to sell, and that encopsing certain areas of woodland would neither yield a worthwhile profit nor allow the inhabitants to benefit from their common; leasing the underwoods in rotation, however, might prove profitable to the Crown.

In September 1587 more than 500 copyholders, freeholders, ancient cottagers and householders, 'inhabitantes and borderers of Duffylde frythe', petitioned the queen against plans to lease the underwoods, and in the process provided an incidental record of other customs exercised there.[61] In addition to common of pasture, they claimed various rights to wood and fuel: 'by all the time of mans remembrance' they had taken 'howsebootes, heyebootes, plowebootes and hedgeboote with convenient and reasonable firewood to burne in their dwelling houses'.[62] Furthermore, 'poore auncient cotagers inhabitinge and borderinge' on

58 TNA, DL 44/305, fos. 6, 7 and 13.

59 TNA, DL 44/305, fo. 13.

60 DRO, D2402 A/PZ 6/1, p. 45.

61 TNA, DL 44/305, fo. 5, 2 Sept. 1587.

62 The 'bootes' claimed were respectively wood to repair houses, to make or repair fences, to make or repair ploughs and to make or repair fences; hedgeboote and heyboote were synonymous: J. Richardson (ed.), *The Local Historian's Encyclopedia* (2nd edn, Barnet, 1986), p. 18. At Duffield,

the Frith had experienced 'great relief', having been permitted 'by the goodness and good favour' of previous Duchy chancellors to enjoy its benefits 'quietly in reasonable sorte'. This popular exploitation, allowed to continue by the grace of the landlord, might be construed as an act of paternalism by the Duchy. It could equally, however, be described as pragmatic because, as both Stanhope's surveyors in 1581 and the commoners in 1587 pointed out, continuing open access to the forest would ensure that its inhabitants would be able to maintain themselves without the need to call on the charity and hospitality of their betters.

In response to the 1587 petition, the Duchy council decided to postpone leasing the underwoods pending further discussion with the Duffield commoners. In June 1588 Stanhope summoned representatives of the 'better sorte' of the tenants to consider how the interests of the Duchy and the commoners might be accommodated in view of the projected leases.[63] In 1587 the petitioners had observed that if their common of pasture were 'taken from us we and all ours shall be utterly impoverished therby and constrained to seeke dwellings other where'.[64] Mindful of the problems that would ensue from such dislocation, Stanhope attempted to assuage the tenants' fears, in particular the possibility of insufficient browse for their animals if the underwoods were leased. Whilst offering to circumvent this, he commented wryly that the Duchy was not obliged to do so for such browsing was not a legal common right but a custom enjoyed by 'curtesy' since 'the deare were decayed in the Frieth'.[65] This veiled attack on the legal basis of their custom spurred the representatives of the tenants to request more time to consider the matter of the projected lease. They also asked for their 'customes of fines, heriottes, and suche like duties from them to her Majestie' to be 'dewlie proved by inquisition and othe'. At this time, copyhold by inheritance was the most prevalent form of tenure at Duffield and this request suggests that these men now wanted the customary level of entry fines on such copyholds to be written down, and therefore fixed, whereas previously they had been fluid. Stanhope certainly interpreted their request in this light.

When the Duffield representatives met with Stanhope again, on 20 July 1588, they were accompanied by Anthony Bradshaw. They were more submissive on this occasion than previously, firstly agreeing to accept as final the Duchy's decision regarding leasing the underwoods; and subsequently refraining from raising the issue of the confirmation of their entry fines. That Stanhope did not want to discuss

'hedgeboote' was only taken every third year and it was for the repair of the fences around the common fields that abutted on the woods (TNA, DL 44/305, fo. 13).

63 TNA, DL 44/305, fo. 3, summons from Edward Stanhope, 27 June 1588.

64 Ibid., fo. 5.

65 Ibid., fo. 1, report by Stanhope of his two meetings with the tenants' representatives, 10 Oct. 1588.

the latter is unsurprising for, as he commented in his report, it was 'no part of the substance of [his] comission'. That the tenants failed to press the issue is more problematic. While the original representatives had recognized an opportunity for the 'confirmacion and putting in certaine of their customes', Bradshaw and those who attended the second meeting let it pass. Their silence was almost certainly deliberate. Given Stanhope's parting shot at the previous meeting and Bradshaw's legal expertise, it seems likely that Bradshaw's presence at the second meeting was anything but coincidental. Stanhope had called into question one of the most important and valuable customs enjoyed in the Frith, that of tenants' animals browsing the underwoods. Perhaps Bradshaw recognized that the validity of customs relating to copyhold entry fines might not have withstood close scrutiny either. By failing to have them confirmed following an inquisition, Bradshaw and his fellow tenants retained the characteristic fluidity of these particular customs but missed the chance to fix the value of entry fines. Although this circumspection theoretically left their heirs prey to financial uncertainty, it was subsequently vindicated since, as we shall see, the failure to have the level of entry fines officially confirmed actually benefited the next generation of tenants.

V

The 1587–88 encounter was only the first of many episodes in which Bradshaw's role was to prove decisive. Indeed the Crown even attempted to harness his well-known expertise to its own interests when in 1595 the earl of Shrewsbury, in his capacity as High Steward of the Honour of Tutbury, appointed Bradshaw as his 'understeward' in the 'Fryth and the manours therein', presumably because the position had become vacant.[66] Although this would have been a lucrative post, its actual value is impossible to quantify since, as Bradshaw later noted, the deputy-steward did not share directly in the fees prescribed by the Duchy: the steward simply paid his deputy at his own discretion and from his own pocket.[67] Shrewsbury would have been only too pleased to delegate the arduous day-to-day management whilst retaining the honour and profits of the stewardship. Bradshaw proved an assiduous deputy, holding the various courts in both the Frith and the manor at the required times, some as frequently as three-weekly.

---

66 DRO, D2402 A/PZ 6/1, p. 60. Although the Frith and manor were separate legal entities, it is clear that he was deputy-steward of both. See TNA, DL 30/37/393–394A; 38/395–400; 38/402–404, records of courts of attachment, woodmote, swainmote and pannage for Duffield Frith during Bradshaw's deputy-stewardship; DRO, 1404/2–4, Duffield court books, 1595–1608 (with gaps), kept by Bradshaw.

67 DRO, D2402 A/PZ 6/1, p. 19.

He carefully recorded the business of each sub-manor 'by distinguishing of the busynes of e[a]ch manour in margynall notes in my court bookes and court rolls'; this consequently 'gave expedicion' to the Duchy auditor who commended Bradshaw's efforts.[68] That Bradshaw took his duties so seriously was to prove both a benefit and a problem to Shrewsbury and to the Crown.

Bradshaw noted that the various ancient customs of both his charges were already preserved at Tutbury Castle in three sets of 'official' documents produced in earlier centuries for the Duchy's use:[69] the Tutbury 'Coucher', 'an attempt at a systematic listing of common rights' in Needwood Forest and Duffield Frith drawn up in the early fifteenth century;[70] a 'custome booke', or custumal recording the customs practised in the manor and Frith, drawn up following the questioning of earlier manorial juries; and 'our charter', a medieval royal document that defined and confirmed rights and liberties granted to inhabitants of Duffield Frith.[71] Bradshaw claimed that all three documents were for 'Duffelds good' because they 'do generally agree/that Duffeld hath theis costomes pure and priviledges free'.[72] That these 'jewells three' might benefit the tenants as well as the landlord is confirmed by Duffield men's entitlement to appeal to them whenever they were 'wronged in there land, or hurt in comon weale'.[73] In theory, these three documents were available for consultation by any tenant who went to Tutbury, where copies could be obtained. Recognizing the enormous potential benefits of these documents to the community, however, Bradshaw took it upon himself to copy them into a small notebook, on the cover of which he wrote: 'Notes of Duffeld Frythe customes and other thinges collected, ABr 1596'.[74] He also rehearsed their contents in his account of a 'discourse and conference' with his friend William Nelson.[75]

68 Ibid., p. 59.

69 Ibid., p. 1.

70 J. Birrell, 'Common rights in the medieval forest: disputes and conflicts in the thirteenth century', *Past and Present* 117 (1987), p. 25. British Library (BL), Harleian MSS 568 and 5138 are respectively sixteenth- and seventeenth-century copies of the Tutbury Coucher.

71 Bradshaw transcribed a version of the charter dated 18 Nov. 11 Edward IV, which confirmed earlier charters (see n. 74 below).

72 DRO, D2402 A/PZ 2/1, fo. 14r (2nd foliation), 'A frends due comendacion of Duffeld Frith', stanza 26. (This source is discussed in detail below and printed as an appendix.)

73 Ibid., stanza 25.

74 DRO, D2402 A/PZ 2/1; fos. 3r–21v (1st foliation) comprise a transcript of much of the Tutbury Coucher, part of which has been published in C. Kerry, 'A history of Peak Forest', *DAJ* 15 (1893), pp. 95–8; fos. 26r–29v comprise 'A copie of Duffeld Fryth ch[art]er', dated 18 Nov. 11 Edward IV; fos. 1–10 (2nd foliation) contain extracts from custumals.

75 DRO, D2402 A/PZ 6/1. Identified only as 'W. N. of C in the Countie of Suffolk, gentleman', it is likely that Bradshaw's companion was William Nelson, a fellow member of the

Bradshaw's stance as a stout defender of custom at Duffield was not necessarily impartial, especially when his own interests were apparently under attack. For example, in June 1596 representatives of the copyholders of Makeney complained in the Duchy court that they were being denied access to the common waste in Chevin ward by certain tenants of Duffield and other manors.[76] Furthermore, they claimed that the offenders had 'gotten into their handes or custodye ... divers court rolles, recordes of survey and perambulacion and divers other auncient recordes wrytinges escriptes and mynimentes' relating to the manors of Duffield and Makeney, and consequently the Makeney tenants were unable to prove their right of common in Chevin. Anthony Bradshaw was one of the Duffield tenants named in the suit: his extensive property in the manor entitled him to common in that ward and by this time he was deputy-steward. Normally manorial records would have been sent to Tutbury and so would not have been available for tenants to consult locally; however, the plaintiffs claimed that the records were in the hands of their oppressors, suggesting that Bradshaw might have abused his position by appropriating them on behalf of himself and his immediate neighbours. The defendants, however, counter-claimed that they knew nothing of records being hidden and that the plaintiffs had no common rights in Chevin. It is almost impossible to separate fact from fiction in such suits; perhaps the greatest significance of the plaintiffs' claim is that they recognized the importance of those writings for verifying their entitlement to common rights.

During his deputy-stewardship Bradshaw kept meticulous records of the business of the various courts of the manor and Frith. His post required him to send the original documents to Tutbury to be kept in the Duchy's muniment room so that the Duchy secured possession of the primary evidence.[77] Recognizing the significance of this, and in order to mitigate its effects, he also made copies of court business which he retained in Duffield. Private record-keeping of this kind was unusual, not to say highly irregular, but it would have been beneficial to all of the tenants for such information to remain accessible locally. In addition to these records, Bradshaw also collected and transcribed by-laws, regulations and customs regarding the conduct and transaction of business within forest

Inner Temple, who, together with Bradshaw and several others, witnessed an enfeoffment in 1586. J. C. Davies (ed.), *Catalogue of Manuscripts in the Library of the Honourable Society of the Inner Temple* (3 vols, Oxford, 1972), vol. 3, pp. 1324–5.

[76] TNA, DL 1/173/F2, Fletcher and Harroppe *v.* William Johnson *et al.*, bill dated 26 June 1596; DL 4/38/16; 39/18, Fletcher and Harroppe *v.* William Johnson *et al.*

[77] Wood, 'Custom', p. 263. The practice of sending the rolls to Tutbury is described in TNA, DL 4/73/30, Attorney General on behalf of Thomas Johnson *v.* Exuperius Bradshaw *et al.*, July 1623, interrogatory no. 5.

and manorial courts, some of a general nature and some relating specifically to Duffield. In 1603 he described eight such books that he had already compiled: a book of forest law relating to the Frith; one of precedents of processes used in the forest courts; another containing the 'paynes ordynances and by laws' to be continually observed in the Frith; 'one other called a lanterne for Copyholders'; two that outlined the leet charge and baron charge of the manorial courts; one 'shewing how carefully orderly and uprightlie Juries ought to cary them selves'; and finally one recording the permitted forms of surrenders in court.[78] Whereas his duplication of court business at Duffield argues for an interest in advancing the economic interests of himself and of his fellow tenants, the sheer volume and variety of these eight books suggest that, as a lawyer, Bradshaw was also interested in the nature and practice of custom and customary law for its own sake.

VI

By their very nature, most of Anthony Bradshaw's extant writings are in starchy prose. Since their purpose was to preserve the customs and land transactions of the manor and Frith, correct legal formulae were obligatory. It is somewhat surprising, therefore, to find that Bradshaw was not averse to making rhymes, the most visible examples being two rhyming acrostics that he had had carved in stone. One sited outside his almshouse, using the letters BRADSHAWGH, asked God to provide others to maintain 'this little Harbor'.[79] The other, at the bottom of his funeral monument, using the letters ANTHONIE BRADSHAWGH AB, asked God's blessing on the lives of his children.[80] But Bradshaw's longest foray into verse does not refer to himself: entitled 'A frends due comendacion of Duffeld Frith', it extols the virtues of that place, its customs and landscape.[81] As the earlier edition of the poem is in a hard to access and in any case imperfectly transcribed, it is printed anew as an appendix to this chapter.

The dating of the 'Comendacion' is problematic. In the top left-hand corner, next to the title, '1588' has been written apparently in the same hand as the

---

78 DRO, D2402 A/PZ 6/1, pp. 61–2.

79 He usually signed his name as 'Bradshawghe'. The almshouse was pulled down in 1804 but the stone is set in a wall outside Duffield Hall, now the offices of the Derbyshire Building Society. The text has been published on several occasions, including Bowles, 'Bradshaw and the Bradshawes', p. 178 and *The Reliquary* 24 (1883–84), p. 50.

80 These verses have also been published on several occasions, including Bowles, 'Bradshaw and the Bradshawes', p. 179 (modernized spelling) and Tudor, *New Light*, pp. 54–5.

81 The original version of the poem is in DRO, D2402 A/PZ 2/1, fos. 12v–15v (2nd foliation).

poem, which seems to be Bradshaw's. As a lawyer he was trained to write in various hands and although the rest of this particular book is in a different hand, the orthography of the 'Comendacion' is the same as that of at least one other of his extant works.[82] Bradshaw did not become deputy-steward until 1595 and the poem has been entered after records dated 30 August 1597 and 19 December 1598;[83] stanzas 2 and 53, furthermore, mention 'King James our gratious Soveraigne' and 'King James our noble prince' and have not been altered from 'Queen Elizabeth'. Although clearly not the year in which the poem was entered in the book, perhaps '1588' refers to the year in which Bradshaw made his original draft of the verses, or at least conceived them, for it was in that year that the validity of the customs of the manor and forest of Duffield were first questioned by Sir Edward Stanhope.

The genre of this 54-stanza poem is perhaps best described as 'chorographical' since it is concerned primarily with place.[84] Literary geographies of this type were often associated with the emerging topos of antiquarianism. Although not named in the various lists of members of the Elizabethan Society of Antiquaries, founded in 1586 by Camden, Bradshaw probably associated with them informally as many of them were, like him, practising lawyers.[85] The actual form of the 'Comendacion', however, is unusual since most chorographies, apart from Michael Drayton's *Poly-Olbion*, were in prose.[86] The content of the 'Comendacion' is also somewhat different from the 'bold, celebratory representations of the land' written by other local chorographers, such as Carew, Stow and Lambarde, for Bradshaw celebrated the management rather

---

82 DRO, D1404/1.

83 DRO, D2402 A/PZ 2/1, fos. 1r–6v (2nd foliation), 'A few rude notes re Duffield Frith collected from various authorities', dated 30 Aug. 1597; fos. 10v–11v, copies of letters dated 19 Dec. 1598, to Thomas Eire and John Bruckshaw, two manorial officials who had failed to carry out their duties.

84 R. Helgerson, *Forms of Nationhood: The Elizabethan Writing of England* (Chicago and London, 1992), p. 132.

85 Eventually most leading English chorographers were members of the Society of Antiquaries. For the activities and membership of the Elizabethan Society, see M. McKisack, *Medieval History in the Tudor Age* (Oxford, 1971), ch. 7; R. J. Shoeck, 'The Elizabethan Society of Antiquaries and Men of Law', *Notes and Queries*, new ser., 1 (1954), pp. 417–21; L. van Norden, 'The Elizabethan Society of Antiquaries' (unpublished PhD thesis, University of California, 1946); K. Sharpe, *Sir Robert Cotton 1586–1631: History and Politics in Early Modern England* (Oxford, 1979), ch. 1.

86 Indeed, even the first part of *Poly-Olbion* was not published until 1613, only a year before Bradshaw's death. J. W. Hebel (ed.), *The Works of Michael Drayton* (6 vols, Oxford, 1933), vol. 4, *Poly-Olbion*. In the 'song' on Nottinghamshire and Derbyshire, Drayton eulogized the forests of Leicester, Charnwood, Sherwood and the Peak, but made no mention of Duffield Frith, pp. 521–34.

than simply the geography of Duffield Frith.[87] Hence, the underlying purpose of what Bradshaw called 'this rude effect ... rashly done'[88] was less to extol the perceived virtues of the Frith than to record the customs by which the forest was governed and the manor was regulated. Stanza 38 explains, for example, that:

> Three sorts of copyhould lands in Duffeld manors bee
> Bond hould att will & mattock land, besydes thos wich be free
> Wich tenures three be held at will, by copye of court roule
> all wich in sondry severall sorts the costomes do controulle

Although the meanings of some of Bradshaw's verses are difficult to unravel, they do provide detailed rhyming accounts of local practices that accord closely with his prose versions. The finished rhymes, therefore, are an idiosyncratic yet highly informative source for the tenurial organization of an early modern forest and manor. These verses also proclaim Bradshaw's pride in and affection for 'the place [in which] ... I could my race best ronne',[89] putting him on an equal footing with the other chorographers among whom 'love and country' was 'their common theme'.[90]

The poetic form of the 'Comendacion' is best understood in the context of the peculiarly close relationship between custom and memory. As already noted, custom was lodged within the collective memory of a community and had been passed down orally through succeeding generations. As aids to that collective memory, mnemonics and rhyme played important roles in the preservation of local custom.[91] In the eighteenth century Thomas Fuller noted that for those who could not read, rhyming was a means 'to make sense abide longer in the memory'.[92] Indeed, Bradshaw himself explicitly confirmed that mnemonics and verse were used to facilitate the memorizing of customs:

> The better sort of Duffeld men, there customes understandes
> and how they do concerne them selves, there houses & there lands

---

87 A. McRae, *God Speed the Plough: The Representation of Agrarian England, 1500–1660* (Cambridge, 1996), p. 237.

88 'Frends due comendacion', stanza 54.

89 Ibid., stanza 4.

90 Helgerson, *Forms of Nationhood*, p. 147. Here 'country' refers to county or neighbourhood as well as nation.

91 Fox, *Oral and Literate Culture*, pp. 24–9.

92 T. Fuller, *Gnomonologia: adagies and proverbs; wise sentences and witty sayings, ancient and modern, foreign and British. Collected by Thomas Fuller, M.D.* (London, 1732), sig. A5.

> The poorer sort and ignorant wich custome bookes have non
> by song may learne some customes now, & memorie alone.[93]

While recognizing the importance of memory, Bradshaw was also making an interesting social distinction. The 'better sort', who held property in the manor, had access to books which recorded the customs relating to that property and which many of them could read. The 'poorer sort and ignorant', on the other hand, could not read; nor did they hold property, but they did need to remember their customary rights claimed in the Frith and manor. The fourth line of this stanza is, however, somewhat ambiguous. Does it suggest that some of Bradshaw's verses were actually based on earlier songs and mnemonics from Duffield? Or, that the 'poorer sort and ignorant' of Duffield would memorize and sing some of his verses? The latter would imply that he intended to circulate them within the community, although evidence that he did so would be impossible to verify. The 'frends due comendacion' nonetheless testifies to Bradshaw's determination that the customs were not only inscribed in the written record, but also perpetuated in oral culture.

This was, indeed, the explicit purpose of another metrical poem, written in 1653 by Edward Manlove, former steward of the Barmote courts of Wirksworth wapentake, just a few miles north of Duffield.[94] These 292 lines of rhyming couplets accurately record the various customs and privileges of the Wirksworth lead miners, customs that were frequently challenged at law by local landlords. It is tempting to speculate that Manlove knew of Bradshaw's 'Comendacion' for he too, concerned that local Derbyshire customs should not be forgotten, was anxious to preserve them in memorable form.[95] Fox has further noted that as well as facilitating memory, verses were also a means of entertainment.[96] Manlove's nineteenth-century editor commented that 'by writing in rhymed verse, and not in prose, he adopted the best means not only of ensuring a lasting remembrance of the practical instruction contained in his poem, but also at the same time of affording a pleasing recreation to them for whom it was written'.[97] Perhaps

---

93 'Frends due comendacion', stanza 51.

94 T. Tapping (ed.), *The liberties and customes of the lead-mines within the wapentake of Wirksworth in the County of Derby ... composed in meeter by Edward Manlove, esquire, heretofore Steward of the Barghmoot court for the Leadmines within the said wapentake* (London, 1653), repr. in W. W. Skeat (ed.), *Reprinted Glossaries* (London, 1873), pp. 9–20.

95 See also the 30-line rhyming acrostic of the words 'William Hopkinson his observation', written sometime after 1637 by William Hopkinson of Ible near Wirksworth, which reproduces some of the customs of Wirksworth. BL, Add. MS 6668, fo. 430r; reference and transcript kindly supplied by Andy Wood.

96 Fox, *Oral and Literate Culture*, p. 26.

97 Tapping (ed.), *Liberties and customes of the lead-mines*, pp. 2–3.

this was also Bradshaw's purpose. His poem, whatever its date, is a forceful reminder that contemporaries were aware of the continued importance of the oral transmission of custom amongst the semi-literate and illiterate.

VII

Although Bradshaw's skills as a competent administrator made him an efficient deputy, his stance as a keen defender of the Frith and of the commoners' rights produced a conflict of interests when the Crown proposed to exploit the forest's timber assets. In March 1608 he was removed from his office of deputy-steward and replaced by Sir John Bentley.[98] Bradshaw complained bitterly about this to Shrewsbury but subsequent events demonstrate that the earl had deliberately removed him from office in order to clear the way for some decidedly dubious dealings, which, given his local loyalties and legal training, Bradshaw would surely have impeded, if not prevented.[99] Later in 1608, as part of a project initiated by Robert Cecil, Earl of Salisbury, to raise revenue by selling Crown woods, Duchy commissioners led by Bentley surveyed and valued the woods in certain parts of the Frith at over £2,500.[100] About a year afterwards, the surveyor Rock Church and others were commissioned to sell the king's woods there on the conditions that whoever purchased the wood (that is, timber) should fell and cart it away within a year, and that whatever remained would revert to Crown ownership.[101] Shrewsbury purchased the woods from Walter Gibson, a member of the second commission, at the knock-down price of about £1,790.[102]

Shrewsbury's cut-price deal aroused Salisbury's suspicions and in May 1609 Church was sent to Duffield to investigate. He reported two possible explanations. Firstly, that the timber in the Frith was of poor quality; however, although Shrewsbury had indeed shown Church some very low-grade timber, the latter was unconvinced that it had actually come from the Frith. Secondly, Bentley

---

98 G. R. Batho (ed.), *A Calendar of the Shrewsbury and Talbot Papers*, II, *Talbot Papers in the College of Arms* (Derbyshire Record Ser., 4, 1968), vol. M, fo. 504, commission, signed and dated by Shrewsbury, appointing Sir John Bentley his deputy and steward of Duffield, 19 Mar. 1607[/08].

99 Ibid., vol. M, fo. 512, Anthony Bradshaw to Shrewsbury, 26 Mar. 1608.

100 TNA, DL 4/79/14, deposition of Francis Bruckshawe, 24 Sept. 1629; DL 1/319 (unnumbered piece), answer of Robert Treswell and Thomas Jaye to the bill of William, Earl of Newcastle, 25 June 1629; DL 4/79/55, examination of Robert Cooke, 28 Sept. 1629.

101 In his tract on woodland husbandry, Church later referred to his work as a royal surveyor: 'my late circuit northward for survey and sale of some of his maiesties woods'. R. Church *An olde thrift newly revived* (London, 1612), p. 21.

102 TNA, DL 1/319, answer of Treswell and Jaye.

claimed that he had overvalued the timber to deter prospective purchasers; Church concluded that if this were true, later sales would necessarily have been at lower rates.[103] Whichever the case, the inference was that Shrewsbury had abused his position as steward by appointing Bentley as his deputy to facilitate collusion over the sale of the timber rights, an exercise in asset-stripping that his previous deputy, Bradshaw, would never have countenanced. Indeed, even Sir Thomas Fanshawe, one of the Crown's own agents, considered the sales at Duffield 'soe preiudiciall' to the Crown that he complained about them at the time.[104] Despite the supposed poor quality of the trees, and the condition stipulated in Church's commission, Shrewsbury and his heirs continued for over 20 years to cut down the timber growing in the woods that he had 'purchased' in 1608.

Whereas the Crown had intended a one-off sale of timber in the Frith, Shrewsbury, disingenuously or otherwise, believed that he had purchased the timber rights forever, and long used the trees for fuel and materials 'in diverse and sundry iron workes, forges and buildinges' in Derbyshire, including his ironworks at Hopping Mill, near Makeney.[105] This discrepancy between intent and practice only came to light when, in March 1629, Charles I – also intending to 'rayse a some of money for his necessarye uses and expences out of the sale of woods uppon his Dutchie' – appointed commissioners to sell woods in Duffield.[106] They found not only that few trees remained standing, but also that the Earl of Newcastle, Shrewsbury's executor, was claiming the latter's timber 'rights' for himself. Had Bradshaw not been removed from office just before the initial commission to survey and value the woods, the outcome would have been somewhat different. As it was, he and the other inhabitants were powerless to prevent this particular Crown project, which actually brought little benefit to the Crown either: Shrewsbury took timber from the Frith over a 20-year period but the Exchequer received only one payment from him. The sale of timber was not, however, the only revenue-raising project attempted at Duffield in 1608.

---

103 Hatfield House, Cecil Papers, 132, no. 60, Rock Church to the Earl of Salisbury, 17 May 1609.

104 TNA, DL 4/79/55, deposition of Sir Thomas Fanshawe, 3 July 1629.

105 TNA, DL 1/319, bill of William Cavendish, 23 June 1629; DL 4/79/14, examination of Andrew Clayton, 24 Sept. 1629. Hammersley has noted that in many areas, although vast quantities of trees were needed to supply sufficient charcoal to fuel the furnaces of iron forges, most iron-masters were careful not to destroy woodlands as these resources were vital to their business. It was contemporary observers who, seeing the short-term effect of such fellings, feared that woodlands were being permanently depleted (Hammersley, 'Charcoal iron industry', esp. p. 612). This was clearly not the case in Duffield, where the woodlands *were* permanently depleted.

106 TNA, DL 1/319, answer of Treswell and Jaye, 25 June 1629.

VIII

Although no longer in office after 1608, Bradshaw continued his interest in the affairs of the manor and Frith. Indeed, taking advantage of his enforced 'retirement', he produced yet another record for the Duffield copyholders. On 25 March 1610 he wrote the preface to his new compilation, in which he explained that he had produced this 'booke of register' not as an official court book but as a record made for the tenants, 'conteyning or mencioning all the surrenders, inquisicions, court daies and yeares and nomber Rolles (recorded att Tutburye) passed and taken before me' while deputy-steward.[107] Its purpose was to enable those tenants who 'hereafter shall desyre or neede notes or copies of such entrees or records' to have them made 'here att home' from 'the said register'. The register was to be kept not at the seat of privilege in Tutbury Castle but in rather more humble surroundings: in a locked chest at Farleys Hall, the key to which would be held in a box in his almshouse, kept by 'one of the most discrete pore people there'.[108] In the chest, the register was to be supplemented both by Bradshaw's 'boke of customes' and by another book that he had 'devysed for better observacion of the customes, (wich I calle "A Lanterne") to light the ignorant the better to see and discerne to kepe the customes'.[109] That these records, kept in Bradshaw's home, would only be accessible via his almshouse was highly significant in both symbolic and practical terms. The records would be located securely and permanently in Duffield, and those tenants wishing to consult them were required to pay a small fee to the keeper of the key, thus supplementing Bradshaw's small local charitable provision.

Although tenants would still have travel to Tutbury to obtain official copies of the terms of their tenancies, it is clear that Bradshaw now distrusted the Duchy and its officials, not least as a result of his displacement from office and its aftermath. He insisted that his book was the copyholders' own accurate archive of their tenurial rights, whereas the records at Tutbury might be '[e]rased, altered, removed, or by any casualtie be lost, ymbeaseled, deteyned, hurt or owtherwise myscaried'.[110] Such losses or alterations would be prejudicial to the tenants' rights since 'the records of customary and copyhold lands' were the tenants'

---

107 DRO, D1404/1. The following quotations are from the verso of the flyleaf.

108 Bradshaw's copies of the deed founding the almshouse and of the regulations governing the inmates, which he wanted to accompany his will, were dated 12 Nov. 1612 (DRO D2402 A/PZ 6/1, 'A Bradshaw's book of customs etc', pp. 65–8). However, the text of the introduction in DRO, D1404/1 indicates that it had been established before 25 Mar. 1610.

109 The 'boke of customes' is the book catalogued as DRO, D2402 A/PZ 2/1. The 'Lanterne' does not seem to have survived.

110 DRO, D1404/1, verso of the flyleaf.

'chief evidences of the same'. Furthermore, he was concerned that the Duffield copyholders should know and observe the customs relating to their holdings because he feared that such tenures might 'growe dangerous' (that is, become endangered).

Indeed Bradshaw's concern for the continuation of copyhold customs and his distrust of record-keeping at Tutbury were not without foundation. In 1608 the Crown had launched two new revenue-raising projects to which Duffield was vulnerable: compositions for fines, targeting the customary entry fines of copyhold tenants; and enfranchisement, seeking to replace copyholds with freeholds on Crown manors. During the early years of James's reign, royal administrators commissioned surveys of the Crown's estates to evaluate its annual landed income.[111] In May 1608 the Earl of Salisbury launched an initiative to increase and then confirm entry fines on both copyholds for lives and copyholds of inheritance, and thus cut through all customary levels of fining.[112] Richard Hoyle has emphasized the astounding audacity of Salisbury's policy, which, contrary to the dictum that 'the local custom must always be observed', 'completely ignored local manorial customs in favour of taking fines at the market rate'.[113] Commissioners were to visit Crown manors and make surveys and valuations of copyhold tenancies, new fines would be calculated on the current value of holdings and all tenants of the manor would then agree to a composition for fixed fines at these rates. Where copyholders by inheritance claimed, but had no written proof, that fines were already 'certain', the Crown recognized that its officers would have to prove otherwise, the fines being respited pending verification.[114] When in 1608 Duffield was targeted in the Crown's policy of increasing copyhold fines, the tenants claimed but could not prove that their fines were certain, and their fines were accordingly suspended.[115] The fact that in 1588 representatives of the Duffield tenants had backed down from having their fines fixed did not, therefore, disadvantage their successors 20 years later. Elsewhere, it is clear that Salisbury's project ran into difficulties, largely because Crown tenants were not backward in 'arguing the fine detail of their manorial

111 Hoyle, '"Shearing the Hog"'.

112 TNA, SP 14/32/76, quoted at length in Hoyle, '"Shearing the Hog"', p. 237. See also R. W. Hoyle, '"Vain Projects": The Crown and Its Copyholders in the Reign of James I', in Chartres and Hey (eds), *English Rural Society, 1500–1800*, pp. 73–104, especially pp. 79–81.

113 '*Et consuetudo loci semper est observanda*'. E. Coke, *The compleate copy-holder* (London, 1641), p. 104, quoted in P. D. A. Harvey, *Manorial Records* (rev. edn, London, 1999), p. 63; Hoyle, '"Vain Projects"', p. 81.

114 Hoyle, '"Shearing the Hog"', p. 237.

115 TNA, DL 44/1147, dated June 1635, includes 'A particular of such fynes uppon surrenders within the mannours [at Duffield] as are due to his maiestie [James I] since the sixte yeare of his raigne of England etc'.

customs'.[116] Duffield was one of the vast majority of Crown manors in which the tenants held out against the offer to compound for fixed entry fines; eventually the tenants of only 26 manors did so, including those of neighbouring Ireton Wood, who intercommoned in Hulland ward.[117] In addition to their new fines, the tenants of the 26 manors had 'their claimed customes confirmed by decree' in the Duchy court in July 1620.[118] To the great financial advantage of Duffield tenants, the Crown made no attempt to collect their respited copyhold fines until the 1630s; and even then collection was unsuccessful, not least because by that time Duffield *cum membris* was no longer Duchy property.[119]

Confirmation of fines was not the only project implemented in an attempt to raise income from the Crown's copyhold tenants. In the summer of 1603 it had been suggested that all copyholders on royal estates should be sold their freeholds.[120] Although attempts were initially made to sell freeholds to the Duchy of Lancaster's tenants in the forest of Clitheroe, the project stalled and was shelved. In 1611 it was revived and the decision was taken to enfranchise copyhold tenants on the Duchy's northern estates.[121] On 12 March Thomas Fanshawe, then the Duchy's auditor, was instructed to carry out a general survey of the Duchy's copyholds, thereby establishing details of tenants' customs. Although the final records of Fanshawe's proceedings have not survived, his itinerary can be reconstructed from the extant account of his expenses.[122] Usually he visited each manor twice: firstly to appoint a jury to enquire into copyholds and customs; secondly to collect the jury's findings and, if the copyholders agreed, to make a composition for their fines and consequently enfranchise them. Thus on 3 June 1611 Fanshawe was at Duffield for 'empanelling of juries of survey for the mannors in Duffeild Frith', and on 18 July he and the other commissioners 'mett for the assessing of the fines' there. Their second meeting

---

116 Hoyle, '"Vain Projects"', p. 82.

117 Ibid., p. 104, App. 2, a list of the compositions made on the duchy of Lancaster estates, 1618–21.

118 TNA, DL 5/28, fos. 368v–80v, decree confirming an agreement between the king and customary tenants of the manors of Wirksworth *cum membris*, and Brassington, Bonsall and Ireton Wood *cum membris*, 5 July 1620; House of Lords RO, PO/PB/1/1662/14C2n55 (1662), Private Act, 14 Charles II, *c.* 23, 'An Act for Confirmation of the Estates of several Tenants and Copyholders of the Manors of Rannes [*recte* Raunds], Irchesten [*recte* Irchester], [...], and several other Manors, Parcels of the Duchy of Lancaster'.

119 For details of the attempts at collection, see Falvey, 'Custom, Resistance and Politics', pp. 166–7.

120 See Hoyle, '"Shearing the Hog"', pp. 233–41. Hoyle's first exploration of the enfranchisement of the Crown's copyholders is to be found in '"Vain Projects"'.

121 Hoyle, '"Shearing the Hog"', p. 241.

122 TNA, DL 28/33/14A (unpaginated).

was inconclusive and on 21 August, for the third time, he was 'at Duffeild to meet with the Tenauntes'. This was the only such extra visit in his entire itinerary. Being simply a list of expenses, Fanshawe's account in the Duchy's archive does not describe the discussions that took place during his various meetings. The proceedings at Duffield are, however, elucidated by a stray document, signed by Fanshawe, which records 21 points raised by the Duffield jurors together with his responses to them.[123] Many of the questions sought clarification of copyholders' entitlements; others tested whether enfranchisement might disadvantage them. There is no record of the jurors' names, but Anthony Bradshaw was almost certainly the prime mover behind their questions. The tenants had wanted time to consider the implications for their tenurial customs of any composition.

Fanshawe's mission to the northern parts of the Duchy was largely unsuccessful and he returned to London on 14 October. However, his responses to the questions of the Duffield tenants had apparently borne fruit: on 30 November, at 'the Dutchye house' in London, an unnamed group of Duffield men appeared before commissioners desiring 'to bee received to composition for purchase of their coppyholde estates in fee farme together with such rite of Common as they now inioye'.[124] But the fruit turned sour: the commissioners stipulated the extortionate purchase price of 50 years' rent and the tenants confessed that they were 'not altogether willinge to coom to that rate'. They beat a hasty retreat, claiming that they needed to confer with 'the rest of theyr neighbours in the cuntry before any conclusion'. There is no record of any further meetings and indeed subsequent events confirm that the Duffield copyholders were never enfranchised: while negotiating the purchase of the manor in 1629, Sir Edward Leech, one of the Masters in Chancery, was still offering to sell tenants their freeholds in return for their support.[125]

Like the Crown's project to fix entry fines, its project to enfranchise copyhold tenants was taken up on very few manors. In general the valuation of the freehold of a property was between 40 and 50 years' rent. As at Duffield, most tenants were either unwilling or unable to pay this significant sum; perhaps they were happy with the *status quo*, particularly on manors where fines had been respited. Freeholding was not always attractive to tenants: although, if valued at 40*s*. or more, freehold bestowed the electoral franchise, it also brought other more demanding responsibilities. Hoyle has even suggested that 'the obligations placed on freeholders,

---

123 DRO, D5195/1/1/1, catalogued as 'Duffield Frith Customs and Laws 1611'. The documents catalogued under D5195 are a miscellaneous collection relating to Duffield's customs but these documents were *not* collected or written by Anthony Bradshaw, most of whose papers are catalogued under D2402 AP/Z.

124 DRO, D5195/1/1/1, Fanshawe's footnote to the document, dated 30 Nov. 1611.

125 TNA, DL 4/98/29, interrogatory no. 5 on behalf of the plaintiffs.

notably that of jury service, were not, as a later tradition might have it, the valued freedoms of politically active men but expensive and time-consuming chores'.[126] Bradshaw was not explicitly named in the documents relating to the projects to fix entry fines and to enfranchise the Duffield tenants – indeed, no names were recorded – but his voice can surely be heard amongst those querying the benefits of either scheme. Ultimately the costs were too high. Agrarian and tenurial practice at Duffield therefore remained entrenched in and driven by its ancient customs.

IX

Anthony Bradshaw died in 1614 and so did not become personally embroiled in the controversies that surrounded two further revenue-raising schemes which aimed to strip Duffield's remaining assets – namely the sale of the manor and, in 1632, the disafforestation the Frith and the enclosure of one-third of each of its three wards.[127] From the examples cited at the beginning of this chapter, it is nevertheless clear that long after his death his writings were still being consulted and given credence, just as he had wished. A brief investigation of the 1641 lawsuit demonstrates how the tenants used Bradshaw's writings to their advantage.

In the late 1620s the manor of Duffield *cum membris* was one of the manors purchased by the Corporation of the City of London as part of the Royal Contract Estates; in 1630 the Corporation sold it on to Sir Edward Leech.[128] Leech was proactive in his ownership of the manor and during the course of the 1641 dispute over entry fines and other customs he complained that some of the tenants, including Bradshaw's sons Joseph and Vicesimus, had possession of certain manorial documents that should have been accessible to everyone.[129] From the exchanges between Leech and his truculent tenants, it is clear that the documents in question had been compiled by Anthony Bradshaw. The most likely scenario is that the 'missing' documents were being held in the chest in Farleys Hall, as he had instructed both in his 'booke of register' and his testament, and that Leech was being denied access to them. During the ensuing examinations,

---

126 Hoyle, '"Shearing the Hog"', p. 253.

127 Falvey, 'Custom, Resistance and Politics', pp. 168–77.

128 BL, Add. MS 6691, fos. 100–106; Corporation of London RO, Deeds RCE 45/9; Falvey, 'Custom, Resistance and Politics', pp. 168–70.

129 TNA, DL 1/360 (unnumbered piece), Attorney General on behalf of Leech *v.* Reyner *et al.*; DL 1/361 (unnumbered piece), Attorney General on behalf of Chaloner *et al.* *v.* Leech.

when another of Bradshaw's records was produced in court, both Joseph and Vicesimus confirmed that the book was indeed in their father's hand.[130]

The dispute raises several interesting points concerning the status of Bradshaw's writings. Firstly, it is clear that in the early 1640s they were valued as evidence of customary practices relating to copyholds in Duffield. Secondly, the fact that the lord of the manor was anxious to secure access to them indicates that Leech believed that Bradshaw's detailed and accurate records would give credence to his arguments. Thirdly, since the tenants were deliberately withholding some of Bradshaw's writings, presumably they also thought that these particular records would bolster Leech's case. Fourthly, the document written by Bradshaw that Leech did succeed in presenting as evidence in court might have been made available to him by the tenants precisely because they knew that it would not support his stance.[131] Bradshaw's stated purpose when compiling his records had been to ensure that the tenants' customary rights and tenures were preserved for posterity because he foresaw that they would questioned and even endangered; by insisting that the documents were kept safely at Farleys Hall, perhaps he also anticipated that on some occasions those rights and tenures could be preserved as effectively by withholding his 'evidences' as by presenting them, just as memories had been 'forgetful' in the past.

X

The fact that Bradshaw's writings have survived the vagaries of time and archival attrition, and were indeed used to defend the customary inheritance of Duffield, is a reflection of his steely determination that they should be preserved. In some respects his writings resemble those of John Smyth of Nibley (Gloucestershire), for Smyth was similarly anxious to capture in writing the essence of the Hundred of Berkeley: its distinctive countryside with its natural boundaries, the inhabitants' sports and traditions, their particular customary laws and, above all, their dialect.[132] Yet Smyth's purpose was essentially antiquarian: to preserve the old ways in the face of change, particularly the 'civilized' language of London and of the court. Bradshaw, on the other hand, not only aimed to provide unbroken access to records of Duffield's ancient customs so that they were exercised continuously but also defended them actively in various courts

[130] TNA, DL 4/98/29, depositions of Joseph Bradshaw, gentleman of Duffield, and Vicesimus Bradshaw, gentleman of Makeney, to interrogatory number 2 for the defendant.

[131] The title of the document (see note 1) suggests that it related more to the customs of the Frith than of the manor.

[132] Rollison, *Local Origin*, ch. 3; Fox, *Oral and Literate Culture*, pp. 76–9.

and transmitted them in verse so that their benefits might be available to posterity. A more plausible parallel can be drawn between Bradshaw's activities and those of Robert Castle of Glatton – gentleman, lawyer, manorial bailiff and substantial tenant – who led several legal battles to preserve tenurial customs against the Cottons on their Huntingdonshire estates in the 1580s and 1590s.[133] And likewise, Bradshaw's verses had a purpose similar to those of Edward Manlove. In themselves, therefore, the three methods by which he sought to preserve the customs of Duffield – in person, in legal prose and in verse – were not unusual.[134] It is their coincidence in Bradshaw, a character of seemingly boundless productive energy, which makes him unique. In recognizing the continuing importance of memory in an age of rising literacy, furthermore, his stance foreshadows Fox's observation there was 'no simple or linear substitution' of writing for remembering.[135] Indeed in the introduction to his 'dialogue' with William Nelson, Bradshaw specifically stated that the purpose of his writings was to aid local memory in the defence and furtherance of Duffield's customs:

> [These I have] now sett downe, the rather to keepe in memorie, the most auntient and laudable customes liberties and privileges ymmunities and freedomes att this day claymed used and allowed, by for and to hir majesties tenants and inhabitantes of and within the said fee, for the better instruccion and cariage of the same tenants and inhabitantes.[136]

As a lawyer, however, he recognized not only the increasing weight given in law to written records but also the crucial role played by access to such records. He therefore determined to preserve his records in a chest in his own home, a location accessible to inhabitants but not to outsiders. That the key to that chest was available only from his own almshouse ensured that Anthony Bradshaw would long continue in the memories both of the poor and of the better sorts of Duffield.

---

133 Manning, 'Antiquarianism', *passim*; R. B. Manning, *Village Revolts: Social Protest and Popular Disturbances in England, 1509–1640* (Oxford, 1988), pp. 146–7.

134 For other examples of all three methods, see Fox, *Oral and Literate Culture*, *passim*; and Fox, 'Custom, Memory and the Authority of Writing', *passim*.

135 Fox, *Oral and Literate Culture*, p. 297.

136 DRO, D2402 A/PZ 6/1, p. 2.

Appendix[137]

1588. A FRENDS DUE COMENDAC[I]ON OF DUFFELD FRITH

1. O auntient pretty Duffeld Frith my love & Comendac[i]on
of due defect I yeld to thee for pleasant habitation
the stately hono[u]r of Tutbury includeth thee as part
And of the Duchy of Lancast[e]r a member fine thou art

2. King James o[u]r gratious Soveraigne of all this lord hee is
And of the Fryth and hono[ur] both, least ought there go amysse
His grace most well appointed hath, his Steward high to bee
His Counsello[r] right Ho[nora]ble, the Earle of Shrewsberie

3. By whose foresight & p[ro]vidence those things well ruled are
By such as he hath substitute to undergoe that Care
As may appeare at Audit tymes not onely in bare words
But also there app[ro]ved is by his highnes Recordes

4. But now t'omytt disgressions more, myself I will retyre
To shew my mynd of Duffeld fryth as first I did desyie
Wheareto my best affecc[i]ons the place hath so much room
That there before all places els I Could my race best ronne.

5. Some reasons w[i]ch so moved me to soch as wish to know
and shale me liston patiently, I will my fancye showe
Craving thiere p[ar]dons for my fault[es] in ev[er]y misprission
in hope where of I will begine fyne Duffeld Fryths description

6. Whoso w[i]th me will take sweete ayre on topp of Cheven hill
most bounds and grounds of Duffeld Fee may vew & take his fill
From Alderwasleigh to Burley yat so north & South it bendeth
From Collins Clarke to Hough P[ar]ke side it Est & West extendith

7. The cheifest towne & mother Church is Duffeld Southward placed
Fast by the river Darwent side no little therew[i]th graced
Her p[ar]ish larg hath Chappeles three to s[er]ve both god & leaig
whose names be called sev[er]allie, Turndych Bealp[er] & Highedge

[137] The original is in DRO, D2402 A/PZ 2/1, fols 12v–15v (2nd foliation) and is reproduced here with the permission of the Derbyshire Record Office. The poem was previously published in *The Reliquary*, 23 (1883), pp. 69–74. This transcript corrects errors there and extends abbreviations. The first four stanzas are very badly damaged.

8. Att Duffeld Place head placed was a statlye Castly & cortyard
where of the Scyte yet beareth name now called Castly Orchard.
The Duke there had great royalties & Forest p[ar]ks & warren
and wards & pleines & waters store, & grounds not verie barren.

9. Duffeld Forest yett heads its name though now not stored w[i]th game
nor venery hath for princly sport w[i]ch want there nor doth blaym
Saving some p[ar]ks replenisht are, disp[ar]kt though others bee
and vert & woods & offic[er]s stands, as I shale showe to thee.

10. This Forest hath hitt four brave woods in midst of it the lye
Hollond Duffeld Colbroke Bearp[er]d the same Castle fast by
Fyne thicks & lands the do conteine & herbidge good the yeld
and skerted w[i]th so sweete asserth as ever man beheld

11. All w[i]ch in order good to keepe such forest lawes as neede
are executed dulie there at woodmote co[u]rts w[i]th speed
The pawnage Tacke rents & duties there of w[i]ch customes raise
Collectors four receive & pay at thaudit tymes alwayes

12. This Forest smale envyrond is with six p[ar]ks yet remaying
Morley Beaurp[er]d Posterne & Shottle & Ravensdale app[er]tayning
All w[i]ch are farmed at this tyme & yeald no deare at all
Save onely Manshall P[ar]ke hath game and yet but verie smale

13. Wherefore those Keep[er]s names shale pass there offic[es] & there Fees
though heretofore the were esteemed ech one there degrees
In Shottle & Posterne tennents had herbage at easie rates
of w[i]ch the are now quite debard & shutt out of those gates

14. This Forest hath Forsters of fee w[i]ch p[ar]tly hold there land
By s[er]vices there in to do, as I do understand
There names be Bradborne Bradshaw Bruckshaw & of the heires of Stone
all w[i]ch at Forest co[ur]ts must be, with others many a one.

15. Corzon esq[uire] leiwtenent is to keepe theis thinges in order
and under him the keep[er]s walke & watch in ev[e]ry border
w[i]ch officers offenders all against vert shold p[re]sent
and for the king in Forest courts are swarne to th[a]t intent

16. Thighe Stuerd hath his boberer to walke & m[ar]ke such trees
as bondhould tenants are alowd For w[i]ch the have some fees
Verderers Rangers & Knaves of Forest & offic[er]s have been moe
W[i]ch now are discontinued place ease I let them goe

17. Besydes the yeerely Woodmote c[ou]rts, a Tacke c[ou]rte muste be kept
and at Lukes day & Martinmas the tack must be collect
Those offic[er]s then a dyner make, ech man must have his pye
and hen therein by antient use,& pay accordinglye

18. If any man his tackeor swyne do wittingly conceale
the same hee forfeytts to the king for shifts will not p[re]vaile
And further for soch fault soch fyne he must endure
as shale be sett upon his head, at the Steward his pleasure

19. Coll[ec]tor of soch wards wherein the Woodmote c[ou]rte is kept
a dyner there he must p[ro]vide & of officers respect
The charge where of the Woodm[en] at after dyner payeth
w[i]ch Co[ur]ts should thus obs[er]ved be & so the custome sayeth

20. And as the offic[er]s for there paynes, allowed are some Fees
So tenants w[i]ch soch duties pay, in wood have liberties
But if wood w[i]thout warrant & livery be felled
soch trespasser a fyne therefore, to pay shale be compelled

21. The Castle ould to thono[ur] now as incydent then being
in Duffeld Fryth had manors eight thereunto app[er]tayning
Duffeld Beurp[er]d Sowthwood Holbrocke & highedge nearly adioyning
Holland Bigging Derichey & Alderwaslye was belonging

22. Where in his grace great royalties hath lets co[ur]ts waif and strayes
Freehoulders good & Copyholders those Co[u]rts attend alwaise
fyve hundreth good & able men this little fryth affored
To s[er]ve his grace at Chancellers bid w[i]th bowes bills & w[i]th swords

23. The soyle all Kynds of corne it yelds, & eke good cattell breeds
and Wooll & lead & Irne & cole, & most things that men needes
On helthy hills & vallis warme men there have habitation
and food & ream[en]t to suffice mens corps & recreations

24. The Chancellars office & the rest sup[e]rior Duchy places
I Could but spare to sett forth them, pr[e]sumpc[i]ons brede disgraces
Of little pritty Duffeld fryth, to speake I did intend
w[i]th due regard desying yet, to please but not to offend

25. This hath Jewells three instore, wher to they may appeale
when the be Wronged in there land, or hurt in Comon weale
The Charter Ch'r[138] & Custome booke, god keepe them in safe hands
to save this Frith inunities, there freedomes & there lands

138 Probably 'C[ouc]h[e]r', i.e. the 'Tutbury Coucher'.

26. W[i]ch Jewells three For Duffelds good, do gen[er]ally agree
that Duffeld hath theis costomes pure & priviledges Free
W[i]ch affter herein p[ar]t to touch, omitting manye moe
If I shale not thee tyre to much, some what I will thee show

27. First Duffeld men showld not be cald, to s[e]rve at sise or sessions
From Juries there the are exempte, & shold not use disgressions
The Duchie offic[er]s duchie men, their Causes governe shold
and may remove all duchie plaints, thether I will uphould

28. No speciall baylies duchie men, in duchie may arrest
unles by bealies not retorne, and non omyttas prest
nor clarke of market may there deale w[i]th weight or mesure ether
nor foren beaylies waives or strayes or rents or duties gather

29. And Inman may by p[ri]viledge, an out mans goods attache
here found in Duffeld liberties, tansw[er] his playnt as gage
Outmen w[i]thout an Inmans pleaydge no Inman here can sue
to strang[er]s here w[i]thout a pledg, no acc[i]on can acrue.

30. no Duffeld man may enter suyt in Foreyn Court a broade
For dept or damage in the frith, if there the make aboade
onles the some amount to forty shillinges or above
on payne to Forfitt forty more, w[i]ch playnt one may remove

31. Through England duchie men are free From paying toll or stallage
For marchandizes w[i]th the use, from picage & from tallage
And other soch exacc[i]ons more ther neds to be recyted
W[i]ch when the cleayme the are full oft of Corporations spited

32. The kinge also hath smale co[ur]ts there where in occa[si]ons to trye
For land or under forty shillings els no can there well by
Justis with speede men may have there when as the nede peas
which for tenants & country men great pleasure is & ease

33. Such helthy plausant hills & valleys warme & sownd
sweete water springs fruyt trees & store of wooded ground
And mynes for Irone slate coale & stone & other p[ro]fitts manye
as Duffeld manors yeld to thee, I know not like or anye

34. What more then this can reason wishe, texpect in Duffeld fee
who this dislikes des[er]vithe lesse & worser plant may hee
And touching customes laudable Freedomes & liberttees
there Ch'r[139] good & custome booke the same right well descrys

139 Could be 'Ch[arte]r' or 'C[ouc]h[e]r'.

35. Which if the keepe inviolate & well together hould
A mightie man cannot then wrest, w[i]th silv[er] nor w[i]th gould
But if the fagott bond ons breake, & stickes flye to & fro
Then Duffeld fryth tornes upsyde downe there welth is ov[e]rthrow

36. If any man obiect & say, Duffeld layes should be inlarged
no, no, in truth say I in large Duffeld is over charged
There comons & there fewell draws more people there to dwell
then all there said comodities, are able to keepe well

37. And now on thord[er]s of those co[ur]ts I will no longer stand
wherein both use & law conioyne, but will retorne to land
Of customes now w[i]ch chiefely touch, the copihouldres state
some soch materiall poynts I meane a litle to debate

38. Three sorts of copyhould lands in Duffeld manors bee
Bond hould att will & mattock land, besydes thos w[i]ch be free
W[i]ch tenures three be held at will, by copye of court roule
all w[i]ch in sondry sev[er]all sorts the costomes do controulle

39. Most of w[i]ch Freeholders land are of a socage tenure
and some be held by knightes service w[i]thout all paradventure
Freehoulds by lawe some s[er]vice do, but not by costams tide
But all the copyhould[er]s have the costames for there gyde

40. The bond hold[er] most bounden is, the costames well to hold
his houses well mayntayne must hee, non there of may be sold
No out man may soch bondhold have, unles he thereon dwell
who th[er]of dyeth seisd must pay, an hariott you know well

41. The bondholder the lord also by torne as Reve must serve
and afterward must halfeswyne be from w[i]ch he may not swerve
w[i]ch services & things to do, to him to be assigned
upon admission to soch lands good pledgs hee must fynd

42. W[i]ch costomes if he careles breake, his lands may then be seised
onles by composic[i]on his lord be well appeased
And for soch s[er]vice by him due, hee hath some Feese allowed
and wood for houses in sett by warrant well avowed

43. Reves also in there office wayfes & strayes may seise & take
and lawfully keepe praise & sell, & there of count must make
And if soch Reve in count be short, or thereon chance to hault
his fellowes of that tenure there, must make up good his fault

44. And all theis Coppyhould[er]s Inheritance have clere
according to the custames pure, of all the manors there
And states the take by surrender, & p[ro]clymations three
and seison & admission & loyall fealtie

45. But if a Copiholder sell land, out of court by deed
And liv[er]y & season thereof give & costome so exceed
Soch lands hee flatly forfeytts as also by exchange
of Copyhold for Freehold allthough it may seeme strange

46. And divers other forfyetures, of Copyholds there bee
and causes eake of seizures, of Copyholds truly
W[i]ch being there well knowne, to speake of them I spare
Wishing all Copyholds, on them for to be ware

47. And all soch Copyholders Inheritance w[i]ch have
surrender may for lyves or yeares, to soch as will them Crave
But out of court state larger non may there make the say
of Copyhold save onely one yeare and a day

48. If a bondholder dye his heire under age beinge
then next to kyn to whome the lande is not dissending
Shale garden be to theire, during minoritie
putting in pledges in that case, as costom telleth thee

49. But if soch men have daughters three, & have no son[n]s at all
those lands should not be p[ar]ted, but theldest have all
Though others lands at will, to cop[ar]teners doe goe
and thus the costomes writt do rule as costomes books doe show

50. Now w[i]th good custumes laudable if tenants keep them well
I know few manors in the land w[i]ch can this Frith excell
W[i]ch to pr[e]s[e]rve I wish & warne that men together hould
then them to hurt non can p[re]veile & there of be then bould

51. The better sort of Duffeld men, there customes understandes
and how they do concerne them selves, there houses & there lands
The poorer sort and ignorant w[i]ch custome bookes have non
by song may learne some customes now, & memorie alone

52. Then sith this Frith doth yeld, all thinges afore recyted
to plant them selves therein, who would not be delyted
And thus I have thee told the reasons of my choyse
and why for pleasant dwelling, Duffeld shale have my voyce

53. God save King James o[ur] noble prince, & p[ro]sp[er] his long Rayne
over this Frith & manors all o[ur] lord for to remeane
God blesse his counsell courts & all the officers of the duchie
the noble Early of Shrewsburye, & of Duffeld Fryth & fee

54. Fare well sweete Chevyn hill w[i]th all thy brave p[ro]spects
w[i]ch temptest me one May morning to writ this rude effect
W[i]ch rashly done, if taken well & censured as I ment
I shale rest loving to this Frith, & think my tyme well spent

Chapter 3

Contested Pasts: Custom, Conflict and Landscape Change in West Norfolk, *c*.1550–1650

*Nicola Whyte**

> Nothing can cause more surprise in the minds of many strangers on their first visiting Norfolk, than to find, on entering the county by Brandon or Thetford, a long stage of 18 miles to Swaffham, through a tract which deserves to be called a desert: a region of warren or sheepwalk, scattered with scanty cultivation, yet highly improvable.[1]

Characterized by large swathes of unimproved heaths, commons and arable open fields, it has long been noted that the 'sheep-corn' regions of west Norfolk became a target for agrarian improvers in the eighteenth century. Denouncing the district as a 'capital disgrace to the country', contemporary writers criticized the environmental and social depravation of villages in the area.[2] In 1769 William Gilpin, purveyor of the picturesque movement, described Breckland as 'a piece of absolute desert almost in the heart of England'. The open heaths were deemed to be unproductive wastes, the unenclosed fields 'ragged and dirty', the people 'dreary and desolate'.[3] Late eighteenth-century ambitions to bring about the improvement of land and people found expression in the physical reorganization and aesthetic enclosure of the land.[4] New boundaries of quickset hedges, linear

---

* My thanks to Richard Hoyle, Paul Warde and Andy Wood for their perceptive and helpful comments on earlier drafts of this chapter. All documents cited are in The National Archives (TNA) unless indicated to the contrary.

1 Arthur Young, *A general view of the agriculture of Norfolk* (London, 1804), p. 385.

2 Ibid.

3 Jon Gregory, 'Mapping improvement: reshaping rural landscapes in the eighteenth century', *Landscapes* 6 (2005), p. 74; William Gilpin, *Observations on several parts of the counties of Cambridge, Norfolk, Suffolk and Essex. Also on several parts of north Wales; relative chiefly to picturesque beauty, in two tours, the former made in the year 1769, the latter in the year 1773* (London, 1809), pp. 28–9.

4 Gregory, 'Mapping improvement', pp. 62–82; Sarah Tarlow, *The Archaeology of Improvement in Britain, 1750–1850* (Cambridge, 2007), chs 2 and 3.

roads and regular plantations were laid out, and existing boundaries and roads straightened. Thus the drawing-board landscape of Oliver Rackham's 'planned countryside' was created.[5]

In recent years historians and landscape archaeologists working on the post-medieval period have become increasingly concerned with notions of boundedness, of social exclusion and cultural separation, identified both in terms of socio-economic relations and in terms of the physical enclosure of the land.[6] From the late sixteenth century the notion of enclosure and improvement gained increasing momentum on the ground as a practical requisite of farming and as a cultural movement propagated by popular husbandry literature.[7] Some writers have viewed the creation of new hedges and ditches as the symbolic manifestation of the rise of individualism, improvement and direct confrontation of 'man' with nature.[8] With this in mind, the continuing operation of open field (and ostensibly communal farming systems) into the late eighteenth century, in a region fully engaged in the commercial production of grain and wool, prompts questions regarding the material and cultural manifestations of capitalism: evidently the relationship between enclosure and ideological change was not straightforward.[9] There are, nevertheless, important parallels that can be made between the making of boundaries – often without obvious physical barriers (to the historian at least) and control of land and resources in light soil villages – and the processes of piecemeal enclosure taking place elsewhere in the sixteenth and seventeenth centuries.

Eighteenth-century distaste for the barren landscape of Norfolk's sheep-corn villages overlooks earlier ideals of the aesthetics of a productive landscape. For preceding generations of elite landowners, far from being unproductive wastes, the heaths and commons were valued as an integral part of a complex 'sheep-corn' farming system.[10] It is generally agreed that the apparent continuity of farming practices into the eighteenth century was a pragmatic response to

---

5 Oliver Rackham, *The History of the Countryside* (London, 1986), p. 5.

6 Steve Hindle, 'A sense of place? Becoming and belonging in the rural parish, 1550–1650', in Alexandra Shepard and Phil Withington (eds), *Communities in Early Modern England: Networks, Place, Rhetoric* (Manchester, 2000), pp. 96–114; Matthew Johnson, *An Archaeology of Capitalism* (Oxford, 1996); Nicholas Blomley, 'Making private property: enclosure, common right and the work of hedges', *Rural Hist.* 18 (2007), pp. 1–21.

7 Andrew McRae, *God Speed the Plough: The Representation of Agrarian England, 1500–1660* (Cambridge, 1996); Tarlow, *Archaeology of Improvement.*

8 Johnson, *Archaeology of Capitalism*; Bromley, 'Making private property'.

9 Tom Williamson, 'Understanding enclosure', *Landscapes* 1 (2000), pp. 56–79.

10 K. J. Allison, 'The sheep-corn husbandry of Norfolk in the sixteenth and seventeenth centuries', *Agricultural History Rev.* 5 (1957), pp. 12–30.

a specific set of environmental conditions.[11] In order to ensure the light, easily leached soils remained in good heart, it was necessary for farmers to keep their land open in order to ensure it received a constant supply of manure deposited by the manorial sheep flock. A corollary of this viewpoint is that it simply was not in the best interests of farmers to enclose their land and thereby risk a deficit of manure and a consequent decline of soil fertility. While there is no denying that farmers faced a harsh environment, such arguments assume that all farmers shared the same economic vision and were essentially conservative in their outlook, being content to continue operating open field systems inherited from the medieval past.[12] Yet, neighbouring lords, tenants and commoners often held different, if not incompatible, ideas about the best and most profitable way to use the land.[13]

Just as enclosure and customary access rights to local resources gave rise to tensions and conflict in wood-pasture, fen and forest villages across the country, the control of land and resources was also a hotly contested issue in arable Norfolk. Following Kett's manifesto of 1549, the tenants of sheep-corn Norfolk presented a petition to Queen Mary in 1553 accusing the gentry of engrossing, increasing rents, overexploiting the commons and abusing their foldcourse rights.[14] Though ineffectual in parliament, the petition by no means marked the end of antagonism between lords and tenants in the area. While large-scale enclosure disputes and riots were generally absent, court records from the late sixteenth and early seventeenth centuries reveal the rumblings of discontent, threatening words and assaults from villages across the region.[15] These localized acts of verbal and physical aggression did not represent the confrontation in any straightforward sense between enclosing and 'improving' landowners on the one hand and disenfranchised and conservative open-field farmers and commoners on the other; the reverse was just as often the case. Historians tend to use enclosure as shorthand for a range of processes culminating in the abolition of manorial jurisdiction over a piece of land. Yet some forms of enclosure, such as the piecemeal consolidation of commonable arable land, often had ambiguous

---

[11] M. Bailey, *A Marginal Economy? East Anglian Breckland in the Later Middle Ages* (Cambridge, 1989), p. 57; E. Kerridge, *The Agricultural Revolution* (London, 1967), pp. 42–5; Tom Williamson, *The Transformation of Rural England* (Exeter, 2002), pp. 55–6.

[12] Williamson, 'Understanding enclosure', p. 58.

[13] Mark Overton, *Agricultural Revolution in England: The Transformation of the Agrarian Economy, 1500–1850* (Cambridge, 1996), pp. 53–5.

[14] R. W. Hoyle, 'Agrarian agitation in mid-sixteenth-century Norfolk: a petition of 1553', *Historical J.* 44 (2001), pp. 223–38.

[15] On the decline of enclosure riots, Andy Wood, *Riot, Rebellion and Popular Politics in Early Modern England* (Basingstoke, 2002), ch. 3.

legal implications. In terms of understanding the shift from a customary 'moral' economy to one based upon individual proprietorship, it is important that we take account of the practical, everyday contexts and meanings of enclosure. For contemporaries, fences and hedges did not necessarily signify individual autonomy over the land.

A central theme of this chapter is an examination of the role of custom in the mediation of local disputes.[16] While some historians have stressed the flexibility of customary rights, which could be adapted to suit changing needs and conditions, far less attention has been paid to what this flexibility meant in practice.[17] The following discussion is based upon the first-hand accounts of witnesses called before commissioners appointed by the equity courts to give their knowledge and recollection of the organization of farming practices and customary rights. Their words reveal the nuances and complexities of late sixteenth- and seventeenth-century attitudes towards enclosure. They also shed light on the concern felt by many tenant households about the decline of local resources. A large number of studies have focused on the achievements of wealthy landowners who profited from large-scale rabbit and sheep farming.[18] But a counter-narrative to that of economic progress and optimism brings to light the impact that their activities had on the sustainability of tenant household economies. As we shall see from the perspective of local inhabitants, the landscape was 'surcharged' – stripped of common grazing, fuel and even corn growing in the open fields. Tenants and commoners experienced the steady rationalization and contraction of customary topographies, not always through the physical enclosure of land but from the diminishing viability of small-scale arable and livestock production. In short, this chapter explores the social and economic dynamics that lay behind the making of a landscape described in such disparaging terms by late eighteenth-century improvers. It falls into four sections: the first considering enclosure and its opponents, the second the impact of the manorial rabbit population on tenant arable economies, and the

---

[16] E. P. Thompson, *Customs in Common* (London, 1991), ch. 3; Andy Wood, 'The place of custom in plebeian political culture: England, 1550–1800', *Social Hist.* 22 (1997), pp. 46–60; and his *The Politics of Social Conflict: The Peak Country, 1520–1770* (Cambridge, 1999), pp. 69–188; Keith Wrightson 'The Politics of the Parish', in P. Griffiths, A. Fox and S. Hindle (eds), *The Experience of Authority in Early Modern England* (London, 1996), pp. 10–46.

[17] Thompson, *Customs in Common*, ch. 3; and Wood, 'Place of custom'.

[18] M. Aston and J. Bettey, 'The Post-Medieval Landscape, *c.*1540–1700: The Drive for Profit and the Desire for Status', in P. Everson and T. Williamson (eds), *The Archaeology of Landscape* (Manchester, 1998); T. Williamson 'The Rural Landscape: 1500–1900, the Neglected Centuries', in D. Hooke (ed.) *Landscape: The Richest Historical Record* (Society for Landscape Studies, supp. ser. 1, 2000), pp. 109–17.

third the exploitation of the heaths. Finally we consider how the openness of this landscape – which so appalled Young and the other commentators – was itself an aspect of landlord power, before drawing the chapter together with some comments on custom and memory.

I

Historians working on East Anglia have long recognized the significance of the foldcourse system for the local economy and society of Breckland and north-west Norfolk.[19] The foldcourse referred to the exclusive right of seigneurial lords, or their tenants, to graze a flock of sheep across all of the land situated within the boundaries of the foldcourse. The movement of the manorial flock was restricted according to the season and status of tilled land. Cultivation was achieved through an integrated system of sheep-corn husbandry; that is sheep were 'tathed' or penned in folds on the stubble after harvest, during the customary period of shack and upon land under fallow. In the sixteenth century a significant shift occurred in the organization and social meaning of the foldcourse. Whereas in the medieval period, as Mark Bailey has shown, tenants were entitled by custom to keep a certain number of sheep in the lord's fold and to erect folds on their own arable strips, in the sixteenth century 'cullet' rights were gradually eroded. By recourse to the central law courts, manorial lords set out to achieve a more systematic and rigorously controlled foldcourse system, which gave them the monopoly over sheep farming and common field grazing rights.[20] Over 50 years ago, Keith Allison made the point that 'by abusing the foldcourse system, landlords were able to enlarge their flocks without recourse to the large scale enclosure and conversion of open field arable land to pasture taking place elsewhere in the country'.[21]

It is important to emphasize that the open fields and heaths were not vast unbounded spaces. Foldcourse territories were carefully, often contentiously, delineated by a series of distinct landmark features situated amid the open fields, commons and heaths. Rather than hedges, fences and ditches, which acted as obvious barriers to movement, route-ways and single landmark features or

---

19 Allison, 'Sheep-corn husbandry'; Bailey, *Marginal Economy*, pp. 65–85; and his 'Sand into gold: the evolution of the foldcourse system in west Suffolk, 1200–1600', *Agricultural History Rev.* 38 (1990), pp. 40–57; M. R. Postgate, 'Field Systems in East Anglia', in A. R. H. Baker and R. A. Butlin (eds), *Studies of Field Systems in the British Isles* (Cambridge, 1973), pp. 281–324.

20 Bailey, *Marginal Economy*, p. 294.

21 Allison, 'Sheep-corn husbandry', p. 24.

'nodal points' were employed.[22] In addition, the practice of folding resulted in the subdivision of open fields by purportedly moveable hurdles. As well as facilitating the efficient manuring of the land, the fold had additional benefits of preventing livestock straying onto adjacent crops, and providing shelter in otherwise open terrain. This last feature has received little comment from historians, yet in north Norfolk such enclosures were deemed to be 'rather beneficiall then hurtfull' for they protected sheep in 'wynter tyme ... in stormye weather' and 'in laming tyme'.[23] In this respect, late eighteenth-century writers noted the benefits of folding in landscapes largely devoid of trees and hedges. Arthur Young reported that a Mr Blythe of Burnham erected folds on his land 'solely by reason of the openness of his farm' – although by this time folding was viewed as both an inefficient way of manuring land and pasturing sheep.[24]

While temporary enclosures were accepted as a practical requisite of open-field farming, by the turn of the seventeenth century it seems local support for the foldcourse was diminishing. No longer included within the lord's folding arrangements, and faced with tighter restrictions placed upon cropping arrangements and grazing rights, the operation of foldcourses gave rise to tensions over the rights of tenants to cultivate the open fields. In contrast to the late medieval period, for which there is evidence that communal cropping arrangements were relatively relaxed, between the sixteenth and eighteenth centuries seigneurial lords sought to compel farmers, often through the courts, to cooperate more fully with their foldcourse operations.[25] In order to ensure enough grazing, they imposed strict regulations on the rotation of tilled land and land under fallows according to a complicated 'shift' system. The 'shift' referred to land under the same state of cultivation, the boundaries of which were flexible, in order to allow adjustments between fallow and cropped shifts, depending on the demand for grain and different soil conditions.[26] Thus in Wighton the rotation of the four Gonge Furlongs involved sowing three with corn and the fourth as 'somerley', used for the feeding and tathing of the foldcourse.[27] In theory the system presented a practical solution to maintaining the balance between grazing (and therefore manure) and arable, but its operation was far from equitable and the levels of compliance required from tenants not

22 Nicola Whyte, 'Landscape, memory and custom: parish identities, *c.*1550–1750', *Social Hist.* 32 (2007), pp. 166–86.

23 DL 4/40/49.

24 Young, *General View*, p. 475.

25 Bailey, *Marginal Economy*, p. 58; Allison, 'Sheep-corn husbandry'.

26 Postgate, 'Field Systems', pp. 299–300.

27 DL 4/18/19.

always forthcoming.[28] Indeed, the extent to which tenant farmers benefited from manure deposited by the manorial flock is unclear; rather concentrated folding took place on the permanent demesne arable and on land to be sown with more profitable crops, such as barley.[29] In a landscape characterized by light soils, prone to excessive leaching and infertility, the allocation of manure was an essential and closely guarded resource, its distribution signifying the division of power over the land. In this environment, arable production relied on an integrated system of livestock husbandry, in practice, and somewhat paradoxically, tensions existed between seigneurial interests in sheep farming on the one hand and tenant cultivators on the other.[30]

The economic and environmental difficulties the tenants faced in the late sixteenth and early seventeenth centuries were, to a great extent, anticipated in the petition of 1553. Regarding the foldcourse, the petitioners sought to restrict the number of sheep kept, to compel owners to observe customary grazing rights and to allow the tenants access to local resources.[31] By the late sixteenth century increasing numbers of sheep resulted in serious logistical problems. The courts heard how it was impossible to drive flocks, often numbering 1,000 and more, without them straying onto and destroying crops belonging to tenants. In seventeenth-century Roxham, for example, the sheep trespassed where the land 'laye open' and in consequence the tenants' corn was 'often tymes spoyled'.[32] Similar complaints were heard in Wighton in 1576: 'it is not possible for any man to dryve a flocke of v or vj^c shepe in the said stey [way] w[i]thout trespassinge' on the tenants' lands.[33] In order to protect their crops from the marauding sheep, tenants responded by setting up their own folds. In Holkham, for example, tenants hindered the run of the manorial flock by sowing their strips on land set aside for fallow and setting up hurdles 'circlewise' in the open fields.[34] Foldcourse owners regarded the tenants' enclosures, with some justification, as a deliberate attempt to disrupt their manorial grazing rights. They complained that such activities went against the customs of the manor and were 'things very mischeevous', and if allowed to continue unchecked 'will tend to the overthrow of very manye foldcourses'.[35]

28 Allison, 'Sheep-corn husbandry'; Postgate, 'Field Systems'.

29 Bailey, *Marginal Economy*.

30 Allison, 'Sheep-corn husbandry'.

31 Hoyle, 'Agrarian agitation', pp. 231–2.

32 Norfolk Record Office (hereafter NRO), PRA 469 380 x 5.

33 DL 4/18/19.

34 Cited in Allison, 'Sheep-corn husbandry', p. 26.

35 Cited in Postgate, 'Field Systems', p. 320; W. Rye, *State Papers Relating to Musters, Beacons, Ship-Money, etc. in Norfolk, from 1626 Chiefly to the Beginning of the Civil War* (1907), pp. 70–71.

Attempting to impose a degree of restraint on foldcourse owners, local inhabitants presented to the courts their own version of the customs of the manor by questioning, for instance, the customary ratio of sheep per acreage of pasture.[36] In Wighton, the tenants maintained that the owner of the manor was entitled to keep 300 sheep on 70 acres of pasture. However, the owner of the manor, James Taverner, was accused of reducing the availability of grazing (both heath and common field) by overcharging the foldcourse with 600 or 700 sheep, 'w[hi]ch amounteth to ix shepe for every acre of pasture'. Deponents gave substance to their answers by contrasting the conduct of the neighbouring Duchy manor of Crabs Castle, deemed to abide by custom and precedent, with the unscrupulous activities of Taverner. According to one deponent, Taverner's actions were 'contrary to all order of foldcourses if ever I have seen or heard time of my remembrance'.[37] Just as foldcourse owners called tenants to account for setting up folds and disrupting manorial grazing rights by recourse to past precedent, tenants and commoners also constructed a version of the past based upon common conceptions of custom to which they claimed manorial lords and their lessees were entitled.

The manorial right to exercise common field grazing or shack rights gave rise to further tensions. Faced with unpredictable corn prices and tighter restrictions placed upon sheep farming, cattle became an important mainstay of tenant households.[38] Reports from Brandon and Thetford indicate that the number of cattle kept by tenants and commoners was increasing by the end of the sixteenth century. While the heaths generally yielded sufficient vegetation to sustain sheep and rabbits, cattle required a greater and more nourishing quantity of grazing. In 1603 James Downing shepherd described Westwick Heath near Thetford as 'for the most p[ar]te barren [and] will yelde small or little feede for greate cattell'.[39] Since fallow grazing and folding rights were strictly limited to the manorial flock, rights of shackage – which usually ran from Michaelmas to the Feast of the Purification of the Blessed Virgin Mary (29 September–2 February, though the dates varied between manors) – provided a vital source of fodder for the tenants' cattle as well as manure for their arable lands. Tenants claimed a degree of flexibility regarding the commencement of shack rights, particularly in years

36 See for example, DL 4/18/19; E 134/10ChasI/Mich51.

37 DL 4/18/19.

38 Particularly in central and eastern Norfolk, see B. M. S. Campbell and M. Overton, 'A new perspective in medieval and early modern agriculture: six centuries of Norfolk farming, *c.*1250–1850', *Past and Present* 141 (1993), pp. 38–105; Susanna Wade Martins and Tom Williamson, *Roots of Change: Farming and the Landscape in East Anglia, 1700–1870* (*Agricultural History Rev.*, Supp. Ser. 2, 1999), pp. 120–25.

39 E 134/1JasI/Trin7.

of late harvest, when grazing began as soon as the corn had been carted from the fields. However, by the turn of the seventeenth century, tensions arose over the attempts of foldcourse owners to impose a more rigorous observance of the customary calendar.

In 1592 the flockmasters of Snettisham were accused of grazing the open fields contrary to custom, which resulted in the destruction of crops still standing in the fields and reduction in the availability of stubble grazing for the tenants' cattle over winter. The tenants claimed that the manor only held grazing rights between the feasts of Saint Michael the Archangel and the Feast of All Saints (29 September–1 November), yet they continued grazing their sheep during the period of common shack until the Feast of Annunciation (25 March). According to Richard Greene of Snettisham, they did not have the right to feed 'any of the corne of the ten[a]nts or inhabitants of Snetish[a]m aforesaid betwene the said feasts'. He knew this to be true for he had seen it used ever since he could remember as he 'hath his abiding in the towne'.[40] Greene's testimony provides a valuable insight into the clash of economic interests between foldcourse owners and tenant farmers.

There emerges a strong sense that the inhabitants of sheep-corn villages did not passively accept the foldcourse institution as the means of ensuring productivity, but for many it was deemed to threaten the viability of their corn production and cattle husbandry. Hence it was the tenants who often sought to enclose their land and exclude the lord's sheep, and the lord and his servants who engaged in acts of hedge-breaking. In 1601 the lessee of Cawston Manor, for example, was accused of breaking into closes belonging to the tenants of the manor, sawing up gates and making gaps in hedges in order to graze his sheep during shack time.[41] Thus physical enclosure did not necessarily represent autonomy over the land.[42] Similar disputes were heard elsewhere. In the case from Wighton of 1576, James Taverner was accused of impounding his tenants' cattle and allegedly slaughtering many as they were driven to what the tenants claimed to be their own pasture closes.[43] Manorial lords exploited their customary shack rights over enclosed land as a means of extending the quantity of grazing for their foldcourses, or as a means of raising revenue by commuting access rights to a monetary payment. Such was the case in Wighton where, by way of compensation, the tenants were allegedly coerced into paying an annual fine to Taverner. Manorial jurisdiction over enclosed or 'half-year lands' continued

[40] DL 4/34/46.

[41] E 134/43&44Eliz/Mich7.

[42] Nicola Whyte, *Inhabiting the Landscape: Place, Custom And Memory, 1500–1800* (Oxford, 2009), p. 106.

[43] DL 4/18/19.

into the eighteenth century. A map of Wighton dating to 1734 shows a number of enclosures in which Sir Charles Turner was entitled to graze his sheep flock during shack time. In many places, abolition of these additional access rights did not occur until parliamentary enclosure.[44] Similar levels of uncertainty and contention, surrounding the attempts of gentry-landowners to dominate common field grazing rights, disrupted the progress of enclosure in champion villages located in sheep-corn villages in central and eastern Norfolk.[45]

The point to emphasize is that the extension and consolidation of seigneurial common field grazing rights, which cemented the authority of the manor over tenants' holdings, had significant consequences in ensuring the survival of open-field systems well into the eighteenth century. Examined at the local level the functions and experience of enclosure in light soil villages is shown to be complex and ambiguous. Unsurprisingly landowners and tenants might support enclosure when it suited them, while simultaneously opposing such changes when their rights were threatened. And, whilst foldcourse owners continued to exercise their jurisdictional rights over their tenants' arable lands and pasture closes (often by intimidation and force), the enclosure of demesne land continued apace. Taking advantage of the sale and redistribution of monastic lands in Breckland, for example, it was reported in 1591 that Sir Richard Fulmerston had enclosed 100 acres of land formerly belonging to the Abbey of Bury on the north side of Lynford.[46] Enclosure was not necessarily an enormous and costly undertaking; many landowners simply left their hurdles up in the open fields, thereby preventing tenants from exercising their shack rights. In Congham in 1598 William Swanton, husbandman, told the court how the most part of the landholders 'do hold up' their closes from the common shack.[47] What had been in previous years temporary folds were thus becoming more permanent structures, reserved for the exclusive use of the owner. For tenant farmers the increasing permanence of such barriers had serious implications: in the words of Richard Greene of Snettisham recorded in 1592: 'not withstanding all the said inclosures so taken from the said tenants and inhabitants' the owner of the manor 'doth still shack and feede in and over all the fields in Snetish[a]m aforesaid as largely & w[i]th as greate nombers of shepe as w[i]thin memory of man were ever kept there before' the enclosing of the grounds.[48] It was not

44 NRO, Ms 21138. And, see for example, the enclosure award for Cawston, NRO, C/Sca2/68.

45 Whyte, *Inhabiting the Landscape*, p. 105.

46 E 134/33&34Eliz/Mich29.

47 E 134/40&41Eliz/Mich21.

48 DL 4/34/46.

merely economic grievances that can be detected in Greene's complaint, but also the injustices felt over the lack of reciprocity shown by the manorial lord.

Alarm over the contraction of common grazing among tenant farmers was heightened by the proliferation of enclosures on the heaths, on what were purportedly arable outfield lands and 'brecks'. During periods of buoyant grain prices parcels of outfield and breck, lying under long restorative fallows, were brought into cultivation. The system had its origins in the late medieval period but became more systematic in the seventeenth century, made possible by increased stocking densities and thus plentiful supplies of manure. Thus in Congham it was reported in 1598 that two years before, a parcel of land containing about 2 acres lying in the East Field had been 'fermed and broken up' and sown 'w[i]th pease and feches' and there upon the parcel of land 'is called Breck lande'.[49] Something of the enormity of the extension of the arable acreage is illustrated in the case regarding access rights to Westwick Heath near Thetford. In 1603 Martin Towler, shepherd, recalled how 30 years previously four 'plough tylthes' out of an allocated 14 were made on Westwick Heath. By the turn of the seventeenth century it was estimated that 110 acres of Westwick Heath had been cultivated and sown with barley and rye.[50] The extension of the cultivated acreage continued apace across the seventeenth century. In 1658 inhabitants of Cranwich reported that the breaking up of the heaths had much increased over the previous 20 years.[51] Yet, due to the nature of the soils it was impossible to till outfield or brecks for more than a few years at a time before the land had to be allowed to revert to heath once again and left to rejuvenate under long fallows.[52]

While the impact of convertible husbandry on raising output, in conjunction with the introduction of fodder legumes, is well attested by historians, less consideration has been paid to the broader social implications of such developments.[53] The decision to plough land that was not obviously different from the surrounding heaths became a point of contention in villages across the region. At the turn of the seventeenth century, 12 inhabitants of Eccles petitioned their manorial lord, Sir Nathaniel Bacon, complaining of the 'wronges and iniuries' done to them by his farmers John and Robert James in breaking and ploughing the heath to which they claimed common rights, 'according

49 E 134/40&41Eliz/Mich21.

50 E 134/1JasI/Trin7.

51 DL 4/104/1658/5.

52 Postgate, 'Field Systems'.

53 Kerridge, *Agricultural Revolution*. For an alternative view, H. Kitsikopoulos, 'Convertible husbandry vs. regular common fields: a model of the relative efficiency of medieval field systems', *J. Economic History* 64 (2004), pp. 462–99.

to o[u]r auncient use and custome'.[54] An attempt was made to resolve such disputes by redress to the past, especially the physical evidence of cultivation. In 1598 80-year-old John Pond remembered seeing 'rigginge and furrowinge' on Goldworthy Hill 40 years previously which then seemed 'verye auncyent'. In comparison, Bakers Close had never been ploughed for he could not perceive any ridge or furrow.[55] In other cases local knowledge of the history of enclosure, including the relative age of each section of boundary, was called upon to verify prior cultivation. In 1601 a 70-year-old labourer, William Chamberlain of Snettisham, told the court that 36 years before, he 'did dike and fence all the west side' of a 10-acre close lying in Westgate called 'More Close'. He went on to say that some four years later, Thomas Crispe 'did dike and enclose the south head therof before w[hi]ch tyme the east and north p[ar]ts therof were annciently enclosed'.[56] The fact that sections of boundary were 'ancient', existing before anyone could remember, was taken to be adequate validation of the right to plough the outfield brecks in question. The evidence from Snettisham further highlights the cumulative impact of boundaries on the landscape.

Providing customary grazing rights were respected, by either removing or making gaps in fences, it was not physical enclosure *per se* that caused controversy in light soil parishes but rather the shift from temporary to permanent enclosures. Landlords or their lessees were accused of keeping gates locked and barring access to the tenants' cattle during shack time, as they have 'anciently accustomed'.[57] In the dispute over More Close and Downe Close in Snettisham – described as 'two closes inclosed yerely and everye yeare' – John Barnard, labourer, revealed that More Close had been enclosed some 30 years previously but had been reopened every year to allow the inhabitants' cattle their grazing during shack time between Michaelmas (29 September) and the Annunciation (25 March). For the last seven years the close had remained enclosed and the gate locked.[58] The courts heard how in some places the tenants and commoners responded by reasserting their customary grazing rights to what they claimed to be common heath. The cattle belonging to the tenants of Snettisham, for example, were impounded by the bailiff of the manor for grazing newly enclosed

54 NRO, MC 571/15.

55 E 134/39&40Eliz/Mich22; usually associated with heavy clay soils and poor drainage, the evidence of 'ridge and furrow' on the light lands of western Norfolk raises interesting questions regarding alternative uses of such earthworks. Judging from the evidence, a form of ridge and furrow may have been used on the light lands to differentiate portions of outfield land.

56 DL 4/43/4.

57 DL 4/34/46.

58 DL 4/43/4.

parcels of land.[59] Similarly the inhabitants of Thetford stated their rights to Westwick Heath by 'forcibly' putting their common herd of cattle on recently tilled brecks. Asked to give his version of events in 1603, Thomas Stallam of Thetford, husbandman, told the court how the rye was 'utterly wasted by the neate cattell of the inhabytants of Thetford' and the barley was 'very much hindered in the growthe' by the 'feeding and treadinge theruppon'.[60]

Just as enclosure and access rights to common land erupted in conflict in wood-pasture and forest villages, similar levels of discontent grew in sheep-corn Norfolk. As any historian familiar with court deposition evidence is well aware, contemporary representations of the past in terms of words and deeds remembered from elderly neighbours and kin were prone to embellishment, if not fabrication. Nevertheless, the oral testimonies convey a strong sense of a landscape deemed (as perhaps every generation experiences) to be in a state of transition, if not decline.

II

It is widely known that mid-sixteenth century writers castigated the growth of sheep farming. In the often-cited words of Thomas Becon: 'Those beastes which were created of God for the nouryshment of man doe nowe devoure man.'[61] But sheep were not the only cause of controversy amongst the residents of Breckland and north-west Norfolk. Since the medieval period the right to stock rabbit warrens was exclusive to manorial lords, and had long inspired resentment within local society. As symbols of status and oppression, warreners' lodges were targeted during the 1549 rebellion. At Snettisham as late as 1601 elderly residents remembered the warrener's lodge being pulled down during the 'commotion time'.[62] Mark Bailey's research on Breckland has shown that warren revenues fell during the fifteenth century as rabbit numbers proliferated and wild colonies became established outside manorial jurisdictions. However, by the late sixteenth century, warrens were once again growing in significance as emblems of social status as well as a lucrative business. The villagers of Snettisham reported in 1601 that the warren had remained unused and decayed for some 50 years following the rebellion, until of late the current owner of the manor had repaired the lodge and 'reedified' its roof again. Not only were the

59 DL 4/34/46.

60 E 134/1JasI/Trin7.

61 McRae, *God Speed the Plough*, p. 43.

62 DL 4/43/12; see also Mark Bailey 'The rabbit and the medieval East Anglian economy' *Agricultural History Rev.* 36 (1988), 1–20, at p. 18.

functions of the lodge reinstated but the boundaries of the warren were enlarged. It had formerly contained 5 acres 'invironed by a dike', but local residents now complained that the warren extended as far as 'Holgate way' and incorporated a number of closes or brecks belonging to the tenants.[63] The destruction of crops caused by the rising number of rabbits, and the rights claimed by warreners to enter enclosures to trap them, gave rise to tensions over the extension of manorial jurisdiction over specific parcels of land. Again, the physical enclosure of land did not necessarily represent private space.

The process of disentangling the complex web of boundaries and customary use rights constitutes an important phase in the landscape history of light soil villages. Litigation focused on the conflicting rights of the manorial warreners to trap rabbits on whatever parcel of land they were to be found and the entitlement of the landholder to exercise autonomy over the same piece of ground. In Snettisham, while the warreners claimed the right to enter newly ploughed brecks in order to trap and kill conies, the farmers saw things rather differently. John Wraske deposed in 1601 that 'such a multitude of conies … do stray onto the arable lands of … [the] inhabitants of Snettisham … and thereby destroy the corn there growing'.[64] The farmers of the brecks led a sustained campaign of intimidation and violence against the warreners to restrict their assumed entitlement to trap and kill conies on their enclosures, and in so doing to push back the jurisdictional boundaries of the warren and protect their crops.[65] In this case and others, contest focused not only on the incompatibility of rabbit farming and corn production but also on the control of land and possession of resources growing upon it.

It was not just outlying portions of arable that were affected. Warreners were accused of maintaining new stores, constructing burrows and overbreeding rabbits, which encroached upon and destroyed the ancient common fields.[66] During a dispute over Brandon warren, 80-year-old Nicholas Tilborough related the words of four old men who, 50 years previously, had told him the boundaries of the warren were defined by a route-way across the open fields and heaths, beyond which no coney should be allowed to burrow and breed. Giving evidence in 1612, he described the arable fields, sown by the tenants and 'the poore' of Brandon, as being overrun with conies.[67] Brandon was so badly affected by the denudation of its arable lands that rabbits were directly linked to the increased poverty of the inhabitants. Deponents reported that the

63 DL 4/43/12.

64 Ibid.

65 Ibid.

66 E 134/34&35Eliz/Mich7; DL 4/22/21.

67 E 134/10Jas1/East27.

tenants and commoners relied upon corn, mainly oats, for the maintenance and commodity of their cattle over the winter months. William Tilbrooke described Brandon as standing 'chiefly upon tillage' but the conies in only a 'short time' had threatened 'the utter decay of tillage and the impovershinge of the most part of the town'.[68]

Late eighteenth-century advocates of improvement took issue with the belief among Breckland landowners that large portions of their estates were unsuited to cultivation. This was certainly the case in central Breckland, where extensive tracts of dry, sandy heath yielded little vegetation and, in spite of the improvers' optimism, was never ploughed.[69] However, the sixteenth- and seventeenth-century tenant farmer made a clear distinction between land designated as warren and arable. In this period local inhabitants perceived the proliferation of rabbits to be gradually eroding what they considered to be workable arable land. In 1578 John Lyster deposed that the rabbits of Methwold Warren 'doo borough and brede' on the arable lands adjoining to the warren, which he had himself ploughed, tilled and sown with corn. He accused the warreners of feeding the rabbits on the borders and not in the middle of the warren as they should. According to a 60-year-old husbandman, Edward Russell, over the 'two winters past' this had resulted in the destruction of 300 acres of corn.[70] Two years later, in neighbouring Feltwell, Adam Parseley (65 years old) remembered his father telling him that certain lands were once cultivated as open field, but due to the great increase in the number of rabbits over the last 40 or 50 years the 'feilds be greatlie distroyed'.[71] The common fields contracted therefore, not with the use of physical enclosures but as a result of viability of cultivation being undermined.

The oral testimonies of witnesses relate a powerful sense of a rapidly changing economic and physical environment. Their memories of a former communal and productive landscape were contrasted with the ravages of more recent times. Recollections of the supposed altruism of former warreners epitomized the belief in the existence of a customary moral economy. The centenarian William Edwards told the court that when he was warrener of Brandon he 'had a speciall care in savinge of other mens corne'. He 'set a man to skare in the coneys from doinge anye harme' and hired one furlong adjacent to the warren, which he did 'cheifly to save his neygboures corne' and 'throughe God's goodnes especially and some care of his owne in lookinge to the coneys and beatinge them owte of his corne, he had comonly good corne borderinge uppon the sayd warren'. He went on to relate the demise of goodwill between warreners and farmers, which

68 E 134/10Jas1/East27.

69 Williamson, *Transformation*, p. 79.

70 DL 4/20/7.

71 DL 4/22/21.

had in former times been sealed by a gift of conies 'for neighborhoods sake and for good will' which he did in respect that 'he knewe veryе well that the coneys … hurte … their cornes'.[72]

By calling upon the memory of elderly inhabitants and kin, deponents presented to the courts a deeply contextualized history of the land. During litigation concerning the extent of Castle Rising warren, Robert Rydde, a shepherd aged 47, confirmed the shrinkage of arable land within his own lifetime. Referring to his father and a number of aged neighbours all now deceased, he remembered them telling him that corn used to grow on sundry parts of the grounds where the warren is now 'pretended' to be.[73] For local inhabitants such dramatic developments became integrated within a shared narrative of place. Evidently people discussed such changes while seeking also to include and indeed explain what they perceived to be the traces of a former customary landscape around them. Just as manorial lords and their farmers employed the physical evidence of the past in order to prove the extension of outfield and brecks, tenant cultivators also used the traces of ridge and furrow in order to challenge the encroachment of manorial jurisdictions. Recalling the words spoken by his elderly neighbours, Rydde told the court that the greatest part of the grounds belonging to the manor of Castle Rising 'hath bene heretofore in ancient time used in tilth as doth appear by the rigges and furrows'. Elsewhere, Nicholas Tilborough remembered in 1612 the 'ancient shiftfields' of Brandon, once in tillage but now consumed by the warren: 'it doth appeare by ridge and furrowe that itt hath bene shiftfield, though now used as warren'.[74] At a time of widespread dearth and inflated corn prices such evocative descriptions of a declining ancient arable field system caused by the avaricious few provide a local context for wider debates concerning the moral deficiencies of engrossment, depopulation and dismantlement of the common field system.[75]

III

From the late sixteenth century, manorial lords sought to expand their jurisdictional rights to the commons and heaths. The work of surveyors, appointed by landowners to ascertain the true nature and extent of their acquisitions, highlighted the ambiguity of boundaries especially across open terrain. Part of the difficulty facing manorial lords was that the heaths were demarcated by

[72] E 178/2166.

[73] E 134&35Eliz/Mich7.

[74] E 134/10Jas1/East27.

[75] McRae, *God Speed the Plough*, p. 46.

various, overlapping customary jurisdictions. Something of the complexity of manorial structures and intercommoning arrangements in Norfolk villages is illustrated in the dispute over Holkham Common in 1592. The common was claimed as part of Wighton manor held by the Duchy of Lancaster across which, so it was claimed, the manor of Peterson (belonging to a former priory in Burnham Thorpe) also had right of a foldcourse.[76] The owners of the manor of Boroughhall in Wighton also claimed liberty of foldcourse in the 'South field wherein Holkham common lies'. In addition, every householder in Holkham had common of pasture for 'great cattell' on the common.[77] By recourse to the law courts manorial lords sought tighter control and rationalization of the range of customary use rights to the commons and heaths. In some places stints were imposed in order to manage the commons. During one such case brought by the tenants and inhabitants of Shernborne, the lessee of the manor was accused of restricting the grazing of cattle and horses to between Michaelmas and the Feast of All Saints (29 September to 1 November), and neat cattle from the Feast of St Andrew the Apostle until the Nativity (30 November to 25 December): this, they maintained, was against their ancient customary rights.[78]

Among late eighteenth-century commentators there was a tendency to associate and blame the impoverishment of the commons and heaths on the activities of poor commoners. But in the sixteenth and seventeenth centuries pressure on the heaths and commons came less from competition for resources within local communities as from the aggressive actions of manorial lords and their demesne farmers, and in particular from their desire to maximize their incomes from the grazing such areas offered sheep and rabbits, and through the extension of arable. Their practices were condemned by tenants and commoners. In 1601 Westwick Heath near Thetford, for example, was described as being 'so commonly fed with sheep and conies and so barren ... it not be worth much'.[79] According to the tenants and commoners of nearby Hargham, the shepherd of the foldcourse had been forbidden to graze the manorial flock on the common during the summer. Yet at the turn of the seventeenth century, his persistence had resulted in the damage of the common, by reason of the 'neate and of the rotte'.[80]

The courts heard how the enlargement of sheep flocks had resulted in an acute shortage of grazing, especially over the winter months. It is interesting to note that one of the main criticisms of folding in the eighteenth century was

---

76 DL4/155/9.

77 DL4/30/28, deposition of Thomas Skott, shepherd.

78 DL 4/18/6.

79 E134/1JasI/Trin7.

80 E134/42&43Eliz/Mich28.

that penned sheep required more food than those left to roam over the fields: 'in short, folding is to gain one shilling in manure, by the loss of two in flesh'.[81] By the late eighteenth century sheep were valued for their mutton and new breeds kept for fattening replaced the old varieties kept for their wool and manure. Nevertheless, the problem of finding adequate feed for sheep, as browse cleared for their feeding in folds and as heathland grazing, gave rise to local tensions. In Roughton in 1570 the inhabitants told the court how the manor overstocked the common known as Roughton Heath with 600 sheep, which resulted in the starvation and death of a number of them.[82] Elsewhere, in Snettisham in 1622, deponents described how in the winter the sheep could be seen on the barren heaths 'beating for their meat'. The attempts of the previous lessee of Snettisham manor to provide sustenance for 2,000 sheep (belonging to the four foldcourses of Snettisham manor) were described in detail by former shepherd John Wraske. He remembered how during the winter 'in the tyme of extraordinarye great snowes' the sheep were brought to the several closes belonging to the manor 'and would in that tyme suffer them when they had eaten their meate to stragle away uppon the said upper grounds and shorte whinnes by the cley pittes' on the common.[83]

Contention arose in places where informal grazing arrangements had arisen in the past, for instance, as a result of particularly severe weather. By recourse to past precedent, the court heard in 1619 how the farmer of Grimston manor maintained the right to drive his foldcourse down the west side of Grimston common in times of 'extraordinary great snowe', where they were foddered with hay until the ground was bare again. Wary of the potential encroachment of the foldcourse at other times of the year, the tenants and commoners strongly refuted his claims and attempted to impound the sheep, maintaining they had no right to enter the common 'neyther in black nor in white weather'.[84] Similarly in Snettisham in 1622 the owner of the foldcourse took the liberty of grazing the sheep on the commons in the winter: 'in the tyme of hard frostes and snowe so covered wth ysses as sheepe cannot feed there'. John Wraske the elder, a 75-year old husbandman, contested their right to do so, noting that in the past they had not done so every year but only in 'hard' weather when there was little or no feed for them within the jurisdiction of the foldcourse.[85] As a result, and to the great detriment of the tenants, the common on the 'upp grounds and shorte whinnes' was 'surcharged'. The poor state of the commons and lack of grazing

81 Young, *General View*, p. 475.

82 DL 4/12/6.

83 DL 4/71/29.

84 E 134/16JasI/Mich17.

85 DL 4/71/29.

had reached desperate levels by the eighteenth century. In 1769 Robert Bird of Hilborough, labourer and 'neatherd', described the commons upon which he kept the common herd of cattle as being 'so bare of grass by the flock of sheep' that he 'frequently drove the herd 10 miles in a day to look about for feed' but there was 'scarce sufficient to keep them alive'.[86]

The burgeoning rabbit population had a particularly serious effect on the grazing potential of heaths and commons. Rabbits stripped the turf, exposing the sand beneath to wind erosion – culminating, in the most extreme cases, in the formation of the mobile sand dunes for which the Breckland district was famous by the eighteenth century. In 1668 the sands of Lakenheath warren engulfed the village of Santon Downham and filled up the River Little Ouse.[87] In 1578 the residents of Congham described the heaths as being 'almost wholly burrowed with conies'. During the same case, the barrenness of the heaths is further attested by reports that rabbits, in 'tyme of harde wether', were fed on the borders of Methwold warren and adjacent to the open fields.[88]

In a number of cases it was reported that the long-term overgrazing by rabbits was responsible for the demise of the foldcourse. During the Methwold warren dispute Thomas Burgesse told the court in 1612 that he had heard his father and other ancient men say that due to the proliferation of rabbits, the number of sheep kept in the Cranwich flock had declined by 300.[89] The decline of sheep farming in Cranwich was corroborated by the oral testimonies recorded some 45 years later. In 1658 Thomas Russell, husbandman of 67, remembered how 50 years previously two flocks of 1,700 sheep each were kept on the heaths, but now the land could only support 800 sheep: the reason being the damage caused by rabbits.[90] Similarly in Congham in 1599, the sheep flock belonging to Sir Henry Spelman in right of his manor of Rustens was reduced 'by reason of the great increasinge of coneys, ther have been so small feede lefte for the feede of the sheepe as they could not tarry ther'.[91] Despite the reduction in grazing, there was an acute awareness among foldcourse owners that their rights might diminish unless they maintained unbroken usage of their customary rights. Landowners like Spelman continued to keep sheep on the heath 'but only for the preservinge of the right and interest in the same'.[92]

86 NRO, HIL 3/16/31; see also Young, *General View*.

87 T. Wright, 'A curious and exact relation of a sand-floud [*sic*] ...' (1668) pr. in Kate Sussams, *The Breckland Archaeological Survey* (Bury St Edmunds, 1996), pp. 180–82.

88 DL 4/20/7.

89 DL 4/59/23; similar reports were made in 1578, DL 4/20/7.

90 DL 4/104/1658.

91 E 134/41Eliz/East5.

92 E 134/41Eliz/East5.

The more systematic and extensive cultivation of outfield and brecks served to heighten local anxieties over the contraction of common grazing. But clearing the heaths for cultivation generated other concerns. As mentioned earlier, shelter was an issue in open landscapes. In 1622 Jeffrey Cremer, owner of East Field foldcourse in Snettisham, was accused of digging up and destroying a 16-acre covert of 'very high' furze which was, in the opinion of John Wraske, 'much better for the harburrence of the sheepe in hard wether' than 'shorte whinnes' on the common.[93] Similarly in Kilverstone in 1594 the heaths were cleared of furze, which had hitherto been preserved for the 'layer and succar' of the sheep.[94] In addition, the underwood growing upon the heaths was a vital source of fuel for local residents. Thomas Constable of Kilverstone told the court how he used to 'take cutt down digge and carrye awaye soe mannye furres, brakes and wood growinge in and upon the heath and lowe grounds as they had occasion to burne or expende in or aboute ther howses'.[95] In the late sixteenth century, the court leet of Thetford noted that 'the poor of the town are ordinarily very much distressed for the want of fuel in the time of the winter by reason of the immoderate course of some who, seeking their own benefit, leave nothing for the rest'.[96] It was not merely commoners seeking their own benefit who were to blame for the denudation of resources.

Visual evidence of destruction caused by the economic improvements implemented by manorial lords and their farmers, particularly in clearing land for arable, heightened concern over fuel supplies. In Thetford 72-year-old Lawrence Fitt, who had known Westwick Heath for 50 years, recalled that brakes used to grow on land now under the plough. Local concerns over fuel and timber shortages were highlighted by the tenants in their petition of 1553, and by the end of the century the deposition evidence portrays a strong sense of alarm at a landscape being stripped of resources.[97] In 1593 deponents from Holkham claimed the right to gather fuel by 'back-burdens' from an area of heath known as the Ollands. They complained how, in the last five years the heaths had been systematically cleared by the farmers of the manor, the furze carried away by the cart load and the land broken up and tilled.[98] Similarly in Snettisham, landowner and improver Nicholas Le Strange was accused of cutting and digging furze up

[93] DL 4/71/29.

[94] E 134/35Eliz/East24.

[95] E 134/35Eliz/East24.

[96] W. G. Clarke 'Some Breckland characteristics', *Trans. Norfolk and Norwich Naturalists Society* 8 (1908), pp. 555–78.

[97] Hoyle, 'Agrarian agitation', p. 231.

[98] DL 4/35/4.

by the roots and carrying them away from 'Southcote' foldcourse in Snettisham, which he then ploughed and sowed with corn.[99]

IV

Historians interested in the eighteenth century have recently shown how the wider productive landscape of the estate needs to be considered as an extension of the designed, ornamental landscape of park and garden.[100] Overall, most studies have focused on the physical enclosure of land, with hedges and the planting of woods and plantations, as a visual and symbolic expression of land ownership. There was, however, meaning and significance in the open landscapes of sheep-corn villages in the sixteenth and seventeenth centuries, which signified the power and status of landowning elites. With tight restrictions placed upon the rights of tenants to keep sheep, by the turn of the seventeenth century sheep farming had become part of the visual apparatus of being a wealthy landowner. The running of large sheep flocks across the open fields and heaths was a spectacle of social, perhaps also aesthetic, certainly economic importance. Celebrated on early maps, the boundaries of foldcourse territories indicated the extent of the landowners' jurisdiction over their tenants' open field grounds and commons. As we have seen, numerous court cases describe the use of sheep flocks to trample (in the most literal way) over local customary jurisdictions, in what amounted to a nascent form of enclosure without physical boundaries. The visual impact of running large sheep flocks across the open fields and heaths as an expression of wealth and status goes some way to explain the attempts of gentry landowners living in sheep-corn villages in central and eastern Norfolk to assert foldcourses where no such rights had existed before.[101] While late eighteenth-century commentators bemoaned the inadequacies of the common fields for being an outmoded and unsustainable system of husbandry redolent of the feudal past,[102] much of what they criticized was in fact the outcome of the ambitions of landowning elites over the preceding two centuries.

---

99 DL 4/15/14.

100 Gregory, 'Mapping improvement'; J. Finch, 'Pallas, Flora and Ceres: Landscape Priorities and Improvement on the Castle Howard Estate, 1699–1880', in J. Finch and K. Giles (eds), *Estate Landscapes: Design, Improvement and Power in the Post-Medieval Landscape* (Woodbridge, 2007); Williamson, *Transformation*, pp. 76–9.

101 Whyte, *Inhabiting the Landscape*, pp. 102–6.

102 Finch, 'Pallas, Flora and Ceres', p. 28; T. Williamson, 'Estate Management and Landscape Design', in C. Ridgeway and R. Williams (eds), *Sir John Vanbrugh and Landscape Architecture in Baroque England, 1690–1730* (Stroud, 2000), pp. 12–30.

Parallels can be drawn between the mapping of foldcourse territories and the representation, even glorification, of rabbit warrens. Contemporary map evidence is particularly indicative of the stark polarization of economic interests between the landowning elite and tenant farmer and commoner. A map of Methwold warren drawn up *c*.1580 shows the warren extending into several surrounding townships, its boundaries clearly defined by a number of landmark features, including medieval stone crosses and named earthwork mounds – many of which were probably prehistoric barrows.[103] The use of ancient relics to define the boundaries of warrens and foldcourses portrays an image of antiquity and stability and, as such, of longevity of landownership. But when considered alongside the contemporary deposition evidence, the fluidity of warren boundaries becomes strikingly apparent. Local inhabitants described the destruction of their 'ancient' arable lands, and subsequent movement of boundaries, not in terms of obvious physical barriers but rather by the line of ridge and furrow left behind as the commonable fields contracted.

The depositions heard before the equity courts convey a strong sense of the alarm felt among local inhabitants at the diminishing quarry of local resources. Minds were cast back to a time when tenants and commoners believed their ancestors enjoyed an equitable system designed for the common good. A moral distinction was made between old manorial lords – the purveyors of custom and tradition – and a new generation of landowners whose activities were deemed to jeopardize the economic and social foundations of local communities.[104] Landowners were accused of conducting campaigns of intimidation and violence against their tenants and commoners. Such reports were heard from Snettisham in 1592, for example, where the servants of the manor allegedly attacked one John Walker, 'being a very poore olde man', as a result of which his face was 'very pore scratcht and disfigured' and he received 'a black iey'.[105] In Wighton in 1576, James Taverner was accused of slaughtering the livestock belonging to the tenants and threatening them that 'if any of them shall depose or speake any thinge againste his inheritance, I will never leave him or he shall never be quiet as long as he is worth a groate'. The tenants complained that they had 'not known such troubles and suits' in the village before the arrival of Taverner and were apparently 'so terrified that any of them dare not present any matter befor the Quene'.[106] Landowners and their lessees were further accused of undermining the authority

[103] Sussams, *Breckland Archaeological Survey*; N. Whyte, 'The afterlife of barrows', *Landscape Hist.* 25 (2003), pp. 5–16.

[104] 'Community' is a problematic term: see the essays in Shepard and Withington (eds), *Communities In Early Modern England*.

[105] DL 4/34/46.

[106] DL 4/18/19.

of the manorial courts by bribery and coercion. According to Richard Greene there had usually been 12 tenants or copyholders of Snettisham, 'being men of knowledge and experience', empanelled on the jury to serve on the court of the Duchy manor 'for the true findinge and p[re]senting of such defaults as they were charged w[i]th', yet the current owner enlisted a smaller jury than prescribed by custom.[107] He was also charged with removing the manor court rolls from the parish chest 'contrary to the said ancient order and custome' of the town. The acquisition of manorial documents was reported elsewhere. In Marsham, for instance, a former bailiff of the manor admitted to the Exchequer court that he was instructed by the lord to burn documents that might prove beneficial to the tenants by counting against his claim to hold foldcourse rights.[108]

Of course, such accusations should not be taken at face value. The hyperbole of the court encouraged exaggeration and embellishment on all sides of disputes. However, the efforts on the part of landowners and wealthy farmers to bring about the rationalization of customary practices and overlapping use rights, thereby consolidating manorial jurisdictions, are real enough. The physical dilapidation and abandonment of tenements in some villages heightened the sense of change occurring within the lifetime of deponents. A 67-year-old husbandman, John Hallyday of Thompson, told the court in 1596 how he once had the occupation of two dwelling houses in Stirston, 'whereof the one is falne downe and thother is pulled downe'. According to John Becke, labourer who was born in Stirston, there were now no dwelling houses left in the parish. Edmond Glasocke, a husbandman aged 50 who had since moved to Tottington, spoke of the decay of the house in which he had once lived and remembered taking 'for his fuell fyrres groweinge uppon the said common and so did other inhabitants of the said towne'.[109] Accounts such as these shed important light upon the experience of village depopulation and perception of the decline of commonality.

A sense of collective impoverishment was used to describe not only the deterioration of economic resources, but also the social and cultural fabric of local life. During the long-running dispute from Snettisham (a coastal village), the withdrawal of manorial patronage from the village had much deeper repercussions for local society. In 1592 Richard Greene told the court that the churchwardens of the town had received fish or money from the owners of every ship that 'dried their fishe upon a c[er]teine place in Snetish[a]m ... called the comen stone'. Traditionally the funds had been employed for the maintenance and reparation of the parish church, until the current lord of the manor took the

107 DL 4/34/46.

108 E 178/4251.

109 E 134/38&39Eliz/Mich9; see also E 134/21&22Eliz/Mich31.

fish money for 'his owne private use ... to the great decay of the said church (the p[ar]ishion[er]s of the towne being very poore people)'.[110]

As in this instance, local inhabitants presented their grievances in terms of the breakdown of manorial patronage and reciprocity. While being attuned to the biases of such evidence, by acknowledging that people interpreted the past, embellishing and manipulating their narratives in order to express their concerns and anxieties in the present, the depositions provide invaluable evidence of the experience of landscape change in the late sixteenth and seventeenth centuries. Moreover, the recurring themes of breakdown and collapse both in terms of land and resources, and the relationship between tenants and manor, which harks back to some golden age of social relations, is in itself important and should not be dismissed out of hand as mere fabrication. The notion that, in the past, social relations had been based upon custom and reciprocity was a viable response to what was a very real threat to the economic subsistence of many households. The construction of networks of genealogical and neighbourhood knowledge, through a process of selective memory, made the past memorable, easily transferable and above all provided a justified response to the inequalities and injustices of the present.

V

The decline of the smallholder and consolidation of landownership among the wealthy few is, of course, a central and well-attested process of the period. By the eighteenth century the light soils of East Anglia had become home to the great estates, a landscape dominated by sheep-walks and warrens. But in some writers' work there is a sense of inevitability about patterns of 'progress', the shift in landholding pattern and accompanied process of engrossment. Certainly by the end of the eighteenth century many considered the land to be unsuitable for anything other than large-scale sheep and rabbit farming.[111] However, the projection of eighteenth- and nineteenth-century attitudes towards the heaths and open arable fields onto the early modern period detracts from another story – one that portrays the experience of tenants and commoners and their determination to make a living out of a harsh environment.

The evidence presented here adds to research carried out over the last two decades on the concept of custom in early modern societies.[112] The strength of

---

110 DL 4/34/46.

111 Young, *General View*.

112 Thompson, *Customs in Common*; Wood, 'Place of custom' and his *Politics of Social Conflict*; J. M. Neeson, *Commoners: Common Right, Enclosure and Social Change in England,*

custom within local communities is illuminated when examined in a particular and changing environmental context. Local inhabitants held clear ideas about sustainability based upon notions of customary rights and manorial reciprocity. The tendency to venerate the past, by (mis)remembering the conduct of past lords and neighbours, fuelled local anxieties regarding the decline of resources, the viability of agricultural production and indeed the fabric of local society itself. Memories of a former customary landscape, of arable fields since overgrown with heath and commons overrun with rabbits and sheep, became integrated within local narratives of place. Dilapidated tenements, the traces of ridge and furrow on the heaths all signified the long history of contention over rights and entitlement to the land.

Just as tenants and commoners called upon the past to verify their rights, wealthy landowners employed a similar language of antiquity in their defence of foldcourse jurisdictions: a legitimate entitlement, stable and fixed in the distant ancestral past. On both sides of disputes, a language of right and entitlement was asserted, manipulated and reinvented in order to bolster claims to land and resources in the present. Wealthy landowners exploited the terms of custom and right in order to maintain and, in some cases, extend their rights to access their tenants' lands. As a result, and contrary to the indignation expressed towards the common fields by late eighteenth-century writers, the consolidation of manorial jurisdictions over the course of the sixteenth and seventeenth centuries effectively fossilized the open fields. But this is not to suggest that the open fields survived in their medieval form into the eighteenth century. The relentless attempts of manorial lords and their lessees to enforce shack rights over the open fields, while simultaneously quashing the additional grazing rights claimed by tenants and commoners, amount to an important phase in the enclosure history of villages in the region. When we consider that many tenant farmers may have wanted to enclose their land, as encouraged by popular husbandry literature, a very different light is shed on the dynamics of post-medieval landscape change and continuity in light soil villages. Moreover, the ambiguous status of much newly enclosed land goes some way to nuance recent discussion of enclosure as a progressive and unified movement. The landscape history of the region was shaped by the gradual rationalization of land use rights, which provided the foundations upon which the general enclosure movement of the late eighteenth century was built.[113]

1700–1820 (Cambridge, 1993).

113 Bailey, 'Sand into gold'.

Chapter 4
The Idea of Improvement, *c.*1520-1700

Paul Warde *

'Improvement' is a word much loved of historians describing a new ethic for agricultural advancement in early modern England.[1] The 'improver' was a determined opponent of custom and of habit. Centuries of agricultural practice could melt into air if found wanting before the court of reason, experiment and experience. Such an ethic extended to the work and person of the improver himself (or, rather more rarely, herself). No text is more emblematic than Walter Blith's *The English Improver Improved* of 1652, an extended version of his first volume published three years earlier.[2] The idea of improvement was allied to the argument that man was not simply a passive recipient of nature's bounty, or the force of providence. Both of these were indeed ineluctable aspects of God's creation. But ever since the Fall the children of Adam and Eve had been subjected to toil, and in the eyes of the improver it was a godly mission not only to harvest what was provided but actively to seek out the truth of how nature functioned, and through this to achieve mastery over it. Nature could be shaped if it could be understood, and this was the task of the true Christian – a sentiment giving rise to Sir Francis Bacon's famous injunction, 'nature is only to be commanded in obeying her'.[3]

There is much truth in this account. Yet in truth 'improvement' was not a word much used by writers on agronomy in the sixteenth and seventeenth

* The author thanks Richard Hoyle, Elizabeth Griffiths and Koji Yamamoto for observations on earlier drafts of this text.

1 For a recent discussion focused on its use in relation to welfare, see the Ford lectures of Paul Slack. P. Slack, *From Reformation to Improvement: Public welfare in Early Modern England* (Oxford, 1999); also A. McRae, 'Husbandry Manuals and the Language Of Agrarian Improvement', in M. Leslie and T. Raylor (eds), *Culture and Cultivation in Early Modern England: Writing and the Land* (Leicester, 1992), pp. 35-62.

2 W. Blith, *The English improver improved or the survey of husbandry surveyed discovering the improueableness of all lands* (London, 1652).

3 An expression that originally appeared in Latin in the *Novum organum* of 1620. For the wider context of beliefs and debates about the functioning of nature and its relationship with the Fall, see C. Glacken, *Traces on the Rhodian Shore: Nature and Culture in Western Thought from Ancient Times to the End of the Eighteenth Century* (Berkeley, 1967).

centuries, at least in what they committed to print. We must be cautious not to elevate a convenient historiographical motif to the commonest currency and guiding light of the day. Nevertheless, the history of this idea *does* bring real insight into the changing disposition of writers on agriculture and, just as importantly, the wider context in which they worked. 'Improvement' was not solely an agricultural term; indeed, the great majority cases in which it was used in print were not related to farming. To be more precise, we are not really dealing with the history of one idea, as we shall see, but tracing the fortunes of a word that passed through a changing world of ideas and became infused with new meaning. This study is very largely based upon published texts; the use of terms in correspondence and conversation is of course another matter, albeit not one we would expect to have taken a very radically different course.

The discussion is divided into four sections, corresponding to phases in the history of 'improvement'. In the sixteenth century the word was employed with quite a narrow technical sense of enhancing rental value, and its use was infrequent. Its appearance becomes more common from the beginning of the seventeenth century, when it began to be used as a metaphor for betterment in a wide variety of walks of life – soon with its content as metaphor becoming forgotten as it came into general usage. The third section deals with the period 1640-60. This was the revolutionary moment for 'improvement', when it emerged as a leading concept among those describing and promoting novel agricultural practices, and it emerges for the first time in the discussion of parliamentary legislation (although this would doubtless have occurred earlier had the Caroline regime called any parliaments during the 1630s). This proliferation was not limited to any one group but was particularly prominent among the republican circles associated with Samuel Hartlib (who, it must be said, succeeded in drawing most of those publishing works on agronomy into his network).

By the Restoration we can see 'improvement' entering into an established status which it maintained throughout the eighteenth century, to be applied not only to Britain but throughout its burgeoning empire. 'Improvement' had become the express mission of government, and the stated intention of laws. The whole surface of the land could be now assigned to two categories: 'improved' and 'unimproved'. But such an ordering applied not just to land but to society as a whole: improved land was a particular aspect of the enterprise of improving England, which was equally a maritime task (as stated in Andrew Yarranton's *England's Improvement by Land and Sea* of 1677-81) and one that embraced 'the improvement too of arts and sciences, and the conveniences of life', in the words of John Locke's *First Treatise*.[4]

I

In the sixteenth century 'improvement' was not a widely used term and had a number of synonyms. Indeed, as late as 1607 John Cowell's early legal dictionary, *The Interpreter*, directed the reader to *approuement*, perhaps largely on etymological grounds.[5] The use of the term was limited in legal parlance to the actual enhancing of rents, or attempts to achieve this:

> *Approue (appruare)* commeth of the French *(approuer, i. approbare, comprobare, calculum albo adiicere)* it signifieth in the common lawe to augment, or (as it were) to examine to the vttermost. For example: to approue land, is to make the best benefite thereof by increasing the rent, &c. So is the substantiue *(approuement)* vsed in *Cromptons iurisd. fol.* 153. for the profits them selues. So is it likewise in the statute of *Merton cap. 4. anno 2. H.* 3 land newly approued, *Old. nat. br. fol.* 79. So the Sheriffes called themselues the kings approuers, *anno 1. Ed. 3. cap.* 8. which is as much in mine opinion as the gatherers or exactors of the kings profits. And *anno 9. H. 6. cap.* 10.

It was precisely this sense that the word conveyed in one of the earliest treatises on economy published in England, Fitzherbert's *Boke of surveyinge and improumentes* (1523). This volume contained much advice on what would, much later, be termed improvements: the use of water meadows, manuring and liming (the latter two called 'mendyinge' the land). But the term was only used twice within the text itself, and in its restricted sense. The more frequent justification for writing was that good practice increased 'profit', and this was indeed a concept far more widely used in early modern agricultural treatises. At the same time Fitzherbert, a knighted member of a prominent gentry and

---

[4] A. Yarranton, *England's improvement by land and sea* (London, 1677-81); J. Locke, *Two treatises of government* (London, 1764), ch. IV, 'Of Adam's title to sovereignty by donation, Gen. I. 28'. In this case Locke was actually briefly discussing the stimulus monarchy can give to population growth in the context of deriving theories of sovereignty from biblical exegesis.

[5] J. Cowell, *The interpreter: or Booke containing the signification of words wherein is set foorth the true meaning of all, or the most part of such words and termes, as are mentioned in the lawe writers, or statutes of this victorious and renowned kingdome, requiring any exposition or interpretation* (London, 1607).

legal family, penned the *Boke of Husbandry* – a more extensive advice manual in the tradition of classical writers such as Virgil, Cato and Xenophon (indeed in the 1530s Fitzherbert's printer published the first English translation of Xenophon).[6] The *Boke of Husbandry* would enjoy at least seventeen imprints in the sixteenth century. It supplied Fitzherbert's readers (who were intended to be not just gentry, but 'poore fermers and tenantes' too[7]) with a long list of agricultural practice arranged largely in calendrical fashion, and much of it was probably entirely familiar to most tilling the land.

Fitzherbert did pay particular attention to timing, and hence to the skill and virtuosity of husbandman – and the best *variety*, not just *species* of crop to sow. Both these themes were very prominent in nearly all subsequent agronomic writing, although they have been curiously absent from much subsequent agricultural history. Another theme that is more familiar is enclosure. Already in the 1520s Fitzherbert noted that enclosed land could bring a higher rent, although he discouraged rack renting as a disincentive to good practice.[8] He argued for the negative impact of unenclosed open pasture because of the indiscriminate mixing of animals and overstocking of the pasture by rich commoners, although stinting could provide some resolution. Again, this theme and argument would be much repeated.[9]

Later sixteenth-century authors and chroniclers described improvements in the strictly financial sense of a higher rent. A letter from the tumultuous year of 1549 argued that such improvements (i.e. higher rents) were justified in the face of inflation but only actually increased profit if accompanied by lower real expenditure: 'improueme[n]t alone maketh no man ryche, but improuement and sparynge'.[10] The author was anonymous, but the arguments chimed well with those of Thomas Smith who wrote his *Discourse on the Commonwealth* while exiled from court that summer, although it was only published a generation later. Smith addressed the tumult over enclosure and, contrary to contemporary popular and political consensus, argued that grain markets should

[6] G. E. Fussell, *The old English farming books from Fitzherbert to Tull, 1523-1730* (London, 1947); R. Drayton, *Nature's Government: Science, Imperial Britain and the 'Improvement' of the World* (London, 2000), p. 51; M. Ambrosoli, *The Wild and the Sown: Botany and Agriculture in Western Europe, 1350-1850* (Cambridge, 1997), pp. 229-31.

[7] J. Fitzherbert, *Boke of surveyinge and improumentes* (London, 1523), fo. iv.

[8] Fitzherbert, *Boke of surveying*, fo. viiiv.

[9] Fitzherbert, *Boke of surveying*, fo. iii; Fitzherbert, *The boke of husbandry* (London, 1533), fo. 53.

[10] The letter was published in T. Knell, *An answer at large, to a most hereticall, trayterous, and papisticall byll in English verse which was cast abrode in the streetes of Northamton, and brought before the judges at the last assizes there* (London, 1570).

be unregulated, even at the cost of short-term price rises, because higher prices and hence profits created the incentive for more people to move into tillage. Thus this enduring debate about whether the national balance between pasture and tillage was desirable was not cast in terms of *yields* but simply how much land was allocated to each; and the way to provide more grain crops was to make growing them more profitable.[11] Social peace would be achieved by a shift in relative prices of agricultural products, but the manner by which those products were produced was not, yet, a matter for serious discussion.

Not that agronomy was entirely moribund in this age. On the continent we see the emergence of *Hausväterliteratur*, tomes also written in imitation of classical works and intended as manuals for the owners of great estates. Most prominent among these was the work of German jurist, estate owner and privy councillor Conrad von Heresbach, whose Latin work swiftly reached English libraries and was translated into English by Barnaby Googe in 1577, seven years after its initial publication. While heavily dependent on authors such as Theophastrus and Pliny, Googe's translation promised that it would also integrate 'the experience and husbandry of our owne husbandes of England, as farre as eyther myne own observations, or the experience of sundry my freendes would suffer me'.[12] Of course, most of Heresbach's originality was in fact based on his knowledge of his native Rhineland. Recovered knowledge was in effect new knowledge, not always of much relevance to the climes of England; but the stated aim of Heresbach's work, and its French equivalent, *La maison rustique* of Claude Estienne – originally published in Latin in 1554 and in the familiar French translation in 1564 – was to convey how to manage a grand estate, not to effect agricultural transformation. The rather more homespun exhortations on husbandry and household management of England's Thomas Tusser, a court musician turned East Anglian farmer, extolled good sense and honest Christian thrift to produce a profitable return.[13] One searches in vain in any of these works

[11] The *Discourse* was published much later by John Hales, and thus until recently was attributed to him, although he in fact disagreed with Smith on the points discussed above. J. Hales, *A compendious or briefe examination of certayne ordinary complaints, of diuers of our country men in these our dayes which although they are in some part vniust [and] friuolous, yet are they all by way of dialogues throughly debated [and] discussed* (London, 1581).

[12] C. Heresbach, *Foure bookes of husbandry*, trans. B. Googe (London, 1577), p. iii; C. Estienne, *Maison rustique, or The countrey farme*, trans. R. Surflet and G. Markham (London, 1616). On the reception of these and the works of Xenophon, Cato, Varro and Palladius, see J. Thirsk, 'Making a Fresh Start: Sixteenth-Century Agriculture and the Classical Inspiration', in Leslie and Raylor (eds), *Culture and Cultivation*, pp. 15-34.

[13] The work was first printed in 1557 and expanded and reprinted many times. T. T. Tusser, *Fiue hundred pointes of good husbandrie* (London, 1580). *Oxford Dictionary of National Biography* (*ODNB*), 'Tusser, Thomas (*c.*1524–80)'.

for an intimation that agricultural revolution, or even a modest growth in farm output, might be achieved. Rather, these works were paeans and guides to the good life as known to the virtuous, ancient and modern.

II

'Improvement' appeared increasingly widely in print after the turn of the sixteenth century. In the Jacobean era the meaning of enhancing rental value became broadened and subsumed into a more general idea of betterment. This was particularly the case with Puritan sermons, where the metaphor presumably appealed to a Calvinist sensibility. It was widely used, for example, by the prolific preacher, poet and courtier Joseph Hall: 'It is from God that these helps can nourish his graces in vs; like as euery flame of our materiall fyre, hath a concourse of prouidence; but we may not expect new infusions: rather know, that God expects of vs an improuement of those habituall graces we haue receiued.'[14] Knowledge of Scripture could improve; but as in Hall's usage, the Christian life could be a course of self-improvement. By the middle decades of the century, as we shall see, the notion of self-improvement would be closely linked to the improvement of the land and commonwealth.

The Edwardian regime had passed a law which came to be called the 'Statute of Improvement', although the word was not used in the text of the statute itself.[15] This facilitated the enclosure of common waste, and essentially reiterated measures in the medieval statutes of Westminster and Merton. It was in this spirit of increasing revenue from land through enclosure (and subsequent changes in land use) that 'improvement' became a favoured notion in official circles between the advent of Robert Sackville, later Earl of Dorset, as Lord Treasurer in 1598 and the Civil War. The policies pursued were not intended as innovations in the practical aspects of land management, but as 'Projects and Improvement of the King's Revenue', as a commission appointed in the summer of 1612 was tasked.[16] The Jacobean and Caroline Crowns made frequent and strenuous efforts, with rather mixed success, to increase revenues from their land either through raising rents or sales. In either case, the sense of 'improvement'

---

14 J. Hall, *Contemplations vpon the principal passages of the holy story* (London, 1614).

15 *Statutes of the Realm* (London, 11 vols, 1810-28), IV (i), pp. 102. 4 Edward VI, c.3. For a further discussion of this statute, see Chapter 6 by Shannon, this volume.

16 Its report can be found in British Library (BL), Add. MS 10038, and an earlier draft in BL Lansdowne 165, fo. 207. J. Thirsk, 'The Crown as Projector on its own Estates, from Elizabeth I to Charles I', in R. W. Hoyle (ed.), *The Estates of the English Crown, 1558-1640* (Cambridge, 1992), pp. 300-301.

was the traditional one, whether a direct rise in annual rentals or offering the potential for higher rents and fines to purchasers who thus allowed the Crown to realize the capital value through sale. Richard Hoyle and Joan Thirsk have discussed the chequered and controversial history of these efforts to bolster the royal finances, culminating in grievances against these Caroline policies finding their place in the Grand Remonstrance of 1641.[17]

Of course, the effort to enhance land values did, in practice, mean changes in use. The draining of marshes and fens, disafforestation and the better management of coppices were all part and parcel of the possibilities; drainage projects especially had already been on the agenda in Elizabeth's reign. 'Improvement' thus became a term more loosely applied to all efforts to transform the value of 'marginal' land – land that was at least marginal in terms of the Crown's ability to extract a satisfactory income stream from it. Reformers were confronted with the problem of 'improving' marginal territory most starkly in the newly subjugated wilds of Ireland, where planters pondered what might be done with their untilled grants in the midst of a hostile country. Improving land would go in tandem with the civilizing of the mere Irish, just as enclosure of the common wastes would raise the lot of poor men who 'now dwell in the woods and deserts as abandoned and forlorn men, deprived of the means to know God or their duties to magistrates'.[18] Ireland became the model for legitimizing property rights in New England, which was made explicit by the Massachusetts court, with an added godly justification: 'what landes any of the Indians, within this jurisdiction, have by possession or improvement, by subdueing of the same, they have just right thereunto, accordinge to that Gen: 1:28, chap 9: 1, Psa: 115, 116'.[19] Whilst this text offered the possibility of natives holding property, it did so based on a judgement of what constituted 'improvement' determined by the court.

The attempts to improve the revenue of Crown woods and forests seem to have been connected to a series of published texts that dealt with contemporary fears of wood scarcity. On a localized level such concerns had become increasingly vocal since the 1550s or even earlier, often in relation to the rapidly expanding demands of industrial users, and resulted in a number of parliamentary bills.

---

17 R. W. Hoyle, '"Shearing the Hog": The Reform of the Estates, *c.*1598-1640' and Hoyle, 'Disafforestation and Drainage: The Crown As Entrepreneur', both in Hoyle (ed.), *Estates of the English Crown*, pp. 204-20, 353-88; Thirsk, 'Crown as Projector', p. 351.

18 John Manwood, author of the leading text on forest law in the 1590s, cited in Hoyle, 'Disafforestation', p. 361; on Ireland, T. Blenerhasset, *A Direction for the Plantation in Ulster* (London, 1610).

19 Cited in W. Cronon, *Changes in the Land: Indians, Colonists and the Ecology of New England* (New York, 1983), p. 63.

Thus surveys of Crown woods that were initiated in December 1607, although focused on sales rather than yields, took place against the context of discussions of 'scarcitie', a discourse which already had a century-long European pedigree.[20] It was one of the Crown's surveyors, Rock Church, who produced the 1612 volume *An olde thrift newly reuiued*, a short manual for better woodland management and a remedy for scarcity based on his experience.[21]

Church's contemporary was Arthur Standish, about whom we know next to nothing. He may have been involved in some way in the Crown surveys, given that in 1611 he wrote that he had been traversing the country investigating the themes on which he would publish for the previous four years. In a series of texts (or more correctly, one gradually expanded text), Standish provided a schema for enhancing the national wood yields such that 'the whole kingdome hereby may be preserved from the ruine that is greatly feared'. His work differed from Church's in that it provided rather less detail on arboriculture, but a rather grander scheme for increasing output that would benefit the entire economy, freeing up land and resources for alternative uses, and through which the careful setting of pollards and hedgerows could eliminate the need for coppice-woods altogether. Standish claimed some royal encouragement and won a laudatory preface from poet and engraver Henry Peacham; but his plans, like so many projects of the time, soon lapsed into obscurity. What however marks out Church and Standish is their intent: they did not speak of 'improvement' but 'profit', but the core of their argument was directed towards the increase of *output* through better practice. Increased revenue was thus incidental to countering the scarcity of an essential resource. Standish was one of the first to differentiate himself from a slow drip of handbooks for very specific crafts, such as bee-keeping, tree-grafting or seed-setting, by projecting a grander project of national renewal.[22]

Crown policy in the early Jacobean years also provides the context for the highly influential *Surveyor's Dialogue*, first published by the surveyor, devotional writer and cartographer John Norden as an illustration and defence of his art.[23]

---

20 In fact commissions to investigate the revenues of coppice woods pre-dated this wider effort. Some of the reports are copied in BL, Add. MS 38444. P. Warde, 'Fear of wood shortage and the reality of the woodland in Europe, *c*.1450-1850', *History Workshop J.* 62 (2006), pp. 28-57.

21 R. Church, *An olde thrift newly revived* (London, 1612).

22 Standish is not mentioned, however, in any of the returns from surveyors and commissioners contained in BL Add. MS 38444. A. Standish, *The commons complaint* (London, 1611), pp. 8-9; Standish, *New directions of experience* (London, 1614); J. Thirsk, 'Agricultural Innovations and Their Diffusion', in J. Thirsk (ed.), *Agrarian History of England and Wales*, V (2 vols, Cambridge, 1985), vol. 2, p. 536.

23 *ODNB*, 'John Norden, (*c*.1547–1625)'.

Norden set out the goal of the landowner and the utility of the surveyor to be in the augmentation of revenue:

> Wherein are to bee considered the Quantities, and Qualities of Land, with the present Rents, and estimate values, by a reasonable improvement: which duly found, to have a due regard to proportion yeerely distributions and expendings, with the annuall Incomes, such sort, as always the present yeere may rather adde unto the next.[24]

The view of improvement was traditional, relating to rent – a sense in which Norden used it extensively in his own surveying reports.[25] Like Fitzherbert, he was keen however to deliver practical recommendations to farmers on matters such as the keeping of meadows and upland pastures, maintaining woodlands and cultivating heaths or boggy ground, while still not describing these directly as 'improvements'. An interest in correctly surveying woods and coastal lands betrays the contemporary preoccupation of the Crown in reclaiming lost revenues. In combining attention to detail and reportage of regional practice with an explication of the surveyor's mission to enrich his landlord, he set the agenda for any self-respecting estate manager.[26]

The most prolific and widely read agricultural writer of these decades was Gervase Markham. He provided an expanded translation of Claude Estienne's *La maison rustique* and a plethora of literary works, as well as writing on veterinary and agricultural themes after retiring briefly to a rural life in the wake of the fall of his patron, the Earl of Essex.[27] Just as in his contemporaries' writing on woods, Markham did not use the term 'improvement' in his long publishing career (a career so prolific that at one point a publisher bound him to cease writing!). Yet despite the fact that much of his work was derivative and repetitive (lifting extensively from Googe's translation of Conrad von Heresbach),[28] he also presented something new: first and foremost, a confidence in the transforming power of knowledge and a sense of destiny for his time. 'The knowledge of our forefathers, compared with the times now present, is but meere ignorance', he proclaimed. His task was to 'nobly and victoriously boast the conquest of the Earth, having conquered Nature by altering Nature, and yet made Nature better than she was before', a line published the same year as Bacon's more famous

---

24 J. Norden, *The surveyor's dialogue* (London, 1607), fo. iiiv.

25 For example, BL Add. MS 38444, fos. 5-6.

26 Norden, *Surveyor's dialogue, passim*.

27 Strangely his biographer in the *ODNB* says next to nothing about Markham's extensive contributions to agronomy. *ODNB*, 'Gervase Markham (1568?–1637)'.

28 Fussell, *Old English farming books*, p. 13.

aphorism. He took sentiments largely implicit in writers such as Norden and built his work around them.[29]

Markham's originality lay as much as anything in the structure of his text. Rather than take the reader through a calendrical list of agricultural tasks, as had Thomas Tusser, or proceeding through the spatial organization of the great estate, as did *Hausväterliteratur*, Markham began with the soil (although Norden too stressed the importance of 'the different nature of grounds').[30] This introduced a novel logic into agronomic writing: traditional practices and yields could be bettered by skilful and informed manipulation of the qualities of the soil, and with the explicit intent to convert the 'sterile' soils of the kingdom to tillage. This encapsulated much of what by the eighteenth century would be termed 'improvement'; and thus later agronomy became, to some degree, a struggle between competing theories of the soil – most notably perhaps in the furore over Jethro Tull's works. Markham believed that he had:

> set downe the best, safest and easiest wayes how to bring the most vilde and barrenest grounds in this kingdome, whether they be clayes or sands, mixt or unmixt, or of what nature soever, to as great fertility and fruitfulnesse in the bearing and bringing forth of corne, as the best and most richest soyle under the suune can doe, and that (all things considered) with as little cost, and much lesse labour.[31]

In doing so he set the literary scene for the discourses of experimental and 'improving' agriculture. Although he explicitly addressed 'the plaine russet honest husbandman'[32] he nevertheless was not aiming at a work that simply raised revenue in the circumstances at hand, but that presented an idealized best agricultural practice: 'I write not according to that which poore men are able (for it were infinite to looke into estates) but according as every good husband ought.' Profit, of course, remained the 'whole aime of our lives in this world', but the discussion of agriculture was becoming both forward-looking and less immediately dependent on the imperative of raising rent.[33]

As Markham wrote, so 'improvement' became a more common term, even if it did not find its way into his writings. In his *History of Henry VII* (1622)

---

29 G. Markham, *Markhams farwell to husbandry* (London, 1620), pp. 3, 9.

30 Norden, *Surveyor's dialogue*, fo. iv.

31 Markham, *Markhams Farwell*, p. 66; although in his later work he reverted to the approach copied from Heresbach and Estienne. G. Markham, *The English husbandman* (London, 1635).

32 Ibid., fo. 3.

33 Ibid., pp. 4, 69.

Francis Bacon wrote of the 'improuement of the *Patrimonie* of the Kingdome' through enclosure, which certainly could simply mean the enhancement of the Crown's own revenue; but that spoke more broadly to a sense of bettering the polity.[34] In another work, published posthumously, Bacon identified the 'helpe of the ground' and named water meadows as 'an excellent improuement, both for *corne*, and *grasse*'.[35] This is possibly the very first use in print that related agricultural improvement solely to enhancing yield without reference to rent, although Bacon's intent is of course to provide advice on how to raise revenue. A trend towards innovation and local pride is visible in the numerous chorographical works that appeared in the early Stuart age, and here too we see 'diversities of improvement' described that 'have much beautified and enriched their soil'. The core of the concept was shifting towards the practices by which the land was enriched rather than the actual revenue received. By this time the standard of the term was sufficiently divorced from legal practice that, in describing 'approvement', Robert Powell had to explain what it was in his 1636 book inveighing against depopulating enclosure of arable.[36]

III

Francis Bacon's work was one of the inspirations for a clutch of writers who established 'improvement' as not just the goal of every right-thinking gentleman but also a national mission in the years after 1640.[37] At the centre of a web of correspondents and writers, often facilitating publication, lay Samuel Hartlib. Hartlib was born of an English mother and a German-speaking merchant father in Elbing, the staple port in the eastern Baltic for the Eastland Company. By the late 1620s, himself exactly as old as the century, he had settled permanently in

34 F. Bacon, *The historie of the reigne of King Henry the Seuenth* (London, 1626), p. 73. Bacon was widely involved in efforts to enhance Crown rents and encourage projects such as the draining of Sedgemoor in Somerset. Slack, *Reformation to Improvement*, p. 69.

35 F. Bacon, *Sylua syluarum: or A naturall historie in ten centuries* (London, 1627), p. 151; although in 1615 Sir John Davies had written in a more general way, explaining increases in litigation: 'that the comodities of the earth being more improued, there is more wealth, and consequently there are more contracts'. J. Davies, *Le primer report des cases and matters en ley resolues & adiudges en les courts del Roy en Ireland* (London, 1615).

36 T. Westcote, cited in A. McCrae, *God Speed the Plough: The Representation Of Agrarian England, 1500-1660* (Cambridge, 1996), p. 249; R. Powell, *Depopulation arraigned, convicted and condemned, by the lawes of God and man a treatise necessary in these times* (London, 1636), p. 56.

37 C. Webster, *The Great Instauration: Science, Medicine and Reform, 1626-1660* (London, 1975); Thirsk, 'Agricultural Innovations'.

England. He had been an early enthusiast for trying to build a utopian Calvinist community in the Baltic, and as a schoolmaster in England he began to turn this sensibility towards the whole of society. During the 1630s he developed a wide network of correspondents across Calvinist Europe, and encouraging flows of information and elevating knowledge became key goals. He supplied the Bohemian educational reformer Comenius with Bacon's texts, and hosted him on a nine-month visit to England in 1641.[38]

This story has an important bearing on the story of improvement because it is in Hartlib's translation of Comenius, appearing as *A reformation of schooles* in 1642, that he first employed the term in print. His aim was 'that learning ought to be used, and improved as the meanes to bring us unto the universall knowledge of all things'. The basis of social advancement was: 'That all things that are, were, or shall bee throughout the world, may be numbred, and summed up, that nothing escape our knowledge', a strategy formed to 'serve to the improvement of our age'.[39] The promotion of knowledge, the exchange of ideas and the unleashing of ingenuity were the goals of the Hartlib circle, keys to a newly virtuous society where godliness enjoined the full flowering of all the talents – the 'improvement of rationality, discretion and prudency' (in the case of this citation to be achieved by the better management of libraries).[40] The valorizing of improvement was a combination of the experimental mien of Bacon, the ambitions of a group of Calvinist clergy who saw the reformation of learning as central to a godly society, and good (by now) old-fashioned projecting. Agriculture was part of this. One of Hartlib's early associates was Gabriel Plattes, author of a utopian tract on a kingdom of Macaria intended for the Long Parliament in 1641 which, among other things, proposed a College of Husbandry among a slew of educational institutions following Comenius' ideas. In 1640 Plattes had also been involved in an unspecified but marvellous 'engin or device' to allow the rapid setting of seed 'for the improving of divers sorts of land, whereby they might get a good advantage to themselves, and procure an inestimable benefit to the commonwealth', and had published a widely admired treatise on agriculture in 1639.[41]

38 *ODNB*, 'Hartlib, Samuel (*c*.1600–62)'.

39 J. A. Comenius, *A reformation of schooles*, trans. S. Hartlib (London, 1642), pp. 4, 24, 56. Comenius would probably have read the call of Bacon for learning to be 'improved and converted by the industry of man', already written in 1605. Slack, *Reformation to Improvement*, p. 80.

40 J. Dury, *The reformed librarie-keeper with a supplement to The reformed-school, as subordinate to colleges in universities* (London, 1650), p. 16.

41 G. Plattes, *A description of the famous kingdome of Macaria* (London, 1641), p. 3 [This work is often still catalogued under Hartlib's name.] Plattes, *Certaine new inventions*

There was a strong religious underpinning to this ethos. According to one strand of Calvinist thinking that had emerged after the Reformation, the land could not be fruitful after Adam and Eve had been expelled from Eden. So much seemed clear from Genesis 3:19. But their toils and travails were not simply punishments visited on the fallen, but the route by which the godly could come back to virtue. According to the Tory clergyman Timothy Nourse, writing at the end of the century:

> What can be more suitable to a serious and well dispos'd mind, than to contemplate the improvements of nature by the various methods and arts of culture: The same spot of ground, which some time since was nothing but heath and desart, and under the original curse of thorns and bryers, after a little labour and expence, seems restor'd to its primitive beauty in the state of Paradise.[42]

Labour was thus neither mere drudgery nor just improved by what we might today call 'human capital', but was the means by which the fertility hidden by God in the soil could be unlocked. In doing this the Christian soul too was elevated. Indeed, the alternative was too awful to contemplate: idleness *not* leading to barrenness and penury could not be. This was also part of the armoury of arguments for extending tillage and against depopulating enclosure, as it seemed to stretch credulity that less labour could lead to more wealth. It also underpinned the conviction of radical Gerard Winstanley, that a godly community could 'improve the waste and common land'.[43]

From 1649 Hartlib had a salaried position based at Oxford, explicitly to facilitate the exchange of information across every imaginable field of knowledge. He became the nexus and publisher of a huge array of ideas, ranging from the reportage of accomplished experimentation to wild flights of fancy. In all he was associated with some 64 works, including key ones on agriculture. The exemplary case of this improving literature could not but be Walter Blith's *The English Improver* of 1649, followed wholly virtuously by *The*

---

and profitable experiments necessary to be known of all farmers, and others, that endeavour to procure benefit to themselves, and plentie to the commonwealth (London, 1640), p. 1; Plattes, *A discovery of infinite treasure* (London, 1639).

42 T. Nourse, *Campania Fœlix* (London, 1706), p. 2.

43 For example, J. Moore, *A target for tillage briefly containing the most necessary, pretious, and profitable vse thereof both for king and state* (London, 1612), p. 14, *passim*; Plattes, *Discovery*; J. O. Appleby, *Economic Thought and Ideology in seventeenth-century England* (Princeton, 1978), pp. 69-70; McCrae, *God Speed the Plough*, p. 129 and on providence rewarding the thrifty and industrious, pp. 212-22.

English Improver Improved in 1652.[44] What better evidence could there be of the new ethos? These books have been described by Joan Thirsk as 'surpass[ing] all others of their time for their practical good sense'. Blith was a prosperous farmer, enthusiastic Parliamentarian soldier and surveyor.[45] His volumes were structured around six 'pieces of improvement', which in the first instance comprised water-meadows, drainage, enclosing and sowing pasture, manuring, planting woods and the wise employment of 'experiences'. Improvement was thus very clearly linked to practical husbandry and tried-and-tested techniques. Nevertheless he was drawing on contemporary theological norms when, in opposition to rack-renting, he argued that allowing the tenant to enjoy the fruits of investment would lead him to:

> act ingenuity with violence as upon his owne, and draw forth the Earth to yeeld her utmost fruitfulnesse; which once being brought to perfection, will easily be maintained and kept up at the height of fruitfulnesse.[46]

Blith's books were more focused on immediate practical remedies than those of Markham, but he followed his predecessor in the emphasis on the quality of the tilth and enhancing the productivity of the soil. 'Improvement' held its double meaning of yield-raising husbandry and financial gain, 'profit'. By now however profit had become the more general end; improvement was not employed specifically to refer to enhancement of rent but to an increased sense of *economic profit* as we would understand it today – the gap between revenue and costs entailed by a particular way of farming.

In this Blith engaged with a new spirit of quantification that had gathered pace in the previous two decades, culminating in grossly optimistic schemes for national reformation through quantification of all manner of behaviour and resources. This was part of the aim ('intelligencing') of Hartlib's office in Oxford. The challenge of introducing more quantitative precision into agronomy was taken up by Sir Richard Weston, a Royalist refugee who penned observations on agriculture in the Low Countries during exile there in 1644: he claimed that he had already 'improved my land as much as anie man in this kingdom hath done both by water and fire'. He contributed to a flow of literature, seed and reports from the continent to the island that had long been established, perhaps accelerating from the 1620s, and which was not reversed until long into

44 W. Blith. *The English improver, or, A new survey of husbandry* (London, 1649); Blith, *English improver improved*.

45 *ODNB*, 'Walter Blith (bap. 1605, d. 1654)'.

46 Blith, *English improver*.

the eighteenth century.[47] Weston wrote with a refined sensibility of profit and loss, backed up by the provision of accounts. There was no such thing, in truth, as 'poor' or 'rich' land; what mattered was net revenue, and thus by the most judicious management poor land was best if it would 'yield more monie than the rich land'.[48] The financial sense of improvement was thus anchored increasingly to a detailed knowledge of inputs and outputs, an approach that would find its greatest flourishing in the farm accounts of the 'new husbandry' over a century later.

The reforming fervour that blossomed among a small but influential minority in the revolutionary decades bequeathed a legacy to agriculture that went beyond the boom in publication, or even the techniques described therein. Hartlib, Blith, Weston, Cressy Dymock, Gerard Boate and John Beale all provided important contributions to agronomy.[49] The productivity of the land became firmly linked to a narrative of national improvement that encompassed economic management, enhanced trade, military prowess and individual virtue. This was to be grounded in education from the earliest age, as Comenius had argued. Improvement was the product of a disposition to ingenuity fostered by information. William Petty proposed:

> That effectuall courses be taken to try the abilities of the bodies and minds of children, the strength of their memory, inclination of their affections either to vice or vertue, and to which of them in particular, and withall to alter what is bad in them, and increase and improve what is good, applying all, whether good or bad, to the least inconveniencie and most advantage.[50]

But the ground of national prosperity was also the land, and knowledge of husbandry: 'amongst all these parts of learning, which relate to a society, I can conceive none more profitable in nature, than that of husbandry ... this is the head spring of al the native commerce and trading.' So wrote the clergyman John Dury in his preface to Gerard Boate's pathbreaking natural history of Ireland (1657), which itself developed the earlier response to colonization as an opportunity for improvement and experimentation. Dury continued: 'there can

47 Sir R. Weston, *A discours of husbandrie used in Brabant and Flanders* (London, 1650). Thirsk, 'Agricultural Innovations', pp. 538-9; Ambrosoli, *Wild and the Sown, passim.*

48 Weston, *Discourse of husbandrie*, p. 1.

49 J. Beale, *Herefordshire orchards, a pattern for all England written in an epistolary address to Samuel Hartlib, Esq* (London, 1657); G. Boate, *Irelands naturall history* (London, 1657); C. Dymock, *The reform'd husband-man* (London, 1651).

50 W. Petty, *The advice of W.P. to Mr. Samuel Hartlib for the advancement of some particular parts of learning* (London, 1647), p. 5.

be no industrie used towards the improvement and husbandry thereof; so except husbandry be improved, the industrie of trading, whereof a nation is capable, can neither be advanced or profitably upheld.'[51] Agriculture was the root of a greater national project. If the ambitious plans for new institutions and state-sponsored development largely foundered after the Interregnum, the sense that every improving landlord was somehow contributing to the public good would linger.

The imperative of improvement, and the possibility of enhancing profit even from apparently low-yielding terrain, came to be mapped over the entire national territory. As Blith put it:

> All sorts of lands, of what nature or quality soever they be, under what climate soever, of what constitution of condition soever, of what face or character soever they be (unless it be such as Naturally participates of so much fatnesse, which artificially it may be raised unto) will admit of a very large improvement.[52]

William Petty, being rather less familiar with the land and more entranced by current transformational notions of chemistry asserted, how one would see 'barren grounds made fruitfull, wet dry, and dry wet, when even hogs and more indocile beasts shall be taught to labour'.[53] Much has been achieved by agricultural revolutions, but not yet draught pigs. As this mental mapping took place, so the whole land was divided into the improved and unimproved, a distinction of great significance which has persisted to the present. In turn, this sharpened arguments over enclosure. Such arguments were in themselves nothing new, but now could more easily be incorporated into narratives of general welfare. Enclosure had always been understood to be improving because it raised rents. But now enclosure was part of a project of national self-improvement.[54]

Any hindrance to enclosure was thus allocated to the world of backwardness and, given the stress on ingenuity and knowledge, ignorance too. Common fields and the admixture of pasture, arable and public ways across the same land prevented obvious possibilities of improvement because the 'carelesnesse or wickednesse of their neighbours or their own children, or servants' discouraged

---

51 Boate, *Irelands naturall history*; Webster, *Great Instauration*, p. 429.

52 Blith, *English improver improved*, p. 17. Much the same kind of claim can be found in C. Dymock and S. Hartlib, *A discoverie for division or setting out of land* (London, 1653), p. 3.

53 Petty, *Advice*, p. 23.

54 See J. Lee, *Considerations concerning common fields, and inclosures* (London, 1653), esp. p. 3.

farmers from innovation.[55] But distrust, lack of capital and inequitable distribution of benefits were all understood to discourage change and make men suspicious of enclosure. 'The remedy whereof may be in commanding them either unto a loving conjunction in the improvement, or else disabling any one to hinder another that is desirous of it.' In other words, a mixture of compensation and legal browbeating was needed to achieve the necessary.[56] The likeliest instigators of change were to be knowledgeable landlords and farmers, confident in their property rights and of sufficient capital to take risks. Thus in 1669 John Worlidge could state in his great synthesis of agronomic knowledge that enclosure was 'a most principle way of improvement, it ascertaineth every man his just and due propriety and interest, and preventeth such infinite of trespasses and injury'.[57]

IV

Many of the key figures in the 'Hartlib circle' were dead or disgraced come the Restoration, their plans largely unrealized.[58] Samuel Hartlib himself died, shunned by parliament and blighted by cataracts, in 1662. But much continued too. The problem of balancing state revenue and expenditure was hardly ever likely to disappear, and hence the emergence of ordinances and statutes for 'improvement' that began in the 1650s continued in subsequent decades. Many of these were concerned with enhancing the land revenues of the Exchequer; but the term 'improvement' came to be used more widely – as well as in the specifically agricultural sense of acts that encouraged Crown tenants 'to manure and improve the said several Lands and Tenements by plowing assarting digging inclosing fencing or building upon the same', or the 'Act for improvement of tillage and the breede of catle'.[59]

The resonance of improvement in agronomy thus has to be understood in the context of a broader discourse of national and individual mission that developed over several decades. In the case of trade, the interests of the public weal had been vigorously contested since the 1620s in discussions over exchange

---

55 Dymock, *Discoverie*, p. 8.

56 Blith, *English improver improved*, pp. 84-6, *passim*; the quotation is from the first edition, W. Blith, *The English improver* (1649), fo. 4v.

57 J. Worlidge, *Systema agriculturae: the mystery of husbandry discovered* (London, 1669), p. 10.

58 Thirsk, 'Agricultural Innovations', pp. 560-61.

59 C. H. Firth and R. S. Rait (eds), *Acts and Ordinances of the Interregnum* (London, 1911), *passim*; *Statutes of the Realm*, V, pp. 636-9, 685-6.

rates, bullion, tariffs and import substitution – commonly grouped by historians under the rubric of 'mercantilism'. One service of the revolutionary period was to more firmly anchor debates about trade to a solid base of agricultural success. Thus the publications of Andrew Yarranton and others sought to encompass the trade and tillage of the country as a seamless whole (a feat not often attempted, and one of which modern historians have also been shy), Yarranton beginning by promoting clover and moving on to geopolitical supremacy over the Dutch.[60]

By the 1690s it is hard to find anything that could not be improved, meaning that the attention to practical detail and the transfer of new knowledge would bring wealth through greater productivity. It was a language, at least, that would have warmed the heart of Francis Bacon.[61] 'England's Improvement' might come from the better cultivation of flax and hemp, for example.[62] It might also come from improving forests, artillery, trade, London's buildings, soldiers, woollens, sail-cloth, ladies' minds, youth, mathematical sciences, fruit trees, navigation, the manual arts, practical godliness, vegetables, writing, single women, financial reform or, in one single publication, 'building, husbandry, gardening, mechanicks, chimistry, painting, japaning, varnishing, guilding, inlaying, embossing, [and] carving'.[63] Indeed, a 1658 dictionary already defined

---

[60] Like Blith, Yarranton had been a Parliamentary officer. He entitled his first volumes in a strikingly similar way. A. Yarranton, *The improvement improved by a second edition, or, The great improvement of lands by clover* (London, 1663); Yarranton, *England's improvement*; *ODNB*, 'Andrew Yarranton, (1619–84)'; Appleby, *Economic Thought*.

[61] Having allegedly died of a chill brought on while trying to freeze a chicken.

[62] [Anon], *Englands improvement, and seasonable advice to all gentlemen and farmers how to prepare the ground fit for sowing hemp and flax seed* (London, 1691).

[63] R. Anderson, *To cut the rigging and proposals for the improvement of great artillery* (London, 1691); Anon, *The interest of England considered in an essay upon wooll* (London, 1694); G. Carew, *Severall considerations offered to the Parliament concerning the improvement of trade, navigation and comerce* (London, 1675); H. Chamberlen, *Several matters, relating to the improvement of the trade in this kingdom* (London, 1700); J. Child, *An essay on wool and wollen manufacture for the improvement of trade* (London, 1693); A. N., *Londons improvement* (London, 1680); Anon, *The perfection of military discipline after the newest method* (London, 1690); Anon, *Reasons for the bill for improvement of the woollen manufactures* (London, 1689); Anon, *Reasons humbly offered for passing the bill for encouragement and improvement of the manufacture of English sail-cloth* (London, 1698); T. Langford, *Plain and full instructions to raise all sorts of fruit-trees* (London, 1696); R. Holden, *The improvement of navigation* (London,1680); M. Astell, *A serious proposal to the ladies. wherein a method is offer'd for the improvement of their minds* (London, 1697); J. Ayres, *The striking copy book* (London, 1687); T. Powell, *Humane industry, or, A history of most manual arts deducing the original, progress, and improvement of them* (London, 1661); R. Allen, *A companion for prayer, or, Directions for improvement in grace and practical Godliness in time of extraordinary danger by Richard Allein* (London, 1684); R. Sharrock, *The history of the propagation and improvement of vegetables*

improvement as 'a thriving or benefiting in any kind of profession'. From 1681 John Houghton published a weekly journal, *A collection for improvement of husbandry and trade*, popularizing the concept to a wide readership.[64]

During the Restoration, publications about the land took on a more gentrified tenor than previously in the century. Some of these authors, like Sir Richard Weston before them, brought back learning from a Royalist diaspora, just as Hartlib's circle had connected to an international network of Calvinist reformers. Given the background of diarist John Evelyn it is perhaps not surprising his preoccupations were more akin to those of the *Hausväterliteratur*: the management of large estates. Evelyn is most famous for his book on arboriculture, *Sylva* of 1664, but he treasured most his writing on horticulture.[65] The much reprinted *Sylva* itself was structured much like a classic manual for maintaining an estate, going through the best ways to grow trees species-by-species, with only relatively short passages on how alleviating a putative timber famine could contribute to 'the glory of this *Nation*'.[66]

Evelyn and others carried forward the notion that the learned man was the source of agricultural improvement. Against him was arrayed the forces of backwardness, suspicion and, in the case of royal forests, the vested interests of Crown officials: 'therefore to design a solid *improvement* in such places, his *majesty* must assert his power, with a firme and high resolution to *reduce* these men to their due *obedience*'.[67] Power of nature meant power over men, at least those who were not possessed of a proper understanding. Hartlib too had suggested that men might be compelled to improve land, just as the power to improve that was used as justification for seizing the American colonies from

(London, 1672); C. Snell, *The pen-man's treasury open'd a new essay for the improvement of free and natural writing in ye English, French, and Italian hands* (London, 1694); E. Stephens, *A letter to a lady concerning the due improvement of her advantages of celibacie, portion, and maturity of age and judgment* (London, 1695); Sir H. Mackworth, *England's glory, or, The great improvement of trade in general, by a royal bank, or office of credit* (London, 1694); R. Neve, *Arts Improvement* (London, 1703).

64 Slack used the British Library catalogue to chart the growth of the word in titles, although this seems to produce an underestimate for the early seventeenth century. Still, usage certainly rose rapidly in the 1640s and 1650s and grew steadily thereafter. Slack, *Reformation to Improvement*, pp. 81, 96 n.89; Fussell, *Old English farming books*, pp. 81-3; These were later collected and published with a preface by Richard Bradley in 1727. J. Houghton, *Husbandry and Trade Improv'd* (London, 1728).

65 John Evelyn, *Sylva, or, A discourse of forest-trees, and the propagation of timber in His Majesties dominions* (London, 1664). See Fussell, *Old English farming books*, pp. 62-7.

66 This appears in fact to be the only use of 'improvement' in *Sylva*. Evelyn, *Sylva*, p. 111.

67 Ibid., pp. 111-12.

their native inhabitants.[68] Some of the programmatic enthusiasms faded, and the steady trickle of new compendia of agronomic ideas became more focused on the gentleman farmer and landlord. But the Tudor and Jacobean suspicion of innovation and rent-raising had largely been erased. Every improver could claim to be moved by the national predicament, no longer overshadowed by the accusation of covetousness that had earlier boomed from plebeian and pulpit alike. The flipside of this argument was that the colonized people who remained mired in their traditional forms of husbandry or pastoralism, or the Fenlanders and others who resisted enclosure, were disloyal, potentially subversive, backward by nature and with a lesser title to the land they used.[69]

Of course, the *actual* dissemination of agricultural novelties and practices doubtless had only a weak connection to the processes described, and historians must be careful to maintain that distinction.[70] But what was also carried forward from the 1650s was a close attention to the detail of agriculture, a respect for the necessary knowledge of local edaphic and climatic conditions, valorizing of experiment and recourse to 'experience' for legitimacy. Indeed the last had nearly always been the case in agronomic literature and would be tiresomely repeated throughout the eighteenth century, often as an alleged distinction with book-bound predecessors. Husbandmen doubtless did not much read Worlidge's *Systemae agriculturae*, the most widely recognized treatise of the age, which was largely a synthesis of all that had gone before. Nevertheless the view was well established that ideally a person directing agriculture should themselves be familiar with the soil: 'every understanding husbandman knowing what sorts best accords with his land', as Worlidge put in his discussion of varieties of peas.[71] In the age of political arithmetic the Royal Society briefly thought to undertake the function that had been suggested for Hartlib's 'Office of Address' by establishing its Georgical Committee to gather reports on the agriculture of the kingdom in 1664. While its work was not completed, it has left a valuable source for historians. The committee demonstrated a close interest in the quality of soils and compiled questionnaires that followed quite closely the concerns of Markham.[72]

---

68 Drayton, *Nature's Government*, pp. 54, 56.

69 See McCrae, *God Speed the Plough*.

70 Joan Thirsk has argued the case that husbandry manuals did have a significant influence on farming practice. Thirsk, 'Making a Fresh Start', pp. 15, 18.

71 Worlidge, *Systemae agriculturae*, p. 37.

72 'Enquiries concerning agriculture', *Philosophical Transactions* 1 (1665), pp. 91-4; R. Lennard, 'English Agriculture under Charles II: the evidence of the Royal Society's "Enquiries"', *Economic History Review* 4 (1932), pp. 23-45, repr. in W. Minchinton (ed.),

Writers did not solely think that the state of the land was a consequence of the will of the cultivator. Clearly there were environmental considerations, above all relating to water. Worlidge could: 'take this as a general observation in *Agriculture*, that most of the barren and unimproved lands in *England* are so, either because of drought, or the want of water or moisture, or that they are poisoned or glutted with too much'; and we may remember that Blith too listed drainage and water meadows high in his list of an improver's preoccupations. It is striking in the literature of the time how much authors were concerned with excess water, the removal of rushes and draining and evening out the ground. Yet this in its own right also created a ranking of land according to its potential for improvement, or the right type of improvement that could be applied.[73]

The idea of improvement had shifted from a limited concept to do with raising rents to a generalized one resting on enhancing practical expertise. But in its application to agriculture, the course of this development had also created a new linkage to chemistry that would endure and eventually become modern soil science. Again, much of the credit for the anchoring of this connection must go to the efforts of those in the revolutionary decades. The burgeoning interest in chemistry and the nature of plant nutrition went back to the works of sixteenth-century adepts and polymaths such as Paracelsus, Bernard Palissy and Hugh Plat. In placing the soil centre-stage in his writings, Markham had provided the platform on which subsequent writers would build. As there was no clear division at this time between the Earth and botanical sciences (indeed, it was believed by some that stones grew in the soil, which anyone with a garden might well believe), there was much interplay between the widespread interests in mineralogy, metallurgy and botany. Most of the chemical speculations, which used an Aristotelian framework of the four elements and humours to describe the soil – spiced with beliefs in some vital universal generational power attributed to various salts, water or an obscure *anima mundi* – were of little or no practical application to husbandry.[74] Yet they crucially encouraged the view that knowledge could be applied to transform the soil, and stimulated experiment. Some of the great controversies of the eighteenth century would in turn rest on competing theories of plant nutrition – whether Jethro Tull's limiting of the function of manure to breaking up the soil during fermentation, or Arthur Young's valorizing of manure as the central agent in sustainable farming. 'Improvement' was thus a scientific enterprise, at least as we would

Essays in Agrarian History (2 vols, Newton Abbot, 1968), vol. 1, pp. 161-86; Thirsk, 'Agricultural Innovations', pp. 563, 566-7.

73 Worlidge, *Systemae agriculturae*, p. 189.

74 Webster, *Great Instauration*, pp. 47-8, 330-31, 377-8, 385; P. Warde, 'The invention of sustainability', *Modern Intellectual History* 8/1 (2011), pp. 153–70.

comprehend the term 'science' today (the term had not yet been borrowed into general usage from the French). By default, agriculture was scientific too, and the developments in chemistry would have a powerful role in shaping agricultural writing long before the emergence of artificial fertilizers – an idea that had already occurred to John Evelyn.[75]

More generally, agriculture and trade were the twin pillars of national greatness; not merely a domestic agriculture and a foreign trade, but the products of the Earth that grew all around the globe when nurtured, shaped and exchanged by ingenious men. Improvement was local and global. At the turn of the seventeenth century Timothy Nourse described this with a popular medical metaphor, proposing a country life now far removed from the bucolic and parochial vision of Xenophon read by early Tudor scholars:

> Profits arising from a country life ... is that great vein by which the blood is distributed through all parts of the body, or rather the very blood itself, since it is diffus'd over the whole, nor can any part or member subsist without it: it is the Foundation of traffick and commerce, forasmuch as all the manufactures and commodities which we export or receive from foreign parts, are but the productions of the Earth at the first or second hand.[76]

---

[75] A. Clow and N. L. Clow, *The Chemical Revolution: A Contribution to Social Technology* (New York, 1952); J. Evelyn, *A philosophical discourse on Earth relating to the Culture and Improvement of Vegetation, and the Propagation of Plants, etc.* (London, 1676), p. 110.

[76] Nourse, *Campania Fœlix*, p. 11.

Chapter 5
The Common Fields of Urban England: Communal Agriculture and the 'Politics of Entitlement', 1500–1750

H. R. French

'Those who would study the early history of our towns ... have fields and pastures on their hands.'[1] So F. W. Maitland, writing in 1898. His *Township and Borough* remains the most systematic investigation of the history of urban open fields and commons, concentrating on the common fields of Cambridge. Maitland emphasized the significance of the subject. He conjectured that in some respects the existence of common fields, pastures and farms within the urban jurisdiction was not as anomalous as it might first appear. 'Time was when we in England had a respectably neat system of legal geography, and when we seldom spoke of parishes ... The whole country (this was the theory, if not precisely the fact) was cut up into vills or towns.' All that had happened was that 'in course of time, we allow[ed] the urban places to appropriate to their exclusive use this good old word, and then we awkwardly distinguish the towns from the townships or borrow "villages" from the French'.[2]

Hence what was anomalous was not that towns possessed and farmed common fields and pastures, but that we came to distinguish between them and the other, smaller, vills in which lands lay, by calling these 'villages' and regarding them as exclusively 'rural'. In setting Cambridge's 1,200 acres of open fields in context, Maitland also sketched the scale of the subject:

> ... if you look at the English boroughs as they stood on the eve of their reformation, as they stood when in 1833 they were visited by the royal commissioners, you will often find that their boundaries have provided wide enough room for fields and meadows and pastures. You will read that 'the local limits of the Borough of Derby contain 1,660 statute acres', that the limits of Northampton comprise 1,520 acres and include

1 F. W. Maitland, *Township and Borough* (Cambridge, 1898), p. 9.

2 Ibid., p. 8.

> 'a considerable quantity of agricultural land', that 'the Borough of Bedford includes the whole town ... which lies nearly in its centre encircled by a broad belt of land; its area being 2,164 statute acres', and, to take one last example, that 'the ancient borough' of Nottingham covered no less than 9,610 acres and 'included a considerable quantity of forest, meadow and common land without the walls of the town'.[3]

As ever, it becomes clear that the more one looks, the more one finds. The best source for parliamentary enclosures is the parliamentary report on enclosure acts published in 1914.[4] It is possible to identify approximately 160 historic towns (excluding suburban London parishes such as Hackney) that obtained enclosure acts between *c.*1720 and 1870.[5] This return omits acts for at least 20 other towns, and one or two more where commons were enclosed piecemeal before the mid-eighteenth century.[6] English Heritage have recently conducted an extensive survey of urban commons and (using a slightly more flexible definition of the term 'town') have identified 314 small, medium and large settlements with historical records of common resources, of which 79 still retain some vestiges of these lands – often as public parks or racecourses.[7] These places include Beverley, Bristol, Cambridge, Doncaster, Godalming, Harrogate, Hereford, Hertford, Huntingdon, Kendal, Lincoln, Newcastle-upon-Tyne, Oxford, Richmond, Shrewsbury, Stafford, Sudbury, Tewkesbury, Tunbridge Wells, Worcester and York.

I

Such lands and rights do not feature particularly strongly in many urban histories, except in cases where these resources have shaped the development of a town, as in Nottingham, or where they remain as prominent features in a city landscape, as in York or Newcastle-upon-Tyne. The reasons for this relative

---

3 Ibid.

4 *British Parliamentary Papers* (*BPP*), 1914, lxvii, pp. 325–412.

5 *VCH Middlesex* X, pp. 92–3.

6 These were Abingdon, Altrincham, Arundel, Bath, Berwick-upon-Tweed, Durham, Gloucester, Huntingdon, King's Lynn, Lewes, Marlborough, Morpeth, Newcastle-upon-Tyne, Norwich, Pevensey, Preston, St Clear, Warwick, Wigan and Woodstock. H. R. French, 'Urban agriculture, commons and commoners in the seventeenth and eighteenth centuries: the case of Sudbury, Suffolk', *Agricultural History Rev.* 48 (2000), p. 173, n. 10.

7 M. Bowden, G. Brown and N. Smith, *An Archaeology of Town Commons in England: 'A Very Fair Field Indeed'* (Swindon, 2009), gazetteer, pp. 83–90. I am very grateful to Mark Bowden and English Heritage for allowing me access to earlier stages of this research.

neglect lay partly in Maitland's observations about the decline in use of the all-embracing term 'vill', and partly in the development of urban and rural history since his day. To avoid messy conceptual overlaps, these histories have tended to define themselves in mutually exclusive terms. Increasingly, urban history has become the study of features, processes, institutions and social or cultural phenomena that are seen to be 'non-rural', while rural and agrarian history has tended not to encroach on the urban, except to study services or processes necessary to the rural economy (such as markets). Urban agriculture, agrarian resources and rights have, therefore, tended to be overlooked (or, at least, not investigated systematically), even in the otherwise excellent and comprehensive volumes of the *Cambridge Urban History*.

Certainly, part of this neglect is because of problems in the available sources. Although many small and medium-sized towns were manorial (the most notorious examples went on to become major cities, notably Manchester and Sheffield, ruled over by courts leet until 1835), most urban manors contained extensive – and untraceable – freehold ownership, or few surviving copyhold court rolls or manorial surveys. Similarly, although other records indicate that common lands were often administered diligently, with pasture use being regulated and listed annually, few such sources have survived. As a consequence, it has been difficult to explore urban agriculture in any systematic way, in comparison with the detailed investigations of land use and ownership undertaken in many manorial histories of rural settlements. While the commons sometimes survive, miraculously untouched in a few cases, it is often impossible to explore the long-term history of their use (from written sources, at least).[8] Yet, if an in-depth understanding of cultivation practices or stinting regimes is probably beyond us, urban records and court cases provide better indications of the kinds of rights enjoyed by urban commoners, and the contests about them – because these sources were designed to register such rights and preserve legal precedents about them.

However, what is the historical significance of such material? There are two important aspects. Firstly, the description of these rights often provides insights into the links between the agrarian and urban economies, and how they intersected both geographically within the urban jurisdiction and economically within the lives of many of its inhabitants. As will be shown below, these rights were often geographically more extensive and (perhaps) economically more intrusive than one might at first suspect. This suggests that we should not dismiss urban agriculture just because (for example) a town's common lands

---

8 For example, significant prehistoric, Roman and early medieval earthworks remain on Oxford's Port Meadow, Newcastle Town Moor and Westwood Common in Beverley respectively. See Bowden *et al.*, *Town Commons*, pp. 11–19.

only comprised a few hundred acres or 'agricultural' occupations were assigned to only a tenth of its testators. Secondly, disputes about these rights often shine a light into the internal workings and power structures of urban government. Such rights were often distributed widely among the lowest tier of freemen as one of the basic rights of enfranchisement. Concerted action in their defence tends to reveal one of two distributions of power: either how this majority organised itself collectively to defend a corporate right; or how splits in urban power structures could be highlighted by contests over these shared resources. These manoeuvres are sometimes hidden beneath legal devices or rhetorical strategies in the 'official transcript' of such sources.[9]

In these two respects, then, the study of urban commons can tell us more both about the role of towns as active participants in the dominant pre-modern 'organic' economy (to use Tony Wrigley's phrase) *and* about the internal 'politics of entitlement' (to use Steve Hindle's phrase) that was a constant accompaniment to such agrarian activity in towns, and by townsfolk.[10]

II

At this point, some definitions are required. The first must be in relation to the term 'town'. In the period 1500–1750 this definition has to include any settlement that possessed, or came to possess, *some* or *all* of the characteristic urban functions: a market, non-manorial forms of government, the borough franchise, concentrations of non-agrarian production or urban 'leisure' facilities and functions.[11] There has to be considerable flexibility in relation to population size because the definition has to include places such as early seventeenth-century Droitwich, with perhaps 200 resident families, as well as centres such as York, with 12,000 inhabitants.[12] However, it should probably exclude 'towns' such as Frodsham in Cheshire which, despite being possessed of

9 J. C. Scott, *Domination and the Arts of Resistance: Hidden Transcripts* (New Haven, 1990), pp. 17–44.

10 E. A. Wrigley, 'The transition to an advanced organic economy: half a millennium of English agriculture', *Economic History Rev.* 59 (2006), pp. 435–80; S. Hindle, *On the Parish? The Micro-Politics of Poor Relief in Rural England, c.1550–1750* (Oxford, 2004), pp. 398–405. This also features in Phil Withington's work on the practices and concepts of civic freedom, *The Politics of Commonwealth: Citizens and Freemen in Early Modern England* (Cambridge, 2005), pp. 180–90.

11 P. Clark (ed.), *Small Towns in Early Modern Europe* (Cambridge, 1995), pp. 1–21.

12 It was reported that there were 151 families resident in 1563, *VCH Worcester*, III, pp. 72–81; E. A. Wrigley, *Peoples, Cities and Wealth: The Transformation of Traditional Society* (Oxford, 1987), p. 160.

common lands, 'burgesses' and stinting procedures (although no corporation or parliamentary representation), was reported by witnesses in 1600 as having only 37 households.[13] Such settlements were towns in name only in this period.

The second definition has to apply to the term 'common rights'. Returning again to Maitland, this term refers first to 'burgensic users in common' – that is, to access and use rights held and exercised in common by all suitably qualified residents.[14] These were different from the rights of 'burgensic users in severalty', held individually by burgesses (usually in the form of leases) in relation to 'land of which the corporation was owner'.[15] From this basic distinction, it is then possible to distinguish at least three separate forms of common rights exercised in such 'towns'. The most obvious was access to arable or pasture commons located entirely within the town boundaries, administered exclusively by corporations or other 'urban' authorities (courts leet and parochial vestries) and determined directly by the possession of rights of freedom, property ownership or rate-paying solely within that jurisdiction. In addition, such qualifications could also govern access to use rights on land not owned exclusively by the corporate body – that is, to 'Lammas land' grazing rights, exercised after harvest, on plots or farms often owned or let in severalty and frequently straddling the borough boundaries. Finally, there was also the exercise of rights in *neighbouring* parishes and manors, through intercommoning on the fallows or after-crop in the open fields or across shared pastures, moors or heaths.

More broadly, we can now begin to distinguish a typology of urban commons by reference to these definitions and to the topography of different regions within England. It is possible to identify four main regional variations in urban commons in England between the sixteenth and nineteenth centuries, although these are based on distinctions that are fairly crude – and in some respects rather arbitrary. In the north-west of England we can begin with the series of small market towns identified by Elliott – some old and established, some new and expanding – which retained their common pasture and arable lands largely within their town boundaries.[16] These included Penrith, Whitehaven and Wigston in Cumberland; Kendal and Kirkby Stephen in Westmorland; Dalton, Ulverston, Clitheroe and Prescot in Lancashire; and Stockport, Wilmslow, Macclesfield and Sandbach in Cheshire. The preservation of their commons and

---

13 The National Archives (TNA), E 134/42 Eliz./East 9, deposition of Robert Jameston, Woodhouse, Cheshire, husbandman aged 76.

14 Maitland, *Township and Borough*, p. 198.

15 Ibid.

16 G. Elliott, 'Field Systems of North-West England' in A. R. H. Baker and R. A. Butlin (eds), *Studies of Field Systems in the British Isles* (Cambridge, 1973), p. 54.

open arable fields seems to have reflected their continuing integration with the agrarian economy of the region until the end of the eighteenth century.

The second region of urban commons in the north was rather different. This was the largely upland, industrializing zone stretching from the West Riding of Yorkshire, through the Derbyshire Peak and into the Staffordshire moorlands and Shropshire. It included towns such as Rotherham, Doncaster, Halifax, Sheffield, Wakefield, Dewsbury and Huddersfield in Yorkshire; Matlock, Bakewell, Glossop and Chesterfield in Derbyshire; and Leek, Newcastle-under-Lyme, Burton-on-Trent, Stone, Stafford and Walsall in Staffordshire.[17] Almost all of these towns were expanding rapidly in population and in industrial capacity in the late eighteenth century. For many, these processes amounted to the urbanization of previously small, sparsely populated, largely rural townships. Almost all of these industrializing upland towns existed within much more extensive parishes. As a consequence, their commons and wastes could be vast. In 1637 it was calculated that 21,363 acres in the parishes of Sheffield, Ecclesfield and Bradfield were 'free commons'; the parish of Doncaster was 8,660 acres at enclosure in 1765; in Wakefield 2,634 acres were enclosed between 1793 and 1805.[18] Much of this upland was some distance from the settlement whose name it took and so it was of less, and perhaps little, use to the townspeople.

As a consequence, enclosure in this region involved disaggregating shared commons, demarcating the boundaries between townships and ending extensive rights of intercommoning, as well as restricting the freedom to take game from these pastures and wastes. As noted in the definition of 'towns' cited earlier, most of these settlements *became* towns in terms of their population levels, economic specialization, market functions and institutional development – the majority in the period 1760–1820, which coincided with the period of the most intense parliamentary enclosure in the region. For them, enclosure was a symbol of their efforts to uncouple themselves from their rural origins, even if particular enclosures appear not to have been related to each other and to have been triggered (like most other enclosures) by the interests of local landowners.[19] Some of these enclosures generated considerable dispute, as they occurred alongside industrial expansion; and (to some extent) the loss of extensive moorland grazing rights and recreational space had adverse consequences for

---

17 *BPP*, 1914, lxvii.

18 G. Scurfield, 'Seventeenth-century Sheffield and its environs', *Yorkshire Archaeological J.* 58 (1986), p. 162; *BPP*, 1874, lii, p. 383 'Return of the acreage of waste lands subject to right of common and of common field lands'; J. F. Broadbent, 'Dewsbury Inclosure, 1796–1806', *Yorkshire Archaeological J.* 69 (1997), p. 209.

19 Ibid.

their labouring populations. This process was documented in most detail for late eighteenth-century Sheffield by Barbara Hammond, almost 80 years ago.[20]

The third region can be described in two ways. On the one hand, we can group together those old-established, relatively populous, corporate towns that existed within the 'classic' Midland open-field region: towns such as Coventry, Warwick, Leicester, Nottingham, Northampton, Huntingdon, Bedford and Cambridge. On the other hand, we can follow Maitland, who saw a similarity in the fact that all these towns were old 'shire-boroughs': that is (except for Coventry), they all gave their names to their shires, and all had extended histories as shire capitals.[21] Using this definition, Maitland also included Oxford, Lincoln, Colchester (shire capital of Essex until 1250), Durham, Gloucester and York. We might also include the developing regional centres of Southampton, Newcastle-upon-Tyne and Preston.[22] While all these other towns were outside the main open field region, they shared a number of characteristics. All were parliamentary boroughs; most were centres of legal administration (assize towns); most had complex and long-established forms of government; and all were quite important reservoirs of distinctively 'urban' functions (manufacturing, marketing, retail, education, service industries, leisure facilities and so on). To such necessary defining characteristics of these ancient 'burghs' we might now add the possession of open-field arable land and/or common rights of pasture.

The fourth region is something of a catchall category. In some ways it is similar, thematically, to the first region. It consisted largely of a disparate series of small boroughs and non-corporate towns, united mostly by their propensity towards population stability or decline, economic stagnation, relatively weak forms of urban government and (consequently) their tendency either to be manorial or to hold common land or use rights from neighbouring manors. Most of these were located in southern and south-west England, and many were decayed boroughs. Examples might include Chippenham, Marlborough and Malmesbury in Wiltshire, Okehampton in Devon, Bodmin in Cornwall, Arundel in Sussex, Basingstoke and Christchurch in Hampshire, Godmanchester in Cambridgeshire, Beccles and Southwold in Suffolk and Hertford in Hertfordshire.[23] None of these towns was particularly dynamic

---

20 B. Hammond, 'Two towns' enclosures', *Economic History* II (1930–33), pp. 258–66.

21 Maitland, *Township and Borough*, p. 201.

22 A. Temple Patterson, *A History of Southampton 1700–1914* (3 vols, Southampton, 1966–75), vol. 1 p. 11; A. Hewitson, *History of Preston* (Preston, 1883), pp. 326–9; E. Halcrow, 'The town moor of Newcastle-upon-Tyne', *Archaeologia Aeliana*, 4th ser., 31 (1953), pp. 149–64.

23 D. Hirst, *The Representative of the People? Voters and Voting in England under the Early Stuarts* (Cambridge, 1975), p. 198; A. R. Stedman, *Marlborough and the Upper Kennet Country* (Marlborough, 1960), pp. 98–9, 122, 270; *Reports from the Commissioners on the Municipal*

in the eighteenth and early nineteenth centuries, and many were among the boroughs that aroused the ire of the Parliamentary Commissioners in 1835, whose reports may accentuate the impression of decay. Of these, Malmesbury, enclosed in 1821, received the most damning condemnation. Here, the ruling body had:

> long since ceased to answer any municipal purposes ... this body is self-selected, irresponsible to the inhabitants of the town, and composed chiefly of labourers without education, and of the least instructed class of retail tradesmen. The present alderman, a pig-killer and chief magistrate of the town, is scarcely able to write his name ... Richard Neale and Christopher Allen, successively chief magistrates, were both of them unable to write, and had no other substance or calling than keeping a few cows ... whether it be owing to the singular distribution of certain town lands which prevails in Malmesbury, or to any other cause, the morals of the labouring class in that town appear to be below the standard of the neighbouring country.[24]

Once again, Maitland made passing reference to such characteristics, noting that only in boroughs 'of the lowest order' were pasture rights connected to particular properties, rights of common held from or shared with manorial lords or exercised by 'inhabitants' rather than burgesses, largely independent of the corporation's authority. He took such individualistic trends to be symptomatic of rural rather than urban organization – an assumption to provoke debate among both nineteenth- and twenty-first-century historians.[25]

III

The diversity of common rights available to, and exercised by, commoners in these towns meant that the contests about them varied considerably even within these loose regions. There were several important reasons for such variation. The first and most obvious of these was the area of the commons available to the town. Alan Dyer noted that Worcester differed from its peers in the Midlands

---

Corporations of England and Wales, First Rep., App. I (London, 1835), pp. 78–9 (Malmesbury); p. 447 (Bodmin); pp. 2236–7 (Godmanchester); p. 2193 (Beccles); p. 2517 (Southwold); W. G. Hoskins and H. P. R. Finberg, *Devonshire Studies* (London, 1952), pp. 284–5; *VCH Sussex*, V (i), pp. 57–8; L. Ellis Tavener, *The Common Lands of Hampshire* (London and Southampton, 1957), pp. 52–3 and 55–8; *VCH Hertford*, III, p. 498.

24 *Municipal Corporations Commissioners*, First Rep., App. I, p. 79.

25 Cf. A. Macfarlane, *The Origins of English Individualism: Family, Property and Social Transition* (Oxford, 1978).

– such as Coventry, Warwick, Leicester, Nottingham or Derby – because it had lost most of its once extensive common fields by the sixteenth century, so that the cultivated area around the city was very restricted. He notes that 'compared with these towns, Worcester emerges as much more markedly urban and industrial in character', with the agricultural sector having only a small role in the town's economy.[26] So, the size of the available commons, or the extent of grazing rights, obviously affected the economic importance of such resources to the urban economy. The bigger they were, the greater their probable significance because the larger the proportion of all freemen they were likely to accommodate (as, for example, in the extensive pastures available in Nottingham and Coventry).[27]

The second, relatively obvious element was the nature of the land and rights available. Coventry, Nottingham, Northampton, Cambridge, Tewkesbury, Hereford and Newcastle-under-Lyme retained a fairly complete system of open-field agriculture and Lammas grazing rights into the early nineteenth century.[28] Elsewhere, however, the agrarian functions of commons could change considerably as they underwent drastic encroachments or piecemeal enclosures. Open fields disappeared in Lichfield in the early eighteenth century. In the seventeenth century the town had been surrounded by at least 12 open fields, where cattle were grazed in the stubble.[29] However, the common herdsman was last listed as an officer in 1731, and Lichfield's enclosure act of 1815 dealt only with 60 acres of marshy common pasture. Coventry and York freemen enjoyed extensive Lammas grazing rights, but over fields largely cultivated in severalty by the later seventeenth century. The same process of piecemeal arable enclosure had occurred in Colchester, Tewkesbury and Burton-on-Trent by the sixteenth century and in Banbury and Tetbury by the mid-eighteenth.[30] However, as the

---

26 A. D. Dyer, *The City of Worcester in the Sixteenth Century* (Leicester, 1973), p. 133.

27 J. D. Chambers, 'Population Change in Nottingham, 1700–1800', in L. S. Pressnell (ed.), *Studies in the Industrial Revolution* (London, 1960), p. 99; J. Prest, *The Industrial Revolution in Coventry* (Oxford, 1960), p. 28.

28 R. B. Rose, 'The City of Coventry: The Common Lands', in *VCH Warwick*, VIII, p. 199; R. M. Butler, 'The common lands of the borough of Nottingham', *Proc. Thoroton Society* 54 (1950), pp. 45–62; H. M. Cam, 'Northampton Borough', in *VCH Northampton*, III, pp. 22–3; Maitland, *Township*, p. 89; A. Brian, 'The allocation of strips in Lammas Meadows by the casting of lots', *Landscape Hist.* 21 (1999), pp. 43–58; S. R. Jones, 'Tewkesbury Borough', in *VCH Gloucester*, VIII, p. 138; *Municipal Corporations Commissioners*, First Rep., App. III, p. 1953 (Newcastle-under-Lyme).

29 N. J. Tringham, 'Lichfield: economic history', in *VCH Staffordshire* XIV, p. 111.

30 C. C. Thornton, 'The common lands', in *VCH Essex*, IX, p. 255; *VCH Gloucester*, VIII, p. 138; *VCH Stafford*, IX, pp. 59–84; P. D. A. Harvey, 'Banbury: agriculture' in *VCH Oxford*, X, pp. 49–54; N. M. Herbert, 'Tetbury', in *VCH Gloucester*, XI, p. 269.

above definition of common rights emphasized, jurisdiction was not essential to the exercise of these rights. In Hertford inhabitants of the town enjoyed two types of common pasture rights: in two meadows owned by, and located within, the borough; but also in nine 'foreign' meadows beyond the borough boundary and in at least three fields held by other manorial lords (and presumably shared with their tenants).[31] In theory, such rights could be expanded by new agreements with other contiguous manors, but their potentially disruptive effects may have deterred many lords. A few such agreements can be traced, as in Tetbury in 1633, as well as disagreements, as in Chesterfield between the Earl of Shrewsbury and two leading burgesses.[32]

Thirdly, the significance of agricultural resources in the urban economy depended in part upon the proportion of the urban population who enjoyed access to them. In a reversal of the situation in most manors, these rights tend to be easier to establish for pasture commons rather than for open arable fields. In part, as Maitland was at pains to show, this was because many established towns like Cambridge had never possessed manorial courts.[33] Many of those that did, such as Preston, did not have much copyhold land, and so lack any registers of land transfers. The best evidence about land tenure often comes from smaller and more marginal towns, where town books or court cases record the apportionment of land among burgesses or corporation members according to custom, in the form of annual or (sometimes) life allotments. Most of these were decayed boroughs such as Marlborough, Malmesbury, Chippenham, Berwick-upon-Tweed and East Retford, but this custom also occurred in larger towns such as Stafford and Nottingham.[34] By contrast, there is a much greater volume of evidence about the size of stints for cattle, horses, sheep or even geese (but rarely pigs) on common lands, and who was allowed to depasture such beasts.

IV

With the variation of rights came differences in the kinds of dispute generated by them. The remainder of this chapter will focus on the three most prevalent types

31 *VCH Hertford*, III, p. 498.

32 *VCH Gloucester*, XI, p. 270; P. Riden, *History of Chesterfield*, II (i), *Tudor and Stuart Chesterfield* (Chesterfield, 1984), pp. 29–30.

33 Maitland, *Township*, p. 18.

34 *Municipal Corporation Commissioners*, First Rep., App. I, p. 85 (Marlborough); p. 78 (Malmesbury); II, p. 1248 (Chippenham); S and B. Webb, *English Local Government: The Manor and the Borough* (5 vols, London, 1906–22), vol. 2, pp. 517–19; *Municipal Corporation Commissioners*, First Rep., App. III, p. 1864; p. 2028 (Stafford); p. 1993 (Nottingham).

of dispute about urban commons and rights. The first of these were contests about attempts to enclose common lands by corporations seeking either to maximize rental income from the town's arable lands or to confine or extinguish grazing rights on their pasture commons, moors or wastes. The second variety were disputes about access rights to these lands, particularly the use or changing of pasture stints, or the introduction of differential access rights through the creation of different grades of freedom. The third kind of dispute was conflict with neighbouring landowners, particularly about Lammas grazing rights or intercommoning in manors adjoining the town, which were often exacerbated when these lands were enclosed and farmed in severalty for the rest of the year.

In the early modern period the first of these disputes seems to have been relatively rare, but not because such activity was unknown. Charles Phythian-Adams demonstrated that in early Tudor Coventry the common lands revealed the tension between the city's 10 wards – who claimed to represent the popular voice in the 'oversight and disposition' of these lands – and the corporation, whose historical roots and popular support were shallow and whose desire for income led it to attempt piecemeal enclosures.[35] He notes riots over access to the commons in 1421, 1430, 1469, 1495, 1509 and 1525. This drive for enclosure in the face of falling population and declining civic income at one end of the period was matched, as Sweet has shown, by corporate ambitions to tap into rising land values and demand for building land in the mid-eighteenth century. She notes disputes between the aldermanic elites and freemen over enclosures or letting arrangements that would curtail common rights in eighteenth-century Nottingham and Newcastle-upon-Tyne.[36] Such disputes also occurred in this period in Oxford, Rye, Bath and Colchester.[37] In general, though, enclosure necessitated such a significant change in property rights that *either* the decision had to involve some level of cooperation or consent from the majority of those exercising these rights *or* it occurred when this body of commoners had shrunk to a number so small that it no longer encompassed a significant proportion of the freemen or burgesses. Where the corporation encompassed large numbers of freemen-commoners, as in Nottingham, Coventry, Oxford or Preston, extensive

35 C. Phythian-Adams, *Desolation of a City: Coventry and the Urban Crisis of the Late Middle Ages* (Cambridge, 1979), pp. 158–9, 182–3, 254–5.

36 R. Sweet, *The English Town, 1680–1840: Government, Society and Culture* (Harlow, 1999), pp. 134–7, 144–5.

37 The corporation's efforts in 1762 to reduce its debts by enclosing Port Meadow were defeated: *VCH Oxford*, IV, pp. 280–82; *Municipal Corporation Commissioners*, First Rep., App. II, pp. 1036–7 (Rye), p. 1120 (Bath). The sale of Colchester's corporate and common lands was proposed after the suspension of its charter in 1742: *VCH Essex*, IX, p. 258.

common rights could persist into the nineteenth century. However, there could be trouble where such corporations sought to enclose.

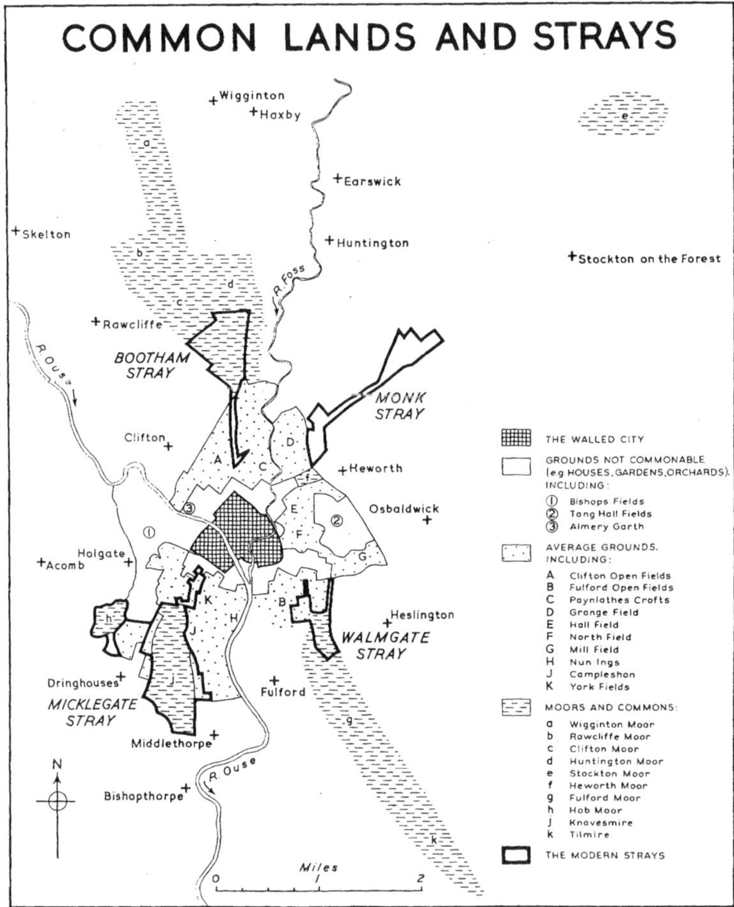

Figure 5.1 York: common lands and strays. Reproduced from *VCH Yorkshire, The City of York*, p. 502

The best documented example of this is at York, the extent of whose common grazings is shown in Figure 5.1. Palliser noted riots over issues of access rights and raising revenue through enclosures in the sixteenth century.[38] Disputes over access were perennial, and will be discussed below. Disputes over enclosure were

[38] D. M. Palliser, *Tudor York* (Oxford, 1979), pp. 45, 49, 84, 294. For the city's financial problems at this time, R. W. Hoyle, 'Urban decay and civic lobbying: the crisis in York's finances, 1525–1536', *Northern Hist.* 34 (1998), pp. 83–108.

rare because it was attempted infrequently, but more serious when they occurred. The most significant events took place in the troubled year of 1536, when the corporation decided, apparently unilaterally, to enclose the several hundred acres of Knavesmire, south of the city (the site of the modern York racecourse). The corporation stated on 3 May 1536 that this measure was 'holly for the common well of this citie'.[39] This was probably a revenue-raising effort at a time when there were repeated complaints about civic poverty, and three years after the observation in the corporation minute book that the city's common lands were often let at below their market value.[40] However, it appears that the purpose of the enclosure was not to extinguish common rights entirely or dismember the common, but rather to police access and restrict rights to freemen in order to make the identification of rights (and charging for them) easier to administer. In practice, it may have been designed primarily to disaggregate these pastures from those shared with the neighbouring parishes of Dringhouses and Middlethorpe outside the borough limits.[41] The order set the rates at 1*s.* 4*d.* per cow, 2*s.* per horse, and limited the stint to two cows or one horse and one cow per freeman. To protect and delimit the common, ditches and gates were constructed.

Predictably, this new measure provoked a riot. At 11 pm on Sunday 14 May, rioters filled in some of the ditches and pulled down the gates at Knavesmire. These events had all the characteristic hallmarks of 'popular politics', as identified by E. P. Thompson, Andy Wood and Ethan Shagan.[42] They began with popular rumour, when the cooper, John Coke, reported that one of the city's MPs, Sir George Lawson, had said in parliament that there should not be any enclosures in York.[43] This quasi-legal justification was then used by seven named tradesmen and others to stir up the riot. This next stage took place in the classic location, the alehouse, where a Thomas Slayter said that he had heard two shoemakers say that the ditches and gates of Knavesmire were going to be thrown down that night. Finally, Alexander Mason, a smith, detailed the practicalities of events when he reported that one of Richard Gibson's servants, a man called Ralph Walker, had called at his house to get a light to set fire to the gates. The last Thompsonian touch was his observation that Ralph Walker was also there – dressed in women's clothing, with his face covered. Events ended in equally

39 A. Raine *et al.* (eds), *York Civic Records* (9 vols, Yorkshire Archaeological Soc. Rec. Ser., 98, 103, 106, 108, 110, 112, 115, 119, 138, 1939–78) [hereafter *YCR*], vol. 4, p. 1.

40 *YCR*, vol. 3, p. 151.

41 *VCH Yorkshire, The City of York*, p. 499.

42 E. P. Thompson, *Customs in Common* (London, 1991), pp. 16–96; A. Wood, *Riot, Rebellion and Popular Politics in Early Modern England* (Basingstoke, 2002), pp. 5–17; E. Shagan, *Popular Politics and the English Reformation* (Cambridge, 2003), pp. 131–61.

43 For the following, *YCR*, vol. 4, pp. 1–12, *passim*.

stereotypical recrimination, with two women – Isabel Lutton and Agnes Cook – being carted round the streets after saying slanderous words, including the wish that the council chamber might be set alight.

The corporation modified their proposal and attempted only to enclose the east side of Knavesmire, in order to rent it out. This was agreed at the end of June, and the lands were let for six years at £14 per annum.[44] In August, slanderous bills were pasted in the city about gifts of wine and venison allegedly given by one George Crayle to the aldermen, possibly in relation to this deal.[45] Ten years later, it was again proposed to 'take in' part of Knavesmire.[46] In December 1546, there were riotous attempts to take down fences in a neighbouring close, and the following September (prior to the Michaelmas opening of the city's pastures) 40 commoners petitioned the common council to have their customary pasture rights restored.[47] The council asked for payment of a rent by commoners in compensation, but were met with a flat denial because this 'wold be to the impoverishing and undoing of the moste parte of the poore comminaltie for ever'.[48] The next month, 15 of the Common Chamber rejected a proposal to let Grange Fields to a servant of the Archbishop of York, and two years later the commonalty again petitioned for the restoration of their customary common rights, and that 'ther be no newe inclosers mayd or hadd aboute this citie' over the winter pasture season.[49]

As has been suggested, these events fall well within the parameters of the classic struggles over enclosure and between aldermen and burgesses over power and civic revenues. Indeed, Andy Wood has emphasized recently how disputes about urban enclosures, or the threat of enclosures, in Cambridge, Norwich, Great Yarmouth, Bristol and Blythburgh heightened tensions significantly in the tinder-box summer of 1549.[50] However, the details sometimes present a slightly less dramatic picture. This was often enclosure to restrict and delimit pasture rights, define the boundaries of the commons on which they were exercised and rent out part of these rights to neighbouring farmers or landlords, rather than to extinguish all such rights in perpetuity. These niceties may not have been obvious to those in York who stood to lose their rights, or have them limited, and whose wishes appeared to be largely ignored by an aldermanic elite

44 Ibid., p. 6.

45 Ibid., pp. 7–12.

46 Ibid., p. 137.

47 Ibid., pp. 148, 160. They also paid 600 marks to help alleviate the city's debts.

48 Ibid., p. 162.

49 Ibid., p. 164; *YCR*, vol. 5, p. 23.

50 A. Wood, *The 1549 Rebellions and the Making of Early Modern England* (Cambridge, 2007), pp. 13–14, 43–4, 49, 60, 62, 121, 124.

desperate to sort out the city's finances. This mid-century crisis seems gradually to have abated after the 1550s. Indeed, the elite may even have responded to these protests after 1561, when the citizens petitioned that the Tang Hall lands on the city's eastern border should not be leased out again, but kept as common pastures for the freemen – subject to the payment of quite large sums for horse and cow 'gates', amounting to approximately 80 per cent of the land's market value each year.[51] Thereafter, considerable enclosure occurred on the lands over which the city's freemen had rights but, as will be shown below, this did not, in most cases, affect the exercise of winter pasture rights on these lands.

Town finances were the main impulse for enclosure and the extinction of pasture rights in Grimsby at the turn of the seventeenth century. Here, inhabitants of the town and neighbouring communities complained that their previously unstinted rights to turn their horses and cattle out onto the town's East Marsh, 120–80 acres of tidal marshes stretching from the town to the Humber estuary, had been curtailed by the enclosure of 30–50 acres in 1598.[52] After this enclosure, witnesses alleged that all such commoners were 'now quite expelled',[53] the enclosure had been surrounded by sea walls and divided between the mayor and aldermen, the 'Company of Twelve', and the 'Company of Four-and-Twenty', to the exclusion of all other users.[54] This action had blocked off a road across the marsh and cut off access to other parts of these lands at high tide.[55] The implication was that the measure had been carried out to increase the corporation's revenue to help pay the fee farm rent to the Crown at a time of decline in coastal trade.[56] Other witnesses pointed out that a large part of the East Marsh remained open to the town's inhabitants, and that the West Marsh (140 acres) had always been leased out to tenants by the corporation, rather than held in common.[57] In this instance, the corporation may have decided that 'improvement' of this waste by walling would prevent previously unfettered access, and that the restriction of access to corporation members only would allow the costs to be recouped more easily, as well as reducing the internal opposition to such a 'land grab'. Similar disputes appear to have happened in Malmesbury, where an enclosure plan in the 1590s was designed supposedly to

---

51 *YCR*, vol. 6, p. 3. They were to pay 7*s*. per horse 'grass', 4*s*. 8*d*. per cow 'grass' and have only one horse or one cow 'grass' each. The city had recently valued Tang Hall at £54 6*s*. 8*d*. p.a. and charged the freemen £43 6*s*. 8*d*. for it. Ibid., p. 5.

52 TNA, E 134/43&44 Eliz/Mich. 12.

53 Ibid., deposition of Nicholas Swindale, Grimsby, shoemaker, aged 60.

54 Ibid., deposition of Gabriel Jackson, Grimsby, yeoman, aged 34.

55 Ibid., deposition of Christopher Hatcliffe, Grimsby, alderman, aged 81.

56 Ibid., deposition of Richard Broxholme, Grimsby, gent., aged 58.

57 Ibid., depositions of Bryan Bailes, Grimsby, miller, aged 60, and Gabriel Jackson.

exclude poor in-migrating weavers; and in Christchurch, where they rumbled on between the 1630s and 1650s.[58] In 1633 there was a trial at the Dorset assizes in a dispute in which the richer townsmen and the mayor of Christchurch had tried to exclude 'poor tradesmen' from the town's (very extensive) commons by an attempted enclosure; but although actions were still being fought in 1657, the commons survived into the nineteenth century.[59]

V

The evidence about *access to* and *control over* the use of commons is both illuminating and frustrating. It is illuminating because the sizes of stints, their social apportionment and disputes about access to common fields and pastures tell us a great deal about Hindle's 'politics of entitlement' in English towns. Commons often became a fundamental fault line in the polity of the corporate town, between those who were entitled, those who were excluded and the authorities (and social mechanisms) who decided between them. As has been shown, Coventry and York provide some of the best illustrations of this process in a series of protests extending from the fifteenth to the nineteenth centuries. In the early seventeenth century in Coventry, Derek Hirst observed repeated disorder in the city over the corporation's control of rents derived from parts of the commons.[60] He notes riots in 1608, 1609 and 1627 and 1628, and riots at the same time in Warwick, Colchester and Chippenham about 'the corporation's misappropriation of town lands in a period of economic hardship'. This tradition of defending the commons lasted into the 1850s in Coventry. By this time, the link between corporate freedom, the vote and rights of pasture meant that although most freemen no longer exercised their common rights popular action defended the commons through the ballot box rather than the enclosure riot. As Prest summarized it crisply, 'no Member of Parliament was going to anticipate the wishes of the freemen in this matter when he depended upon their favour for his re-election'.[61]

This evidence is frustrating, though, because it is extremely difficult to identify what proportion of freemen actually exercised these rights, particularly in the

58 R. B. Manning, *Village Revolts: Social Protest and Popular Disturbances in England, 1509–1640* (Oxford, 1988), pp. 103–6.

59 Dorset RO, DC/CC/I 7/1, Petition of burgesses of Christchurch to Lord Chief Justice of King's Bench, 26 July 1633; 8/1 Resolution to defend inhabitants' rights of common, 15 Aug. 1657; Tavener, *Common Lands of Hampshire*, pp. 55–8.

60 Hirst, *Representative of the People?*, pp. 51–2.

61 Prest, *Industrial Revolution in Coventry*, p. 29.

period before municipal corporation enquiries or enclosure acts. While we know that in Coventry in 1835 'not above a fourth' of the freemen actually exercised their rights of common – which might still have been 700–800 individuals from the approximately 3,000 freemen – it is difficult to project this proportion back to earlier periods.[62] Similarly, in York in 1700, while the corporation (led, in a happy historical accident, by Alderman Edward Thompson!) spent at least £562 10*s*. on an Exchequer case to defend common rights at Nun Ings and York Fields, few witnesses were prepared to testify that these rights were of benefit to the majority of the city's population.[63] Robert Jebb, a Quaker, was reluctant to specify the monetary value of such grazing rights, but observed that while 'both rich and poor make benefit by it ... most benefit is made by the middle sort of people'.[64] William Smith, a York 'chemist', was a little more specific. He stated that the poor derived 'little or no benefit ... for that they have no cattle to depasture thereupon', whereas cattle ownership was restricted mainly to 'the better sort of men' in the ward.[65] The same complaint was made in Elizabethan Hertford.[66] Even where there is more precise information about commoners – as in the smaller, and much more manageable, boroughs of Sudbury and Clitheroe – further problems arise in respect of entitlements. In the former, as in nineteenth-century Coventry, only about a quarter of entitled freemen turned out animals on the commons. However, this entitlement had been cut in 1654 by the stipulation that no freemen paying an entry fine of less than £5 would be allowed rights of common. Without such rights the fee was £2. Similar differentials existed in Arundel, Tewkesbury and (seventeenth-century) Oxford.[67]

There were further difficulties. In Clitheroe a supposedly transparent allocation of rights to the holders of 78 defined burgage properties was almost completely subverted in practice. Assignments of rights were so rife that although in any one year about one-third of burgage owners exercised their rights, almost none did so for the properties to which they were entitled.[68] This

62 *Municipal Corporations Commission* (1835), Rep. XXV, p. 431.

63 TNA, E 134/6GeoI/Mich. 33, deposition of John Brack, York, gent, aged 38.

64 TNA, E 134/12WmIII/East. 18, deposition of Robert Jebb, York, baker, aged 63. This was a rare contemporary use of the term 'middle sort of people', possibly in response to the interrogatory which asked 'what sort of people receive the most benefit ...?' See H. R. French, *The Middle Sort of People in Provincial England, 1600–1750* (Oxford, 2007), pp. 90–140.

65 TNA, E 134/12WmIII/East.18, deposition of William Smith, York, chemist, aged 45.

66 TNA, C 2/Eliz/C19/56, bill of complaint of Edward Casson, Middle Temple, London, gent.

67 *VCH Sussex*, V (i), p. 58; S. R. Jones, 'Tewkesbury Borough', in *VCH Gloucester*, VIII, p. 138; *VCH Oxford*, IV, p. 280.

68 H. R. French, 'Urban common rights, enclosure and the market: Clitheroe Town Moors, 1764–1802', *Agricultural History Rev*. 51 (2003), pp. 56–8.

hidden market in commons' rights was the economic mechanism by which rights that were tied inflexibly to properties could be detached and linked to people, without the properties themselves changing hands. By this means outsiders and residents of the 50 or so other properties in the town without rights could be accommodated. Subletting of rights occurred (or was forbidden) in Coventry, Leicester, Nottingham, Tewkesbury, Arundel and Calne. It was permitted in Doncaster and Chippenham.[69] It may also have been the reason for prohibitions against butchers exercising pasture rights, as in York.[70] So, it can be very difficult in practice to discover the actual identity of the urban commoners, and where we can, the 'politics of entitlement' begins to look very tangled indeed. In the larger corporate county towns rights were being sublet even in the sixteenth century, with an increasing number of poorer burgesses foregoing or transferring their stints to wealthier freemen; and the process was embodied (in a few instances) by the introduction of differential rights of freedom that distinguished between commoners and non-commoners.[71]

However, if by the seventeenth century only between a quarter to one-third of all those entitled actually used these common rights, comprising only a fraction of the total population of a town (particularly in some of the larger ones), then is historical neglect of the phenomenon understandable? Clearly, except in the most bucolic of rotten boroughs, agricultural occupations rarely predominated among townsmen. The presence and functions of commons indicate that to search for agriculture as a primary occupation in towns is surely to look for it in the wrong place. Even if it sustained only a few urban households directly, agrarian activity remained perhaps the most important *by-employment* for urban dwellers. For example, in Sudbury between 1710 and 1728, different social groups appeared to use the commons in different ways.[72] The bulk of the freemen who exercised their rights of common were prosperous 'middling' tradesmen, 38 per cent of them in clothing trades in this cloth-producing town. Of these, two-thirds favoured horses and mares over cattle. For them, the commons were

---

69 'The City of Coventry: Common Lands', *VCH Warwick*, VIII, p. 199; Butler, 'Common Lands ... of Nottingham', p. 55; W. H. Stevenson *et al.* (eds), *Records of the Borough of Leicester* (7 vols, 1899–1974), IV, p. 542; *VCH Gloucester*, VIII, p. 138; *VCH Sussex*, V (i), p. 58; *VCH Wiltshire*, XVII, p. 80.

70 *YCR*, vol. 2, p. 181.

71 Restrictions were imposed in Northampton in 1556, *VCH Northamptonshire*, III, p. 22; in Calne, Wiltshire, in 1657, R. C. Richardson and T. B. James (eds), *The Urban Experience: A Sourcebook. English, Scottish and Welsh Towns, 1450–1700* (Manchester, 1983), pp. 54–5; burgesses enjoyed more rights than freemen in seventeenth-century Tewkesbury and eighteenth-century Malmesbury, *VCH Gloucestershire*, VIII, p. 138, *VCH Wiltshire*, XII, p. 207.

72 French, 'Sudbury', pp. 40–68.

an overnight town-centre subscription animal pound. While clothiers exhibited the same bias towards traction rather than dairy animals, weavers, other cloth workers and woodworkers were almost twice as likely to depasture cattle rather than horses. One other group displayed this tendency – widows of freemen. For those closest to the economic margins, and most subject to the fluctuations in the cloth trade, cow keeping on the commons provided a second income and a form of social security. The extent of cow keeping among freemen's widows also shows how this second *household* income might form a primary income stream for these urban women, during and after marriage.[73] Freemen without animals also exhibited a distinctive social profile. They received payments out of the money levied from commons' users and, of the 108 whose occupation can be identified between 1710 and 1728, 64 per cent were cloth workers and weavers, while only 8 per cent were cloth manufacturers. By contrast, in Clitheroe, where the ratio of burgesses to available common acreage was more favourable, labourers and tailors made a little more use of these pastures in the third quarter of the eighteenth century. Even so, these rights remained predominantly in the lands of 'middling' trades of this small, Pennine market town – notably food producers (butchers, in particular), leather workers, carpenters and blacksmiths.[74] In York, at the end of the seventeenth century, it was noted that commons offered opportunities not only for cow-keeping and the use of horses for traction, but also allowed ordinary people to make money out of horse hire when their animals were not otherwise being used.[75]

In these ways, the agrarian influence on the urban economy might be greater than the bare numbers of town-dwelling 'husbandmen' or 'yeoman' suggests. This influence extended out into by-employments in urban families, particularly for women, as sources of alternative seasonal employment, or as opportunities for 'windfall' profits from the subletting of rights, or as stores of (often overexploited) resources – wood, furze, peat, gravel, marl, stone, fish and game – even if their contribution to household budgets is difficult to determine.[76]

---

73 See J. Humphreys, 'Enclosure, common rights and women: the proletarianization of families in the late eighteenth and early nineteenth centuries', *J. Economic History* 50 (1990), pp. 17–42.

74 French, 'Clitheroe Town Moors', pp. 54–8.

75 TNA, E 134/12Wm3/East18, deposition of Benedict Horseley, York, painter-stainer, aged 72.

76 Bowden *et al.*, *Town Commons*, pp. 33–44.

VI

As has been suggested, town commons generally existed as part of a wider agrarian landscape within the borough boundaries. Consequently, commons could exist within complex jurisdictional arrangements, and highly variegated patterns of tenancy and ownership. This proximity had two effects.

The first was illustrated by the situation in Sudbury in the late seventeenth century. Here, the commons were dwarfed by several hundred acres of privately owned land (at least 338 acres in St Gregory's parish) divided up into a patchwork of smallholdings of arable and meadow.[77] These were held either as functioning farms of more than 20 acres or smallholdings of less than 10 acres. While most appear to have been owned or leased by the same more prosperous tradesmen who dominated the commons, they provided seasonal by-employment for weavers, labourers and women, who reported experience as hired harvesters and tithe-gatherers rather than as cultivators.[78] This suggests that even where poorer inhabitants were denied access to commons, either by being priced out of animal husbandry or off the commons, such additional agrarian resources might assist them in efforts to patch together a household 'economy of makeshifts'. However, there is little consistent evidence of such expedients in the surviving urban sources.

By contrast, the second effect is much better documented. This was the conflict that emerged between towns and adjacent parishes over intercommoning arrangements. These disputes seem to have been the most frequent cause of equity disputes about urban common rights. As noted before, surviving commons, or areas set aside wholly for communal use (such as the York strays or the freemen's commons of Lincoln, Nottingham, Cambridge, Oxford, Leicester or Beverley), never encompassed the full extent of common rights available in such towns. In particular, pasture rights extended beyond the town's boundaries, into intercommoning or 'Lammas' grazing rights in neighbouring settlements, and even further afield.

York possessed one of the most complex systems of pasture grazing rights. As indicated, in addition to the permanent pastures reserved exclusively for freemen (Bootham, Monk and Knavesmire strays), the citizens possessed winter pasture rights over lands owned by the Archbishop and Dean and Chapter of York located immediately adjacent to the walled city (Bishop's Fields, Tang Hall and Almery Garth), and rights of intercommoning with townships bordering

---

77 Suffolk RO (Bury St Edmunds), FL 634/1/1, St Gregory's Parish Book, 1661–1829, account of lands in the parish, 1696.

78 TNA, E 134/11&12Anne/Hil2, depositions of Robert Haxall, Long Melford, husbandman, Jonathan Lee, Sudbury, sayweaver, and Samuel Jones, Sudbury, sayweaver.

the city – in Clifton Fields, Fulford, Dringhouses, Rawcliffe, Huntington, Wigginton, Heworth and further out on Stockton Moor. As Palliser has noted, these distinctions created 'two concentric but very irregular areas', in the latter of which York's citizens were required to project their rights into fields and management regimes from which they were excluded at other times of the year. As a result, conflicts over pasture rights were endemic. The published volumes of *York Civic Records* refer to at least 16 separate disputes about these rights between 1480 and 1590, particularly in pastures immediately adjacent to the city.[79] These recurred frequently at Nun Ings, Camplesham Pasture and York Fields next to Knavesmire, south of the city, and in the highly contentious Tang Hall estate, which was set in the middle of Hall and North Fields immediately north-east of the city, in which freemen had less contentious rights.

While the personalities and places varied, the issue remained the same. The exercise of common pasture rights over lands owned (if not always farmed) in severalty produced friction between commoners, owners and tenants, particularly when owners and tenants were denied access to their lands in 'average' time (when common pasture rights were exercised, generally between Michaelmas and Lady Day). Landlords and tenants often responded by trying to exclude freemen's cattle and horses from their lands. Some of the most contentious disputes occurred in the 1480s and 1490s, between the corporation and Sir James Danby and with the Vicars Choral over lands next to Tang Hall fields, in Hall Field and the adjacent Vicars' Lees.[80] In both cases the owners and tenants tried to exclude burgesses' cattle from these fields. This provoked 'riots', in which commoners made gaps in fences or hedges and filled in ditches, actions which mirrored the customary opening of closes by the pasture-masters of each ward on uncontested land.[81] The corporation sought to apply pressure on Sir James by forbidding any freeman from taking a lease of his property in the city while he claimed common cause with the Vicars Choral. In October 1494 it was reported that he had suggested to the sergeant representing the city: 'tell thy Maisters that the vicars part shalbe my part ... and therfor like as they purvey for the Vicars let theym provyd for me ... and if any tenaunt of myn be so hardy to giff any mony again the vicars he shuld never hold any land of me ne dwell on my ground'.[82] A month later, several persons were indicted for a riot at the

[79] These were in 1480, 1483, 1487, 1488, 1490, 1494, 1501, 1517, 1524, 1534, 1536, 1539, 1546, 1549, 1567 and 1574. *YCR*, vol. 1, pp. 32–3, 81, 177; *YCR*, vol. 2, pp. 38, 83, 93–4, 109–10, 163; *YCR*, vol. 3, pp. 36, 92, 169; *YCR*, vol. 4, pp. 1–3, 38, 148; *YCR*, vol. 5, p. 23; *YCR*, vol. 6, pp. 125; *YCR*, vol. 7, pp. 91–2.

[80] *VCH Yorkshire, The City of York*, pp. 498–506.

[81] *YCR*, vol. 2, pp. 93–4.

[82] Ibid., pp. 109–10.

nearby Vicars' Lees after two priests and their servant were seen chasing away the citizens' sheep from these lands.[83] Robert Clerk, carpenter, confessed that he had pulled down a gate and posts, while John Chalke, weaver, admitted being with about 50 people the following evening who had demolished a 'tile house' and hedges on these lands, having been ordered there by his master. Ultimately, the city asserted its rights over Sir James's land, but conceded defeat to the Vicars Choral in 1495.[84] This loss was not forgotten, however. Twenty-two years later, Nicholas Roger complained bitterly about the choice of George Kyrke as Mayor. Kyrke had last held the office in 1495, and Roger called him 'a false traitor and myddyng knight' because 'he lost the Vycar Lees'.[85]

Over 200 years later, the same issues of access rights generated further disputes. In 1700 the corporation sued Robert Squire, tenant to the Archbishop of York of lands in Camplesham Pasture, Nun Ings and York Fields, immediately adjacent to Knavesmire stray. By this time, in York as elsewhere, issues about the exercise of pasture rights had been complicated by enclosure. Increasingly around York, the lands on which *common* pasture rights were exercised in winter were farmed in severalty during the spring and summer growing season. This was accompanied by the physical enclosure of such lands by hedges, fences, rails and ditches. When the pastures were 'opened' for grazing, the pasture-masters of Micklegate ward had to go to each enclosure and ensure gates were opened, or gaps made in hedges or fences so that cattle could roam freely across these fields.[86] In fact, across the farming year access rights were sometimes even more complicated. According to citizens defending the corporation's rights, the owners and tenants had exclusive rights to these fields from Lady Day until Michaelmas. They also had exclusive pasture rights after the harvest, or the first hay crop, until Michaelmas. After this time they had no individual entitlements on these lands, but might turn out animals *either* through their rights as citizens or as part of the small communal stints allowed the tenants of the manors of Fulford and Dringhouses on these lands.[87] There was dispute between the parties in the 1700 case about whether or not access was denied to these parcels when winter wheat had been sown on them, which seems to have occurred on other lands in the area on which there was no formal right of common, but which were opened to commoning when they were set down to pasture.[88] Deponents reported that the largest such enclosure had occurred in 1656, when Col. William White had

83 Ibid., pp. 110–11.

84 Ibid., p. 123.

85 *YCR*, vol. 3, p. 36.

86 TNA, E 134/12Wm3/East18, deposition of William Lister, York, grocer, aged 43.

87 Ibid., deposition of Robert Jebb.

88 Ibid.

fenced off Camplesham Pasture out of York Fields. He had attempted to bar access by commoners, but eventually relented, and gaps were made at Michaelmas each year in the hedges on this land for freemen's cattle.[89] Only when Robert Squire had attempted to exclude cattle from his newly planted field of rape seed did these rights again come into dispute. The language used was reminiscent of 200 years earlier. When the pasture-masters visited these enclosures to open them for cattle, one said that if he was refused access he would 'beat a drum and raise the rabble to pull the said inclosure down', while Alderman Thompson told the City's Common council that he was prepared to spend all he had down 'to his coat or shirt' in order to defend these rights.[90] More prosaically, but still in line with manoeuvres in the later fifteenth century, Robert Squire had offered to settle the matter through a cheap action of trespass at common law, or to accept a mediation (possibly involving only the symbolic annual assertion of freemen's common rights to these lands).[91] Squire eventually lost his case, but we are left to wonder whether these statements from the York civic elite represented (in the Thompsonian lexicon) not so much an assertion of 'moral economy' as the elite playing to (and with) the 'theatre of the crowd', a crowd who increasingly by 1700 were bystanders on the common rather than commoners themselves.

Similar disputes occurred at the edges of other well-defined common pastures. In Beverley in 1609 the corporation claimed rights to fields adjoining to the south of the largest of the town's three common pastures, Westwood.[92] Like much of Westwood in the sixteenth century, these fields had been unenclosed woodland until the latter part of Mary's reign, when they were enclosed and felled. The freemen continued to claim pasture rights here from Michaelmas to Lady Day, although few witnesses were able to testify to continuous usage since the enclosure.[93] By contrast, inhabitants of neighbouring manors continued to exercise pasture rights in Swinemoor into the early nineteenth century.[94] The same issues occurred at Droitwich in the 1620s and 1630s. Here, again, enclosure had led to the disruption of rights of common grazing held by the burgesses and associated with the unusual 'burgage' rights in this salt-producing

---

89 Ibid., deposition of Jane Syers, Bishopthorpe, Yorks., aged 61.

90 Ibid., depositions of William Smith and Thomas Hammond, York, bookseller, aged 43.

91 TNA, E 134/6GeoI/Mich33, depositions of Michael Fothergill, York, gent, aged 55 and Henry Bewley, Dringhouses, York, yeoman, aged 70.

92 TNA, E 134/7Jas1/East8.

93 Ibid., depositions of John Coats, Beverley, aged 80 and John Greene, Beverley, glover, aged 80.

94 *VCH East Riding*, VI, p. 214.

town, in which enfranchisement was tied to owning a share of a salt 'fat' or pan.[95] Despite several agreements between local landlords about common rights in the sixteenth century, meadows and fields totalling 17–18 acres had been enclosed by a tenant, Philip Pardoe, at the turn of the seventeenth century, and freemen of Droitwich excluded.[96] A series of inconclusive court cases were initiated, ending in a damning verdict in favour of the town in 1635 in which the enclosures were described as 'very intollerable' because they denied freemen common rights, and which overrode earlier agreements.[97] Other disputes occurred, as in Elizabethan Leominster, Jacobean Burton-on-Trent, Interregnum Leicester and early eighteenth-century Stafford, between corporations and neighbouring manorial lords about corporate rights to pasture or income from lands well *outside* the town boundaries in jurisdictions over which these towns had no other interest.[98]

VII

It is evident that the lands and other resources held in common by towns in early modern history have a more extensive history than is sometimes suggested by the existing literature – and one that may be somewhat more important in understanding urban development, government and society than is sometimes allowed. In particular, these urban common rights provide two new opportunities for historical study.

Firstly, they provide new information on the workings of the urban economy. Along with research into market gardening, they allow us to consider the significance of agrarian by-employments in towns. While it is obvious that commons rarely provided a living for the entire household, even in a tiny rural borough such as Clitheroe, it is equally apparent that opportunities for cow-keeping or horse-hire offered the lucky minority a significant additional income stream. Debates about access to these rights also reveal extra dimensions to the 'politics of entitlement' that ebbed and flowed in urban society throughout

95 TNA, E 134/5ChasI/Mich10; E. Cruickshanks, S. Handley and D. W. Hayton (eds), *The History of Parliament: The House of Commons, 1690–1715* (5 vols, Cambridge, 2002), vol. 2, p. 709.

96 TNA, E 134/10ChasI/Mich23, depositions of John Pennell, Salway, Worc., husbandman, aged 33 and Roger Glasbrooke, Upton Warren, Worc., gent, aged 81.

97 TNA, E 134/5ChasI/Mich 10, deposition of William Creswell, St Peter's near Droitwich, Worc., husbandman, aged 60; E 178/5732, Decree n.d. (but associated with E 134/10Chas1/Mich23?).

98 TNA E 134/32Eliz/East9; *VCH Stafford*, IX, pp. 59–64; TNA E 134/1651/Mich15; *Municipal Corporations Commissioners*, First Rep. App. III, p. 2028.

the period. They illustrate how the seemingly artificial hierarchy of corporate membership was translated into the much more tangible hierarchy of rights, and how this reflected social fissures in towns. As in Coventry and York, they also show how such a resource could be a touchstone for discontent within the urban polity through the generations. However, even where stints and entitlements were recorded in official registers, the surviving evidence suggests that in practice the allocation and use of these rights was often complicated by subletting and exchanges. These trends may have favoured those formally excluded from the exercise of rights, but were probably more likely to let in butchers or enable a few wealthier commoners to exceed their stints.

Secondly, they invite us to adopt a new perspective on themes that are already familiar. The most prominent of these is the very nature of the 'urban' in urban history. If agriculture, agrarian activity, the farming economy, questions of land tenure and resource management extended right up to the town-dweller's front door, then it was not merely the air in towns (to borrow another phrase from Maitland) that 'smacked of the farmyard'. While it is surely right to base our definitions of the 'urban' on those elements of town living that were different from the surrounding rural world, we should not ignore this world when we find it within the town boundaries. Here, new forms of entitlement and management were created, forms that reflected the different social organization and pressures on resources in towns. These can usefully be compared *both* with other urban rights (such as charities, trade privileges and prerequisites) *and* with rural forms of allocating resources (such as the structure and policing of open-field agriculture or pasture stints).

In addition, the fact that most equity disputes about common rights seem to relate to lands *beyond* the borough boundaries, or outside the formal area of corporate commons, reminds us that towns were bound up intimately in the rural economy and farming system of the manors and townships immediately surrounding them. In these respects, then, the 'politics of entitlement' were not merely between different categories of urban dweller, but also defined in contests between townsfolk and their rural neighbours. As has become clear in some studies of rural intercommoning in the sixteenth century, attempts to 'enclose' urban commons, or extinguish Lammas grazing rights, were often efforts to reserve rights to a particular settlement rather than to 'privatize' such rights within that settlement. The fact that many of these disputes were recorded most often in the period 1500–1640 suggests that the history of urban commons also provides new angles on the timing of enclosure campaigns. Cash-strapped corporations always eyed common resources enviously, and did not need eighteenth-century agrarian 'improvers' to tell them that letting them to the highest bidder would produce a better return than farming them in common.

Although debates about 'urban decline in Tudor England' stalled years ago, there may have been more such moves before 1600 than after that date. Conversely, there may have been a greater temptation among such governing bodies to tap into rising leasehold rents and building demand after 1750 than there had been a century earlier. In addition, the court cases about Lammas grazing in York in the later seventeenth century are also suggestive. By this time, disputes reflected the incongruity of *common* rights being exercised over otherwise wholly *enclosed* lands. The freemen of the city were sufficiently wealthy, numerous and well connected to continue to assert these rights, as were their peers in Leicester and Nottingham. Elsewhere, though, the evidence is that piecemeal enclosure began to extinguish such practices, particularly from the early seventeenth century.

In fact, the fate of these common rights and resources often provides an insight into the power structures of such urban polities. Clearly, in some places (such as Nottingham, Coventry, Oxford or Preston) the openness of the corporation created a political majority with a vested interest in their preservation. By contrast, though, did they also endure in oligarchic Cambridge, Colchester, Sudbury, Beccles or Huntingdon, precisely because these corporations were able to defend them against popular encroachment? It may be that corporations' desire to preserve these resources intact, and occasional financial or electoral dependence on them, fossilized these commons to a greater extent than in many rural manors. They appear finally to have succumbed not because of an inability to defend them, but because this became untenable in the face of a potent combination of the rhetoric of agricultural improvement, municipal and electoral reform and the desires of the New Poor Law to undermine systems of outdoor relief.

Urban common rights were, in many respects, anachronistic by the early modern period – a legacy not only of a time when the English did not distinguish linguistically between town and village, but also (perhaps) of a time when they had little need to do so in economic and social terms. By the sixteenth century such resources and rights were increasingly vestigial in relation to the numbers who benefited from them and the scale of the benefit obtained by them. In this sense, these rights became more and more *symbolic*. However, as symbols, commons, commoners and common rights continued to be powerful, indicating deeper distributions of power and contests over its exercise within corporate communities and between them and their neighbours. In particular, they marked out literal and metaphorical territories in which contests were fought between increasingly disenfranchised freemen and civic elites, and between subsistence and profit-oriented forms of agriculture. As a consequence, the historical significance of urban commons may be much greater than is suggested by their measurable economic contribution or the extent of their use by townsfolk in this period.

Chapter 6

Approvement and Improvement in the Lowland Wastes of Early Modern Lancashire

*Bill Shannon**

'Waste', said John Cowell (1607), 'seemeth to be called waste, because the Lord cannot make such profit of it, as he doth of other of his land.'[1] From the landlord's perspective, the problem was that 'at the same moment, several persons might have and be actually enjoying rights of a proprietary kind in the same plot of ground'.[2] These usage rights had been protected by the *Statute of Merton* (1236), which had stated that a landlord's free tenants ought to have sufficient pasture, 'as much as pertains to their tenements'.[3] However, *Merton* had gone on to say that, providing those tenants had 'sufficient pasture with free entry and exit, as aforesaid, then may the lords lawfully and freely make their profit from the residue'. Thus a manorial lord could, by statute, enclose a part (but only a part) of his waste without the need for anyone else's consent. The eighteenth-century legal writer Blackstone regarded this provision as being 'extremely reasonable', making the point that such enclosures were, from a legalistic perspective, 'no injury to any one, so no one is entitled to any remedy'.[4] The term given to this form of enclosure was 'approvement', defined as:

---

* All documents cited in this chapter are in The National Archives (TNA). Extracts from contemporary printed sources and manuscripts are reproduced with capitalization in accordance with modern practice. I would like to thank Angus Winchester, my PhD supervisor, for his encouragement and enthusiasm throughout this project. I am also grateful to numerous members of the British Agricultural History Society at their spring and winter conferences for their help in clarifying my thoughts.

1 John Cowell, *The Interpreter* (Cambridge, 1607), 'Waste', unpaginated but p. 286 in the copy accessed via Early English Books Online (EEBO).

2 F. W. Maitland, quoted in John Hudson, *Land, Law and Lordship in Anglo-Norman England* (Oxford, 1994), p. 7.

3 *Statutes of the Realm* (11 vols, 1810–28), vol. 1, p. 2, 20 Henry III, cap. IV.

4 Sir William Blackstone, *Commentaries on the Laws of England* (4 vols, Oxford, 1765–69), III, ch. 16, pp. 236–53, 'On Disturbance'.

> Where a manne hath common in the Lordes waste ground, and the Lord encloseth part of the wast for him selfe, leaving never the lesse suffycient common, with egresse and regresse for the commoners: This enclosure is called approvement.[5]

This right to approve was so enshrined in *Merton* that Coke referred to it as the 'Statute of Approvements'.[6] However in the changing economic conditions of the sixteenth century, lords sought not to convert waste to arable, as *Merton* had assumed, but to convert arable to pasture. Enclosure became equated with depopulation and the whole concept was thrown into disrepute, while Protector Somerset's misguided proclamation against enclosure 'ministered occasion of a foule and dangerous disorder' as people took it upon themselves to enforce the law.[7] It was against this background that *Merton* and the related *Second Statute of Westminster* (1285) were re-enacted in 1549 as 'An act concerning the improvements of moors and waste grounds'.[8] The key point, though, is that the 1549 Act did not repeal *Merton*; it merely increased the penalties for breaching it, and added some new clauses. Indeed Prothero felt that the legislation might in fact have been specifically pro-enclosure, 'intended to increase the amount of tillage by bringing new land under the plough in exchange for that which had been laid down to grass'.[9]

Thirsk also suggested the same thing, in a footnote to the effect that 'the repetition of these two acts was evidently intended to encourage lords to improve wastes.[10] This interpretation is perhaps supported by noting that the committee to which the House of Lords referred the 'Bill for approving of commons and waste grounds' after its first Lords reading in January 1550 comprised the Bishops of Ely and Lincoln, Lords Wharton, Paget and Monteagle and Justice Hales.[11] These are men who might be presumed to have been more in favour

[5] John Rastell, *An exposition of certaine difficult words and termes of the lawes of this realme* (London, 1st edn *c.*1523; the 1579 edn is used here), fos. 23–4.

[6] See for example Sir Edward Coke, *The Second Part of the Institutes of the Laws of England* (1642 edn, repr. 1979), p. 87.

[7] P. L. Hughes and J. F. Larkin (eds), *Tudor Royal Proclamations* (3 vols, New Haven, 1964–69), nos 327, 451. The quotation is from R. Holinshed, *Chronicles* (6 vols, 1808 edn), vol. 3, p. 916.

[8] *Statutes of the Realm*, vol. 4, p. 102, 3 and 4 Edw. VI, c. 3. Note that it was not actually enacted until January 1550 (new style).

[9] R. E. Prothero (Lord Ernle), *English Farming Past and Present* (London, 1936 edn), ch. 3.

[10] Joan Thirsk, 'The Crown as Projector on its own Estates, from Elizabeth I to Charles I', in R. W. Hoyle (ed.), *The Estates of the English Crown, 1558–1640* (Cambridge, 1992), pp. 297–352.

[11] *Lord Journal*, vol. I (3 Jan. 1550), p. 1. Note that the *Journal* mistakenly lists *Domino Mountague*, whereas the names of the lords present on that day makes it clear Lord Monteagle is meant.

of wasteland enclosure than otherwise, and likely to have a working knowledge of, if not a personal interest in, the subject. Leaving aside the two Fenland bishops, Wharton had been Member of Parliament for Cumberland and came from Kirkby Stephen, a district with extensive upland wastes: Paget was at this date Chancellor of the Duchy of Lancaster, with its extensive lowland and upland wastes in Lancashire, and had himself acquired the Lancashire priories of Conishead and Burscough, together with their lowland wastes. Monteagle was based at Hornby in the Lune Valley, again an area with extensive wastes; while even their legal adviser, Justice Hales, had been a counsel in the Duchy Chamber. Yet early modern and subsequent commentators appear to have regarded wasteland approvement as a dead letter. Thus, in 1580, John Kitchin wrote in his *Jurisdictions* that:

> when the statutes ... were made for improvements, immediately the lords have improved their wastes as much as they could, or otherwise they were so moved with charity and pitty to the poor that more they would not improve for charity. I pray God that that may continue.[12]

Nearly 300 years later, Charles Elton, in his magisterial *Treatise on ... the law of approvement* stated that while for centuries after *Merton* approvement by the lord of the manor had been 'the most usual method of extinguishing rights of common', nevertheless 'there was at one period great popular opposition to this method of enclosure', namely at the beginning of the reign of Edward VI.[13] Elton did not make it clear whether he thought that the 1549 Act actually allowed approvements to continue for a little while – or that the Act had led to their immediate demise. One way or another, though, so far as Elton was concerned:

> the Statutes of Approvement fell into disuse for centuries ... [it being] seldom that any common was sufficiently extensive to afford a surplus of any moment after the claims of

---

[12] J. Kitchin, *Jurisdictions, or the lawful authority of courts leet etc* (3rd edn, London, 1656), p. 183. The first edition in French appeared in 1580: it was subsequently translated into English and was frequently reprinted. For Kitchin see *Oxford Dictionary of National Biography* (*ODNB*). The wording in the 1590 edition was 'que quant les estatutes ... fueront faits pur improvements, immediatement les seigniors adonques ount improve de les wastes quant ils puissont, ou autrement ils fueront issint moue oue charitie et pitty al poore, que pluis ne volunt improve que charitie (ieo pria dieu que ceo continue)', fo. 99.

[13] Charles I. Elton, *A Treatise on Commons and Waste Grounds with Special Reference to the Law of Approvement* (London, 1868), pp. 170–71, 204–5.

> those who had a right of common on it were satisfied ... insomuch that in modern times there is scarce an instance of an approvement, as it is technically called, taking place.[14]

Perhaps in consequence, little attention has been paid to approvement in the literature of enclosure, although Gonner was an exception when he listed approvement as one of the means by which enclosure might be brought about.[15] At the same time, though, he noted that:

> throughout the copious literature dealing with commons and inclosure, approvement, if referred to at all, is never mentioned as a means whereby inclosures are being effected or could be effected.[16]

This conclusion was echoed by Butlin, who said that 'evidence for enclosure by approvement in the seventeenth century is relatively scarce'; while Eric Kerridge, although recognizing approvement as important, perhaps muddied the waters by claiming that 'it became usual for approvement to be conducted under a formal agreement. In the long run it was the easiest way of going about the business.'[17]

Before going on to try to restore approvement to its proper place in the enclosure history of those districts where the common was sufficiently extensive to afford a surplus, an important distinction needs to be made between 'approvement' as a legal process of enclosure and 'improvement', the physical process of extracting value from that enclosure. 'Improve' and 'approve' in fact have the same roots, and *Catholicon Anglicum*, an English–Latin wordbook of 1483, translated 'To approwe' as '*Approare, sicut domini se faciunt de vastis* ie as lords approwe (or improwe) themselves of wastes.'[18] Early in the sixteenth century, though, 'to improve' began increasingly to separate itself from 'to approve', the latter retaining its original narrow legal meaning and so falling out of popular usage; while 'improvement' came to mean making the land itself, any land, more valuable, by whatever means.

Thus John Fitzherbert (1523) used 'to improve' as a reflexive verb, as in 'woodes ... where the lorde may improwe himselfe thereof'.[19] However,

---

14 Ibid., pp. 171, 172, quoting *Report of the Select Committee on Inclosures*, 1795.

15 E. C. K. Gonner, *Common Land and Inclosure* (London, 1912, repr. 1966), pp. 43–69.

16 Ibid., p. 50.

17 R. A. Butlin, 'The Enclosure of Open Fields and the Extinction of Common Rights in England, *c.*1600–1750: A Review', in H. S. A. Fox and R. A. Butlin (eds), *Change in the Countryside: Essays on Rural England, 1500–1900* (1979), pp. 65–82. E. Kerridge, *Agrarian Problems in the Sixteenth Century and After* (London, 1969), p. 95.

18 See *Oxford English Dictionary* (*OED*), under 'Approve, approw'.

19 J. Fitzherbert, *The boke of surueyeng and improumentes* (London, 1523), fo. v.

Fitzherbert also used the word in its 'modern' sense in the title of his work *The boke of surueyeng and improumentes*, while by the middle of the seventeenth century the meaning had shifted further and had begun increasingly to carry the implication that, whereas the beneficiary of 'approvement' had always been the landlord, the beneficiary of 'improvement' could or should be the country as a whole. Some writers indeed became convinced that improvement was not just an economic necessity but a religious duty.[20]

Sylvanus Taylor was one such, and his pamphlet *Common-Good* (1652) had a wide-ranging agenda, driven at least in part by his view that commons were one of the two 'great nurseries of idleness and beggary' (the other being ale-houses).[21] He argued that parliament should legislate to enclose the wastes, setting aside a quarter of the land so enclosed – part to be given to cottagers on subsidized leases, the remainder being leased out to pay for workhouses and other poor relief. However, in:

> Lancashire, and other of those northern counties that do abound with commons and ignorance, I desire ... that by dividing those large commons into five equall parts, and that one fifth part thereof should be subdivided, the one moyety thereof to maintain a free schoole in every parish ... The other moyety of the fifth part may be well imployed for the maintenance of a Latin free schoole and these to be seated in the severall counties.[22]

I

Whatever may have been the truth of Taylor's conclusion with regard to ignorance in Lancashire, he was certainly correct with regard to the abundant commons. Indeed, for many outsiders it was the wastes, and specifically the mosslands, that defined the county. Mosses, also known as raised mires or raised bogs, comprise thick layers of peat, a fibrous organic material formed under anaerobic conditions from partly decomposed plant remains. Peat, known locally as turf, is an excellent fuel when cut and dried; but the mosses in their waterlogged natural state, covered predominantly with *sphagnum* together with cotton-grass, sedges and heathers, had little economic value. Camden for example noted in 1586 the presence in Lancashire of 'certaine moist places and unwholsome called *Mosses*',

20 Paul Warde, 'The Idea of Improvement, *c*.1500–1700', Chapter 4 of this volume.

21 Silvanus Taylor, *Common-Good: or, the improvement of commons, forrests, and chases, by inclosure* (London, 1652), p. 51.

22 Ibid., pp. 39–40.

while Michael Drayton (1622) wrote of 'those gross wat'ry grounds' near the Alt, which he featured in personified form on his accompanying map.[23]

Today 'there are no completely intact examples of lowland raised bog left in Lancashire'.[24] Back in 1500, though, there would have been extensive tracts of living moss, a landscape vividly described in a court case concerning Angerton Moss in 1546 as:

> so full of water and a depe shakinge and salowe mosse that no maner of catell can pasture the same nor no maner of proffet thereof was ever taken nor so farre as we can perceive can ever be taken.[25]

This was the landscape which the Lancashire natural historian Dr Charles Leigh (1662–1701?) called the *white morass*.[26] However, a reference in a lawsuit in Heysham in 1627 to a 'parcell of grounde ... gayned from the Greate White Mosse by graving of turves from and of the same' is a reminder that this landscape was far from static.[27] A map of 1571 (Figure 6.1) shows such a landscape, with the undivided *White Mosse*, surrounded by turbaries, apparently divided into two grades, perhaps reflecting Dr Leigh's *grey* and *black morasses*.[28] The boundaries of the surrounding townships reach only to the edge of the black moss and comprise a ring of unenclosed pastures, while the enclosed arable lands of the townships lie beyond; and there is a strong sense that each of these zones is encroaching upon the next, as through the action of man white moss gives way to black, and black moss to open grazing or enclosed fields.

As to the extent of the Lancashire wastes, Hall *et al.* are probably correct in their assertion that the mosses had reached their maximum extent by the start of the sixteenth century.[29] Saxton's map of 1577 (Figure 6.2) names *Chatmosse*, *Pyllyn mosse*, *Marton mosse* and a fourth, referred to merely as *the Mosse*, running

---

23 William Camden, *Britain: or a chorographical description of the most flourishing kingdomes ... etc* (London, 1637, trans. Philemon Holland, first pub. 1586), p. 745: The 1586 version reads '*nisi uliginosis quibusdam minus salubribus locis* Mosses *vocant*'. Richard Hooper (ed.), *The Complete Works of Michael Drayton* (3 vols, London 1876), vol. 3, p. 176, 27th song, line 78.

24 David J. Dunlop, *Mossland Report* (Lancashire Biodiversity Partnership, 2001) www.lancspartners.org/lbap/plans/Mossland_Final_2001.doc (accessed 20 Nov. 2008).

25 DL 3/48/R5k.

26 Dr Charles Leigh, *The natural history of Lancashire, Cheshire and the Peak in Derbyshire* (Oxford, 1700), pp. 19 and 58. For Leigh, see Stan A. E. Mendyk, *Speculum Britanniae: Regional Study, Antiquarianism and Science in Britain to 1700* (Toronto, 1989), pp. 222–3.

27 DL 4/77/35.

28 MPC 1/63: Leigh, *Natural History of Lancashire*, p. 58.

29 D. Hall, C. E. Wells and E. Huckerby, *The Wetlands of Greater Manchester* (Lancaster, North-West Wetlands Survey, 2, 1995), p. 125.

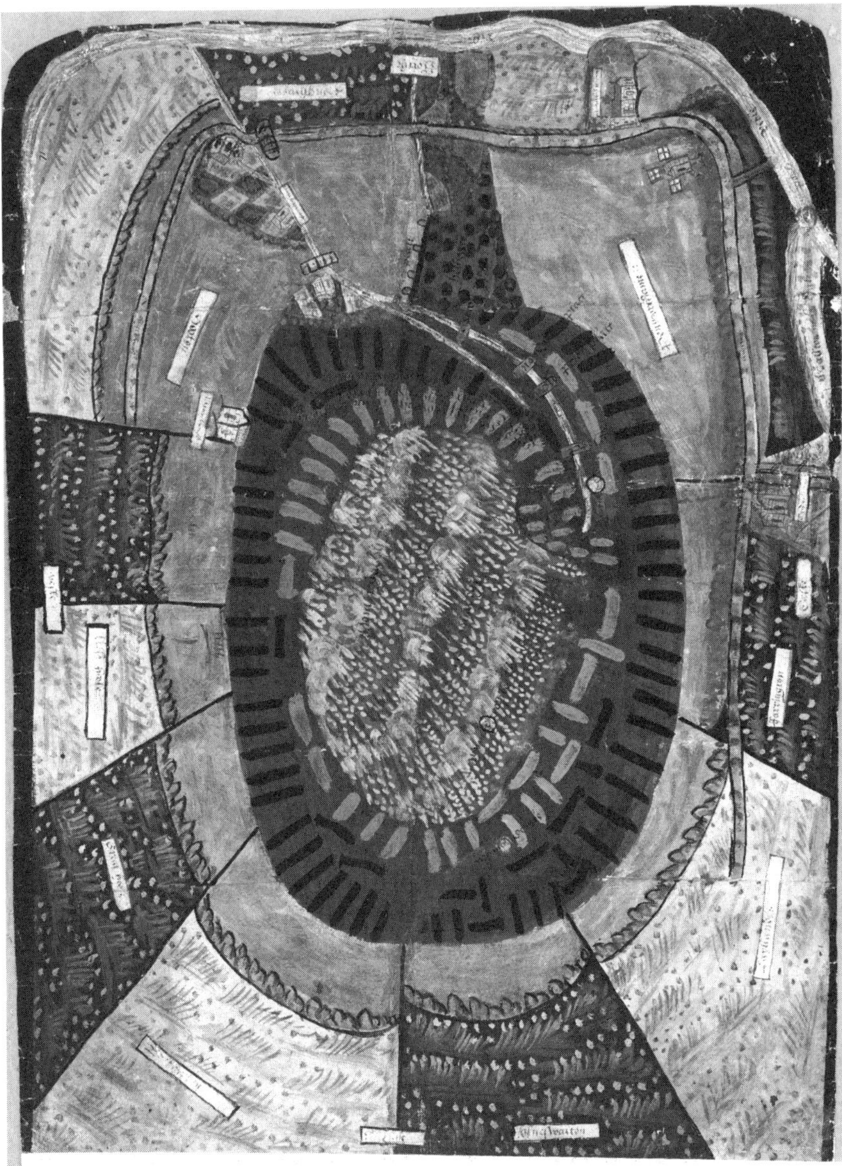

Figure 6.1 The White Moss. TNA, MPC 1/63, 1571. Reproduced with the permission of The National Archives

On this map, which was produced in evidence in the Duchy court, are shown (clockwise from top right) the townships of Penwortham, above Walton-le-Dale, then Farington, Leyland, Ulnes Walton, Brereton, Great Hoole, Little Hoole, Longton, Hutton and Howick, which is separated from Penwortham by the 'helhooles', an area of peat 'mining'. Note that the township boundaries do not extend onto the moss.

Figure 6.2 The mosses on Saxton's map of Lancashire, 1577 (author's collection)

along the coastal strip from Formby to Hesketh, However, it would be unwise to regard this map as anything other than a very generalized indication of the location of these features. Indeed it is a futile exercise to use any early map to study the original extent of the wastes or their subsequent changes.[30]

[30] Surprisingly, though, this task was attempted by Middleton *et al.*, who reproduced Saxton's and Speed's maps to show 'the distribution of peat in the Fylde in 1577 and 1610 respectively' – without apparently being aware that Speed's Lancashire map is entirely derived from Saxton, the differences between them merely reflecting a different engraver's interpretation of identical data. See R. Middleton, C. E. Wells and E. Huckerby, *The Wetlands of North Lancashire* (Lancaster, North-West Wetlands Survey 3, 1995), fig. 89, p. 208. Hale and Coney appear to fall into the same trap in depicting Martin Mere on Saxton's map and four others from the Harleian manuscript map

William Yates's map of 1785 was the first with any claims to being an accurate depiction, and Harley calculated that Yates showed 34,500 acres of moss – yet by then the mosses had already reduced considerably in extent.[31] The only other attempt at calculating the original extent of Lancashire's lowland wastes is by Rodgers, whose data can be reanalysed to show wasteland accounting for 49 per cent of the lowlands.[32] This, however, almost certainly overstates the true position. A new map and estimate of the original extent of the waste was therefore undertaken for the present study, based upon geological and soil surveys together with the work of the North-West Wetlands Survey, as well as other sources.[33] Without going into detail, the conclusion was that the lowland wastes of Lancashire would at their greatest extent, *c.*1500, have accounted for at least 160,000 acres, equivalent to something over one-third of the surface area of lowland Lancashire.[34]

Although these wastes included lowland moor, heath, carr and marsh as well as moss, it was the latter which dominated, and the district was characterized in particular by three main groupings of mosses of regional importance, each of which formed a boundary zone between hundreds. Elsewhere there were other substantial mosses which almost without exception lay between rather

of 1598 to Bowen's map of 1745, all of which are merely redrawings of Saxton. See W. G. Hale and Audrey Coney, *Martin Mere: Lancashire's Lost Lake* (Liverpool, 2005), fig. 4.1, pp. 46–7.

31 J. B. Harley, *William Yates' Map of Lancashire, 1786* (Historic Society of Lancashire and Cheshire, 1968), p. 19.

32 H. B. Rodgers, 'Land use in Tudor Lancashire: the evidence of the Final Concords, 1450–1558', *Trans. Institute of British Geographers* 21 (1955), pp. 79–97.

33 C. E. De Rance, *The superficial geology of the country adjoining the coasts of south-west Lancashire* (London, 1877), p. 80; De Rance, *The geology of the country around Blackpool, Poulton and Fleetwood* (London, 1875), p. 10; E. Crompton, *The Soils of the Preston District of Lancashire (Sheet 75)* (Harpenden, 1966); B. R. Hall and C. J. Folland, *Soils of the South-West Lancashire Coastal Plain (Sheets 74 and 83)* (Harpenden, 1967): B. R. Hall and C. J. Folland, *Soils of Lancashire* (Harpenden, 1970); G. R. Beard, T. R. E. Thompson and J. W. Lea, *Soils of the Liverpool District (Sheet 108)* (Harpenden, 1987); R. W. Cowell and J. B. Innes, *The Wetlands of Merseyside* (North-West Wetlands Survey 1, Lancaster, 1994); Hall *et al.*, *Wetlands of Greater Manchester*; Middleton *et al.*, *Wetlands of North Lancashire*; M. D. Leah, C. E. Wells, C. Appleby and E. Huckerby, *The Wetlands of Cheshire* (North-West Wetlands Survey 4, Lancaster, 1997): M. D. Leah, C. E. Wells, P. Stanger, E. Huckerby and C. Welsh, *The Wetlands of Shropshire and Staffordshire* (North-West Wetlands Survey 5, Lancaster, 1998): D. Hodgkinson, E. Huckerby, R. Middleton and C. E. Wells, *The Lowland Wetlands of Cumbria* (North-West Wetlands Survey 6, Lancaster, 2000). The final volume, R. Middleton, M. J. Tooley, J. B. Inne *et al.*, *The Wetlands of South Lancashire* (North West Wetlands Survey 7), is in press.

34 The evidence in presented in more detail in my PhD thesis, W. D. Shannon, 'Approvement and Improvement in Early-Modern England; Enclosure in the Lowland Wastes of Lancashire, c.1500–1700' (unpublished, Lancaster University, 2009).

than within townships, and which in 1500 would in many cases have been intercommoned or otherwise shared by their neighbouring manors. The existence of wastes which were not neatly divided between manors had been recognized by the statute Westminster II (1285), but this was a particular issue in Lancashire where not only common *per cause de vicinage* but also true intercommoning might be found – the latter being where all neighbouring lords claimed full rights in the *whole of* the waste and where all parts were equally open to all the freeholders of all the manors that intercommoned there.[35] This concept cannot have sat easily with developing early modern ideas of private property.[36] Moreover, as under Westminster II a lord could not approve a waste which was not his exclusive property, in order for the lord to make profit from such a waste, partition would have to have been the necessary first step.

II

Despite the legal complexities, it seems clear that a significant part of these extensive Lancashire wastes disappeared into several ownership during the sixteenth and seventeenth centuries. If there is a consensus in the literature as to how that enclosure might have occurred, it is summed up by Yelling, who appears to have regarded piecemeal enclosure as having been the norm in Lancashire at this date. Yet, quoting Tupling and Porter, he also stated that 'in certain cases tenants joined with the manorial lord to agree a complete or partial general enclosure of the wastes'.[37] Both Tupling and Porter, however, were solely concerned with upland enclosure, and are poor guides as to what was happening in the lowlands. As for the evidence from elsewhere in England, Leonard had demonstrated that, in the seventeenth century, enclosure agreements between lord and tenant were on occasions made certain by collusive cases in the Courts of Chancery and Exchequer involving the formal enrolment of a decree.[38] In 1979 Beresford reported that a search had revealed 260 such decrees, the largest number of which probably date from the middle years of the seventeenth century.[39]

35 Elton, *Approvement*, p. 201.

36 These ideas were developed further in my MA dissertation, 'Approvement, Encroachment, Agreement' (Lancaster 2004).

37 J. A. Yelling, 'Agriculture, 1500–1750', in R. A. Dodgshon and R. A. Butlin (eds), *An Historical Geography of England and Wales* (London, 1978), pp. 151–72.

38 E. M. Leonard, 'The inclosure of common fields in the seventeenth century', *Trans. Royal Historical Society*, new ser. 19 (1905), pp. 101–46.

39 M. W. Beresford, 'The decree rolls of Chancery as a source for economic history, 1547–*c*.1700', *Economic History Rev.* 32 (1979), pp. 1–10.

However, most of these decrees refer to open-field enclosure in the Midland counties, and only one of Beresford's 260 cases originated in Lancashire.[40] The reason for this absence, as Beresford pointed out, lay in 'the separate jurisdiction of the courts of the Duchy of Lancaster [which] gives analogous documentation for the Duchy estates all over England'. But the prospect of the records of the Duchy yielding a similar harvest of agreements to that of Chancery had already been flagged up by Tate, who had written, regarding enclosure by decree, 'it is likely enough that much enclosure in Lancashire ... may have been carried out by rather similar means'.[41]

The Court of Duchy Chamber was an equity court which met in Westminster, its jurisdiction comprising 'all pleas reall and personall, which concerne any of the Duchie lands, now in his Majesties hands and parcell of the crowne'.[42] Its importance lies in the fact that its mode of trial was by the administration of interrogatories and the taking of sworn depositions by a commission meeting at a place convenient for the witnesses. The records of the court have been available to scholars since their transfer to the Public Record Office (PRO) in 1868, including the Duchy's own manuscript catalogue of entries relating to decrees and orders prior to the death of Charles I, known as 'Great Ayloffe'.[43] A considerable part of this refers to the county of Lancashire: yet of all the decrees indexed for Lancashire, only a dozen actually use the words 'enclosure', with a further three mentioning 'improvements'. There is nothing whatsoever here to suggest a heavy workload of collusive cases involving enclosure agreements analogous to those found by Beresford in the Chancery decrees. Of course, it may be that decrees concerning such agreements are to be found in the records of the Lancashire Palatinate court rather than the Duchy. However, in 1622 the boundary between the respective jurisdictions was set at £10, so anything worth more than that after that date – which by analogy with the Beresford Chancery decrees would have been the great majority of such putative agreements – should

---

40 TNA, C 78/491/18.

41 M. W. Beresford, 'Habitation Versus Improvement: The Debate on Enclosure by Agreement', in F. J. Fisher (ed.), *Essays in the Economic and Social History of Tudor and Stuart England* (Cambridge, 1961), pp. 40–69: W. E. Tate, *The English Village Community and the Enclosure Movement* (London, 1967), p. 47.

42 John Stow, *A Survay of London* (London, 1598); Sir Thomas Smith, *The commonwealth of England* (London, 1565, 1640 edn), p. 232.

43 Edward Jennings, 'Decrees and orders of Duchy of Lancaster, Edward IV to Charles I, arranged in counties, transcribed from the ancient calendar known as "Great Ayloffe"', manuscript, PRO (1910). The list was originally compiled by Benjamin Ayloffe, keeper of the Duchy Records for 30 years from 1685. See OBS 1/512 and R. Somerville, 'The Duchy of Lancaster records', *Trans. Royal Historical Society*, 4th ser., 29 (1947), pp. 1–17.

have been heard in the Duchy Chamber.[44] Nevertheless, irrespective of what may have occurred in the Palatinate court, the clear conclusion is that the Duchy Chamber itself was not to any significant extent used for ratifying enclosure agreements by decree in the way Chancery and Exchequer appear to have been.

There are, however, other records in the Duchy archives, namely the depositions and interrogatories, which provide much information about enclosure – both specifically and in passing. Recognizing that focusing on these records alone ignores both the pleadings with which the cases commenced and the decrees which record their ending (albeit only for a relatively small proportion of the total number of cases), nevertheless a sampling exercise of these depositions was carried out, involving four 20-year periods – 1540–59, 1580–89, 1620–39 and 1660–79. There were across these four periods a total of 3,673 files, of which 1,545 referred to Lancashire. These files were examined for references to enclosure of the lowland waste, but to be included in the analysis the cases did not have to be *about* enclosure – enclosure merely had to be mentioned or implied somewhere in the documentation. The importance of this is that the cases studied were not just dealing with contested enclosure, which would have perhaps given a distorted view as to process. Some 130 such files were found, making up the fundamental data set for the research. However, as some hearings were carried forward from one year to the next, these 130 files actually resolved into 96 different legal cases, of which 32 were located in the first sample period, 40 in the second, 18 in the third and 6 in the final period (Table 6.1).

This pattern was not dissimilar to that of the total Duchy workload, but the number of files mentioning wasteland enclosure rose initially more slowly than the Duchy files as a whole, while their fall thereafter was much more dramatic. A chi-squared test was applied to test the statistical significance of these differences, allowing the assertion to be made that these cases do not merely reflect the general litigiousness of the period, but show real differences compared with the distribution of Duchy cases as a whole, thus allowing the conclusion that the enclosure episodes which lay behind these cases were far more common in the Tudor period than in the Stuart – but that these episodes had more or less come to an end by the time of the Restoration.[45]

44 R. A. Forrester (ed.), *Bennett's Chancery of Lancashire Practice* (London, 1933), p. 10.

45 The null hypothesis that the lowland waste files were distributed across the four periods as per all Duchy files was tested. The result was that there is a 99.98 per cent probability that the observed difference is a real one: that is, that these files are *not* distributed across the periods in the same way as all Duchy files. Two other null hypotheses were also tested: a) that the lowland waste files were distributed as per all Lancashire files: and b) that all Lancashire files were distributed in the same way as all Duchy files. These produced results in test a) that there is a 99.28 per cent probability and in test b) a 99.99 per cent probability that these files are *not* so distributed.

Table 6.1 Lancashire approvement cases: protagonists within or between townships

	1540–1559	1580–1599	1620–1639	1660–1679	All sample periods
Between townships Lord vs neighbouring lord, or lord vs neighbouring freeholder/tenant(s)	10	21	6	1	38
Within townships					
Lord vs lord	10	5	2	1	18
Lord vs tenant/freeholder(s)	12	12	6	0	30
Tenant/freeholder(s) vs tenant/freeholder(s)	0	2	4	4	10
Total within townships	22	19	12	5	58
Total cases	32	40	18	6	96

Source: Four 20-year samples of cases from the Duchy depositions (as described in the text).

A close examination of the cases themselves reveals, with one possible exception, no hint of the sort of collusion found by Beresford.[46] Thus these cases record genuine grievances, not legal fictions. It follows that the plaintiffs must have felt litigation in the Duchy Chamber to have been worthwhile in terms of their chances of a successful outcome, balanced against the time, effort and costs involved. As to who those plaintiffs were, and who the defendants, two trends in Table 6.1 are discernible over time, of which the first is the increasing 'democratization' of the cases, with the first two periods dominated by lords (or the Crown) as plaintiff, while in the final period (1660–79) four of the six cases were brought by tenants or freeholders.

This same general trend is discernible among defendants too; but Table 6.1 also highlights the second major trend, which is that cross-border cases peak in the late Tudor period, to be replaced by proportionately more disputes within rather than between townships. This distribution is almost certainly related to the increasing certainty of township boundaries, as by the 1620s – if not before – the great majority of boundaries had been fixed, often as a result of those earlier disputes.

Looking at the plaintiffs and defendants in more detail, it is clear they were overwhelmingly local gentry, with relatively few complete outsiders. The same well-known local family names crop up over and over again. Apart from the

46 DL 4/77/46. This case includes a reference to an enclosure agreement of 1618, given certainty in the Palatinate Court in 1620. Note that this is prior to the date, 1622, when the boundary between the two jurisdictions was defined.

Crown (which initiated seven cases, took on another on behalf of a freeholder and was defendant in another case), the record for litigiousness is held by the Gerard family, with seven cases (six as plaintiffs). Next comes the Faringtons with six cases (two as plaintiff) and thereafter 15 family names with between three and five cases each.[47] In so far as it is possible to generalize, then, it seems fairly clear that the 'typical' case was one brought by one manorial lord against a neighbour, both of them being members of the established squirearchy of lowland Lancashire.[48] Indeed, the very men who appear as plaintiffs or defendants in one case may very well turn up as commissioners in the next.

III

Turning to the nature and substance of the cases, there is an immediate problem in discussing the different types of enclosure in that the language of the period is anything but precise. Contemporary writers and commentators seldom if ever gave precise or consistent legal meaning to words such as 'inclosure', 'intake' or 'encroachment'; and the same is true of the Duchy court. It is indeed normal, especially in the bills of complaint which launch the cases, for several words to be used to ensure that the suit does not fall to a challenge over the correctness of the language. The lawyers or their clients thus routinely used doublets such as 'inclosed and made several', 'improvements and incroachments' and the like.

Unsurprisingly, the single most commonly occurring word for the process in these files, whether on its own or in these phrases, is *enclosure* (and its variants), used in 76 of the 96 cases. *Improved* and its variants is used in 49 cases, although in only one of these is the *approve* variant used, in a case of 1588.[49] The fact that this occurred in an interrogatory, which would have been drafted by a lawyer, rather than in a deposition, supports the suggestion that the word had by this

---

47 Both the Gerards and the Faringtons were extended local landowning families who played a significant part in the administration of county and Duchy. Sir Gilbert Gerard was bailiff of the royal manor of West Derby and vice chancellor of the County Palatine, as well as Master of the Rolls under Elizabeth. The Faringtons were virtually hereditary farmers and stewards of the royal manor of Penwortham throughout the Tudor period, while a member of a junior branch of the family was steward to Lord Derby.

48 This pattern contrasts markedly with that found by Hoyle in Chancery tenure cases, where tenants were plaintiffs in 87 per cent of the cases. R. W. Hoyle, 'Custom, Chancery and Institutional Restraints on Landlord Income 1540–1640' (End of Award report to the ESRC, 2003), p. 9.

49 DL 4/30/25.

date gone out of popular use – and that the distinction between 'approvement' and 'improvement' in ordinary usage had been lost.[50]

For the rest, there is no discernible pattern. The words appear to have been largely interchangeable in casual contemporary usage. However, it is clear that there were indeed different legal forms of enclosure going on, and a more precise terminology is required to identify and separate them. Five terms were therefore adopted for the different types of wasteland enclosure recognized in these cases:

> *Approvement* – enclosure by a lord of part of his waste;
> *Intake* – enclosure under the lord's licence, and thus itself a special form of approvement;
> *Encroachment* – illicit enclosure which might be regularized later;
> *Agreement* – enclosure by the lord and his freeholders and/or other tenants, acting together;
> *Partitioning* – the division of an intercommon by neighbouring proprietors into separately owned wastes.

Starting with this latter point, the attitude of the Duchy court towards intercommoning is of particular interest. While it would be untrue to claim that intercommoning was the norm, nevertheless in a definite 27 cases (plus another 11 possible cases) there is evidence for intercommoning either between townships or within townships held in coparcenry or moieties. The term *enter comon/entrecomyn* is only specifically used in two of these cases, but its use, together with legal terms like *by cause of vicinage* and *pro indiviso* (= for an undivided part), shows a grasp of the subject on the part of some at least of the lawyers involved.[51] The whole question of the legal status of intercommoning is, however, a difficult one; but the Duchy Chamber seems to have aimed at regularizing it into clear, several manorial ownership.

The fact that almost a third of the cases in the data set were about, or resulted in, the partitioning of a waste which had been jointly owned, or claimed to have been held at a higher level than the manor, suggests that the Duchy Chamber was effectively playing the same part in the dividing of these wastes as did the

---

50 Evidence from cases studied outside the data set suggest that the clear distinction in ordinary usage between 'approve' and 'improve' disappeared quite early. Only one example of the use 'approve' has been found in bills later than the reign of Henry VII, DL 1/58/C2. For earlier use, see DL 1/1/ B10; DL 1/2/W2.

51 Enter comon, DL 4/81/38 (1632): entrecomyn ... by cause of vicinage, DL 3/66/R5 (1554): pro indiviso, DL 3/64/H2 (1554).

Scottish Commonty Act of 1695.[52] As an example, in a case concerning events in the 1530s, one lord rejected another's claim that they were tenants in common of the waste of Burtonwood and that their beasts should pasture 'together and undevydet'. The case was resolved by the division of the waste by the court, for which the certificate of measurement survives.[53]

In more than a further quarter of the cases, at least part of the dispute revolves around similar issues of superior or chief lordships. In these, as in other cases, the court saw its main role as arbitrator, rather than merely coming down on one side or the other; and in at least half a dozen cases commissioners were appointed to measure, or survey or inquire into issues like sufficiency prior to drawing up new boundaries. In clarifying ownership, such actions had the possible outcome that enclosure could thereafter have taken place quietly, without recorded dispute, as now being a process internal to a manor. Indeed, far from being hostile to wasteland enclosure *per se*, the court was actually the principal agent of enclosure in some cases, awarding parcels of the waste to compensate for loss of access to a turbary, or for loss of right of way.[54] On the other hand, its attitude to illegal enclosures was wholly unsympathetic, for example ruling that encroachments which were under 10 years old should be pulled down and returned to the waste.[55]

Moving from the attitude of the court to the actual legal process of enclosure, there are several different ways of looking at the evidence. The simplest is to take the 96 cases and try to put each into just one of the five defined categories (Table 6.2). This ignores whether the enclosure event mentioned was recent or earlier, and also ignores the fact that many of these cases reveal more than one enclosure event – indeed, often of more than one enclosure type. It also ignores the acreages involved, which might be trivial in the case of encroachments while normally being substantial in the case of agreements. However, it has the advantage of showing a clear pattern.

---

52 Statutes (Scotland) 1695, c.69, *An Act Concerning the Dividing of Commonties*. See also I. H. Adams, 'The legal geography of Scotland's common lands', *Revue de l'Institut de Sociologie* 2 (1973) and Robin Callander, *The History of Common Land in Scotland* (Caledonia Centre for Social Development: Commonweal of Scotland Working Paper 1 (Issue 2), 2003).

53 DL 3/40/L4. For earlier information on the same case, see DL 1/21/L17; DL 1/20/B10; and DL 1/21/L15.

54 For example DL 3/53/F1.

55 DL 3/72/P3.

Table 6.2 Lancashire approvement cases: probable main type of enclosure involved in each case

	1540–1559	%	1580–1599	%	1620–1639	%	1660–1679	%	All sample periods	%
Partition	8	25.0	1	2.5	0	0.0	0	0.0	9	9.4
Agreement	3	9.4	3	7.5	6	33.3	1	16.7	13	13.5
Encroachment	6	18.8	4	10.0	1	5.6	1	16.7	12	12.5
Intake	6	18.8	13	32.5	2	11.1	2	33.3	23	24.0
Approvement	9	28.1	19	47.5	9	50.0	2	33.3	39	40.6
Approvement plus intake	**15**	**46.9**	**32**	**80.0**	**11**	**61.1**	4	**66.7**	**62**	**64.6**
Total cases	32	100.0	40	100.0	18	100.0	6	100.0	96	100.0

Source: Four 20-year samples of cases from the Duchy depositions (as described in the text).

Partition – either within or between townships – primarily occurred in the first period and is not found at all in cases in the third and fourth periods. *Agreements* became more important over time from the first to the third period (1620–39), at which time they accounted for a third of the cases (6 out of 18). There were, in all periods, a modest number of cases where the main enclosure type was *encroachment* – but this was only really significant in the first period (19 per cent, 6 out of 32 cases), and mainly related to the commissions set up on behalf of the Crown to reveal encroachments on former monastic estates. It should be pointed out that squatter-type encroachments would perhaps normally have been dealt with at manorial court level, not in Westminster, and so might not be expected to feature strongly here. However, the lack of even passing references in these cases to squatters is striking.

Approvement was the main enclosure type in 39 of the 96 cases overall (40 per cent), and accounted for the largest number of cases in each of the four periods. *Intakes*, which, as stated before, are themselves a type of approvement, were the main type in 23 out of 96 cases (24 per cent), and were particularly important in the second period (1580–99) – at which time 80 per cent of the cases (32 out of 40) involved either an approvement or an intake event. The data was also reviewed in various other ways, for example looking at all passing references to enclosure in the files and not just the main event. This analysis revealed more (uncontested) agreements and more partitions, the latter particularly in the middle two periods. Nevertheless, approvements continued overall, as well as in each period separately, to be the main enclosure type mentioned.

The question therefore had to be asked whether the types of enclosure recorded in these cases reflected the actual distribution of enclosure events or whether it was in some way a function of the cases themselves. In other words, were certain types of enclosure more likely than others to feature in cases before the Duchy court and, in particular, was approvement more likely than other types to be contested? This question was tested by contrasting those cases where an enclosure event was central with those where the main issue was something else. It might be expected that these would show different patterns, with the first being influenced in some way by the nature of the cases. However, both in those cases where enclosure was central and those where it was not, the main type of enclosure found was approvement. Moreover, allowing that intakes are a special case of approvement, then taking the two together, approvement plus intakes accounted for 58 per cent (24 out of 41) of the cases where enclosure was central, but 69 per cent (38 out of 55) of the cases where it was not.

Thus there are no good grounds for suggesting that the type of case before the court significantly biased the evidence for the process involved; or for suggesting that the distribution of the different types of enclosure revealed by these cases is anything other than a fair picture of how wasteland enclosure actually happened in lowland Lancashire at this time. Far from enclosure being dominated by agreements and encroachments, which has perhaps been the impression given in other studies, the normal method by which enclosure was achieved was approvement (often following partition), either at the direct initiative of the lord or in the form of licensed intakes. This is not to deny that agreements were important, but it would appear that they were not very common (except, perhaps, in the first half of the seventeenth century); while encroachments were never more than a temporary stage prior to the closes either being laid open or regularized by retrospective licence.

What is noticeable in all periods and for all cases is that opposition to the enclosure act itself – that is, contested enclosure – was relatively rare. Although the question of sufficiency of pasture lies behind more than a dozen cases, references to loss of common are found in no more than one in five of all the cases in the data set; while over time challenges on grounds of loss of common, never particularly widespread, became increasingly rare. On the other hand, issues of ownership cropped up in all periods, including such matters as claims to being sole lord or claims of one lord to share in the profits of another; disputes over rent, encroachment and other manorial issues – and including, above all, boundary disputes. The boundary dispute was a special case of the manorial claim, and such disputes lay behind nearly half the cases in the first two periods. However, legal challenges over the ownership of the land being enclosed, like claims to loss of common, reduced over time as more and more of the cases came to refer instead to specific issues arising from the enclosure process itself. Nevertheless, taken together, all these essentially manorial claims and objections add up to 71 cases – three-quarters of the total.

Wordie had claimed that the absence of an 'outcry' about enclosure was itself evidence for the absence of extensive wasteland enclosure in the Tudor period.[56] Yet here there is considerable evidence for enclosure without outcry, while the single biggest objection was not loss of common, as might have been expected. Instead, the 'typical' case involved a claim by one lord that another lord had infringed his territorial rights by crossing boundaries. This has interesting implications. The only enclosure events visible in these court records, by definition, are those which came before the court for one reason or another. Such cases arose predominantly because enclosure was taking or had taken place on a disputed part of the waste, either within or between townships. It is reasonable to surmise that such contested parts of the waste would only ever have been a relatively small part of the total lowland waste of Lancashire. At the start of the early modern period the wastes were at their most extensive, and thus we may suppose there could have been many enclosure events occurring during this time where the lord, secure in his undisputed title, quietly got on with enclosing a part of his waste without upsetting his neighbours or – providing he left sufficient residue – his freeholders or tenants. Very large acreages could have been approved in this way without leaving anything behind in the way of evidence in these or other courts, other than perhaps the occasional passing reference in a case which was concerned with some other matter – or, of course, in the surviving estate records of Lancashire families such as the Cliftons, the Molyneux and the Faringtons, which have not been searched as part of this present study.

Another significant conclusion from these sample cases is that there is no hint here of the 'village revolts' which Manning regarded as typifying wasteland enclosure, or of the 'outcry' which Wordie expected to find.[57] Nor indeed is there any sign of the landless poor being a party to any of these disputes. It might be argued that the Duchy court would not have taken up the cases of the landless poor as plaintiffs and that the poor would instead have gone to the Court of Requests (known as the poor man's court). Similarly the poor as defendants would perhaps have been pursued through the manorial courts, or at the Quarter Sessions or assizes, rather than in the Duchy Chamber. However, poor men could and did sue in the Duchy court, with attorneys acting '*in forma*

56 J. R. Wordie, 'The chronology of English enclosure: a reply', *Economic History Rev.* 37 (1984), pp. 560–62.

57 R. B. Manning, *Village Revolts: Social Protest and Popular Disturbances in England, 1509–1640* (Oxford, 1988). Wordie, 'Reply'.

pauperis', granting what amounted to legal aid for poor people who had a case but not the means to pursue it. There is, though, no such case in this data set, the nearest being a case in 1662 where the plaintiff was described as a 'gentleman pauper'.[58]

Far from there being 'village revolts', it would seem that most of the 'riots' alleged in these cases were no such thing, but merely a necessary device used by the plaintiff to secure a hearing for his bill in the Duchy court. The alleged riot – whether riotously digging a marl pit, or turves, building a house, cutting down trees or even riotously fishing – seems generally to have involved no more than the presence of a number of men carrying the appropriate tools for the job in hand.[59] Even in those few cases where the violence was real enough, the protagonists more often than not were the lords, or their servants or tenants, taking direct action against a neighbouring lord, his servants or tenants. In other words, these riots were not 'popular' disturbances at all, let alone revolts. Instead, they were part and parcel of the manorial system and its associated power bases and relationships.

Taking all the cases together, accusations of riot or other violence occur in 30, plus possibly two others, out of the 96 cases. Such charges are relatively most common in the earliest period, with 42 per cent involving an accusation of riot. However, only one of these early cases appears to have involved an actual breach of the peace. In this case a fight had apparently broken out spontaneously when the plaintiff's reeve tried to stop the defendant's men from taking turves in what the defendant regarded as his enclosed turbary. The first blow seems in fact to have been struck by the reeve, not by the alleged 'rioters'.[60] In the second period 35 per cent of the cases involved accusations of riot, but that accusation was probably only justified in the modern sense of the word in a single case.[61] In the third period 17 per cent of the cases involved allegations of riot, but there were no such accusations at all in the final period.

The real significance in these figures lies in the fact that at a time when many men routinely carried knives or swords, as well as having ready access to bills, hooks and other potential weapons, there is in fact so very little evidence of their use in acts of aggression. Although it has been alleged that the Lancashire gentry of this period 'helped to ensure a low threshold of violence in an infamously unruly society', all the evidence from these cases suggests that the 'rule of law' was as applicable then as now.[62] While there can be no doubt that violence was

58 DL 4/106/9.

59 The riotous fishing accusation is in DL 4/35/31.

60 DL 3/39/H7.

61 DL 4/33/68.

62 J. K. Walton, *Lancashire: A Social History, 1558–1939* (Manchester, 1987), p. 7.

sometimes resorted to by lords and their servants, such direct action tended to initiate rather than settle the dispute. Protagonists were far more likely to meet each other in court than in an affray.

IV

For the larger-scale events, the first step towards improvement would have been the measuring and allotment of parcels, generally carried out by manorial officers of the respective lords – although there is some evidence for outside professionals being used.[63] In the early days the normal method of surveying was by perambulation and estimation. Yet the growing number of references to allocating plots of closely defined sizes must imply something more than just doing it by eye. In one case the waste had been measured by viewing and pacing.[64] In another a 'measuring prick' had been used, the land to be enclosed then being laid out with line and/or cords.[65] In two later cases a surveyor's chain was used.[66] Whatever the method used, measuring was a public process, designed to ensure fairness, and one which witnesses could readily recall many years later. Once measured, the aim was to allocate the land 'equall and indiferent ... according to the goodness of the common or lande'.[67] Sometimes the process involved casting lots as to who was to get which parcel, again the aim being to avoid disputes.[68]

Physical separation as such is not essential for a legal enclosure, but some form of marking-out and fencing-off probably normally took place at or very soon after any allocation or lord's licence to enclose. Ditches are specifically mentioned in about 15 cases, around or between as yet unimproved parcels; and where the enclosure was of mossland rather than the drier carr, heath or moor, ditching served a dual purpose – both physically separating the close while at the same time starting the improvement process by initiating drainage. Thus in Stalmine it was suggested that the unenclosed residue of the wastes could be made 'much more beneficiall and profitable by droweing the water from the same'.[69] It may be, though, that drainage activity was so normal as to be unremarkable, and

63 DL 4/36/20; DL 4/92/33.

64 DL 4/30/25.

65 DL 4/33/68.

66 DL 4/85/34; DL 4/92/33.

67 DL 4/85/34.

68 DL 4/33/49.

69 DL 4/95/10.

we only hear about it when unforeseen consequences arise, such as when a ditch dug around a new enclosure caused the flooding of the adjacent turbary.[70]

The subsequent process of turning poorly drained waste into productive farm land was lengthy and costly. Although enclosure might have been undertaken for pasture, involving little or no improvement, or for meadow or even for turbary, most of the large-scale enclosures found in these cases were intended for arable – specifically mentioned or implied in about a third of all the cases, although detail is rare. One particular technique for converting waste to arable which may have been widespread, though only hinted at in the documentation, was paring and burning – the skimming away or 'flaying' of the top layer of growing sods, which were then burned, the ashes being spread over the newly exposed soil or peat, as described by Dr Leigh.[71] Certainly this seems to have been the technique utilized in Bryning, where, following an enclosure of *c.*1587, the tenants were said to have 'for one yere nowe last past plowed upp burned and sowed with rye a greate part of the wastes in Kellemerghe'.[72]

The process of initiating reclamation by removing the turf layer can also be seen in other cases. In Worsley a parcel which had been 'made fyrme lande by digging of turves' was now bearing corn.[73] It is not always clear, though, whether this was a planned step or whether enclosure had merely followed the exhaustion of what had been a productive turbary. However, even where the improvement process had begun as the almost accidental by-product of some other activity, the creation of good agricultural land out of exhausted or decayed turbary or from ill-drained rough pasture was hard, expensive work, and was far from guaranteed success. Occasionally we hear accounts of the full sequence of activities involved, as in Chadderton, where the process involved:

> ridding, stubbing, grubbing, gutteringe and ffenceinge ... also marleinge of the same parcells and ploweing them up to make them fertile and profitable grounde.[74]

Yields, however, did not always live up to expectations, and we learn of an enclosure in Knowsley *c.*1636 concerning a barley crop, where:

> There was hopes of a good Cropp But it proved so poore and slender that it was not neither cold be cut downe or shorne but was to this deponents best remembrance all

70 DL 3/48/R5.

71 Leigh, *Natural history of Lancashire*, p. 65.

72 DL 4/33/49.

73 DL 4/37/30.

74 DL 4/85/35, interrogatories on behalf of Adam Taylor *et al.*, defendants.

> of the same corne sold for three shillings to one Thomas Houghton who confessed so muche and that he must be forced to pull it as they do flaxe and songle [glean] it.[75]

On the other hand elsewhere we hear of land which before improvement had been poor grazing not worth 2*s*. an acre *per annum*, but was now yielding crops of barley and oats valued at £4 an acre – 'yeeldes as good as most in Salford hundreth'.[76] The initial investment in stubbing, ridding and marling made in the late 1620s had amounted to £8 8*s*. 4*d*. an acre. Even allowing that the total investment – after adding in other costs such as the fine and annual rent, plus the outlay on seed, ploughing, sowing and reaping – probably ended up more like £16 than £8 an acre, nevertheless the tenant improver would still have achieved a fairly rapid pay-back on his initial investment, in perhaps as little as four years.

Although *worth* is perhaps generally taken to be the 'true value' – that is, how much the land would produce *per annum* after paying rent – in the interrogatories and depositions of the cases in the data set the word seems to have had a number of meanings, depending upon the context.[77] However, it is probably safe to assume that whatever is meant in a particular case, the same meaning applied both to the 'before' and 'after' figures, thus allowing us to establish the extent to which enclosure added value in this period. Thus one late case, referring back to an enclosure of *c*.1631, showed that some 3 or 4 acres which had at the time of enclosure not been worth 20*s*. a year were now (40 years later) worth £5 a year, a five-fold increase in value since enclosure.[78] Although such an increase in value through enclosure is impressive enough, a case in Knowsley, though a little more difficult to interpret, could imply a far more spectacular increase in value, whereby land which when it 'lay open and unenclosed ... was not then worth twelve pence *per annum*' (4*d*. per acre) was now (1663) worth 15*s*. an acre, 45 times its pre-enclosure value.[79]

In setting rents for new holdings there appears to have been a clear distinction in landlords' attitudes towards different types of enclosure, related partly to the scale of the activity and partly to whose initiative it was. Thus the rents charged by landlords for one-off licensed building on the waste were usually extremely modest in all periods, and a late-Tudor builder of a licensed cottage could expect to pay no more than 2*d*. to 4*d*. a year, perhaps equivalent to a day's wage for a farm labourer. Early small-scale intakes or retrospectively licensed enclosures

75 DL 4/107/7, deposition of John Aspinwall of Melling, husbandman.

76 DL 4/85/35, deposition of George Kenyon of Heap in Bury, husbandman.

77 C. Clay 'Lifeleasehold in the western counties, 1650–1750', *Agricultural History Rev.* 29 (1981), pp. 83–96.

78 DL 4/113/8.

79 DL 4/107/7.

appear to have had similarly modest rents, such as the 2*d.* an acre, plus service, recorded for land enclosed in the 1530s.[80] However, generous landlords and rents of pennies per acre were the exception, and a business-like approach was generally adopted to enclosure rents as far back as Henry VIII's reign. The earliest evidence for rents in this data set, a commission enquiring into encroachments, shows that 80 acres of Angerton Moss enclosed in the 1530s were averaging a fraction over a shilling a year per acre for 'errable lande and meadow'; while 20 acres of more recent encroachments, again arable and meadow, were assessed by the commissioners in 1546 to be 'worth to be latten every acre j^{s} iiij^{d}'.[81] In the following year a tenant in Penwortham who had made an encroachment of 7 acres on which no rent was currently being paid had offered to pay 4*d.* an acre – but the king's steward of the manor demanded a more realistic 2*s.* an acre.[82]

By the end of the sixteenth century and into the seventeenth, many landlords expected substantial returns per acre even on newly leased but still unimproved land. Thus lands in Upper Rawcliffe in 1657 were let for 21 years at 5*s.* an acre a year, while lands enclosed in Middleton *c.*1616 were let 'green side up' (that is unploughed, unimproved) for 6*s.* 8*d.* per acre per year.[83] Land in Stalmine, enclosed *c.*1610–20, was said in 1640 to be worth 8*s.* 'with the green syde up, and better if it be tilled'. Indeed in some parts, this same land was worth as much as 11*s.* an acre, again 'greene syde upp'.[84]

From the landlord's perspective, though, rents may often or even always have been less important than the fines, particularly where the landlord was motivated more by the desire for a lump sum *now* rather than long-term income. At the same time, low rents may reflect a recognition on the part of some lords that a heavy initial investment would be required by the tenant to improve the lands. Thus an enclosure in Stalmine in the 1590s generated fines of £1, £2 or £3 an acre, presumably dependent upon the quality of land; but rents generally seem to have been pitched at 1*s.* an acre *per annum*.[85] Another case, following the enclosure of Audenshaw Moss in *c.*1608–11, showed a wide range and mix of fines and rents, perhaps implying robust negotiation.[86] The best land had been assessed at fines of £6 an acre, payable over nine years, plus 1*s.* 6*d.* rent per year for 21 years. The poorest land raised a £2 fine and no rent for 21 years. Some other land paid no fine, but 2*s.* 6*d.* or 2*s.* 8*d.* an acre a year in rent. Taking them

80 DL 4/33/49.

81 DL 3/48/R5.

82 DL 3/50/P2.

83 DL 4/106/9; DL 4/74/20.

84 DL 4/95/10.

85 DL 4/73/28.

86 DL 4/71/26.

altogether, though, if, as is possible, some 100 acres were enclosed in this event, then at an average fine of, say, £4 the landlord, Lady Booth, would have received around £400 in fines. Before the enclosure, all she was getting from the same land was around £2 a year from selling turves.

Clearly, then, wasteland enclosure was capable of delivering substantial added value to both owner and occupier. However, unlike contemporary projects such as the draining of the Fens, the capital costs of improvement in lowland Lancashire, as seen from these cases, seem to have been borne largely, or even exclusively, by the tenant.[87] As a result, the landlord's costs appear to have been restricted essentially to two classes of expenditure: professional costs (lawyers, surveyors) and the cost of making boundaries (often in the form of ditches). Although detail is generally lacking, it is probable that lords finding themselves involved in a contested boundary or enclosure case could have been faced with costs of many tens of pounds. However, in terms of cost per acre, particularly where tens or hundreds of acres were involved, this was hardly excessive. In uncontested cases the investment on the part of the landlord would have been absolutely insignificant compared with that required from the incoming tenant to improve the land, which would have been from £2 an acre to £9 or more. Add to that an entry fine of up to £12 an acre, although possibly averaging £4 or so, then an initial outlay of anything from £6 to £20 *per acre* was required on the part of the tenant before the first crop could be planted.

Before enclosure the lord, as owner, was entitled to sell the product of the wastes, such as fuel, marl, building materials and the like. In certain restricted places there were commercial turbaries producing fuel for sale with a value to the lord of, say, 10*s*. an acre or more.[88] This, though, was rare, and it can be assumed that under normal circumstances the returns from pasture, turbary and the like on unenclosed manorial wastes added really very little to the lord's total annual income. Enclosed and divided, however, the land might be let for anything from a few pence to 5*s*. or more an acre. Moreover, although we do not hear of fines in every case, it is likely that the fines were a major consideration, generating an immediate lump sum of many hundreds, or perhaps in some cases thousands of pounds.[89] Such sums must have been very tempting indeed for Lancashire

---

87 The first Lancashire drainage project of anything like similar ambition to the Fens was the agreement drawn up in 1694 by a group of neighbouring landlords to drain Martin Mere. See Hale and Coney, *Martin Mere*, pp. 125ff.

88 DL 4/71/26 (1621, Ashton under Lyme). Turf was sold at 3*d*. per load and the lord was getting 40–50 loads per year per acre from *c*.4 acres of turbary = 10*s*. to 13*s*. an acre.

89 DL 4/71/26 (1621, Ashton under Lyme).

landlords who generally had incomes of less than £250 a year.[90] In addition, for the landlord there was always the prospect of taking back the land at the end of the lease, at which time the improved and productive land could have been let at a current market rate. Finally land which before enclosure could not be sold in parcels because others had usufruct rights in it, could, as several land, now be freely sold or mortgaged.

From the occupier's perspective, before enclosure the lowland wastes provided both rough grazing and moss rooms (turbary), worth perhaps a low number of pence per acre. After enclosure, where the land remained as pasture, the *product* may not have increased significantly, although there may have been additional, less quantifiable benefits to the tenant, such as improved quality of stock. However, where the improvement resulted in prime arable land, despite initial improvement costs and fines amounting to several pounds per acre, pay-back would have been achieved in a relatively low number of years, after which a regular annual income 'above all reprizes' of several pounds an acre could be hoped for. A new holding comprising a relatively small number of such acres could thus have produced a decent income for a seventeenth-century husbandman, of the order of £10–20 a year. On the other hand, there are reports of poor yields, and the same investment on poor land could produce a nil return. It is probable that quite a few of the parcels mentioned in these cases quietly returned to rough grazing at the end of the lease or before, having never paid back the tenant's investment. And even where the new holding produced a respectable living, there was one additional huge risk for the tenant: at the end of his lease he had no rights to compensation for his expenditure.

In addition to landlord and tenant, there were other beneficiaries of wasteland enclosure. Where there was an agreement involving sharing out the waste between a lord and his freeholders, the latter too acquired new land which they could work themselves or lease to others. Though their improvement costs would have been the same, not being faced with fines or rents other than their ancient rent, the freeholders' total investments would have been less than those of the tenants. Their rewards would have been as variable as those of the tenants. But while the potential for spectacular returns was as good for the freeholders as for the tenants, they had one big advantage over them: freeholders acquired the asset, and retained in perpetuity the benefits of their improvements.

A second group of beneficiaries was the tithe owners, rarely mentioned in discussions of enclosure, but under the *Statute of Tithes* (1549) newly enclosed

---

[90] B. G. Blackwood, 'The Catholic and Protestant gentry of Lancashire during the Civil War period', *Trans. Historic Society of Lancashire and Cheshire* 126 (1976), pp. 1–29.

land became liable for tithes after seven years.[91] The rectors and lay impropriators must have benefited hugely, with absolutely no risk or input required on their part. Finally there was a third group who should not be ignored – those who acquired homes on small parcels of former waste from which they could pursue their occupation as weaver, miner, potter or whatever. These settlers were not 'squatters', but licensed cottagers who gained a home at a cost in rent of only a day's wage or so a year. These too must be counted among the list of the beneficiaries of wasteland enclosure.

V

Using the evidence from the cases in the data set and making a number of fairly bold assumptions, it may be that some 40,000 acres of Lancashire's lowland waste were enclosed in the early modern period, representing perhaps a quarter of the waste which had existed in 1500 – equivalent to a 12 per cent increase in the farmland of the district, a significant part of which would have been enclosed for arable.[92] While perhaps not keeping pace with the population growth of the era, this would nevertheless have made a real contribution towards feeding those extra mouths.

The partitioning of the wastes would also have had an impact on the landscape, both real and imagined. What the inhabitants of Pilling said of their moss – 'Pilling Moss, like God's grace, is boundless' – was equally true of much of the rest of the county in 1500, both in terms of the seeming vast extent of the wastes and in their literal lack of boundaries.[93] Many wastes were genuine intercommons, but even where there were mere-stones or other boundary markers, uncertainty could exist, and ownership in many places was, at best, fuzzy. By 1600 or not long after, this situation had changed. A century of informal and formal boundary agreements had resulted in the partitioning of the great majority of the formerly boundless wastes, even where no actual enclosure had subsequently taken place. Add to that the extensive enclosure and it is probably no exaggeration to say that hundreds of miles of hedges and ditches, fences and rails now divided up this formerly empty landscape. In its place, a new landscape was emerging, a landscape of rectangular fields in many ways indistinguishable from a later parliamentary enclosure landscape.

---

91 *Statutes of the Realm*, vol. 4 pt 1, p. 55, 2 & 3 Edward VI, c. 13, An Act for payment of Tithes.

92 Shannon, 'Approvement and Improvement in Early-Modern England'.

93 De Rance, *Geology of the Country adjoining the coasts of south-west Lancashire*, p. 80.

The enclosure model found in this district, based upon partitioning, approving and improving the waste, often for arable, peaked in the late-Elizabethan period but appears to have almost completely disappeared by the 1630s. Research elsewhere in England has shown enclosure, including wasteland enclosure, generally increasing in the seventeenth century and perhaps peaking in the post-Restoration years. In lowland Lancashire, though, it may be that by the 1630s population growth had slowed, inflation had stopped and the impact of the Little Ice Age was beginning to be felt in the mosslands. In the absence of capital-intensive projects, it may also be that the technological limit had been reached, and what *could* be achieved by the individual tenant with spade and plough had by then *been* achieved, as local landowners settled for a modest reward for no risk rather than undertake a high-risk project – a strategy which the later problems surrounding the drainage of Martin Mere perhaps showed to have been the right one.[94] It may even be that, with a quarter of the original waste having disappeared into enclosures between *c.*1500 and 1650, the act of approvement itself was becoming more difficult to achieve, requiring as it did the leaving of sufficient pasture in the residue. However, for whatever reason, around or just before the time of the Civil War the enclosure phase which had been associated with, and driven by, partition and approvement came to an end.

---

[94] Andrew Gritt, 'Making good land from bad: the drainage of west Lancashire, *c.*1650–1850', *Rural Hist.* 19 (2008), pp. 1–27. See also Hale and Coney, *Martin Mere*, pp. 125ff.

Chapter 7

'A Country Life': Sir Hamon Le Strange of Hunstanton in Norfolk, 1583–1654

Elizabeth Griffiths

This chapter is about 'a country life'[1] and what it meant to a gentleman living on his Norfolk estate in the first half of the seventeenth century. It is based on the experience of Sir Hamon Le Strange of Hunstanton (1583–1654), who is best known in academic circles as the husband of Lady Alice (1585–1656) – the author of a remarkable series of household accounts, and the subject of a major research project.[2] While Hamon is remembered in local histories for leading the defence of King's Lynn against the Parliamentary forces in 1643, Alice is credited with running a substantial household, managing the estate and for being the sober brains behind this leading gentry family whose male members had a reputation for dashing and reckless behaviour.[3] The vast archive she left is testimony to her role. However, the impression conveyed by the documents is misleading. Sir Hamon was, in his own time, a renowned bibliophile, musician, sportsman, soldier, theologian, architect, engineer, agriculturist, educator and family man. As a very young man, he appeared destined for a life at court; famously he and Sir Robert Carey rode to Scotland to inform James VI of the death of Queen Elizabeth, for which he received a knighthood. But for some unknown reason, on his marriage to Alice in 1604 he retired from royal service and opted for a life in the country. However, he did not entirely forsake the capital. The performance of public duties was central to the identity of a seventeenth-century country gentleman and often required attendance in London. He was elected MP for Norfolk in the parliaments of 1614 and 1621 and in 1625 represented Castle Rising; locally he served as a Justice of the Peace, colonel of the militia, high sheriff in 1608 and from 1625 as a deputy lieutenant.

1 Ben Jonson, 'The Praises of a Country Life', in A. Fowler (ed.), *The Country House Poem* (Edinburgh, 1994), pp. 70–73.

2 J. C. Whittle and E. M. Griffiths, *Consumption and Gender in the Early Seventeenth-Century Household* (Oxford, forthcoming).

3 R. W. Ketton-Cremer, 'Sir Hamon Le Strange and His Sons', in *A Norfolk Gallery* (London, 1948), pp. 56–94; Ketton-Cremer, *Norfolk in the Civil War* (London, 1969).

Interludes in London were clearly no hardship, providing opportunities for dealing with financial and legal concerns and, more particularly, for socializing and shopping for luxury goods – one of Sir Hamon's weaknesses.

In his pursuit of learning and excellence, Sir Hamon was truly a Renaissance man; what makes him unusual is the evidence he left of putting his knowledge into practice, whether it was designing watercourses and buildings, specifying the style and materials for his new coaches, ordering new uniforms for the militia, playing the viols, collecting and writing books, hunting with hawks or commissioning portraits of his wife and himself. We know about his beliefs, interests and activities from the books he wrote, the library he assembled and the memoranda books he kept – full of scribbled notes, sketches, measured diagrams, details of building projects and reminders to himself.[4] From these documents, drawings and jottings we see a man with surprisingly strong Calvinist convictions and a clear vision about how to order his life and engage with his environment.

The memoranda books show the thinking and planning behind Alice's meticulous field books and estate accounts, the newly commissioned surveys and the notebooks of their son, Sir Nicholas (1604–55), who undertook the drainage of the coastal marshes at Hunstanton, Heacham and Holme in the 1630s and 1640s.[5] Working as a team, the family rebuilt their estate 'out of the ground', as Alice explained in her summary of the family finances.[6] Systematically, they tackled the medieval hall, the decayed farmhouses, the neglected pastures, the barren heaths and the malarial marshland. Without a doubt, Alice played a key role in this process, modernizing the estate records, generating useful information, controlling expenditure and ensuring that Sir Hamon and Sir Nicholas had sufficient funds to pay for their schemes. Women were not unknown to estate management, particularly as widows, but few performed the task on this scale and with this level of aptitude, or worked so closely alongside their husbands. Sir Hamon had the utmost respect for her abilities and encouraged her at every turn. On the front of the fifth Household book, romantically concealed under a flap, we find a message 'who shall finde a virtuous woman for her price is above pearls, the very heart of her husband trusteth in her

---

4 All documents cited are in the Norfolk Record Office (NRO). LEST/NE1; Memoranda books: LEST/Q38, Q37, Q36.

5 Maps: LEST/AO1; OC1; OC2; OB2; OB5, OB6. and see also n. 47 below. Field Books: LEST/BH1–2; EH4–5, EH10; IC55, IC58; DH19, DH22, DH23. Alice's Estate Accounts: LEST/BK7–9, BK15; EK4–8; IC64, IC65; IB84, IB85, IB89, IB90. Sir Nicholas's notebooks. LEST/KA6, KA9, KA10, KA24.

6 LEST/P10. Alice's household accounts are LEST/P6–P10.

... she overseeth the way of her household and eateth not the brede of idleness'.[7] In his will he thanked her for 'ever incessant industry, in straynes of knowledge above her sex, to the just, faithfull and laudable advantage and advancement of my estate'.[8] In these few words, he expressed not only his love and gratitude to Alice, but also his philosophy of life. For him, the management of his estate was an intellectual and productive endeavour with a moral and even godly purpose.

The idea of this chapter is to draw attention to Sir Hamon Le Strange as an estate improver and his role as leader, thinker and project manager. We recognize in him that rare commodity: a blue sky thinker with the commitment, flair, technical expertise and management skills to carry out his ideas. But where did this ability and purpose come from? What motivated him and shaped his mental outlook? How far was he influenced by the books contained in his library? We hear about culture inspiring cultivation, but there is little empirical evidence of this actually happening on the ground. At Hunstanton this interaction appears to have been a two-way process, with Sir Hamon and Sir Nicholas using their knowledge of science and mathematics to effect improvement; and at the same time being shaped and influenced by their environment, family traditions and local custom. How did they balance these sometimes conflicting concerns? How far did Sir Hamon's approach differ from his forebears and successors? Can we detect those changes in language and attitude to the land identified by McRae in his work on husbandry manuals?[9] Space prevents us considering Sir Hamon's passion for music, theology and politics, but we understand that his relationship with the land and landscape was part of a much broader philosophy as to what constituted a country life.

I

Sir Hamon was very much a product of his history and locality. Born in 1583, he was the scion of an ancient Norfolk family whose association with Hunstanton dates back to the early twelfth century. The first Sir Hamon, a hero of the Battle of Crecy, built the original medieval gatehouse, while his great-grandfather, Sir Thomas Le Strange (*c.*1490–1545), served Henry VIII at the Field of the Cloth of Gold. Later, Sir Thomas benefited greatly from the dissolution of the

---

7 LEST/P8.

8 LEST/AE8.

9 A. McRae, 'Husbandry Manuals and the Language of Improvement', in M. Leslie and T. Raylor (eds), *Culture and Cultivation in Early Modern England: Writing and the Land* (Leicester, 1992); A. McRae, *God Speed the Plough: The Representation of Agrarian England, 1500–1660* (Cambridge, 1996).

monasteries and secured the most prestigious offices in the county. But he never lost his commitment to his estate and neighbourhood. This was the central point made by Oestmann in his account of the Le Strange family and the village of Hunstanton in the first half of the sixteenth century.[10] Through a benevolent farming system, Sir Thomas worked in harmony with the village community and accommodated their divergent interests. The most striking and recurring feature was his protection of smallholders from large commercial farmers. By his generosity and good lordship he averted conflict and earned the loyalty and gratitude of his locality. Significantly, when other Norfolk landowners suffered at the hands of their tenants protesting against enclosure, the Le Stranges were left unscathed.[11]

This close relationship between lord and village owed much to the geography of the area. Hunstanton, situated on the coast, supported a rich and diverse economy based on land and sea. The shoreline of the Wash at Hunstanton is shallow; at low tide the sea retreats up to a mile from the shore, revealing a long stretch of sandy beach ideal for mussel gathering and inshore fishing. Fishing rights to the sea fisheries, dating from the Domesday Book, were also available to smallholders. Inland, coastal marshland provided ample summer grazing for cow-keepers, while the light sandy brecks over to the east afforded scope for large farmers to extend their corn and sheep farming enterprises. Sir Thomas, like Sir Hamon, leased his lands and foldcourses, and moved in and out of farming as it suited him – grazing sheep, setting up dairy and cattle units but rarely cultivating grain, which he left to the villagers. So, there was room for all to prosper. With the marshland and resources of the sea and shore, Hunstanton men were able to pursue and combine a range of activities, which included wild fowling, reed gathering and pasturing as well as more traditional by-employment such as brewing, building, crafts and textiles. This happy state of affairs seems too good to be true, but in fact the Le Stranges were not entirely altruistic in their approach. It paid them to tolerate and even encourage these arrangements as they benefited from the ready pool of labour and the goods and services they provided: this stimulated a vibrant local economy in this remote corner of Norfolk and secured social stability.

At the heart of this economy was the demand generated by the Le Strange household. Oestmann and Whittle have both described the lord's household as a market, where the family relied on local provisioning by a network of small peasant suppliers, and sold their own surpluses of corn, livestock, dairy products

---

10 C. Oestmann, *Lordship and Community: The Lestrange Family and the Village of Hunstanton, Norfolk in the First Half of the Sixteenth Century* (Woodbridge, 1994).

11 A point made to me in conversation with Professor Andy Wood.

and building materials.[12] They travelled further afield only for luxuries, specialist building work and furniture making. This was the type of household, estate and community inherited by Sir Hamon when he came of age in 1604. It was a conservative but productive type which, McRae has observed, reinforced the pre-existent order on the estate yet permitted new possibilities and development.[13] Custom clearly did not preclude improvement; in fact it played a prominent part in promoting economic success and social stability at Hunstanton. Sir Hamon remained firmly wedded to this paternalistic philosophy. Where he differed from his forebears was in the scale of his reforms, and the planning and thought that went into them. The remainder of this chapter will show how he reconciled a system rooted in custom with his new schemes for improvement, inspired by his learning and forced upon him by sheer economic necessity.

II

The late sixteenth and early seventeenth centuries have long been identified as a period of intense economic and social stress, marked by an acute demographic crisis which placed huge pressure on traditional agriculture. The open-field system, designed for self-sufficiency, could no longer meet the demand of the rising population for food and resources; farmers had to make better use of the land available to them.[14] Rising prices created opportunities for food producers; but if farmers and landowners were to benefit from the growing market they needed to intensify their farming regimes, expand cultivation, modernize their procedures and place their business affairs on a commercial footing. These changes often challenged custom and proved controversial in the sixteenth century. Even as prices soared in the 1580s and 1590s, Elizabeth I and her elderly advisers baulked at such ideas, preferring to live off old rents and at peace with their tenants in the interest of political and social stability.[15] James I had no such qualms. From a younger generation and a different cultural background, which placed more value on improvement and increased productivity, he actively promoted agrarian reform. He himself set the pace with his radical reorganization of the Crown lands, so badly neglected by Elizabeth. Surveyors, lawyers and agents were engaged to prepare it for sale and development. The

---

12 Oestmann, *Lestrange Family*; Whittle and Griffiths, *Consumption and Gender*.

13 McRae, 'Husbandry Manuals', p. 37.

14 M. Turner, J. Beckett and B. Afton, 'Agricultural sustainability and open-field farming in England, *c.*1650–1830', *International J. Agricultural Sustainability* 1 (2003), pp. 124–40.

15 R. W. Hoyle (ed.), *The Estates of the English Crown, 1558–1640* (Cambridge, 1992), p. 436.

Crown itself rarely had the funds to invest directly in the land; its role was to strip away feudal restrictions and legal impediments and then sell, with the prospect of improvement. This shift in attitudes to the land led by James I was of the utmost significance. By its example, the Crown permitted the wholesale commercialization of land management and encouraged landowners to do the same. From the 1600s, they could proceed with their surveys, acquisitions and reorganization in a thoroughly professional way, in the knowledge that their actions met the approval of the Crown and were in accordance with the prevailing ethos of the court, elite society and educated circles. Sir Hamon's uncle and guardian, Sir Henry Hobart, was an expert in such matters; he served on the Exchequer Commissions and was later appointed Chancellor to the Prince of Wales, in succession to Sir Francis Bacon, another kinsman of the Le Stranges. Between 1596 and 1625 he purchased a vast estate in Norfolk by using his legal acumen and a policy of local surveys designed to identify the 'scope for improvement'.[16]

The message of improvement, advanced by the Crown, was reinforced by the literature of the day. Increasingly, writers, poets and scholars espoused the case for agrarian reform. Low argues that the translation of Virgil in 1589 proved a turning point.[17] In the 1590s Edmund Spenser revised the aristocratic idea of leisure and grace to one that valued effort, persistence and hard-won achievement.[18] Virtue, for the first time, was equated with productive labour. In the context of the war with Spain, the agricultural reformer was presented as hero and patriot. Spenser also stressed the civilizing power of agriculture in taming empty and uncultivated lands, and the need for right-minded Protestants to lead the British people to a new and better society. Sir Hamon was very much of this world and mindset. His guardians and trustees included not only Sir Henry Hobart but also Sir Henry Spelman, the renowned antiquarian and jurist, and Sir John Peyton, the Elizabethan soldier, courtier and associate of the Earl of Leicester and the Sidneys of Penshurst – celebrated in Ben Jonson's famous country house poem.[19]

Economic imperatives and the cultural climate of the day necessitated a new approach to estate management, but it is clear that Sir Hamon also experienced

[16] E. M. Griffiths, 'Sir Henry Hobart: A new hero of Norfolk agriculture?', *Agricultural History Rev.* 46 (1998) pp. 15–34.

[17] A. Low, *The Georgic Revolution* (Princeton, 1985), pp. 13–98.

[18] Low's references to Spenser include *The Faerie Queen* (1596), a copy of which Sir Hamon had in his library.

[19] *Oxford Dictionary of National Biography* (*ODNB*), 'Spelman, Sir Henry (1563–1641), 'Peyton, Sir John (1544–1630); Ben Jonson, 'To Penshurst', in Fowler (ed.), *Country House Poem*, pp. 53–62.

and brought to the task a most unusual upbringing and education. Orphaned at the age of eight, he and his estate passed into the care of trustees who cared for his affairs for more than 10 years. The trustees included not only Peyton and Spelman but also the family lawyer, Richard Stubbe of Sedgeford. These men belonged to a close network committed to the family and locality; in 1602 they arranged Sir Hamon's marriage to Stubbe's daughter Alice.[20] Sir Hamon and Alice were both cousins and neighbours. Alice's mother, Anne Goding, was first married to Sir Hamon's uncle, John Le Strange of Sedgeford, and their daughter Elinor married Henry Spelman in 1590; their family, brought up at Holme Parsonage, often feature in the household accounts acquiring books for their cousin's new library. In her widowhood and settled on her Sedgeford estate, Anne Le Strange married Richard Stubbe in 1582; their daughter Alice was born in 1585 and inherited the Sedgeford estate from her father when he died in 1619. Both Spelman and Stubbe acted as mentors to the young boy, and later steered the young married couple through their early difficult years. Sir Henry Hobart and Sir John Peyton – connected to Sir Hamon's maternal family, the Bells of Stow Bardolph – performed a more distant role, although the relationship with the younger Bells and Hobarts remained close. Following Spelman's example, Sir Hamon attended Cambridge and entered the court; and then, like his kinsman, he opted for the country life, improving his estate and cultivating his mind – a decision commended by James I and entirely in tune with the spirit with the times.[21]

III

Alice Le Strange maintained household books and general disbursement books throughout her married life. These include summaries of her receipts, allowing a detailed assessment of the Le Strange's income and expenditure to be made. They form the basis of the figures and are presented in summary form in the appendix. Figure 7.1 shows the Le Strange's receipts from 1607 to 1652, highlighting and explaining those years in which receipts were especially high.

Sir Hamon and his young wife started their long married life from a relatively low base. At the end of her first experimental book of receipts and disbursements

[20] LEST/A66–72.

[21] James I, 'Counsel for Ladies and Gentlemen', in Fowler (ed.), *Country House Poem*, p. 101; L. Marcus, 'Politics and Pastoral: Writing the Court on the Countryside', in K. Sharpe and P. Lake (eds), *Culture and Politics in Early Stuart England* (Basingstoke, 1994), pp. 139–59.

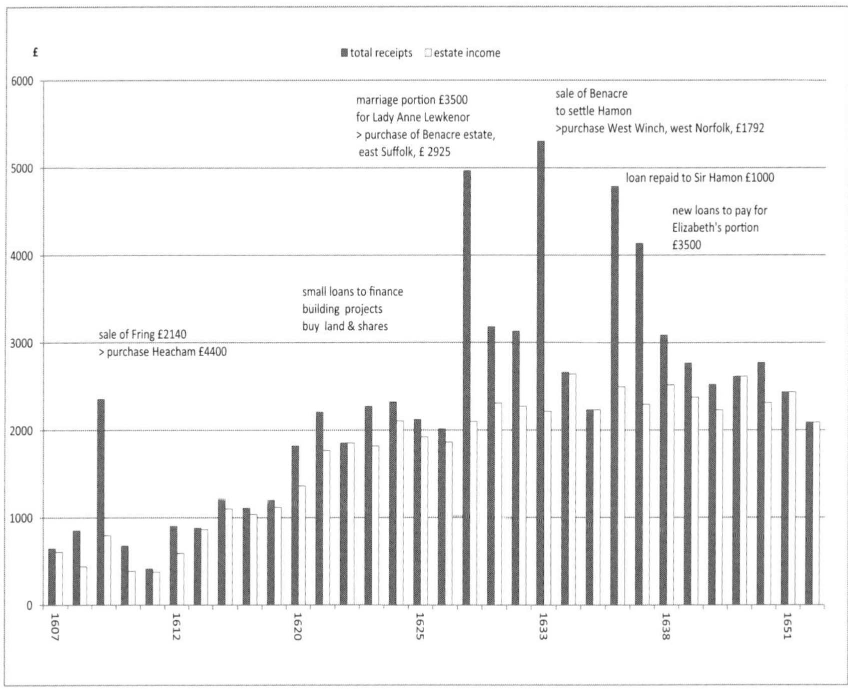

Figure 7.1 Summary of receipts, 1607–53

(1610–13), Alice calculated their yearly income at £905.[22] From this sum Sir Hamon paid an annuity of £160 to Lady Cope, the widow of his father Sir Nicholas Le Strange, and a further £140 to Richard Stubbe, leaving them with £605 to cover the cost of 'the house'. Alice estimated this at £264, with a further £60 for 'livery and wages'. In 1616 Hamon made 'a note of his revenue', which then totalled £1,247.[23] The higher figure was based on his estimate for Hunstanton of £331 but the receipts never reached this figure, indicating that while significant improvements were made at Hunstanton in those early years, Sir

22 Richard Stubbe collected the rents before handing over to Alice in 1613 'pennyworth paid into the hands of Lady Alice Le Strange within time of this account as appear in the said Lady Alice's receipt book', LEST/R9. Alice valued Hunstanton at £120, Heacham Manor £215, Calyes £120, Great Ringstead £120, Barrett Ringstead (Parva) £100 and Gressenhall £230 – making a total of £905.

23 LEST/Q38, In 1616 Sir Hamon noted revenue from Hunstanton as £331, Hunstanton parsonage £51, the park and the other ground in my own use £60; Heacham Lewis (Manor) £226, Calyes £124, Ringstead Great £111, Ringstead Parva £114, Gressenhall £230 – making a total of £1,247.

Hamon may have diverted some of the income into his own pocket. In 1617 the receipts from the estate, recorded by Alice, amounted to no more than £1,100.[24] In a later book of disbursements, Alice provides a retrospective summary of the family finances, including their debts from 1632 onwards (Figure 7.2).[25] In this she noted that the trustees had left substantial debts and neglected the estate:

> my husband was left in debt by his father's executors, with money due to his uncle Roger Le Strange £1500. He was left neyther household stuffe nor stock and his chief house halfe built and all his fearme houses in such decay so he hath built most of them out of the ground.[26]

Alice also felt hard done by by her father. On two facing pages she set out how his estate had been settled between her half-sister and herself, concluding that she had received substantially less in land and money – £5,142 compared to Dionisia's £6,377. However, much of her half-sister's portion was used to repay the debts of her husband, Sir Henry Yelverton of Rougham, while Alice received assets in land, property and goods. Significantly, the £1,000 Stubbe paid Sir John Peyton for the release of Sir Hamon's wardship on Alice's marriage was paid out of her inheritance, which may partly explain her grievance against the trustees.[27] This apparently unequal treatment did not, however, disturb a close relationship between father, daughter and son-in-law. The entries in the household accounts show the old man taking a keen interest in their growing family, lending them money, collecting rents, giving the grandchildren sheep and offering advice. However, despite their efforts the couple were never free of debt, as can be seen in Figure 7.2.

Their experience, reinforced by the Yelvertons, drove Sir Hamon and Alice to improve the management of the estate. Norfolk in the early seventeenth century provided countless examples of families unable or unwilling to adapt to economic necessity, and of enterprising gentlemen, often lawyers, ready to take advantage of their predicament. Notable among these were Sir Edward Coke, Sir Nicholas Bacon and Sir Henry Hobart, who capitalized on the failure of leading families like the Howards, the Cleres, the Heydons and indeed the Yelvertons. The Le Stranges were determined not to be among the latter group. Success was not, however, confined to lawyers and high officeholders able to deploy vast amounts of capital. Another group of well-established families,

---

[24] Alice's second Household Book (1614–16) does not survive, so we cannot make a direct comparison for 1616 between Sir Hamon's calculation and Alice's receipts.

[25] LEST/P10.

[26] LEST/P10.

[27] LEST/A73.

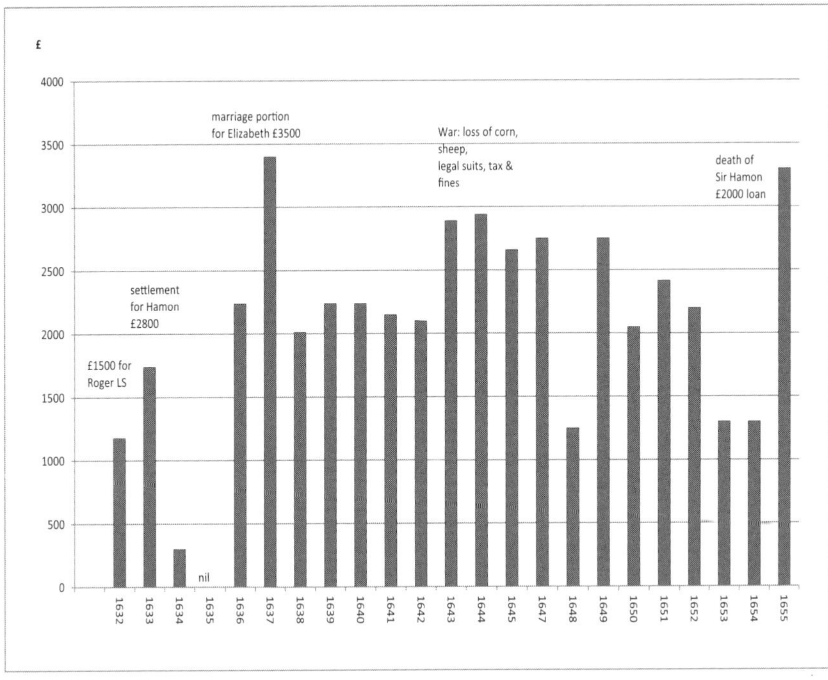

Figure 7.2 Level of debt, 1632–55

including the Windhams of Felbrigg and the Townshends of Raynham, showed that estates could be enlarged and incomes increased by careful marriages, good management and the profits of Norfolk agriculture. This was the path chosen by Sir Hamon and Lady Alice. From the start they followed the example of their industrious kinsmen and neighbours, and were dismissive of those, like the Yelvertons, who were unable or unwilling to change. In their battle for survival, books formed an important part of their armoury.

Books played a central role in Sir Hamon's life. The library catalogue – with entries dating from the 1590s when he lived under Spelman's guidance, to the early 1700s as his successors continued to add to it – lists nearly 3,000 volumes, making it one of the most important book collections in the country.[28] One of

[28] Sir Hamon's library consisted of 2,659 volumes of printed books and 37 manuscripts. The total compares with 2,448 titles owned by Sir Thomas Browne, the philosopher, J. Finch, *A Catalogue of the Libraries of Sir Thomas and Dr. Edward Browne, His Son* (Leiden, 1986); Sir Edward Coke's library of 1,237 volumes, W. O. Hassall (ed.), *A Catalogue of the Library of Sir Edward Coke* (Yale, 1950); Sir Thomas Knyvett's 1,400 volumes and 70 MSS, D. McKitterick, *The Library of Sir Thomas Knyvett of Ashwellthorpe, c.1539–1618* (Cambridge, 1978). The same

his first projects was to construct a library to house the growing collection.[29] In the manner of the true bibliophile, he arranged his books by subject, with the shelving numbered and marked with letters. The catalogue also contains an index of authors, giving the reader easy access to the different titles associated with particular authors. This level of organization is most unusual, if not unique for the period, indicating that he was acting under expert guidance. The library was clearly designed for a purpose and meant to be used. Its range was extensive. As we would expect, religious works dominate, with literally hundreds of books of sermons, Bibles and devotional works intended to prepare one for the godly life. The ancient classics feature extensively, as do contemporary works by Spenser, Sydney, Jonson and Bacon espousing the virtues of country living.[30] Warming to the task, Sir Hamon acquired every sort of self-improvement manual, covering topics such as how to run a household, improve an estate, design houses, plant trees, make a garden, concoct medicines, bring up children and acquire the accomplishments of a gentleman.[31] The description in the catalogue suggests a close familiarity with certain volumes: for example, two copies of 'Gouge, his Domesticall Duties' (1634) and 'Will Gouge his whole Armour of God: 8 Treatises of Domesticall Duties 1622' and 'Crook's Anatomy' (1616).[32] Sir Hamon also had a particular interest in astronomy and mathematics, buying not only books but all sorts of instruments, globes and surveying equipment to

volume tells us that Sir Henry Spelman owned 400 volumes. In comparison, Sir Roger Townshend owned a meagre 300 volumes, R. J. Fehrenbach and E. S. Leedham-Green (eds), *Private Libraries in Renaissance England* (Marlborough, 1992). My thanks to C. Wilkin-Jones of the Norwich Millennium Library for these references.

29 LEST/Q38.

30 The catalogue includes E. Spenser, *The faerie queene* (1596); P. Sydney, *The Countess of Pembrokes Arcadia* (1590); B. Jonson and W. Hole, *The workes of Ben Jonson* (1616); F. Bacon, *Of the advancement and proficience of learning* (1640); F. Bacon, *Sylva sylvarum* (1627).

31 For example, W. Gouge, *Of domesticall duties eight treatises* (1622); W. Lawson, *A new orchard and garden* (1618); T. Elyot, *The castell of health* (1595); T. Cogan, *The haven of health* (1636); T. Vicary, *The English mans treasure* (1613); J. Gerard. *The herbal or Generall historie of plants* (1633); P. Barrough, *The method of physick* (1596); W. Clever, *The flower of phisicke* (1590); W. Langham, *The garden of health* (1597); J. Goeurot, *The regiment of life, whereunto is added a treatyse of the pestilience, with the book of children, latelye corrected and enlarged by Thomas Phayer* (1546); P. Scot, *A fathers advice or last will to his son* (1620); R. Brathwaite, *The good wife or a rare one amongst women* (1618); H. Peacham, *The compleat gentleman* (1627); G. Markham, *Cavelarice, or The English Horseman* (1607); J. Berners, *Hawking, hunting and fishing* (1586); and G. Turbeville, *The booke of falconrie or hawking* (1611).

32 Gouge, *Of domesticall duties*; H. Crook, *Mikrokosmographia. A description of the body of man* (1616).

measure his estate.[33] The husbandry titles are relatively few, but include Barnaby Googe's translation of Conrad Heresbach, nine volumes of Gervase Markham and, most particularly, Richard Surflete's translation of *Maison Rustique*, which inspired Markham's work and reflects most closely Sir Hamon's holistic strategy for his estate.[34]

Joan Thirsk was surprised to realize how zealously the English read *Maison Rustique* or *The Countrey Farme* (1616), and how fully they digested it.[35] This all-encompassing work contained not only a full description of farming methods, but also advice on everything that was required for the creation of a beautiful and productive unit. It was divided into seven books. The first contains sections on farm buildings, the duties of the farmer, the housewife and farm servants; the second concerns the making of gardens for the kitchen, physick and pleasure; the third, the planting of fruit trees; the fourth, the making of meadows and fishponds; the fifth, the measuring and cultivation of arable grounds; the sixth the growing of vines; and the seventh the making of a warren, the planting of trees, methods of imparking and aspects of hunting and hawking. Only in the making of wine, betraying the French origin of the book, did the Le Stranges diverge from this model. Sir Hamon's preoccupation with health – he collected far more medical books than manuals on agriculture – and Alice's growing of herbs, processing of food and making of medicines indicate that this volume played an important part in their lives. It also suggests that they were motivated by a genuine desire to create a consciously healthy lifestyle. The French authors were both doctors of physick, and clearly made the link between farming, food and good health. The Le Stranges went to great lengths to create the type of productive and healthy environment described in the book.

---

33 Ptolemy, *The compost of Ptholomeus, prince of astronomye, very necessary, vtile and profitable for all such as desire the knowledge of the science of astronomye* (1562). Sir Hamon's edition is undated, but was in Latin.

34 C. Heresbach, *Foure bookes of husbandry ... newely Englished and increased by Barnabe Googe* (1586); G. Markham, *Farewell to husbandry or the enrichment of all sorts of barren and steril grounds in our kingdome* (1638). For the *Maison Rustique*, see the next footnote.

35 Conversation with Joan Thirsk. *Maison Rustique*, as the description of the book states, was originally 'Compyled in the French tongue by Charles Stevens and John Liebault, Doctors of Physicke. And now translated into English by Richard Surflet, practitioner in phsicke. Now newly reviewed, corrected and augmented with divers large editions out of the works Serres his Agriculture, Vinet his Maison champestre, French. Albyterio in Italie and Spaine, reconciled and made to agree with ours here in England by Gervase Markham.' Sir Hamon acquired this edition which Markham brought out 'to suit English conditions'; this might explain why he had no copies of Markham's two earlier works, *The English Husbandman* (1613) and *The English Housewife* (1615), both based on *The Countrey Farme*.

Their concern with health may well have been connected to their location on the coastal marshes. Hunstanton Hall lies in a hollow among numerous slow-moving watercourses. Such areas were notoriously unhealthy, plagued by malaria and other water-borne diseases, as the authors of *The Countrey Farme* noted.[36] Mary Dobson has shown how death rates in marshland parishes were often four times higher than in those parishes out of the range of the mosquito.[37] Contemporaries were acutely aware of the unhealthiness of marshland. John Norden described the low places about the creeks which gave rise to the most cruel quatern fever.[38] Sir Francis Bacon, who knew this area well, particularly noted the problems with salt marshes: 'Marshes and other Fenny places that are overflowed with salt tides are unwholesomer than those overflowed with fresh land water'; the 'unhealthful ayre' shortened men's lives.[39] In the 1580s and 1590s his step-brother, Nathaniel, undertook an extensive programme of drainage, dredging and enclosure further along the north Norfolk coast at Stiffkey.[40] Today we associate marsh drainage with the destruction of natural habitats, resources and traditional lifestyles, but before the advent of modern medicine, perceptions would have been very different. In Sir Hamon's day it represented improvement in its fullest sense, facilitating not only the expansion of cultivation but also offering the prospect of a longer and healthier life to those living in areas blighted by disease.

From their actions, it looks as if *The Countrey Farme* played an important role in their strategy, providing technical information and advice; but we do not know for sure. The library does not survive so we cannot point to annotated volumes as proof of their use. However, the notebooks contain references to texts and almanacs, sometimes with passages copied out – for example, on interest rates, weights and measures and tithing tables – indicating an ongoing dialogue with the texts listed in the catalogue. But no direct reference to *The Countrey Farme* has been noted. The influence of various texts can also be seen in the organization of the notebooks which appear with indexes and come to resemble manuals in their own right. Those of Sir Nicholas contain instructions

---

36 Houses built in 'waterie and marsh places' will impair 'your owne health as also the health of those of your family ... especially in winter', *Countrey Farme*, p. 14.

37 M. Dobson, *Contours of Death and Disease in Early Modern England* (Cambridge, 1997), pp. 287–367.

38 J. Norden, *The Surveyor's Dialogue* (1607). The fifth book deals with the benefits of marsh drainage.

39 F. Bacon, *The historie of life and death with observations naturall and experimental for prolonging life* (1638).

40 A. H. Smith and G. M. Baker (eds), *The Papers of Nathaniel Bacon of Stiffkey*, III, *1586–95* (Norfolk Record Soc. 53, 1990), pp. xvi–xvii.

to the reader directing them to refer to a certain text. On the cost of developing marshland, he writes: 'Look a little back and there you shall finde the total sums of expense every year under the title or heads of every general work, which sums agree precisely, and were drawn out of the epitome of the abstract which containes all the particulars of this book.' Later, he explains his calculations: 'I wrought all the uses by the table of interest in Ponds Almanacke for 1638.'[41]

There is plenty of evidence that the notebooks were used – as was surely intended – by later generations. In one of Sir Hamon's memoranda books, his great-grandson, another Sir Nicholas, explains:

> This book I found in ye old evidence house w[i]th a decayed and worm eaten cover thrown by and neglected. But upon perusal meeting with severall things relating to building and every material and likely to prove of use, I put an index or table to that part of ye Booke, such other observations as might possibly prove of service and convenience to refer to upon occasion.[42]

Later, he noted: 'An index of ye several things in this part of this book. This mark * prefixt signifies the same to be found at ye other end of the book under Sir Hamon's hand'. His purpose is quite clear – he was constructing a manual of information about the estate for the benefit of future generations. Most usefully, he drew up a table summarizing the repairs and building initiated by Sir Hamon from 1617 to 1651, updating it and including his own improvements undertaken between 1687 and 1721; this provides a complete picture of the building on the estate from 1617 to 1721.[43] Figure 7.3, which shows Sir Hamon's expenditure on building projects and repairs between 1606 and 1653, indicates the scale of the enterprise. Similar updates can be found for the drainage schemes, the administration of the 'Hunston Fishery' and the handling of whales on Hunstanton beach. Referring directly to Sir Hamon's observations of whales, and other written texts, he added his own ideas and sketches, and included detailed diagrams for the construction of new fishing nets. Sir Nicholas also updated the field books, commissioned new surveys of the estate and continued the habit of buying books and adding to the library catalogue. Clearly, Sir Hamon used his library, encouraged his children and grandchildren to do the same and established a tradition of reading, using and writing books in the family. So, although we have no books, we know that they used them and understood the role that information played in the modernization of a landed estate.

---

41 LEST/KA 6.

42 LEST/Q38.

43 LEST/Q38.

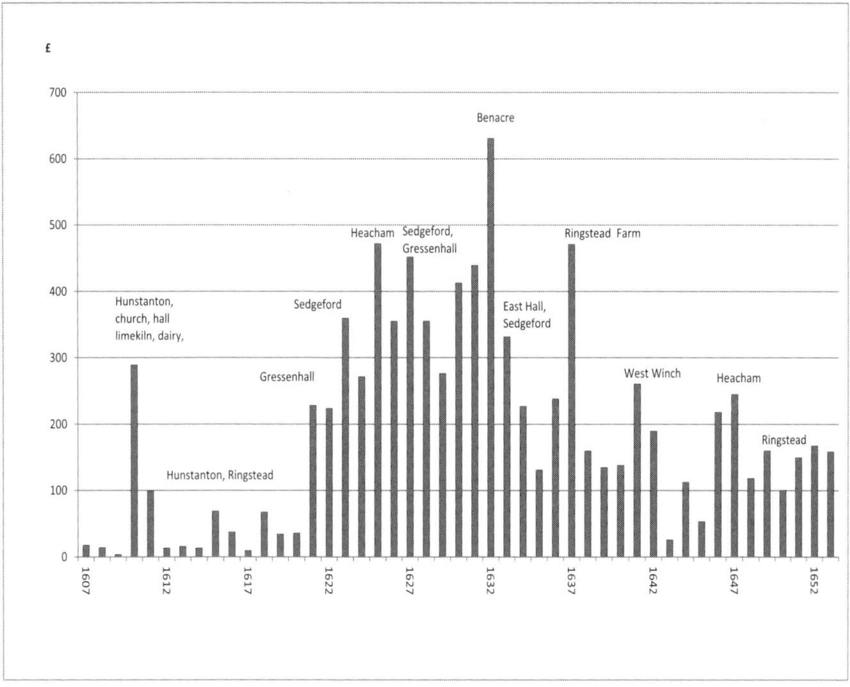

Figure 7.3 Building projects and repairs, 1607–53

The records that survive show a gentry family learning from books, consulting texts and practising their science on the ground in the age of the scientific revolution.[44] Significantly, their work predated the creation of the Hartlib circle, underlining the intellectual and bookish origins of the approach.[45] Like true scientists, they created their own knowledge, observing, experimenting and recording it for the benefit of their successors. In this way invaluable information on the estate was handed down from generation to generation, and we can see how ideas and practices developed over time. Stephen Shapin identified one of the problems associated with the scientific revolution as the difficulty of pinning it down.[46] The ideas and discoveries 'float', when they need to be firmly located in their cultural and social context. Historians want to know and understand the concrete human practices by which ideas were made, what people did when they

44 C. Webster, *The Great Instauration: Science, Medicine and Reform, 1626–1660* (London, 1975).

45 The catalogue included a copy of *Hartlib of Husbandry, 1651*, the book he produced with Sir Richard Weston, *A discours of husbandrie used in Brabant and Flanders, shewing the wonderful improvement of land there, and serving as a pattern for our practice in this Common-wealth* (1650).

46 S. Shapin, *The Scientific Revolution* (Chicago, 1996).

made an observation and to what use they put the information. Who wrought these changes? What did they think a reformed natural philosophy was good for? How did it sit with more traditional beliefs and practices? The example of Sir Hamon Le Strange and his family helps to answer these questions and provides a rare insight into how early modern science was understood and formulated.

IV

Sir Hamon embraced the new learning and adhered to a new moral philosophy. But how, in practice, did these ideas work out on the ground, and how far was he able to accommodate traditional beliefs and local custom? One of his first steps, in keeping with best practice, was to commission surveys of the estate, starting with Holme in 1605, followed by Thomas Waterman's surveys of Hunstanton (1615), Brisley (1622), Heacham (1623) and Gressenhall (1624), and John Fisher's surveys of Sedgeford (1630) and Ringstead (undated).[47] These maps, combined with the field books, provide an almost complete picture of the landholding structure and the topography of the estate in the early seventeenth century. The maps reflect a point in time, but the field books, redrafted at intervals, record changes in the size and occupation of holdings. For example, those for Hunstanton survive for 1618/23, 1648, 1671 and 1689, and show little alteration in the layout of field patterns before the 1670s and 1680s. At that time, as corn prices declined, freeholders sold their lands to Sir Hamon's great-grandson, Sir Nicholas, allowing him to consolidate strips and enclose holdings. In contrast, Sir Hamon and his eldest son, Sir Nicholas, like their forebears, worked alongside the open-field system and concentrated their efforts on neglected pasture, breckland and marsh which lay within their immediate control; they did not seek advancement at the expense of the local community or the dismantling of traditional social structures. To be honest it was not in their interest to do so; ownership in the open fields was far too fragmented. As we have seen, it was much better to focus on those areas with the greatest scope for improvement and to utilize the plentiful supply of local labour which the open fields supported.

The map of Hunstanton made in 1615 shows the sense of their approach. The parish was divided into 56 furlongs which lay in two precincts, amounting to some 1720 acres. The first precinct, furlongs 1–16 on the map, included the Hall, park, East Field and marshland to the north, comprising 750 acres:

---

[47] See n. 5 above. 'The maps of Brisley, NRO, MF, RO/402/7 and Gressenhall, NRO, Hayes and Storr, 72 are in different collections following the sale of these estates in the eighteenth century.

310 acres of meadow, permanent pasture and marsh, 200 acres of park and 240 acres of arable, of which 89 per cent was controlled by the Le Stranges. Of the remaining 86½ acres, half was in hands of a single freeholder in furlongs 3 and 5, while the rest was scattered between 12 men in furlongs 11 to 16, giving Sir Hamon almost a free run in this area. In contrast, the second precinct, West Field, consisting of furlongs 17–56, amounted to 972 acres – of which 960 acres were in arable strips, of which nearly 50 per cent were in the hands of 100 or so freeholders and copyholders who rented the remainder from the Le Stranges.[48] This pattern of settlement can be explained by geography and custom. The better soils lay to the west of the parish, were intensively cultivated and supported the well-populated village; villagers had the right to graze their animals on the open-field stubbles prior to the sowing of spring barley, giving them every incentive to retain the existing system. The lighter soils to the south and east, with the marshes to the north, dictated a more extensive regime – with livestock grazing permanent pasture and being folded on the sandy brecks to increase fertility. Unlike in West Field, the Le Stranges enjoyed rights of foldcourse over East Field and in the neighbouring parishes of Great and Little Ringstead, where three flocks grazed the sheepwalks and heathland.[49] In the manner advocated in *The Countrey Farme*, Sir Hamon's aim was to intensify these farming systems by restocking flocks, ploughing up and subdividing degraded pasture, making meadows and ponds, erecting buildings to house shepherds, dairies and cattle units, draining marshes and imparking. This sort of programme required money and commitment, but the freedom from mixed ownership and legal impediments, the availability of labour and the return on capital made it a worthwhile investment in the long run. Figure 7.4 shows the growing proportion of corn, sheep and wool included in estate income.

The Le Stranges had focused on this less fertile area for some time. Among Sir Hamon's first entries in the memoranda book is his description of the imparking undertaken by his father in the 1580s; by purchasing 94 acres of strips he almost doubled the size of the park from 100 to nearly 200 acres.[50] Sir Hamon increased his holding in East Field by acquiring a further 77 acres, and another 21 acres where the park abutted West Field to the south; this can be seen on the map where he noted the planting of acorns in 1636. The new triangle of parkland, so created, extended the view from the new South Wing of Hunstanton Hall, which contained the living and entertaining rooms of the family. Against the new boundary, which rises up from the valley where the Hall stands, he erected

48 Oestmann, *Lestrange Family*, pp. 30–38.

49 S. Wade Martins and T. Williamson, *Roots of Change: Farming and the Landscape in East Anglia, c.1700–1870* (Exeter, 1999), pp. 9–12.

50 LEST/Q38; LEST/BK1; LEST/R9.

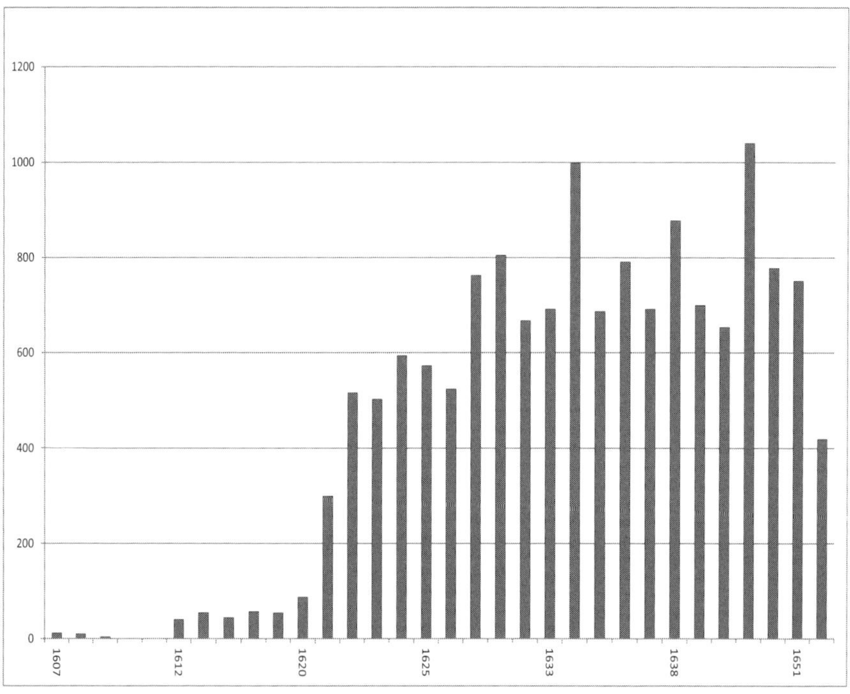

Figure 7.4 Income from corn, sheep and wool, 1607–52

palings and placed strategic plantings of trees, screening the park from the open fields and protecting the house from the coastal winds. Reorganization can also be detected in the open field in front of the Hall. In the field book of 1618/23, furlongs 10 and 11 included several strips, but only a few appear on the map, with a later note saying 'enclose[d] 1655'.[51] Furlongs 12–16 show further work in progress, with strips enclosed and hedges planted. To the north of East Field, several furlongs have been renamed and subdivided. For example furlong 7, Lords Close, appears in Alice's estate account of 1632 as the Two Lower Closes; furlong 8, also Lords Close, as the Two Upper Closes; furlong 10, Lower Furlong, appears as the Newe Close and 'a close against the New Close'; while Poole Close has been divided into the First and Second Pool Close.[52] Two of the marshes, Marsh Close and Bushey Close, have been renamed Brimble Close and Normans Close to avoid confusion with Bushey Close in furlong 6 and Hall

51 LEST/BH1.

52 LEST/BK15.

Marsh in furlong 9. This reorganization predates the initiatives of Sir Nicholas and can be attributed to Sir Hamon in the 1610s and 1620s.

To help new tenants, Sir Hamon sometimes concluded sharefarming agreements, providing the seed corn and halving the crop. Thus in 1613, with his servant, Thomas Ketwood, he 'sowed of barley to halves in the upper close, 10 c, in the lower close 5 c'; and with Will Cobb he 'sowed of gray pease and fetches to halfes with me in Poole close'.[53] In Ringstead he went to great lengths to support the three foldcourses, leasing the flocks to syndicates of farmers and sowing the arable to halves.[54] He provided incentives for shepherds, allowing them to place 100 sheep in each flock of 800 sheep, and building houses for them to be near the flocks.[55] In 1620, when he leased the Ringstead North Flock, he promised to tolerate the North Flock coming into the East Field of Hunstanton after St Andrew's Day (30 November) until Lady Day (25 March) for the 'succour of the flock', and he continued to share the costs of cultivating the arable.[56] Later, they divided the brecks into 11 and operated an 11-year rotation, compensating farmers at 2*s*. 8*d*. per acre when they were laid down to pasture and grazed by the sheep.[57] In 1617 much expense, labour and effort went into the building of Ringstead Yards, at the southern end of Hunstanton Park, where cattle were kept and fattened.[58]

V

The most tangible expression of Sir Hamon's learning, vision and technical skill lies in his building work, which formed the largest regular item of expenditure between 1618 and 1654 (Figure 7.3). The table drawn up by Sir Nicholas in his great-grandfather's memoranda book, running to 30 pages, indicates the scale of the task.[59] By 1620, expenditure on building had reached such a level of complexity that Alice created a separate account for it.[60] At first, Sir Hamon concentrated his energies on Hunstanton Hall and its environs. When he inherited the estate, the Hall consisted of a moated site, with the fifteenth-century gatehouse facing what appears to have been a medieval hall. This was in fact the half-built element

53 LEST/BK3; LEST/P6.

54 LEST/R8; LEST/Q38, fo. 8.

55 LEST/Q38; LEST/Q37. A new lease to the inhabitants of Ringstead in 1650 allowed them to place 300 sheep in the flocks, Sir Hamon and Sir Nicholas 300 and the shepherds 100.

56 LEST/Q38, fo. 42.

57 LEST/Q37, contained in the new lease of 1650.

58 LEST/Q38 fo. 17–20.

59 LEST/Q38, fos. 201–30.

60 LEST/P7.

of the 'chief house' to which Alice referred; it had been constructed in 1577 and was known as the 'Elizabethan Wing'.[61] In 1618 Sir Hamon added the elaborate porch, bristling with classical detail, as a first step in the completion of the house.[62] The stone was supplied by Mr Thomas Thorpe of High Cliffe, Northamptonshire – the father of John Thorpe, the noted architect who may have played a part in the overall design.[63] The pyramids, escallop and coats of arms on the porch were made by Hans Weller, a Dutchman lodging in Southwark.[64]

The decoration of the porch, combining classical detail and medieval elements was typical of the period. With this device fixed on porches and gates, an early seventeenth-century gentleman displayed his classical and humanist credentials alongside his ancient lineage. Sir Hamon repeated this theme, respecting the past while embracing the new, throughout the rebuilding at Hunstanton. In the 1620s he completed the house by constructing two T-shaped wings from the north and south of the gatehouse, linked back to the Elizabethan wing to create a courtyard.[65] The new elevation repeated the symmetry of the Elizabethan wing but with the addition of a crenellated parapet linking the new building to the medieval gatehouse. In front of the gatehouse, where a few scattered barns and stables can be seen on the 1615 map, he built a new walled courtyard with a huge stone gate – 'the upper freestone gates' – where lions, unicorns and coats of arms sit astride a pure classical design. He himself produced the sketches for the gates and the crenellations of the courtyard walls.[66] In this way, the house achieved stylistic coherence and a conventional double courtyard structure with a grand inner porch, late medieval gatehouse and outer gates. This treatment focused the attention of the visitor on the ancient and illustrious status of the family and Sir Hamon's newly acquired identity as a Renaissance gentleman.

Sir Hamon's enthusiasm for building extended to service and farm buildings. As advocated in *The Countrey Farme*, he erected houses and structures to cater

61 The Elizabethan Wing was burned down in the fire of 1853, but a sketch, LEST/MS 21219, shows a house with a symmetrical front, closely resembling Corsham Court, built and reputedly designed by Thomas Symthson in the 1570s; it too replaced a decayed medieval manor house. M. Girouard, *Robert Smythson and the Architecture of the Elizabethan Era* (London, 1966) p. 65; N. Cooper, *The Houses of the Gentry, 1480–1680* (New Haven, 1999), pp. 141–53; C. Hussey, 'Hunstanton Hall', *Country Life* 10, 17 Apr. 1926.

62 LEST/Q38, fol. 11. The porch miraculously survived the fire of 1853 and now stands as a roundabout in the centre of the courtyard, which is now open to the gardens beyond. The ornamentation, with pyramids, classical columns, coats of arms etc., resembles that of Cranborne Manor, Dorset, *c.*1608. Girouard, *Smythson*, p. 221.

63 LEST/Q38, fos. 54, 70, 72.

64 LEST/Q38, fo. 11.

65 See Hussey in *Country Life*, 17 Apr. 1926, for a plan of the house.

66 LEST/Q38, fo. 114.

for pets, hunting animals and leisure interests: hawks' mews, dogs' kennels, stables and a coachhouse were built to the north and east of the Hall, while the Bowling Ground and Octagon, where he practised on his viols, could be seen from the South Wing. The Octagon, a classical design topped with crenellations, repeated the theme of the Porch, Upper Gates and the North and South wings, combining classical and gothic elements. Similar attention to detail can be found in the stables, bridge and miles of garden, moat and courtyard walls. At a more practical level, he built barns, granaries, a dovehouse, a hen house, bakehouse, brewhouse, larder, dairy, slaughterhouse and scullery, and workshops for carpenters, plumbers and ploughmen. Several were upgraded, like the dairy with pipes and pumps, the granary with a new roof and upper floor and the stables where the walls were raised and a new roof fitted.[67]

Sir Hamon did not confine his efforts to Hunstanton Hall. He spent vast sums building manor houses and farmhouses with proper facilities across the estate. At Ringstead, he rebuilt the manor house for his second son, Hamon, as he did at Gressenhall, leased to his cousin Phillip Calthorpe. The newly acquired properties of Heacham Manor and Sedgeford received particular attention. At the former, the 'very ancient' house was rebuilt with dovehouse, mill house and barns, while at Sedgeford, two new farmsteads were constructed at East Hall and West Hall. Sir Hamon had an acute understanding of the type of buildings required to improve agricultural production: housing for animals and storage for grain and hay; and the need for specialist units for producing, processing and preserving food, such as dairies, slaughterhouses, mills, malthouses and larders. His notes also show his deep interest in technology. In 1618 the plan for the new brewhouse and bakehouse at Hunstanton included three rooms 46 feet long, divided into the bakehouse; the cooler 'wortfatt' (wort vat), where the malt fermented; and the firehouse, copper and 'mashfatt' (mash vat) – the copper was to stand on the east side and a cistern for drains on the west.[68]

The systematic nature of the building programme suggests that Sir Hamon was working to a plan. From the start he managed the project, often acting as his own architect, drawing designs, managing the employment of labour, procuring material and equipment and relying on Alice to keep a tight rein on costs. Typically, for a particular task he drew up an agreement with a craftsman or tradesman, specifying rates for the job. With his rolling programme of building and repairs, he gradually built up a local team and local expertise. In this way he created an informal estate yard, equipped with all the necessary skills for the maintenance of an estate. For specialist tasks – notably for glazing, stonework

67 LEST/Q38, fo. 201.

68 LEST/Q38, fo. 29.

and decorative finishing – Sir Hamon went further afield, but increasingly he relied on local families specializing in carpentry, lead and ironwork and general building work. By acting as his own clerk of the works he was able to control and reduce costs, and build more. Between them they created an efficient system. Figure 7.3 summarizes the expenditure on building projects and repairs, contained in the books of disbursements, undertaken between 1606 and 1654. The sudden increase in 1610 indicates the start of their enterprise, when they built a limekiln, a house for the limeburner and a dairy for Alice costing over £150. It also marks the point when Alice took responsibility for the household accounts and provided a framework for managing expenditure. The next sharp increase occurred in 1621 soon after she inherited the Sedgeford estate from her father; average expenditure rose from 3 per cent of estate income between 1617 and 1620 to 15 per cent over the next six years (1621–25). It was the extra building work that required the creation of designated building accounts. These consist of two to four pages every half-year at the end of the general disbursements. From that point expenditure gathered momentum as they were able to predict and manage their cash flow and maintain their programme of building and repairs. Between 1630 and 1641 expenditure averaged 10 per cent of a significantly larger estate income, before falling in the 1640s and averaging 6 per cent between 1650 and 1653. Following the advice of Henry Peacham, Sir Hamon did not ignore the 'Mechanical Arts' – to the great benefit of his estate.[69]

VI

By 1630, when his eldest son Sir Nicholas married and joined the family management team, Sir Hamon had achieved much; but more remained to be done on the coastal marshes at Hunstanton and Heacham, and the brecks at Sedgeford. Sir Nicholas tackled this venture over the next 25 years, recording the details in a series of farming notebooks, of which four survive.[70] He built on his father's work, but developed his own method and style. The layout of the notebooks, which is meticulous and resembles his mother's approach, indicates a carefully planned enterprise very different to the haphazard entries in the memoranda books. Pocket-sized for taking on site, and written in a clear, round hand with indexes, summaries and commentary, the notebooks were explicitly designed to instruct and inform. Sir Nicholas was also more concerned with profit and loss, keeping his own accounts, costing and analysing expenditure using

69 H. Peacham, *The Compleat Gentleman* (1627).

70 LEST/KA6, KA9, KA10, KA24 for Hunstanton and Sedgeford survive; those for Heacham, LEST/KA4–8, are missing.

mathematical tables and almanacs, and calculating the return on the enterprise. He seems to have learned basic accounting skills from his mother, but acquired a more sophisticated understanding of financial management from textbooks. The result confirms McRae's observations that the language of improvement changed during the course of the seventeenth century.[71] However, apart from a more modern approach, the underlying philosophy remained the same.

The first notebook details the imbanking and the draining of the marshes at Hunstanton – known as The Marsh, Bogge and Meeles (sand dunes) and part of Holme Marshes – where he worked in partnership with his father, sharing the costs 'in a PARTIBLE way of charge and profit'.[72] Like his father, he entered into sharefarming agreements with tenants and labourers, halving the costs of 'levelling, tumbrelling and barrowing' and of 'cutting and bunching osiers', thereby sharing the risks of improvement. This process was followed by ploughing, harrowing, sowing and reaping, and the construction of new farmsteads at Hunstanton. In the ploughing and sowing accounts for 1643–53 Sir Nicholas sets out in three columns the time of year, the crop, the work to be done and the costs. For example, on Hunstanton Marsh in June 1643 they weeded 'miscellane', harvested it in August and threshed it in January; in November they threshed wheat; in February they ploughed for beans and oats, sowing in March.[73] In other years they grew coleseed, wheat, pease and vetches. The land continued to be improved with sand carried from the Meeles and 'spread unto some rancke stiff places', and new drains were cut. At the foot of each account, 'Miscellanie Charges' noted sums expended on the maintenance of drains, posts, rails and fences, the weeding and making of hay and any new ventures undertaken, such as the new Horse Bridge in 1653. This was the format for each account, detailing every process, activity and the time of year when it occurred.[74] Similarly, the building accounts for the same period record every detail of the construction of the new farmhouses under headings listing the work of masons, carpenters, joiners, smiths, thatchers and glaziers, all much more systematically than Sir Hamon had done.[75] The work included interior decoration and the setting out gardens with herbs and fruit trees; Thomas Church, 'our Gardiner', was paid to go to nurseries to choose particular varieties. Their methods differed, but father and son both looked after their tenants, provided employment and accommodation, invested in their wellbeing and shared the risks of improvements. These risks could prove extremely costly. The

71 McRae, 'Husbandry Manuals'.

72 LEST/KA6. The payments for Sir Hamon's share appear in Alice's accounts, LEST/P7.

73 LEST/KA6. Miscellane – probably meslin or mixtlyn, a mixture of grains.

74 LEST/KA6, KA9.

75 LEST/KA10.

detail from Heacham appears to be contained in the four missing notebooks, but we know from a summary of the drainage work undertaken that 176 acres of marsh in that parish were 'drowned ... undrowned and enclosed'.[76] The enterprise, undertaken in partnership with Sir Hamon, ran into severe difficulties, as Alice noted in her summary of their finances; they lost £600 on Heacham Marsh, with a further £500 adventuring on Boston Fennes.[77]

A theme that runs through the memoranda books is Sir Hamon's passion for wildlife, natural history and field sports, which he shared with his sons and grandsons, friends and neighbours. Complying enthusiastically with the requirement in *The Countrey Farme* to manage one's estate for pleasure as well as profit, they engaged in hunting, hawking and fishing, as well as extending the park, creating ponds and planting trees to enhance the landscape. An early entry in Sir Hamon's memoranda book includes 'a catalogue of the number of hawks, falcons and tassels which I have taken at the cliffs since 1604 when I came of age'.[78] One of his first building projects was to construct mews for the hawks at Hunstanton Hall; between 1606 and 1626 he spent £121 buying nets, bells, hoods, muzzles, jesses, leashes, bags, lure and gloves.[79] In 1626 he commissioned Tom Stokesby of Upwell to make him eight ladd nets for fishing the sea channels.[80] One of Sir Nicholas's earliest plans for Hunstanton Marsh involved the planting of osiers for 'fishing, fowling and brooke-hawking'.[81] The aim for Hunstanton Common was to make it 'handsome for gunne and hawke' by creating a new haven and 'pitts for handsome flying'. He also constructed 'a handsome riding passage through Murton's Bogge along my new drains'. At Holme Marsh they built 'breast works and blinds ... to gaine shoots at the fowles'. Although Sir Nicholas carefully costed the drainage enterprise, and tried to avoid disaster, father and son were clearly motivated by the idea of enjoying land as an amenity and creating attractive landscapes.

This all presents a charming picture; but how successful was improvement on the Hunstanton estate, and how far was it achieved within a moral and godly framework? More to the point, did it pay? They appear to have lost money on the drainage of Heacham Marsh, but how did they fare elsewhere on the estate? From the care Alice lavished on her accounts, we can be sure that such considerations were important to the family. Figures 7.1–7.4 show precise calculations of income and expenditure and a genuine attempt at financial management, keeping their

76 LEST/KA24.

77 LEST/P10. These figures appear in Alice's list of 'Losses in my Husbands Estate'.

78 LEST/Q36, fo. 1.

79 LEST/P6, P7.

80 LEST/Q38, fo. 91.

81 LEST/KA6.

level of debt under control. In 1635 they paid off all their debts with the sale of the Benacre estate in Suffolk (Figure 7.2). However, they soon resorted to further borrowing to finance Elizabeth's portion and the settlement of their second son, Hamon.[82] These arrangements appear overgenerous, but they may have been sustainable in the context of a steadily rising income.

The receipts from the estate vary from year to year as the returns made by the bailiffs represent net receipts with allowances deducted at source. Further expenditure on the estate, principally on building projects and the lands held in hand, was recorded in the books of general disbursements. No receipt book survives for the years 1642–50 and the final book only covers the years from 1650 to 1652.[83] As we have seen, the family received a significant boost in 1621, when Alice inherited the Sedgeford estate from her father. This was worth about £460 and lifted the rental, using Sir Hamon's optimistic estimate, to £1,700 a year – but more conservatively to about £1,450. Figure 7.1 shows that receipts rapidly rose to £2,000 a year, reaching a peak of £2,640 in 1641. Between 1630 and 1641 they averaged £2,572, representing an increase of between 50 per cent and 75 per cent since 1622, depending on the base figure used. By the 1650s the average had fallen to £2,300.[84] The increase in estate income in the 1620s and 1630s was achieved entirely through improvement, partly from the uplift in farm rents, but also from the growing sale of corn, sheep and wool.

Figure 7.4 the income derived from the sale of corn, wool and sheep rose from minimal amounts in 1617 to an average of £710 a year between 1622 and 1641; it fell to £650 in the 1650s. This was principally due to the losses of sheep in 1643, which continued to have an impact. However, by the 1650s sales of 'marsh wheat' and 'marsh barley' from Heacham regularly appear in the receipts; the average for corn alone actually increased from £472 to £503. At Heacham income rose from £350 in 1616 to £584 by 1636, with £160 paid in corn. The loss of £600 incurred at Heacham draining the marshes was significant; but by 1650 the rental had increased to £503, reflecting the investment in buildings and also the extended acreage available for corn growing and grazing for cattle and sheep. At Sedgeford income rose from £464 in 1621, with £287 paid in corn, to £690 in 1636, with £418 paid in corn in 1636. Sedgeford was a particular success story, undertaken without the risks associated with marsh drainage. From 1621 they started the careful reorganization of the Brecks to facilitate the more intensive cultivation of

---

[82] Hamon's settlement included Holme parsonage left to him by his grandfather, a farm at Ringstead and a small estate at West Winch.

[83] In the run from 1607 to 1653 there are gaps from 1614–16, 1627–29 and 1642–50.

[84] By the 1650s the average had fallen to £650.

corn; this culminated in the survey of 1630 and the building of new farmsteads.[85] Improvement was not confined to the income from corn, wool and sheep; money rents increased at a steady pace from £177 in 1621 to £314 in 1652. There was also a ready demand for buildings for storage: in 1652 John Ellgar paid an extra £3 a year for three years for 'part of the great barne' at Sedgeford.[86]

The returns from Hunstanton, Ringstead and Gressenhall are more difficult to disentangle, as farms were leased to members of the family on what appears to be a concessionary basis, and the likelihood is that Sir Hamon diverted income from Hunstanton into his own pocket.[87] Nevertheless, Alice's sheep accounts, combined with her receipt book, show an increasingly efficient organization of the three flocks they held in hand – one at Sedgeford based on the new brecks and the other two at Ringstead.[88] The receipts from the sale of sheep, lambs and wool between 1622 and 1643 averaged £228 a year. No receipt book survives for the period 1642 to 1649, but the sheep accounts suggest an average of £64 following the loss of 1,695 sheep at the hands of Captain Poe and his soldiers in 1643.[89] For several years after 1643 the Le Stranges relied on tenants and neighbours placing cullet sheep in their flocks. By 1650 they had partially rebuilt their stock, and for the three years to 1652 receipts averaged £148. The impact of the Parliamentary forces was compounded by fines and a lawsuit which dogged Sir Hamon until his death in 1654.[90] But for a policy of improvement and collaboration with their communities the family might not have survived this catastrophe. As we have seen, across the estate rent levels were maintained, benefiting from the investment undertaken in the sunny years of the 1620s and 1630s. Figure 7.3 shows they continued with their building projects, albeit at a reduced level; in the 1650s, the shepherd Osborne paid £4 2*s*. for the South Shepherds House and Barne at Ringstead, while Goodman paid £3 5*s*. for the North Shepherds House.

Some idea of what the Le Stranges achieved can be gleaned from Alice's account for Hunstanton from 1632 to 1653. At the end she made 'A note of what lands are in the Lord's Hands 1653 and how they are rated'. She valued the park and closes, amounting to some 462 acres, at 6*s*. 8*d*. per acre, a single

85 Alice's farming records for Sedgeford are being edited as a volume for the Norfolk Record Society.

86 LEST/P11.

87 Phillip Calthorpe, Sir Hamon's cousin, leased the estate at Gressenhall; the rent actually declined from £237 in 1621 to £143 in 1652. For many years receipts only amounted to £112.

88 LEST/P10 includes Alice's sheep accounts which she kept from 1618 to 1653. The Le Stranges also worked closely with the farmers leasing the remaining three flocks: the North and South foldcourse at Sedgeford and with the North flock at Ringstead; see p. 221 and n. 56 above.

89 This figure might be too low as the receipts give a fuller picture of income.

90 See n. 88 above

meadow at 10*s*., a few acres of brecks for 5*s*., 44 acres of the Marsh, Bogge and Meeles and another meadow at 6*s*. This compared to rents for open field arable, situated on the more fertile soils to the west of the village, ranging between 2*s*. and 4*s*. per acre, with an average of 3*s*. per acre. Apart from a modest increase in Ringstead, from 2*s*. to 2*s*. 4*d*. and 2*s*. 6*d*. per acre, these rents remained static for the entire period of the account from 1632 to 1653, in contrast to the improvement achieved elsewhere.[91] So, it appears that significant progress was made without encroaching on the livelihoods of villagers; they also benefited from the improvement undertaken on the marshes, the brecks and in the park.

The pursuit of improvement required landowners to be vigilant and hardheaded in the protection of their rights; in this respect the Le Stranges were no exception. They were sticklers for record keeping. One memoranda book was designed to contain precisely this kind of information.[92] It includes 'a note of sundry matters to bee understood to bee rectified ... according to law', which identified the nature of copyhold rents and fines, restrictions on felling timber, the areas of shackable lands at Heacham and Sir Hamon's claim to the lordships of Great Ringstead and Holme – each with its vast expanse of waste, commons, marshes and meeles (dunes) full of rabbits over which the lord enjoyed sole privilege.[93] Disputes were frequent. At Heacham, where Sir Hamon had been misinformed on the stocking rates of Caly Foldcourse, when his knowledge was 'raw and imperfect', he insisted that it should be 'inquired into, altered and reformed in such a manner ... as may be thought reasonable'.[94] The election of the sea bailiff at Holme was another bone of contention. Traditionally, he was chosen from the copyholders of the town 'by turn of tenement'. What the sea bailiff found on the shore he was supposed to send to the manor house at Ringstead. But 'in late years the water bailiff had appropriated wrecks to themselves allowing the lord but half the value'.[95] As the lord became 'more sensible of the abuse' they denied the rights of copyholders to hold the office and appointed their own water bailiff. These two examples emphasize the value of common grazing and the sea shore in this part of Norfolk and the need for Sir Hamon to be wary. The tenants, copyholders and freeholders were only too eager to encroach on his rights. In 1698 Sir Nicholas benefited from his great-grandfather's scrupulous care as he was able to refute the claims of a purchaser of a small estate at Ringstead to rights of warren on the sand dunes.[96]

91 The small increase at Ringstead reflected investment in the foldcourses.

92 LEST/Q37, transcribed and annotated by Sir Nicholas Le Strange.

93 LEST/Q37.

94 LEST/Q37, fo. 27.

95 LEST/Q37, fo. 27.

96 LEST/Q37, fo. 34.

To all appearances, their improvements were made with the acquiescence of the village community of Hunstanton. It is only when we look outside the family's own archive that we gain a sense that all was not quite well. In 1638 Hamon Le Strange sued Robert Cremer of Little Massingham and Robert Stileman of Snettisham co. Norfolk, gent, his uncle, for delivering a petition to the justices at the Norwich assizes and making scandalous speeches against Le Strange. These turned on two matters: an allegation that Le Strange's steward had borrowed a copy of the court roll from Cremer and altered it by erasing some words and interlining others to deprive him of some of his land; and a claim that Le Strange had incorporated some of Cremer's land into his drainage scheme despite his objections. Indeed, Cremer was said to have tried to lie down in front of Le Strange's workmen to stop them erecting a seabank over his land. Cremer seemed to have a legitimate case against Le Strange for his heavy-handed behaviour. Le Strange answered this by taking Cremer's attempts to seek retribution as a slur on his good name and used the Court of Chivalry to force a public submission – a sort of gagging order. The larger issues – of forgery and the inclusion of Cremer's lands in Le Strange's scheme – remained unanswered.[97] We gain a sense of the grievances and complaints about Le Strange's improvement which may have circulated but which could not be articulated openly.

In his day, Sir Hamon would have won plaudits for his firmness and attention to detail, an essential part of an improvement strategy designed to benefit the commonweal. Today, with a longer perspective, we might take a different view, depending on our cast of mind. However, from the sentiments expressed in his will, when he thanked Alice for 'the just, faithful and laudable advantage and advancement of my estate', we can be sure that Sir Hamon believed he had achieved his objectives: a virtuous circle satisfying his moral concerns, cultural preferences and agricultural imperatives.[98] In his desire to live harmoniously within his physical and social environment, we recognize the modern ideal of a country life; he displayed an understanding of how to manage a fragile environment, embracing heath and marshland, in a productive and sustainable way without sacrificing the wider interests and the wellbeing of those living in this remote corner of Norfolk. He seems to have managed that rare feat of accommodating the aesthetic and profitable development of his estate with a genuine commitment to rural community.

---

[97] The suit is summarized in R. P. Cust and A. J. Hopper (eds), *Cases in the High Court of Chivalry, 1634–1640* (Harleian Society, new ser. 18, 2006), pp. 164–6 without mentioning the improvement aspect of the case. For the full court record, see http://www.court-of-chivalry.bham.ac.uk/index.htm.

[98] LEST/AE8

Appendix

A Summary of the Income and Selected Expenditure of Sir Hamon and Lady Alice Le Strange, 1607–1653

	1607	**1608**	**1609**	**1610**	**1611**	**1612**	**1613**	**1614**	**1615**	**1616**	**1617**	**1618**	**1619**	**1620**	**1621**	**1622**	**1623**	**1624**	**1625**	**1626**	**1627**	**1628**	**1629**	**1630**	**1631**
Receipts																									
Cash receipts	379	342	719	224	296	225	422				99	8	41	36		2		20							24
Bailiff accounts	135	86	65	51	61	224	326				862	877	942	1014	1274	1257	1204	1315	1255	1258				1280	1412
Corn	1		4	1	1	40	52				28	53	42	83	290	307	290	382	373	247				599	570
Sheep	11						2				6	5	8	4	5	91	105	86	92	183				164	148
Wool		10									10		4		5	117	107	126	108	94				1	87
Wood	70			105	13	101	56				28	64	46	200	118	48	57	108	61	18				12	26
Dairy, cows							5				32	14	18	11	13		6	19	10	9				24	9
Horses, hawks	12	5	8		6		2				32	12	16	10	37	5	34	46	18	10				10	19
Lime, reeds, wax			1	8	4	3	2				3	5		3	5	3	4	3	5	9				9	4
Ships, boats, sea															23	25	12		1	37				1	10
Estate Receipts	609	443	797	389	381	592	867				1100	1038	1117	1361	1769	1855	1819	2105	1923	1865				2099	2308
Sale of land		210	1440	185	20	30	14										76								76

	1607	1608	1609	1610	1611	1612	1613	1614	1615	1616	1617	1618	1619	1620	1621	1622	1623	1624	1625	1626	1627	1628	1629	1630	1631
Sale of shares																		217						59	
New Loans	40	199	120	105	16	281					98	71	80	460	439		378		200	150				160	800
Loans Repaid																									
Legal Damages																									
Marriage Portion																								2650	
Total Receipts	649	852	2357	679	417	903	881				1198	1109	1197	1821	2203	1855	2274	2321	2123	2015				4968	3184

Major Expenditure																									
Purchase Of Land			4400										48				326		80					2925	400
Legal Costs, War, Fines																									
Marriage Portion																									
Building	18	14	4	289	99	13	16	13	69	38	10	67	35	36	228	224	360	271	272	355	452	355	276	413	439
Marsh Drainage																									
Total Expenditure	****			642	509	919	686	1023	1188	1107	1235	1224	1097	1779	2263	1791	2391	2115	2021	2288	2051	2274	2372	5228	2935
Debt	1500																								

	1632	1633	1634	1635	1636	1637	1638	1639	1640	1641	1642	1643	1644	1645	1646	1647	1648	1649	1650	1651	1652	1653
Receipts																						
Cash Receipts	14		1	30	2		22			41									30	30	114	
Bailiff Accounts	1423	1452	1492	1453	1635	1454	1562	1567	1521	1473									1472	1584	1520	
Corn	436	559	598	342	650	471	616	470	426	864									619	566	319	
Sheep	116	93	395	124	137	149	166	168	122	129									55	111	82	
Wool	116	40	5	221	5	72	94	61	107	57									104	74	19	
Wood	58	10	41	25	14	27	4	30		5									7		4	
Dairy, Cows	6	29	17	26	33	13	6	23	8	20									12	43	25	
Horses, Hawks	71	10	35		15	50	32	50	45	19									3	19	1	
Lime, Reeds, Wax	3	6	10	4	5	11	14	6	2	6									9	7	5	
Ships, Boats, Sea	30	15	47	8		48																
Estate Receipts	2273	2214	2641	2233	2495	2295	2517	2376	2230	2614									2311	2434	2089	
Sale Of Land	441	2200	20		500	580	171												10			
Sale Of Shares	38																					
New Loan	380	891			740	1260	400	390	100										450			
Loans Repaid					1053																	
Legal Damages									190													
Marriage Portion		5305	2661	2233	4788	4135	3088	2766	2520	2614									2771	2434	2089	
Total Receipts																						

	1632	1633	1634	1635	1636	1637	1638	1639	1640	1641	1642	1643	1644	1645	1646	1647	1648	1649	1650	1651	1652	1653
Major Expenditure																						
Purchase of Land		1792											159	50			281	69				
Legal Costs, War, Fines							222					300	200	225	385	314	93	136	683			
Marriage Portion					3500																	
Building		331	227	131	238	471	160	135	138	261	190	26	113	53	218	245	118	160	101	149	168	158
Marsh Drainage					107		307		472	400	129											
Total		5402	2535	2260	4566	4367	3065	2396	2711	2661	2135	2883	2775	2552	2644	3348	3031	2565	2930	2247	2253	2447
Debt		1741	300		2240	3400	2010	2240	2240	2150	2100	2890	2940	2660	2750	1230	1850	2050	2300	2414	2200	1300

Chapter 8

Between the Corporation and Captain Flood: The Fens and Drainage After 1663

*Julie Bowring**

Rowse up you Corperration and do not stand
for Captaine Floud you see hath seased your land
for Captain Floud is arived in the Fenn
and theire designes to quator all his men
He theire designs this winter to abide
He hath broke the south banck and the north banck tried.
O you Corperation, we wish their had nere bene none
for it is the Corperation that hath the Fenns undon.[1]

So begins the 'Song against [the] Corporation', an anonymous, libellous ballad circulated in the Great Level of the Fens at the end of the seventeenth century whose target was the Corporation of the Great Level, also known as the Bedford

---

* This chapter is based on research carried out with the support of a Social Sciences and Humanities Research Council (SSHRC) Doctoral Fellowship. In addition to the acknowledgements I have made within the notes, I would like to thank Heather Falvey for her assistance with the transcription of the 'Song against [the] Corporation' and for discussion of its content; Hugh Gunz for his comments on an earlier draft of the chapter; Keith Wrightson for his comments and advice through its development; and Jonathan James for his timely provision of tea and friendship. An earlier version of part of this chapter appeared in Susan Oosthuizen and Frances Willmoth (eds), *Drowned and Drained: Exploring Fenland Records and Landscape* (Cambridge, Institute of Continuing Education, 2009).

The following abbreviations have been used for manuscript collections: BLC refers to the Bedford Level Corporation archive, held at the Cambridgeshire Archives and Local Studies (formerly Cambridgeshire Record Office), reference R/59/31; S/B/SP is the catalogue number at the Cambridgeshire Archives for the petitions submitted to the Bedford Level Corporation; and EDR has been used for the Ely Diocesan Records held by the Cambridge University Library, Manuscripts and Archives. Extracts from MSS are printed with their original spelling, except that 'ff' has been rendered as a capital 'F' when appropriate.

[1] R/59/31, uncatalogued records, box 2, bundle 4: 'Song against the Corporation' (hereafter 'Song'), printed below as an appendix. The poem is undated; Falvey has suggested that it dates from *c.*1698–99. Heather Falvey, 'Custom, Resistance and Politics: Local Experiences of Improvement in Seventeenth-Century England' (PhD thesis, University of Warwick, 2007), ch. 5.

Level Corporation. This was the private company founded by the fourth and fifth Earls of Bedford and their fellow investors, who in 1630 famously – or infamously depending on the account – began a project to improve this large tract of peat wetland by drainage. They undertook to do this in exchange for ownership of one-third of the drained fens, most of which had, until then, been used as common grazing lands. But equally as famously, their project was met with strident opposition from the inhabitants of the fenland, who denounced it as a scheme to deprive them of their commons and, as with similar drainage projects in the Lincolnshire Fens, a protracted series of riots erupted against the drainers and their enclosures which lasted through the 1630s, 1640s and 1650s.[2]

Between the riots and the confusion of the Civil War, some of the drainage projects were derailed; but the Bedford project in the Great Level continued. The drainers there had the support of both the Interregnum and Restoration governments through two Acts of Parliament of 1649 and 1663, and the aid of the military in suppressing riots.[3] By 1663 the drainers had been confirmed in their authority over the drainage works, in the possession of their enclosures, and established as a perpetual Corporation to oversee the maintenance of the drainage works.

As the title of the song suggests, feelings about the drainers and the Corporation they founded did not generally improve in the decades after the riots were suppressed. Six of its seven verses are taken up with castigating the Corporation and its officers for their arrogance, ignorance and negligence, such as the Register who comes down from London 'so wounderos rare', or the Board of the Corporation who do 'meet and sitt in state/they put on their clocks and then they look so grate'. But these cloaks failed to disguise that (as the singer claims) 'their witts was very small/for it is the Corp[o]r[a]t[atio]n thatt hath undone us all'.

But even though this is a 'Song against [the] Corporation', there is another villain: Captain Flood. As the personification of the river floods that at times covered the low-lying fens, he first appears in a well-known ballad from the first quarter of the century, 'The Powte's Complaint', as a champion of the fens against other would-be drainers.[4] By the end of the century he had become a threat to the fenmen, as an invading force that breaks banks and drowns meadows, fields and houses. The harshest criticism of the Corporation is reserved for how their negligence had left the fens vulnerable to the captain and his watery forces. And,

2 Keith Lindley, *Fenland Riots and the English Revolution* (London, 1982), gives an overview of the riots across East Anglia; Falvey, 'Custom, Resistance and Politics', gives a more detailed analysis through a case study of the town of Whittlesey, Cambs.

3 Lindley, *Fenland Riots*, pp. 182–3.

4 Falvey, 'Custom, Resistance and Politics', ch. 5.

despite the repeated refrain of how the Corporation 'hath the Fenns undon', the last stanza makes a complete turnabout, as the singer promises the Corporation that if they would 'send [Wa]rrants to sease Captain Floud/we will Assist you with all our powers & mights'. Given a choice between the Corporation and Captain Flood, the singer chooses the Corporation, for (as the song plaintively ends) 'if Captain Floud bent taine [be not taken], we shall be all undon'.

This may seem surprising considering the apparently vociferous opposition to drainage only a few years before. But to understand the relationship between the fenlanders and the drainage works in the later seventeenth century we need to reassess their relationship with the fens themselves, both before and after drainage. Their opposition to the draining – as opposed to the enclosures – was more ambivalent than has been implied in recent literature.[5] Moreover, both the drainage and the subsequent enclosures wrought their own changes on the landscape of the level, physical and human. Not only did the drainage have unforeseen consequences, including lowering the surface of the peat fens, but the enclosures by both the drainers and by others within the level had reorganized land use into patterns which were themselves dependent on the continued good functioning of the works. This dependence can be seen in the crises that developed as the works broke down over the later seventeenth century and in the conflicts that emerged between different communities and regions over which would be drained at the expense of another.

As an act of improvement, the draining of the fens was, of course, unique – just as the landscape was unique. But the continued experiences in the Great Level also force us to confront the complexities of conflicts over agricultural improvement: to take issues of environment and landscape seriously and to understand how the changes wrought by improvement created new interests, even as old grievances were not wholly forgotten.

I

The fen drainage schemes of the early and mid-seventeenth century were some of the most ambitious improvement projects pursued in early modern Britain. More recently they have become notorious as examples of unwanted and unnecessary 'improvement' imposed by elites as a means to improve their own fortunes at the expense of the customary rights of the inhabitants of the place.

---

[5] Notably Lindley, *Fenland Riots*, introduction; Christopher Newbold, 'Historical changes in the Nature Conservation Interest of the Fens of Cambridgeshire', in Hadrian Cook and Tom Williamson (eds), *Water Management in the English Landscape: Field, Marsh and Meadow* (Edinburgh, 1999), pp. 210–26.

The rights in question were use-rights within the vast fen commons of eastern England. These low-lying and seasonally flooded wetlands were unsuitable for arable agriculture, but were instead used by the fen and fen-edge communities as summer grazing for the livestock which were the mainstay of the region. They also provided such valuable products as fish and fowl, turf for fuel and reeds or sedge for thatching, baskets and flooring. In the early seventeenth century there were an estimated 600,000 acres of flooded fenlands in eastern England around the Wash. The Great Level, as the fens on the south side of the Wash between Cambridge and Wisbech were known, was the largest of the fen levels to be drained at this time, and included over 300,000 acres of fenlands mostly used as common.[6]

The proponents of drainage claimed that new drainage canals and flood protection banks would improve the quality of these lands by securing them against the winter flooding which contributed 'not only to the great hurt and damage of the same grounds but also of the whole comon wealth'.[7] Drainage would transform this 'wildernesse of water' into 'a goodly green meddow', perhaps even arable land, to the benefit of both the region and the nation as a whole.[8] This was their justification for pushing the projects forwards against the will of the majority of the inhabitants. The drainers in the several projects were engineers, well-to-do landowners and/or courtiers who offered their expertise and/or finance to construct these works. But in exchange for their investment they demanded ownership of a proportion of the drained lands: in the Great Level, the Earls of Bedford and their fellow investors were awarded 95,000 acres, about one-third of the land deemed to be hurtfully surrounded.[9]

---

6 H. C. Darby, *The Medieval Fenland* (Cambridge, 1940), pp. 21–85; Joan Thirsk, *English Peasant Farming: The Agrarian History of Lincolnshire from Tudor to Recent Times* (London, 1957), pp. 6–48; J. R. Ravensdale, *Liable to Floods: Village Landscape on the Edge of the Fens, AD 450–1850* (Cambridge, 1974), *passim*. The estimate of fenland acreage is taken from George Bland, *The humble remonstrance of the benefits of drayning fenne lands of the severall Counties of Yorke, Lincolne, Cambridge, Norfolk and Huntington* (1628).

7 EDR, A/1/8, fos. 50–61: draft of bill of 1604; also Mark E. Kennedy, '"So glorious a work as this draining of the Fens": The Impact of Royal Government on Local Political Culture in Elizabethan and Jacobean England' (PhD thesis, Cornell University, 1985), pp. 132–6.

8 H. C., *A discourse concerning the drayning of fennes and surrounded grounds in the sixe counteys of Norfolk, Suffolke, Cambridge, with the Isle of Ely, Huntington, Northampton and Lincolne* (London, 1629); also Bland, *Humble Remonstrance*, and I. L., *A discourse concerning the great benefit of drayning and imbanking, and of transportation by water within the Country* (1641).

9 The 'Lynn Law' of 1630, printed in Samuel Wells, *The history of the drainage of the Great Level of the Fens, called Bedford Level; with the constitution and laws of the Bedford Level Corporation* (2 vols, London, 1828–30), vol. 2, pp. 98–119.

The spokesmen for the opponents of drainage argued that the drainage was not necessary and that the drainers had lied about the productivity of the unimproved fens. Far from being 'so much useless ground',[10] the common fens bred 'infinite numbers of horses, mares, and colts, and all sorts of cattel', as well as 'great flocks of sheep' and 'great store of osier, reed and sedg' and other necessities which set 'many poor on work'.[11] And rather than seeing periodic floods as a problem, it was argued that many areas within the fens were 'bettered by overflowing'.[12] The Bishop of Ely, for example, asserted that there were many grounds within the level 'which are never drowned, but as all meadowes are', and others which were 'not hurtfully surrounded but are better and more fruitfull by being sometymes overflowne and surrounded'.[13] Indeed, the inhabitants of Cottenham in 1621 testified that they received 'more benefit then hurte' from the floods and, when not overflowed, 'the white fodder decayeth, and the growndes turn muche to a kinde of small hamersede which the cattell like not so well'.[14] Having lied about the fens and subverted the political process to gain their drainage contracts, the drainers had simply forced through what would serve their own private gain, the opponents charged, for all that they claimed that drainage was a public good.[15]

Most recent historians would agree with this assessment. Despite their challenging environment, the fenlanders were not poor; their fields may have been small, but the inhabitants sustained a comfortable, even at times prosperous, livelihood utilizing the common resources of the fen wetlands.[16] Indeed, Margaret Spufford has suggested that access to these common resources mitigated the economic pressures which, elsewhere in southern England,

---

10 Sir William Killigrew, *Sir William Killigrew his answer to the fenne mens objections against the Earl of Lindsay his drayning in Lincolnshire* (1649), p. 15.

11 *The humble petition of the owners and Commoners of the town of Islelham in the county of Cambridge* (*c.*1653), p. 4.

12 *The anti-projector, or, the history of the Fen project* (*c.*1653), p. 8. This pamphlet has been re-dated by Willmoth to 1646 to *c.*1653: Frances Willmoth, *Sir Jonas Moore: Practical Mathematics and Restoration Science* (Woodbridge, 1993), p. 94. It is also clearly authored by or highly derivative of Sir John Maynard, the author of *The picklock of the Old Fenne Project* (1650).

13 EDR, A/8/7, fos 1–5: 'Excepcons offered by Mathew Bishop of Ely, and the Dean and Chapter of Ely' [*c.*1646].

14 British Library (BL), Add. Ms. 33466, fo. 184 (also quoted in Ravensdale, *Liable to Floods*, p. 64).

15 *Anti-projector*, p. 6. This accusation appears frequently elsewhere within the opposition discourse.

16 Assessment based on Darby, *Medieval Fenland*; Ravensdale, *Liable to Floods*; Thirsk, *English Peasant Farming*; and Thirsk, 'The Isle of Axholme before Vermuyden', *Agricultural History Rev.* 1 (1953), pp. 16–28.

contributed to growing rural inequality and landlessness.[17] And the motivation of the drainers was most definitely profit. They, like any modern contractor bidding to construct a public work, did not spend hundreds of thousands of pounds for the good of the commonwealth, but for the increase of their own fortunes.[18] In this they were actively supported by significant landlords within the fens, including the Crown and its lessees, who were themselves looking to make more money out of their own estates after drainage through their rights of approvement: that is, the right to enclose land from manorial wastes such as the fen commons.[19] Their political support was key to all the drainage schemes: in the Great Level it was what allowed the approval of Bedford's original contract of 1630 by the Court of Sewers, a commission of landowners personally chosen by the pro-drainage Charles I, and helped his son gain the subsequent Act of Parliament in 1663 (following on one of 1649) which confirmed the drainers' project and their ownership of the 95,000 acres.[20]

Yet even such apparently black and white situations have their grey and muddy bits. As the inhabitants of the fens rioted against the drainers and their enclosures, their relationship with the wetlands and the possibilities offered by drainage were more ambivalent than recent literature has suggested. Though the drainers clearly exaggerated the low productivity of the fens, their opponents were very selective in their own arguments. Some areas of the Great Level certainly were bettered by overflowing: after the drainage, the town of Over asked to set down a tunnel in the river bank to purposely re-flood their fens because they found that the grass was 'very much inriched by the winter fluds'.[21] Over, however, is in the south-west corner of the Great Level; its fens were, as one seventeenth-century fenman put it, the best fens, nearest the hills, 'soonest drowned and soonest drayned',[22] such that the water did not rest upon them as

---

17 Margaret Spufford, *Contrasting Communities: English Villagers in the Sixteenth and Seventeenth Centuries* (London, 1974), pp. 165–7.

18 Margaret Albright Knittl, 'The design for the initial drainage of the Great Level of the Fens: an historical whodunit in three parts', *Agricultural History Rev.* 55 (2007), p. 25 quotes the fourth Earl of Bedford regarding his investing his 'shrunk fortune' in the draining. The Corporation later claimed that the drainers in the Great Level had spent £200,000 constructing the works: BLC 11/15, fo. 13 (1696).

19 For more on the right of approvement, see Shannon's chapter in this volume.

20 Kennedy, '"So glorious a work"', discusses political support for drainage to 1625; Lindley, *Fenland Riots*, after 1625; also Joan Thirsk, 'The Crown As Projector on Its own Estates, from Elizabeth I to Charles I', in R. W. Hoyle (ed.), *The Estates of the English Crown, 1558–1640* (Cambridge, 1992), pp. 297–352.

21 S/B/SP/045, Letter to Richard, Lord Gorges, Surveyor General of the BLC from the town of Over, 17 Nov. 1670.

22 Quoted in Ravensdale, *Liable to Floods*, p. 42.

long as it did elsewhere. The productivity of the fenlands varied widely across the Great Level, and those towns with the best-drained fens not only reported higher values for their lands but also had much higher population densities. In an assessment of the rent-value or equivalent of their fens before the draining, Over's neighbouring town of Cottenham claimed that its half-several fens were worth between 12*s*. and 20*s*. an acre. But the best fens of March, in the centre of the level and drained by the problematic River Nene, were thought by the local inhabitants to be worth only 5*s*. an acre, while 1,000 acres of 'moorish and mossy ground' (most likely bog) in Woodwalton were valued at 18*d*. an acre.[23] Thousands of acres of fens – including the largest fen commons – were apparently exactly as one drainage proponent had claimed: 'drowned land ... not worth 5*s*. by the yeare'.[24] Contemporaries were well aware of this; one early seventeenth-century petition of the inhabitants of the fen towns along the southern fen-edge contrasted their own fens, which were 'firme ground' and 'of good value', with the 'low and bottom grounde within Isle of Ely and other counties', in the centre of the level, 'which be little or nothing worth'.[25] And while the commons of fen-edge parishes like Cottenham, Over or Willingham supported as many or even more people per acre than conventional arable communities, the parishes with the largest fen commons – those in the centre and west of the level, such as Doddington, which included the hamlet of March – only supported a very low population density. On the evidence of the 1563 diocesan returns, Cottenham had an estimated 16.75 families per 1,000 acres, and its neighbouring towns of Willingham and Over 22.53 and 33.72 families per 1,000 acres respectively. But Woodwalton was reported as having only 9.49 families per 1,000 acres and the parish of Doddington only 5.32 families.[26]

---

23 BL, Add. MS. 33466, fos. 172, 176, 184. Ash has noted some very interesting overestimation in another set of local assessments submitted in 1620, but there is no reason to believe that the value of fens was underestimated. Eric Ash, 'Pushing and pushing back: Central vs. local interests in draining the English Fens', unpublished draft paper presented at The Johns Hopkins University, 2007.

24 Bland, *Humble remonstrance*.

25 EDR, A/8/1, p. 104, petition of the fen towns in Suffolk and Cambridgeshire 'without the Isle of Ely' [*c.*1605].

26 These figures are derived from a comparison of the 1563 Ecclesiastical Census as published in Alan Dyer and D. M. Palliser (eds), *The Diocesan Population Returns for 1563 and 1603* (British Academy Records of Social and Economic History, new ser., 31 Oxford, 2005) with modern parish acreages in *VCH Cambridgeshire*, II, pp. 136–40 and *VCH Huntingdon*, I, pp. 101–5. Serious doubts have been expressed regarding the accuracy of the 1563 census: Nigel Goose, 'The Bishops' census of 1563: a re-examination of its reliability', *Local Population Stud.* 56 (1996), pp. 43–53. However, the overall pattern of population density in sixteenth-century Cambridgeshire and Huntingdonshire as derived from this source closely follows known

It should also be noted that the idea of draining was not an alien one in the fens. From the early medieval period forwards, the landowners and inhabitants of the fens had sought to mitigate and control both tidal and river flooding by constructing protective banks and redirecting and/or straightening rivers to run more directly to the sea.[27] Much of the silt fens nearer to the coast had been already reclaimed by the sixteenth century.[28] These areas were excluded from the later drainage proposals because they were already deemed to have been sufficiently drained. Within the peat fens, the area of interest to the seventeenth-century drainers, rivers were redirected and embanked to improve the draining of some parts: in the late fifteenth century, Bishop Morton oversaw the construction of an artificial drainage canal very similar in design to the new rivers which were constructed by the Bedfords some 150 years later.[29] It was also in the middle ages that the Crown established the Courts of Sewers, ad hoc commissions of local gentry, to oversee the maintenance of these drainage works by the adjacent landowners and commoners. But by the seventeenth century serious questions were being raised about both the adequacy of the existing works and the Court of Sewers within the Great Level. As Mark Kennedy has shown, the late sixteenth and early seventeenth centuries saw several serious floods in the fens and complaints from the inhabitants regarding the poor condition of their lands. And it was the inadequacy of these works and the apparently intractable disputes between different parts of the Great Level over them that first attracted the attention of the central government and secured the support of James I for a comprehensive drainage project.[30]

In a close reading of some of the opposition to drainage in both the early and mid-seventeenth century, one can see how these disparities and history played out in the ambivalence shown towards drainage itself. Though some opponents of the drainage claimed that they did 'disavowe the worke and do disagree to all manner of drayninge',[31] others denied that they were against

landscape patterns, as well as the population densities derived from both the 1674 Hearth Tax and the 1801 census in each county, suggesting that these inaccuracies do not reduce the pattern to noise. They also match the patterns of wealth per square mile in *c.*1524/25 as mapped by John Sheail, *The Regional Distribution of Wealth in England as Indicated in the 1524/25 Lay Subsidy Returns* (2 vols, List and Index Soc., Special Ser., 28–9, 1998), vol. 2, pp. 71, 104, 121, 129.

27 David Hall and John Coles, *Fenland Survey: An Essay in Landscape and Persistence* (London, 1994), *passim*.

28 Robert Silvester, 'Medieval Reclamation of Marsh and Fen', in Cook and Williamson (eds), *Water Management*, pp. 122–40.

29 Darby, *Medieval Fenland*, pp. 167–8.

30 Kennedy, 'So glorious a work', p. 242, *passim*.

31 BLC 9/3, second section, fo. 3: Notes taken at the Committee for the Fens, 10 June 1646.

drainage in principle.[32] Indeed, one opposition paper distributed in the name of the landowners and commoners in southern Lincolnshire claimed that they knew 'none in England that opposeth drainings'; nor did they believe 'that any in England think us such fools or mad men, that we need guardians for our estates'.[33] Whether *their* specific fens needed draining or how drainage was to be paid for was another matter. Opponents on the edges of the Great Level, for example, protested against being included in a project which they claimed would only benefit the fens within the centre of the level, including 'the Earl of Bedford's hurtfully surrounded land, as Thorney Abbey and Whittlesey';[34] others claimed that new works would not be required if only landlords (particularly those interested in new works) would pay their share in maintaining the existing works, 'the neglect whereof hath been the cause of the decay of those countries'.[35]

And, of course, this ambivalence towards drainage did not at all detract from the very real, and very adamant, opposition to enclosures to pay for that draining. The fenlanders were upset by the reduction of their commons and angry at how it went forward without their consent.[36] Perhaps it is not even possible to separate drainage from enclosure or the restriction of common right. The fens continued to exist as extensive commons precisely because they were seasonally flooded and thus unsuitable for arable or more intensive pastoral cultivation; they had offered little temptation to expanding farmers or manorial lords who might have enclosed a larger proportion earlier. A reduction in the

---

32 'It is suggested that the inhabitants are not willing to have those countries drayned which is not so', EDR, A/8/1, p. 49, petition from the inhabitants of Sutton, 24 June 1605. Maynard, *Picklock*, p. 10, also distinguished between illegal and legal draining, saying that the latter was 'good for the common-wealth, because it is with their free consents'.

33 *A reply to Sir William Killigrews dispersed papers, by the owners and commoners in Lincolnshire* [after 1650].

34 *Petition of ... the town of Islelham*, p. 6; also *A reply to a printed paper intituled The state of the adventurers case, in answer to a petition exhibited against them by the inhabitants of the Soake of Peterborow* (1650), p. 4. In this, they echoed earlier objections: EDR, A/8/1, p. 49, petition from the inhabitants of Sutton, 24 June 1605; p. 104, petition of the fen towns in Suffolk and Cambridgeshire 'without the Isle of Ely' [*c.*1605]; pp. 122–4, petition of Bottisham, Swaffam Bulbeck and Prior, Burwell, Wickin, Soham, Fen Drayton, Swavesey, Over, Willingham, Cottenham, Rampton and Waterbeach [*c.*1605].

35 EDR, A/8/1, pp. 62–7: 'Reasons of the Inhabitants of the Isle of Ely why the aforesaid Bill should not pass' [*c.*1604].

36 The consent of the majority of the commoners had been required for undertakings by the General Drainage Act of 1600/01 (43 Eliz., c.11), but the drainers used the Courts of Sewers to avoid this procedure; lack of consent was raised as the first objection in The National Archives (TNA), SP 16/339/27 [*c.*1636], 'Reasons which the inhabitants ... do make againste the drayninge of the fenns'.

size of the commons might result in a restriction of common right. In the late sixteenth and early seventeenth centuries, rights of pasture were still relatively unlimited in many of the large common fens of the Isle of Ely, and were not restricted to the owners of certain houses, or land in the arable fields or in the number of animals allowed to be pastured – as was usual elsewhere.[37] But pasture rights had already begun to be restricted in some of the better-drained, smaller commons of the fen-edge parishes.[38] Some opponents feared that if the fens were improved by drainage, and were thus more desirable, the drainers' enclosures would themselves be followed up by further enclosures of the remaining fen commons by the 'incroaching lords';[39] common rights were likely to become more restricted. And these fears were justified, as we shall see, as both of these outcomes followed the draining and enclosure of fenlands in the Great Level.

But when looking at the relationship between the fenlanders and drainage in the later period, it is important to remember that while the drainers may have been unwanted, their draining was not the focus of the opposition. Indeed, the riots in the Great Level did not begin when the work on the projects began in 1630, but only after the first enclosures. Heather Falvey has pointed out that, in the case of Whittlesey, accusations that the fenlanders attacked major drainage works are unsubstantiated.[40] There were even a minority of farmers and landowners who supported the drainage projects, as can be seen by their testimony on the drainers' behalf before a parliamentary committee in 1646.[41] One Robert Pinchbacke testified that six years before the draining, Well and Welney had been 'so wett in sumer as they had no meate [fodder] but what they gott in the water up to the Bolly'; the ground had been worth 4*d*. an acre, but now was worth 4*s*. or 5*s*. an acre and 'the stocke as much increase'. He also testified that a farm his father had rented in 1600 for £20 was now let at £60.[42] Whether his father could have afforded this three-fold increase in rent he did

37 BL, Harl. Ms 5011, fo. 28v, decree of the court of Exchequer, dated 27 May 1590, notes that it was the custom in the manor of Doddington and 'the most parte of the townes and parishes within the said isle' that common of pasture was available by residency, and also denied to absentee house-owners.

38 Ravensdale, *Liable to Floods*, p. 78; Spufford, *Contrasting Communities*, p. 139. The relationship between size of commons and eligibility for common right is demonstrated through the comparative study of common lands in Martina de Moor, Leigh Shaw-Taylor and Paul Warde (eds), *The Management of Common Land in North-West Europe, c.1500–1850* (Turnhout, 2002).

39 H.C., *Discourse concerning the drayning of fennes*, B2, quoting an objection to drainage.

40 Falvey, 'Custom, Resistance and Politics', ch. 5.

41 BLC 9/3, second section. Falvey also notes the split in Whittlesey, with the majority of the inhabitants against the project and a minority of tenants and landowners in favour, 'Custom, Resistance and Politics', ch. 5.

42 BLC 9/3, second section, fos. 10v–11 (30 June 1647).

not say, but he was quite adamant that the draining had brought a significant increase in the productivity of those fenlands.

II

Understanding that the opposition to drainage was based on social and political grounds rather than considerations of what would be best for the productivity of the fens[43] helps us understand better the context in which the relationship between the fenlanders and drainage developed in the decades after the suppression of the riots, including their relationship with the institution which oversaw those works: the Corporation of the Great Level. This body was established by the 1663 Act and had evolved from the private drainage company formed by those who had 'adventured' their capital in the construction of the new drainage works in the Great Level and thus received part of the 95,000 acres in proportion to their investment. As shares in the 'Adventurers' lands', as the 95,000 acres were known locally, began to be divided up and sold off, the new owners also became members of the Corporation. By the eighteenth century there were over 500 owners of Adventurers' lands, all of whom were members of the Corporation, though voting rights were subject to a property qualification of 100 acres.[44]

As part of their agreement, Bedford and the other drainers had also taken on the responsibility of maintaining the drainage of the level in perpetuity. This was financed through rates (which contemporaries always referred to as 'taxes') on the Adventurers' lands which were then spent on the maintenance of the major rivers, banks and sluices of the level, known as the 'public works'. But the 1663 Act appointed the Board of the Corporation to act as the Commissioners of Sewers for the Great Level, replacing the traditional royally appointed commission. As the Court of Sewers, the Corporation's authority extended not only over their own works but also over the many private drains and ditches and, indeed, over any behaviour that could be to the detriment of the drainage of the level – as the numerous by-laws against dams and weirs in the rivers and cattle or carts on the banks testify.[45] The Board of the Corporation and the Court of

43 The lack of consent and the subversion of the Commissions of Sewers were serious issues and not just Civil War rhetoric. See TNA, SP 16/339/27 [*c.* 1636] and EDR, A/8/1, pp. 119–22 [*c.* 1605]; and the discussion in my forthcoming dissertation.

44 Dorothy Summers, 'The Constitution of the Bedford Level Corporation, 1663–1920' (MA thesis, University of London, 1971), p. 82. Three hundred of the members held less than 100 acres.

45 For example BLC 10/*, fos. 36r–v (27 June 1666): general orders.

Sewers were notionally two different bodies and kept separate records for their meetings; but as they were always the same men, their policies and actions ran in parallel.

This authority did not go unchallenged; nor did tensions between the drainers – as represented by the Corporation – and the inhabitants of the level end with the suppression of the riots. There continued to be disputes over the drainers' enclosures and the other rights they claimed. In 1666 several tenants of the Adventurers' lands in Whelpmore fought a legal battle for their lands against Sir John Cutts and even paid men to guard their fens at night[46]; in 1674 William Drury complained that he had been kept out of 100 acres of Corporation land for several years by the commoners of Littleport, who themselves claimed that the drainers had taken 'more then their due' out of the said fens.[47] By the terms of the 1663 Act the Corporation had also been granted the fishing in the new rivers and the grazing on the banks and foreshore within 60 feet of the major rivers; these rights were then leased to Corporation members, often at very low rates. But the lessees complained of being 'forced to severall tryalls att lawe att theyr great charge' to defend their titles.[48] In 1670 Mr Bullmer of Isleham threatened to impound the Adventurers' cattle on the wash between the river and the Adventurers' lands there[49], while in 1680 the Board was informed that:

> notwithstanding the severall verdicts against Henry Foster for fishing in the Gull Hole [in Old Bedford River] the said Foster had lately pr[e]sumed to fish in the same place againe.[50]

Several inhabitants of the town of Mepal demolished one of the Corporation's cottages which was on disputed land,[51] but in 1694 Roger Jenyns, a prominent Board member, apparently had less luck removing the cottages of 'severall poor people' erected on the bank of the Old Bedford River which he leased, as the town of Welches Dam can be found in the same place today.[52]

---

46 S/B/SP/021, petition of John Berry and seven others of Littleport, tenants in Whelpmore in the 95,000 acres, n.d. [*c.*1666].

47 S/B/SP/074, petition of William Drury of Earith, gent, read 2 July 1674.

48 BLC 11/8, fo. 33 (10 Feb. 1675/76), *passim*.

49 BLC 11/6, fo. 5 (16 June 1670).

50 BLC 11/10, fo. 4 (12 Feb. 1679/80). See also BLC 11/9, fos. 2v (8 Feb. 1676/77), 30–30v (12 Dec. 1678), 31 (13 Dec. 1687).

51 BLC 11/12, fo. 23v (5 July 1688).

52 BLC 10/6, fol. 26 (5 Apr. 1694). It was specified in the complaint that the cottages were on the bank near Welches Dam, and no settlement has been noticed here from before 1660.

Conflict also emerged over the drainage works – and the Corporation's exercise of its authority to maintain them – and other uses of the space within the fens. The construction of the new rivers and banks, not to mention enclosures and division ditches, naturally disrupted both land- and water-based transportation networks within the level. As Dorothy Summers has pointed out, the needs of drainage did not necessarily coincide with those of navigation; the professional watermen frequently butted heads with sluice-keepers over when the doors of the waterways would be open.[53] Local networks were also disrupted. The small hamlet of Manea was cut off from its parish town of Coveney and the market at Ely by both of the new Bedford Rivers; in 1652, and again in 1663, they complained of how they had no 'passage neither to mille nor markete' and how even in good conditions they were 'forced to goe and com tenn miles about'.[54] The Corporation's new embankment in Methwold blocked a navigation canal from some private fens there; the two gentlemen who leased this land from the king were incensed. Not only had the Corporation taken 'not soe few as 350 acres' of their land 'under pretence of improvement', but now many of their under-tenants 'did throw upp their farmes' and they were forced to let the grounds at 'very low and under rates' because of the charge of getting commodities away.[55] Similarly, the many new drainage and division ditches, which marked out enclosures just as hedges did in drier countries, disrupted the droveways and cartways of the fens. Some petitioned the Corporation to provide them with bridges,[56] while others simply went ahead and made dams in the ditches to cross into their common or several fens, an offence which was prosecuted in the Court of Sewers as a threat to the draining of the level.[57]

Albeit in an unintended way, the works also created new transportation networks. To the disgust of the Corporation, many of the raised banks which they had constructed at great cost to prevent floods also became very popular with the inhabitants for carting and driving their cattle along. After all, they were solid and higher than the rest of the fens, and they ran in convenient straight lines.[58] But, as stated in the presentment of William Walter of Stowbrinck in

---

53 Dorothy Summers, *The Great Level: A History of Drainage and Land Reclamation in the Fens* (Newton Abbot, 1976), pp. 108–9.

54 S/B/SP/001, petition of the inhabitants of Manea, 20 Apr. 1652; S/B/SP/005, petition of the inhabitants of Manea, read 1 Oct. 1663.

55 S/B/SP/031, petition of Charles Fleetwood and Symon Smyth, Esqs, read 29 May 1668.

56 For example S/B/SP/188, petition of the inhabitants of Littleport, 4 Apr. 1688; S/B/SP/203, petition of William Stafford of Denver, read 6 Apr. 1692.

57 BLC 10/3, fos. 33v–34r (4 Apr. 1683): 'severall persons have made damms and cartwayes' over drains in the level.

58 Summers has made the same observation: *Great Level*, p. 118.

1689, the loaded wagons could 'breake and subvert' the soils of the banks, to their 'great decay and damage'.[59] The records of the Corporation and Sewers contain repeated orders against this practice – as well as suits or fines against those defying those orders[60] – and the Board also instructed their officers or lessees to set up narrow horse-bridges or rails and posts on affected banks.[61] But they had trouble enforcing those orders: rails and posts were torn down[62] and their own sluice-keeper apparently ignored several orders to stop the 'great and continuall passage' over the bridge at Stanground sluice, despite how the adjacent bank was being 'much worne and trodden down'.[63]

Nor were these the only conflicts over bank usage: just as they were used to move about the fens, banks were also used by fenlanders in the course of keeping their livestock. Thomas Powell was presented in 1687 for having kept his cattle on or near the bank of the 20-foot drain in Sutton because they 'tread downe the said banck', while Thomas Grimwood of Upwell was presented at the same time for having placed 'severall stacks of corne' on the bank of Popham's Eau to make a feeding place for his cattle. The court ordered him to put up a hedge 'for preventing strawe falling into the draine and cattell from treading into the same'.[64] Pigs were the worst offenders due to their habit of digging into the already beleaguered banks. In this matter the Corporation again met strong resistance: even after a generous bounty had been offered for any pigs seized on the banks, the 'Hoggtakers' found that the pigs were 'driven from them [so] that they could not gett them to the pound'.[65]

More seriously for the sake of the works, there were also challenges to the Corporation's claim to have the right to dig earth from the forelands – the area within 60 feet of a river – and commons of the fens for the repair of banks. While

---

59 BLC 9/12, fo. 35 (3 Oct. 1689).

60 For example BLC 11/4, fo. 30 (31 July 1667): suit against Thomas Bentley of Ely for carting upon the banks; BLC 11/5, fo. 17v (2 Apr. 1668): 'Court being informed that some of the persons that had been arrested for carting upon banks had repayred the same but other were refractory'. See too the presentments: BLC 9/12, fos. 9, 40, 57v.

61 For example BLC 11/5, fol. 9v (29 Oct. 1668); BLC 11/7, fo. 39 (4 Feb. 1674/75).

62 BLC 11/16, fo. 37v (2 July 1702): William Baggerly and William Nicholls, inhabitants of Crowland, arrested for cutting and pulling down the posts and rails on Peakirk Bank; also for throwing earth into the river and for 'discharging the Corp[ora]c[i]ons Workemen', charged at the Lincoln assizes. Also BLC 9/12, fo. 61 (2 Nov. 1698): Adam Sennis of Leverington presented 'for breaking down and forcing the barrs upon the great north bank of Mortens Leam at Willyses near Northas Gravell'.

63 BLC 10/7, fo. 9v (9 Apr. 1695); 11/16, fo. 30v (18 Feb. 1703).

64 BLC 9/12, fo. 3 (21 Oct. 1687).

65 BLC 10/4, fo. 24v (4 June 1687).

some were willing to accept compensation for the damage,[66] others refused. In May 1696 one Butler of Clayhithe stopped the workers who were cutting earth from his land within 60 feet of the river to repair the nearby bank and threatened to sue them. Later that year the Corporation's attorney was asked to appear for several persons who took earth from Mrs Coventry's grounds for the repair of the Corporation's banks, just in case she decided to sue them.[67] And at Swavesey a dispute over the Corporation's right to dig in their common fens erupted into a riot in 1674 in which the corporation's workmen were harassed, struck and even threatened with pitchforks.[68]

But even as they contested the rights of the Corporation to cut earth with which to repair the works, the inhabitants of Swavesey petitioned them that same year, requesting that the sluice in the bank near their town be repaired.[69] Indeed, though many in the level ran into conflicts over the works, just as many ran into problems rather with their failure. Requests for improvement to the drainage works were the largest single category of petitions to the Corporation in the late seventeenth century, and were more likely to be the large petitions submitted by towns or groups of towns. About half of the surviving petitions from those identifying themselves as 'the inhabitants' or the towns of the fens concerned requests for improvements to their local drainage.[70]

In fact, if one could say that there was a discourse of being 'bettered by overflowing' in the opposition to drainage, then the petitions and complaints in the late seventeenth-century fens were rather a lament of how their fens were 'overflowed and drowned'.[71] As early as 1663 the decay of banks and silting up of the drain near the town of Stoke and its neighbours in Norfolk meant that not only were the Adventurers' lands damaged, but also 'every downfall of water or swelling of the river ... doth surround the greatest p[ar]t of all the s[ai]d comons', leaving 'many of the poore Inhabitants ... near undunn not only by losing the feed for their cattle but also the losse of the fother and winter meate for thim'.[72] At about that time, the inhabitants of Stretham and Thetford also

---

66 For example BLC 11/7, fo. 11r–v (13 Nov. 1673): the town of Over desired money to be distributed to the poor for certain lands in Over cut for the repair of Swavesey banks; order that the lands in question be assessed and the value returned to the town.

67 BLC 11/15, fos. 6v (15 May 1696), 16v (3 Dec. 1696).

68 BLC 11/7, fos. 17v (26 Feb. 1673/4), 31r–v (30 July 1674). Also R/59/31, uncatalogued records, box 15, bundle 2.

69 BLC 11/7, fos. 22v–23r (4 June 1674).

70 Based on an analysis of S/B/SP/1–232.

71 Quote from S/B/SP/106, petition of the Inhabitants of Methwold, n.d. [*c*.1679?].

72 S/B/SP/3, petition of the inhabitants of the several towns of Stoke, Wretton, Wereham, West Dereham and Roxham, read 29 Sept. 1663.

reported that 900 acres of their several land and commons had been drowned for nine months, 'to the undoeing of many of your petitoners'.[73] In 1675 the inhabitants of Methwold described themselves as 'very great sufferers' from the 'great inundacons on the common of Methwold',[74] while in the year before, the inhabitants of Haddenham and Sutton were also 'great sufferers' due to the 'unusual inundacons and overflowings' of their lands, rendering their fens 'very unprofitable'.[75] Fenlanders complained when the Corporation's works disrupted not just their navigation but also their drainage.[76] They asked the Corporation to enforce the maintenance of the smaller drainage works by other landowners or inhabitants in the level[77] and complained bitterly when the actions of other inhabitants hurt the draining of their lands, such as by setting down a dam in a drain or fishing weirs in the rivers.[78] And, of course, the 'Song against [the] Corporation' itself begins with an account of floods due to breaches in the banks; the singer is upset because the Corporation has allowed Captain Flood to drown 'our hay & corne thus & our Housses two'.[79]

III

It was complaints such as these which led H. C. Darby to conclude in 1940 that the drainage works in the Great Level had begun to break down just a few years after they had been completed, and that what had seemed to be an achievement in 1652 was a 'tragedy' by 1700.[80] The causes of this failure are well known. Not only had the drainers failed to deal with one of the ultimate causes of the flooding – the silting up of the river mouths by the strong Wash tides – but the initial success of the draining also bred its failure: as the peat of the

73 S/B/SP/2, petition of the inhabitants of Stretham and Thetford, read 1 Oct. [*c.*1663].

74 S/B/SP/84, petition of divers of the Inhabitants of Methwold, read 17 June 1675.

75 S/B/SP/66, petition of the inhabitants of Haddenham and Sutton, read 9 Apr. 1674.

76 S/B/SP/160, petition of the inhabitants of Southery, read 8 Apr. 1685.

77 S/B/SP/55, petition of Thomas Cooke, Thomas Lemberd and Thomas Bensted, on behalf of themselves and others the inhabitants of the town of Bottisham, read 9 Apr. 1673, asking for an order for Thomas Parker, gent, to scour out Bottisham Lode; S/B/SP/91, petition of Robert Cole of Littleport, read Apr. 1677, asking for an order for the inhabitants of Littleport to scour out Cammell Lode.

78 BLC 10/2, fo. 13 (8 Apr. 1674), petition of the inhabitants of Manea against a dam set down by Mr Dymond in Daisy Lode; S/B/SP/90, petition of several inhabitants of Nassingborough hundred and the lord's tenants in Peterborough Great Fen, read 21 Feb. 1677, against a dam in the 12-foot and 18-foot drains set down by Francis Underwood, Esq.

79 'Song'.

80 H. C. Darby, *The Draining of the Fens* (Cambridge, 2nd edn, 1956), p. 113.

fens dried, it began to shrink and erode away.[81] Between these two problems, the rivers and drains of the level became 'much growne up and full of dirt and soyle and silt' and were at times higher than the surrounding fens.[82] Thus, even as the drainage succeeded in lowering the water table in the fens, the changes this caused in the landscape made drainage more difficult and left the lowered fens themselves more vulnerable to floods, especially after a breach in the banks protecting them.[83] These problems were also exacerbated by fatal flaws in the design of the works. The amount of water flowing from south-west to north-east along the New and Old Bedford Rivers, for example, overwhelmed the Ouse just downstream of Denver Dam; the dam was often kept closed to keep this water from running back up the Ouse. But that just caused the upstream Ouse water to back up and flood the once relatively better-drained southern part of the level.[84] In this sense, the Corporation and the drainage works really had 'the Fenns undon', though unintentionally.

At the same time, there was also a serious flaw in the design of the institution meant to maintain the draining. Though the drainers had promised to maintain the works from their own lands (the 95,000 acres) alone, the revenue from the rates on these lands was not enough to handle the ever-increasing costs of maintenance; as Dorothy Summers has shown, the Corporation's works were constantly underfunded, leading to both serious debt and neglect.[85] For those who had unwillingly paid for these works with the loss of their lands, this neglect added insult to injury. The townsmen of Burwell, for example, complained about how since the making of Burwell Lode, the 'Adventurers have not expended any money in clearing or scouring' it,[86] which must have been galling after 700 acres

---

81 Ibid., pp. 94–112.

82 Quote from S/B/SP/228, petition of the inhabitants of the town of Methwold, 7 Apr. 1702. In 1673 the inhabitants of Bottisham complained that the bottom of Bottisham Lode was higher than the soil around it (S/B/SP/57, case of Mr Parker's tunnel at Bottisham, received 15 May 1673). Wicken Lode was described as being 'grown almost level with the quick soyle, and consequently useless' (S/B/SP/012, petition of the inhabitants, landowners and landholders of Wicken, n.d. [*c.*1664?]). For another petition complaining that the rivers were grown up and in 'worse condicon than before the draineing', see S/B/SP/59, petition of the Town of Ely and parts adjacent, [that is] Stretham, Thetford, Wilburton, Haddenham, read 24 Apr. 1673.

83 Several serious floods followed breaches in the banks of the major rivers, notably in the winter of 1673/74. BLC 11/7, fos. 18v (23 Mar. 1673/4), 21 (21 May 1673).

84 Darby, *Draining*, pp. 98–9; see below for further discussion.

85 Summers, 'Bedford Level Corporation', pp. 108–52.

86 S/B/SP/156, petition of the townsmen of Burwell, n.d. [*c.*1685?]. Similar complaints were made in S/B/SP/108, petition of the inhabitants and parishioners of Haddenham, read 9 Apr. 1679; and S/B/SP/161, petition of the inhabitants of the Town of Lakenheath, read 8 Apr. 1685.

of their common fens had been granted to the drainers in order to sustain that work.[87] Several landowners and occupiers in Whittlesey were more pointed in their request for the repair of Thorney Dyke, as they stopped to remind the Corporation that the drainers 'hath and doth enjoy a considerable part of the said lands for dreyning and securing of the rest'.[88] And this neglect is the primary criticism in the 'Song against [the] Corporacon' – that 'the Corporaton might have kept him out/if they strict gardes the bancks had sett aboute'.[89]

However, there was more than just pique to these complaints: as the last verse laments, 'we poore fenn mens harts be all moust deade/scarcely Able to houlde up our heads'. The enclosures which were so much part and parcel of the drainage project had themselves changed the shape of the fens profoundly and made the inhabitants there more dependent on the successful functioning of the works. It was not just the drainers' enclosures that affected the fens; just as opponents had feared, the initial draining and enclosures had been followed by subsequent enclosures by lords and commoners in the expectation of improvements to the fens through drainage. The drainers' enclosures had already increased the amount of enclosed land within the level from about 20 per cent of the fenlands in 1635–36 to about 50 per cent.[90] But in addition to the drainers, both the lords of manors and the owners of commonable houses chose to enclose fen commons – some in agreements before the Civil War,[91] but also many under a clause in the 1663 Act which allowed them to 'to improve, sett out, inclose, divide and sever' portions of the common wastes – in lieu of their rights in those specific fens.[92] From between 1663 and 1685 there are 359 surviving decrees for the enclosure of parts of the fens, including 66 for the lords of manors and 286 for the owners of commonable messuages, from over 50 towns.[93] The total proportion of the Great Level enclosed by lords and tenants is not known. Many of these decrees could be quite small: in one award for Stow cum Qui there were 38 lots of between 0.75 and 2.75 acres in Hoe fen (perhaps for turf digging),

[87] TNA, C 225/1/9; also schedule from the St Ives Law of Sewers, 1637, printed in Wells, *History*, vol. 2, pp. 253–339.

[88] S/B/SP/172, petition of landowners and occupiers of lands at Willow Hall and Priors Fen in the parish of Whittlesey, read 7 Apr. 1686.

[89] 'Song'.

[90] Based on an analysis of the tax schedule from 1638 in BLC 9/1A, fos. 192–8, fair copy of TNA, C 225/1/9.

[91] Falvey, 'Custom, Resistance and Politics', ch. 5 discusses enclosures at Whittlesey in 1638; Lindley, *Fenland Riots*, refers to several enclosures by lords, including in Soham, where the first riot in the Great Level was sparked off by Sir Robert Heath's enclosure of 500 acres in 1632 (p. 83).

[92] 15 Car. 2 c.17, clause 35.

[93] TNA, C 229, Boxes 1–8.

adding up to only 34.5 acres.[94] But others could be much more substantial: the lords of the manor of Littleport enclosed 862 acres of fen, followed in the same year by the enclosure of a further 3,000 acres by the commoners, most receiving between 20 and 30 acres per messuage and 2–5 acres per cottage.[95] In Manea, 1472 acres and 3 roods of fenlands were enclosed; this is the equivalent of 26 per cent of the modern parish.[96]

These enclosures were not necessarily eagerly embraced by the inhabitants. In most manors or towns the lord was the first to enclose, followed by decrees for the tenants sometimes months or even years later. Eligibility for common rights – and thus for lots in lieu of those rights – was also restricted to the owners of commonable houses, a change from the late sixteenth century. In Manea the 33 owners of 35 commonable messuages claimed to be the only legal commoners in those fens, though there were 62 households reported in the Hearth Tax of 1674.[97] And as with previous attempts by lords and tenants to enclose, they also faced opposition from the other inhabitants and those claiming right of common; there were riots against the lords' enclosures at Peterborough Great Fen in 1667 and at Mildenhall in 1669 and 1684.[98]

Nor did these enclosures represent a sudden transformation of the fenland economy from a pastoral to an arable one. Though there is evidence that some of the new lots and Adventurers' grounds were put to growing crops, livestock remained the mainstay of the region.[99] For example, in 1688 one Oliver Kent of Doddington held 34 acres of lot ground (that is, enclosures made for commoners from the fens), of which he planted 19 acres with coleseed, but that year he also 'held and enjoyed' 21 acres of pasture ground and 65 acres of fen in Ransomemore and owed tithes on eight calves, 20 lambs and the fleeces of 60 sheep.[100]

But even as livestock remained very important to the region, the private fens were being used more intensively than the common fens had been before the draining. Indeed, the population of several central parishes – the ones with the

---

94 TNA, C 229/8/3. My thanks to Richard Hoyle for his suggestion on the use of these lands.

95 TNA, C 229/2/28, 3/12, 3/39, all from 1666.

96 PRO C 229/3/52, 1665: Manea decree, compared to acreage of 5,642, given in *Kelly's Directory* (1929 edn).

97 TNA, C 229/3/52, 1665; Norman and Vicky Uffindell (eds), 'Hearth Tax Assessment Cambridgeshire, 1674' (unpublished transcript, Cambridgeshire RO, 1987), p. 57.

98 Lindley, *Fenland Riots*, pp. 230–31.

99 Falvey, 'Custom, Resistance and Politics', pp. 352–3, notes that this was true of earlier lots made at Whittlesey.

100 TNA, E134/3W&M/Mich44.

lowest population density before the draining – appears to have increased in the years after 1650, though they also had had the highest proportion of their commons enclosed for the drainers. In 1670 the town of March petitioned to become a market town because the population of the Isle of Ely and the 'trade of the said countrey inn cole-seede, all sorts of graine, hemp, flax, cattell, butter, cheese, and other comodities is greatly increased'.[101] That this population growth was dependent on the draining is further supported by the fact that the population in the rural towns fell again by the end of the century as the works themselves failed.[102]

Although few of the initial investors in drainage were resident in the level, their tenants were, and over time the Adventurers' lands began to be 'divided into many small parcells' which increasingly rested 'in country peoples hands'.[103] These farmers, and the owners and tenants of the lords' and commoners' enclosures, constituted a significant landholding interest within the level who were dependent on the quality of the drainage of their lands for their profits. At the same time, the remaining commons were themselves also more dependent on the Corporation's works because they were reduced in size. After all, while a flood in part of a large open common would be bad, any grazing cattle could be moved. But once a farmer – whether grazier or ploughman, commoner or tenant – was committed to only one small part of that fen, then a flood concentrated on the wrong place could be disastrous.

The failure of the drainage was caused by problems in its design, by neglect and also by the unforeseen environmental changes wrought by drainage. But when these failures came, they caused crises because people had come to expect drainage and had begun to use the fens in ways that required it. Things could not just return to the way they had been before; the inhabitants of the Great Level – commoners and landowners alike – were dependent on the works, and the Corporation which was supposed to maintain them.

And when there were problems with the drainage, it set off new conflicts within the fenland. It could set farmers against fishermen, as when the inhabitants of Ely, Stretham, Wilberton and Thetford complained about the 'the numerous company of fishing wares' in the Ouse which so obstructed the river that it caused their grounds 'to be drowd much worse and longer'.[104] And it could and

101 S/B/SP/42: petition of the JPs for the Isle of Ely to the king, read 25 May 1670.

102 Based on an analysis of the parish records of Littleport, Downham, March and Ramsey (from transcriptions in the Cambridgeshire RO). March, by then a market town, was the only parish whose population did not fall, but instead continued to grow.

103 BLC 11/10, fo. 30 (10 Nov. 1681).

104 S/B/SP/64, petition of the inhabitants of Ely, Stretham, Thetford and Wilburton, read 8 Apr. 1674.

often did set one part of the fens against another, as actions taken to drain one area threatened another. Over and Willingham submitted a petition in 1696 against Swavesey's request for a sluice or tunnel through the river bank there, claiming that it would inevitably 'drown many thousand acres for the drayneing some few'.[105] And there was a flurry of petitions and counter-petitions in 1694 and 1695 concerning a tunnel under Hilgay or Wissy River, which the towns of Hilgay and Southery wanted to be opened ('they haveing noe other outfall for their water') but which eight towns on the north side of the river requested to be locked shut to prevent the water coming onto their lands.[106] Twenty years later, they were still arguing about whether Hilgay could run the waters of their fens through the other towns' lands.[107]

These disputes could even erupt into threats to the works themselves. In 1673 the Corporation was informed of a summons 'in the name of the inhabitants of Haddenham and townes adjacent of an intention in a ryotous manner to cutt open the damm att the head of Downham Eau'.[108] Though this was prevented, it was only part of a long grievance between the towns in the south of the level and those in the Norfolk Fens near Downham Eau as to whether the Ouse waters should be allowed to run that way, around the almost permanently blocked Denver Dam. Five days later, the Corporation received a petition from the city of Ely and four adjacent towns which complained about how Downham Eau, which had been made 'for the benefitt of that whole contry', was now stopped up and only for the use of 'some particular persons': since the stopping, 'the waters of the Ouse and of the whole contry stands still like a poole without any currant'.[109] But, as the inhabitants of the 17 towns in Norfolk downriver of the dam later claimed, it was feared that if the Ouse waters were run through Downham Eau,

105 S/B/SP/221, petition of the inhabitants of Wivelingham [Willingham] and Over, read 26 Nov. 1696.

106 S/B/SP/214, petition of the inhabitants of Stoke, Wretton, Wereham, West Dereham, Roxham, Fordham, Denver and Downham Market, read 4 Apr.1694. Also BLC 10/6, fo. 18 (4 Apr. 1694); BLC 10/6, fo. 29 (10 Apr. 1695), petition of Mr Spencer, Mr Towers and other the inhabitants of Hilgay and Southery; BLC 10/6, fo. 30 (11 Apr. 1695), petition of several of the landowners of Fordham, Denver and Downham Markett in Norfolk on behalf of themselves and others.

107 S/B/SP/243, petition of owners and farmers of Fenlands in Hilgay, response dated 6 Apr. 1709; 244, petition of the landowners and occupiers of Denver and Fordham, ND [*c.* 1709–10];/262, petition of the inhabitants and landowners of Hilgay, read 4 Apr. 1716.

108 BLC 11/7, fo. 2 (19 Apr. 1673).

109 S/B/SP/59, petition of 'the towne of Ely and partes adjacent', Stretham, Thetford, Wilburton and Haddenham, read 24 Apr. 1673.

it would 'be the certain occasion of making them all a fishpond'.[110] The matter was subject of 'lardge debate'.[111] It arose again in 1674, 1682, 1689, 1692, 1693, 1694 and 1695, and each time the landowners and inhabitants of one side or the other complained that they were 'very much drowned' as the dam was opened or closed.[112]

A similar dispute emerged over Bevill's Leam, a major drain near Whittlesey. It had been dammed to protect the fens below Whittlesey Dike towards Guyhirn, which were 'very lowe lands'.[113] But just a year later the Corporation received the news that some inhabitants of Whittlesey had attempted to cut the dam, while a petition from several tenants in the fens above the dam complained that its placement there had flooded their lands.[114] It was replaced by a sluice that could be opened and closed, but this did not help matters. When it was open, several inhabitants of March and others complained that the water from the sluice, as well as that from two water mills, spread 'it selfe over all [their] said lands being on a great flatt'.[115] But when it was closed, it was again a target of vandalism and the sluice was 'maliciously pull'd up by some persons with horses' in 1696.[116]

As with drainage, conflicts of these sorts were also not entirely new to the Great Level. In the late sixteenth century, a dispute over whether to open the Shire Drain at Clowes Cross had set the hundred of Wisbech against all of its neighbours to the south and west, and drawn the attention of the Privy Council to the problems of the fens. In the fourteenth century, the damming of a river to drain the manor of Coldham led to similar complaints of the ill-effects on everyone else upstream.[117] Drainage in the fens has always been interconnected, and any changes to the draining of one part will have an effect on another. The use of windmills sparked off further conflicts because they removed water from one fen only to dump it on another.[118] But the frequency of the disputes and

---

110 S/B/SP/151, petition of the inhabitants of Hockwold, Wilton, Feltwell, Methwold, Northwold, Stoke, Wretton, Wyreham, West Dereham, Roxham, Southery, Hilgay, Fordham, Denver, Downham, Wimbotsham and Stow Bardolph, read 17 Nov. 1682.

111 BLC 11/7, fo. 8 (19 June 1673).

112 Quote from S/B/SP/105, petition of landowners and tenants bordering on the River Ouse above Denver Sluice, read 5 Apr. 1693.

113 BLC 11/10, fo. 31v (1 Dec. 1681).

114 S/B/SP/146, petition of the tenants of George Keale, Esq, read 11 May 1682; BLC 11/10, fo. 34v (11 May 1682).

115 BLC 10/6, fol. 17v (4 Apr. 1694).

116 BLC 11/15, fo. 7v (21 May 1696).

117 Kennedy, '"So glorious a work"', pp. 54–5; Sir William Dugdale, *The history of imbanking and drayning of divers fenns and marshes* (1662), p. 301.

118 Falvey, 'Custom, Resistance and Politics', ch. 5; R59/31 uncatalogued records, box 2, bundle 4, 'Reasons against the Mills', n.d.

attacks on the Corporation's works when they were seen to prejudice the local draining is an indication of how the physical and organizational changes to the fenland had made the region dependent on drainage, even as their disregard of the Corporation's authority suggests that it still lacked legitimacy in the eyes of many fenlanders.

IV

As an agricultural improvement, the seventeenth-century draining of the fens left much to be desired. Having been forced on the inhabitants against their will, it did result in some increased productivity and trade, but much of this was short-lived; at the same time legal common rights became more restricted on the remaining common fens.[119] The protests of pro-drainage pamphlets aside, by the end of the century this was not a landscape in which the floods were 'muzzled, and the ocean tam'd ... [and] heaps of water turn'd to land'.[120]

But it did profoundly change the landscape and created new interests within the level, much as other agrarian changes like engrossment and enclosure by agreement were changing the landscape and creating new interests among land-users elsewhere in seventeenth-century England.[121] The authority and legitimacy of the Corporation continued to be challenged throughout the eighteenth century: in 1777 there was a major riot when it attempted to lay rates on the whole of the level to pay for the upkeep of the major drainage works.[122] But over those same decades, groups of landowners within the fens began to petition parliament for permission to create local drainage boards which would themselves have the power to collect rates from all of the landholders within a given district, and which would take over the regulation and maintenance of local drains from the Corporation. The opposition to these boards appears to have come primarily from the Corporation; certainly there was none of the open protest from the inhabitants of the fens such as that which the seventeenth-century proposals had engendered. The first local board was established at Haddenham in 1727, and by the end of the century there were over 20 in the South Level alone.[123] By forming private drainage districts, the landowners and farmers in the fens further

---

119 More research is required on the illegal use of common rights. For a discussion of *de jure* and *de facto* common rights, see Falvey, 'Custom, Resistance and Politics', ch. 3.

120 *History or narrative of the Great Level of the Fenns* (London, 1685), p. 72.

121 M. Overton, *Agricultural Revolution in England: The Transformation of the Agrarian Economy, 1500–1850* (Cambridge, 1996), pp. 132–92.

122 Summers, *Great Level*, p. 128.

123 Ibid., pp. 119–21.

undermined the Corporation, reducing its significance even as they lightened its responsibilities. But they had also clearly committed themselves to drainage and cultivation of the fens in severalty. How much capital they were willing to invest in making this happen would rise and fall with agricultural prices;[124] and to what extent their feelings were shared by other members of fenland society is a matter for further research. But the future of the Great Level and the interests of its more prominent inhabitants had been set in a pattern that would not be seriously challenged again until the twentieth century.[125]

---

124 See Christopher Taylor, 'Post-Medieval Drainage of Marsh and Fen', in Cook and Williamson (eds), *Water Management*, pp. 152–6.

125 With the lessening importance of agriculture to the British economy and concerns over biodiversity, some areas of the Great Level had been reflooded and plans have been made to extend this to other areas. See here Wicken Fen (http://www.wicken.org.uk) and the Great Fen Project (http://www.greatfen.org.uk).

Appendix

'Song against [the] Corporation'[126]

The poem is written on a single sheet of paper, originally folded into thirds. It was written out with each stanza separated by a line, though the poem was not lined by rhythm but simply by space. The copy below has been relined. The handwriting is archaic for the late seventeenth century, and the spelling is very idiosyncratic. The paper appears to have been addressed as a letter, though damage to the paper and subsequent dirt obscures some of the text. The address looks to be a similar hand to the poem: 'To Mr Burly [or Barly] one of y^e [...]ers of y^e [...] sise to be left at ye W[h]ite hart In march p^rsent'. The paper was labelled 'Song agst Corporation' in another hand, across what would be the top of the paper when folded in three and stacked in a bundle, as it was filed by the Corporation. At the bottom of the song the original writer has noted that it was to be sung 'to ye tune of "London show yor Lyallte"'. A song with that refrain and the same rhythm as this song was printed in London in 1682 (Bodleian Broadsheet collection: Ashm. G 15(65) G 15(65), 'London's Joy And Loyalty on Duke of York's return').

> Rowse up you Corperration & do not Stand
> for Captaine floud you see hath seased yor Land
> for Captain floud is ARived In ye ffenn
> & theire designes to Quator all his men
>
> he theire designes this winter to Abide
> he hath broke y^e ~~Nort~~ South banck & ye North banck tried
> O you Corperation we wish their had nere bene none
> for it is ye Corperation y^t hath ye ffenns undon
>
> ye Corporaton might have Kept him out
> if they strict gardes ye bancks had sett Aboute
> but Captain floud he came so vigorosly
> that for want of fresh Recruets he made them flie

126 Cambridgeshire Archives, R59/31, uncatalogued records, box 2, bundle 4. The poem is printed with the kind permission of Cambridgeshire Archives and Local Studies.

he came so vigoros & so wondros grate
that emeditly he did ye ffenns besett
o you Corp^{rtn} we wish their had nere bene none
for it is this Corp^{r} that hath ou^{r} fenns undon

ye Conseruater he is grone so grate
& y^{e} [...] Rec^{r} he did talk & prate
that ye Bancks was all secuered & made so good
y^{t} ye ffenns could nere be tayne by Captain floud

but captain floud he came so woundros ~~grate~~ stoute
y^{t} emeditly he hemd ye ffenns Aboute
O you Corp^{rn} what doe you mene to due
to drouend ou^{r} hay & corne thus & our Housses two

At Ely there they meet & sitt In state
they put on their Clocks & then they Look so grate
he that bares ye mace he Looks so prodagall
if he met ye King hed scarcely give ye Walle

theirs Thorny Just because his witts was grate
he ryd out ye bancks would niver brake
but now we fiend their witts was very small
for it is the Corp^{rtn} y^{t} hath undone us all

their Regester he coms downe so wounderos Rare
he is [... A hopfull? ...] sparke I do declare
& his coming downe we now well understand
was to sell ye Corp^{rn} nastey Land

& noe we ffenn men I think be well fitted
ye Corp^{rn} hath us over witted
& we poore harts hath cause A nufe to wepe
Captain floud hath seased our Lands & doeth pursesshon Keep

they have so maney offecers I say
that A thousand pound A year doth scarcely pay
& they were uniust stuards now it is Known
or else ye banck we are sure had never flons[?]

theres the Rider of ye banck upon my Life
he had so much Respect for Barnets Wife
whilest he Lay craming Sargent barne[ts] henn
Captain floud he brocke ye banck & drownded all ye ffenn

[sideways down paper]

Now Corp^rn if you think it good
pray you send [Wa]rrants to sease Captain floud
we will Assist you wth all our powers & mights
for its tenn times worce then paying for our Lights

for we poore fenn mens harts be all moust deade
scarcely Able to houlde up our heads
o this fatell year we wish we had niver Knone
if Captain floud bent taine we shall be all undon
Finis

Chapter 9

'All towards the improvements of the estate': Mrs Elizabeth Prowse at Wicken (Northamptonshire), 1764–1810

*Briony McDonagh**

Despite decades of research on the rural aristocracy, landed estates and the agricultural changes of the long eighteenth century, very little has been written about female landowners and the role they played in managing and improving their estates. Amy Erickson and others have recognized that despite coverture and primogeniture, early modern women actually controlled significant amounts of property as widows and co-heiresses.[1] Yet by focusing on country-house women's roles in household management, garden design and charitable projects – all spaces in which women are traditionally seen to have been active – historians have tended to overlook female landowners' involvement in estate

* The initial research for this chapter was undertaken as part of the Arts and Humanities Research Council (AHRC)-sponsored 'Changing Landscapes, Changing Environments' project based at the Universities of Hertfordshire, Lincoln and Sussex. Further research was funded by a Leverhulme Early Career Fellowship based at the University of Nottingham. Short sections of this chapter previously appeared in B. McDonagh, 'Women, enclosure and estate improvement in eighteenth-century Northamptonshire', *Rural Hist.* 20 (2009), pp. 143–62 and are reprinted with the permission of Cambridge University Press.

1 A. L. Erickson, 'Possession – and the other one-tenth of the law: assessing women's ownership and economic roles in early modern England', *Women's History Rev.* 16 (2007), pp. 369–85; J. Bailey, 'Favoured or oppressed? Married women, property and "coverture" in England, 1660–1800', *Continuity and Change* 17 (2002), pp. 351–72; M. Finn, 'Women, consumption and coverture in England, *c.*1760–1860', *Historical J.* 39 (1996), pp. 703–22. Little quantitative information is available on the proportion of land held by elite women, although further down the social scale Seeliger has suggested that female tenants held up to one-fifth of the land in many Hampshire parishes between the mid-sixteenth and mid-nineteenth centuries. S. Seeliger, 'Hampshire women as landholders: common law mediated by manorial custom', *Rural Hist.* 7 (1996), pp. 1–14. For a contrasting view, see E. Spring, *Law, Land and Family* (Chapel Hill, 1993), who points to a long-term decline in women's property and rights which reached their lowest ebb in the eighteenth century.

management and agricultural improvement, areas which have generally been thought of as distinctly 'male' spheres of activity.[2]

This is perhaps surprising given the growing recognition that aristocratic, gentle- and middle-class women participated in a variety of other arenas traditionally seen as the preserve of men. For example, scholars working on women's relationship to the economy have recently drawn attention to single and widowed women's independent involvement in business enterprises, formal credit provision and the stock market, while others have highlighted women's involvement in politics, electioneering and activism in the anti-slavery movement.[3] At the same time, historians have recognized the contributions

[2] J. Martin, *Wives and Daughters: Women and Children in the Georgian Country House* (London, 2004); S. Tillyard, *Aristocrats: Caroline, Emily, Louisa and Sarah Lennox, 1740–1832* (London, 1995); T. Lummis and J. Marsh, *The Woman's Domain: Women and the English Country House* (London, 1990); S. G. Bell, 'Women create gardens in male landscapes: a revisionist approach to eighteenth-century English garden history', *Feminist Stud.* 16 (1990), pp. 471–91; A. Hunt and P. Everson, 'Sublime horror: industry and designed landscape in Miss Wakefield's garden at Basingill, Cumbria', *Garden Hist.* 32 (2004), pp. 68–86; L. L. Moore, 'Queer gardens: Mary Delany's flowers and friendships', *Eighteenth-century Stud.* 39 (2005), pp. 49–70; R. Larsen, 'For want of a good fortune: elite single women's experiences in Yorkshire, 1730–1860', *Women's History Rev.* 16 (2007), pp. 387–401; J. Gerard, 'Lady Bountiful: women of the landed classes and rural philanthropy', *Victorian Stud.* 30 (1987), pp. 183–210. S. Dunster, 'Women of the Nottinghamshire elite, c.1720–1820' (unpublished PhD thesis, University of Nottingham, 2003) includes a brief consideration of Nottinghamshire women's role in estate management, while A. Mitson, 'An exchange of letters: estate management and Lady Yarborough', *Women's History Rev.* 7 (1998), pp. 547–66 offers a useful analysis of a late nineteenth-century woman managing a landed estate.

[3] On women's role in the economy, see L. Davidoff and C. Hall, *Family Fortunes: Men and Women of the English Middle Class, 1780–1850* (Chicago, 1987); H. Barker, *The Business of Women* (Oxford, 2006); N. J. Phillips, *Women in Business, 1700–1850* (Woodbridge, 2006); J. Spicksley, 'Usury legislation, cash and credit', *English Historical Review* (*EHR*) 61 (2008), pp. 277–301; P. Sharpe, 'Dealing with love', *Gender and History* 11 (1999), pp. 209–32; D. R. Green and A. Owens, 'Gentlewomanly capitalism? Spinsters, widows and wealth-holding in England and Wales, *c.*1800–60', *Economic History Review* (*EcHR*) 56 (2003), pp. 510–36; C. Wiskin, 'Industry, investment and consumption: urban women in the Midlands', in J. Stobart and N. Raven (eds), *Towns, Regions and Industries: Urban and Industrial Change in the Midlands, c.1700–1840* (Manchester, 2005), pp. 62–79, citing S. Hudson, 'Attitudes to investment risk among West Midland canal and railway company investors, 1700–1850' (unpublished PhD thesis, University of Warwick, 2001), p. 113; J. Rutterford and J. Maltby, '"The widow, the clergyman and the reckless": women investors in England, 1830–1914', *Feminist Economics* 12 (2006), pp. 111–38. On their place in politics, see K. Gleadle and S. Richardson (eds), *Women in British Politics, 1760–1860: The Power of the Petticoat* (Basingstoke, 2000); A. K. Mellor, *Mothers of the Nation: Women's Political Writing in England, 1780–1830* (Bloomington, 2000); H. Rogers, *Women and the People: Authority, Authorship and the Radical Tradition in Nineteenth-Century*

made to household economies by the wives of farmers and labourers, principally through practices like dairying, caring for animals and helping with harvest work.[4] Yet far less has been said about aristocratic and gentlewomen living in rural areas and the part they played in managing family estates, partly because of the difficulties in accessing women's hidden histories but also because elite women seen to have been active in farm management in the seventeenth century are understood to have increasingly retired into domesticity in the eighteenth.[5] As a result, the history of elite women's involvement in the agricultural changes of the long eighteenth century is largely to be written.

Evidence from Northamptonshire – a county which experienced particularly high levels of parliamentary enclosure – demonstrates that elite women were active in estate management, enclosure and improvement in the second half of the eighteenth century. Wealthy widows like Lady Elizabeth Dryden of Canons Ashby kept detailed estate ledgers in which they recorded receipts and expenditure along with memoranda about the estate's tenancies, whilst more middling landowners like Mrs Jane Ashley of Ashby St Ledgers personally collected rents and organized repairs to tenants' farmsteads. Like male landowners, these women also lobbied parliament for enclosure acts and negotiated with freeholders and stewards about purchases and exchanges. Jane Ashley, for example, carefully calculated the profits she expected to make from the enclosure of Ashby in 1764, and in the two decades after enclosure she reorganized the tenancies and more than doubled her rental income whilst maintaining the vast majority of

England (Aldershot, 2000); E. Chalus, 'Kisses for Votes: The Kiss and Corruption in Eighteenth-Century English Elections', in K. Harvey (ed.), *The Kiss in History* (Manchester, 2005), pp. 122–47; C. Midgley, *Feminism and Empire: Women Activists in Imperial Britain, 1790–1865* (London, 2007), pp. 41–86.

4 N. Verdon, '" ... subjects deserving of the highest praise": farmers' wives and the farm economy in England, *c.*1700–1850', *Agricultural History Rev.* 51 (2003), pp. 23–39. See also A. Clark, *Working Life of Women in the Seventeenth Century* (London, 1919), pp. 5, 50, 60–62; M. Roberts, 'Sickles and scythes: women's work and men's work at harvest time', *History Workshop J.* 7 (1979), pp. 3–28; B. Hill, *Women, Work and Sexual Politics in Eighteenth-Century England* (Oxford, 1989), pp. 24–46; D. Valenze, 'The art of women and the business of men: women's work and the dairy industry, *c.*1740–1840', *Past and Present* 130 (1991), pp. 142–69.

5 A. Vickery, *The Gentleman's Daughter: Women's Lives in Georgian England* (New Haven, 1998), p. 2 reviews the literature; Hill, *Women*, p. 123; L. Stone, *The Family, Sex and Marriage in England, 1500–1800* (London, 1977), p. 396; S. D. Amussen, *An Ordered Society: Gender and Class in Early Modern England* (Oxford, 1988), p. 187; C. Hall, 'The history of the housewife', in Hall, *White, Male and Middle Class: Explorations in Feminism and History* (Cambridge, 1992), pp. 43–71. See J. Thomas, 'Women and capitalism: oppression or emancipation? a review article', *Comparative Stud. in Society and History* 30 (1988), pp. 534–49 for a review of some of the early literature on the impact of capitalism on women's position in society.

her tenants on their farms. Other women supervised the enclosure of family properties even where they were not identified in the act or award. During her son's long minority, Mrs Mary Cotterel consolidated and improved the family estate at Aynho, established new plantations and negotiated a parliamentary enclosure act. Her son's name appeared on the 1792 award, but he was then on his Grand Tour and it was Mary who travelled to Aynho to see the new hedges laid out and the new farmhouses erected, later writing to her son to tell him how things went on. Other women reorganised tenancies and raised rents in the wake of enclosure, thereby increasing the value of their estates by creating – rather than simply preserving – wealth which could be passed on to future generations.[6]

This chapter further explores women's role as agricultural managers and innovators through a detailed case study of one particular female landowner: Mrs Elizabeth Prowse of Wicken, a widow who controlled a 2,200-acre estate in the south of Northamptonshire for more than 40 years between 1767 and 1810. The first part of the chapter offers a brief biography of Elizabeth, along with some discussion of her management of the estate finances. The second part of the chapter uses her estate and personal accounts, notebooks and memoirs to chart the broad range of social and agricultural improvements Elizabeth introduced to the newly enclosed estate. The third part of the study examines Elizabeth's attitude towards estate improvement, drawing attention to evidence that she was aware of the social costs of enclosure at the same time as being concerned to rationalize and improve the estate. As a corollary to this, the chapter explores how propertied women accessed ideas about estate management and landscape improvement, and the role family members and stewards played in the circulation of ideas, knowledge and expertise.

I

Elizabeth Sharp was born in 1733, one of the nine surviving children of Thomas Sharp, prebendary of Durham, and his wife Judith Wheler.[7] The Sharps were a moderately wealthy clerical family, and in 1762 Elizabeth married George Prowse, the son of a Somerset MP, Thomas Prowse, who held property in Gloucestershire and Somerset as well as an estate at Wicken (Northamptonshire)

6 For a more detailed discussion of these examples, see McDonagh, 'Women, enclosure and estate improvement'.

7 Gloucestershire Record Office (hereafter GRO), D3549/14/1/2, pt 3, hereafter cited as Prowse, 'Memoir', pp. 2–3; *Oxford Dictionary of National Biography* (*ODNB*), 'Sharp, Thomas (1693–1758)'.

which he had acquired in right of his wife. As first cousins once removed, George and Elizabeth were already acquainted and apparently well suited, though George was four years Elizabeth's junior. They lived in London with his family during the first years of their marriage, but in 1764 Thomas granted his son the Wicken estate. The couple moved into the house in October, full of ideas about how to improve it, having spent the journey to Wicken 'forming our plans for living there'.[8] Yet George died just three years later, an event that more than 40 years later Elizabeth still considered 'The very greates[t] shock and affliction I ever received'.[9] Moreover, after only five brief years of marriage, Elizabeth and George had no children.

As a childless widow, Elizabeth might have expected to be provided for by means of an annuity or yearly cash sum, like the £400 jointure agreed as part of the marriage negotiations between the Sharp and Prowse families.[10] Yet Elizabeth's jointure was payable out of the Northamptonshire estates, and she seems to have quickly arranged with her mother-in-law that she would manage Wicken herself.[11] Her husband's family seem to have been very happy to leave the estate in Elizabeth's hands, not least because in 1767 there was no suitable male relative available to manage it: George's father and only brother were dead and both his sisters were unmarried teenagers. Yet five years later, in 1772, Elizabeth's mother-in-law confirmed the arrangement despite the fact George's sister was now married with a young son, Charles Mordaunt. In exchange for surrendering her jointure and agreeing not to remarry, Elizabeth secured the Wicken estate for life. Elizabeth's decision to forego remarriage was probably informed by a number of considerations, not least her commitment to the programme of estate improvements she and George had devised together. Given her modest family background, she may have felt that it was unlikely that she would marry well enough to better her position as lady of the manor at Wicken. The decision perhaps also reflects the Prowse family's preference to have a resident landowner oversee the Northamptonshire estate, as well as a sincere belief that at only 39 and with a potentially long widowhood ahead of her, Elizabeth was capable of managing Wicken for the benefit of the eventual Mordaunt inheritor.

Whilst both male and female landowners without direct heirs are sometimes supposed to have let their estates run down, Elizabeth was a careful bookkeeper

8 Prowse, 'Memoir', p. 18.

9 Ibid., p. 25.

10 A. L. Erickson, *Woman and Property in Early Modern England* (London, 1993), pp. 3–26; Elizabeth's jointure arrangements are reported in her memoir, pp. 41–2.

11 The spirit of negotiation between Elizabeth and her mother-in-law also extended to the furniture and contents at Wicken, the whole of which Elizabeth took in lieu of her rights to the contents of Berkeley and elsewhere (GRO, D3549/13/2/13).

and a committed improver.[12] She no doubt felt she owed her husband's family – and especially her mother-in-law, whom she later described as having 'been as a real mother to me' – to manage the estate with care.[13] Moreover unlike some widows who never met the distant male relatives in line to inherit their estates, Elizabeth was closely involved in the Mordaunt family's lives, noting her nieces' and nephews' births and childhood illnesses in her memoirs, organizing for their inoculations in London and exchanging regular visits with them in Warwickshire.[14] Her brother-in-law, Sir John Mordaunt, also negotiated with the tenants over tithe payments on her behalf in 1796, and Elizabeth later appointed his younger son John as rector of Wicken.[15] Such close family ties no doubt contributed to her willingness to invest both time and money in the Wicken estate.

The surviving ledgers and notebooks provide good evidence of the seriousness with which Elizabeth approached the task of managing the estate, and of her close personal scrutiny of the accounts.[16] Elizabeth's ledgers begin in May 1768, nine months after her husband's death. The three surviving volumes cover the periods 1768–71 and 1774–84, and include what might be broadly thought of as personal, household and estate accounts. Personal clothing, travel and pocket expenses were accounted under separate headings, as were Elizabeth's meticulous records of money she was owed by various relatives and friends. The household accounts were organized under a variety of headings, including expenses for general housekeeping, linens, coal, servants' wages and clothing, the stables, cellars and repairs to the house. The estate accounts were organized under three main headings: firstly, the expenses of the farm in hand, including a detailed record of the sums raised from the sale of butter, cheese, wool, livestock and grain; secondly, the expenses of the cottages; and thirdly, the Wicken estate, including money spent on the tenants' farms.

---

[12] Mitson, 'An exchange of letters', pp. 555–7, for example, notes how the trustees of the third Earl of Yarborough's estate in Lincolnshire accused his widow of being grasping, greedy and self-interested, despite evidence that she actually reduced the estate's indebtedness during the six years she managed it.

[13] Prowse, 'Memoir', p. 62.

[14] See, for example, Prowse, 'Memoir', p. 58. By contrast, Jane Ashley never met the man who inherited Ashby St Ledgers (Northamptonshire) at her death in 1784, despite his promises to visit her on the estate (Northamptonshire Record Office (hereafter NRO), ASL 357 and 362).

[15] Prowse, 'Memoir', pp. 91 and 93.

[16] The main sources for Elizabeth Prowse are three estate ledgers, a cash book and two notebooks for the Wicken and Grafton Park estates (all preserved at Northamptonshire Record Office), plus a copy of her memoirs, her brother Granville Sharp's letters and James Sharp's collection of pamphlets and drawings (at Gloucestershire Record Office). No letters written by or to Elizabeth have yet been identified.

The first year's entries are in a hand other than Elizabeth's – almost certainly that of her brother, James Sharp. It was for James that Elizabeth acted as housekeeper in London before her marriage, and it seems likely that he returned the favour by helping her to manage the estate and keep her accounts in the first year of her widowhood. James planned the layout of the ledger, writing the headings for each section of the accounts and ruling the pages. Yet by May 1769 Elizabeth had assumed full responsibility for keeping the estate, household and personal accounts, and the remainder of the ledgers are written in her hand. Despite some early confusion about exactly what should be entered where, the ledgers represent a highly organized and methodical record of the estate's finances.[17] Each item was carefully cross-referenced against other entries in the volume as well as with a series of cash books, only one of which appears to survive.[18]

It is clear from the ledgers that the estate steward, housekeeper and cook also kept accounts, all of which were audited by Elizabeth. Thus, for example, a few days after returning to Wicken in May 1769, Elizabeth looked over her steward's cash book and settled his account for the winter months she had spent in London and Berkeley (Gloucestershire). She then copied his receipts and expenditure into her own ledger and cross-referenced the items against entries in the general, cottage and estate accounts elsewhere in the volume.[19] Elizabeth was resident at Wicken during the summer and autumn 1769, and entries were regularly made in the ledger as she reimbursed the steward for the sums he laid out for bills and wages on the estate and home farm. These entries disappear during the winter of 1769–70 which she spent in London, but she once again audited her steward's accounts when she returned in April 1770.[20] Much the same was true in subsequent years. Rather than being professional land agents employed by a London firm, Elizabeth's stewards were local men who lived on one of the estate farms or – as in the case of her first steward, Joseph Foxley – in the rooms above the stables.[21] All this implies that it was Elizabeth, rather than her steward, who had overall control of the estate and its finances, even if her

17 See, for example, NRO, 364p/67, fos. 28, 36–7.

18 NRO, 364p/70, which covers the period from 1 May 1774 to 31 Aug. 1781.

19 NRO, 364p/67, fos. 45–8.

20 Ibid., fos. 49–59.

21 S. Webster, 'Estate improvement and the professionalisation of land agents on the Egremont estates in Sussex and Yorkshire, 1770–1835', *Rural Hist.* 18 (2007), pp. 47–69; NRO, 364p/67, fo. 40; Prowse, 'Memoir', p. 37. Whilst she did not employ professional land agents, Elizabeth did occasionally rely on London-based solicitors. Thus, for example, a lawyer called Lally drew up the tenants' new leases in March 1768 and later provided legal opinions and advice (Prowse, 'Memoir', p. 27; NRO, 364p/68, fos. 200 and 207).

senior servants regularly took over the day-to-day management of the house and estate whilst she visited friends and family in the capital and elsewhere.

Elizabeth's meticulous record-keeping is also evident in the accounts she kept for the home farm. Somewhat unusually, she charged herself an annual rent of £73 for the tenancy, a sum which rose to £100 in the late 1770s when she brought additional parcels of land in hand. She also kept detailed accounts of her expenditure and receipts on the farm, itemizing the money she made from the sale of butter, cheese, eggs, livestock, grain, wool, hay, sheep skins and tallow. Some of the produce was sold to local farmers and the rest consumed in the house and stables at Wicken Park. This included food for the table and hay for the stables, as well as more unusual items such as lime from the kiln on the farm which was used in the building works at the house, all of which was carefully charged to the appropriate accounts elsewhere in the ledgers.[22] When, as in 1776, Elizabeth forgot to charge hay produced on the farm to the coach-horse stables where it had been eaten, she chastised herself for her mistake, writing in her ledger that 'next year I must be more particular & have an account what is used in that stable'.[23]

II

As well as carefully managing the estate's finances, Elizabeth tirelessly improved the house, park and estate during her 43-year widowhood. Wicken Park House had been rebuilt on a new site outside the village in 1717, but Elizabeth and George planned significant additions and improvements to the house (Figure 9.1).[24] Plans for two new wings and a third storey to the main block were drawn up by Elizabeth's father-in-law, although work continued for more than a decade after Thomas and George's deaths in 1767.[25] Thus, for example, the corridors of the new building were papered in 1768 at the same time as the parlours, bedrooms and staircase were painted, and the new drawing room was fitted up in 1777.[26] Work on the cellars was still being undertaken as late at 1787.[27] Coals were used in the house for the first time in 1766, probably to fuel new heating apparatus bought from Elizabeth's brother James, a London ironmonger.[28] Elizabeth bought several more of James's American stoves in the 1770s and early

22 NRO, 364p/68, fos. 6–16.

23 Ibid., fo. 10.

24 *VCH Northants*, V, p. 418; Prowse, 'Memoir', p. 18.

25 Ibid., pp. 19, 21.

26 NRO, 364p/67, fo. 40.

27 Prowse, 'Memoir', p. 73.

28 NRO, 364p/67, fo. 76.

1780s, and also installed a water closet in the house in 1781, when she paid more than £4 for various parts sourced by James.[29]

Elizabeth's ledgers and memoirs also provide good evidence for her improvements to the gardens and parkland. Examples include new gravel walks laid out in Park Copse to the north-west of the house in 1771 and a ha-ha dug between the pleasure grounds and the stables in 1778.[30] Sadly no plan for the gardens now survives, and it remains unclear how far Elizabeth's visits to important picturesque gardens like Stowe (Buckinghamshire), Studley Royal and Hackfall (Yorkshire) and Thoresby and Clumber (Nottinghamshire) or her 1785 tour of key sites of picturesque tourism, including the Lake District and the Scottish Highlands, influenced the design of the gardens at Wicken.[31] More is known about the estate woodlands, where at least four new ridings were laid out in the 1770s and 1780s.[32] These functioned to emphasize the house's woodland setting, and also mirrored and extended the elaborate pattern of rides which criss-crossed the neighbouring Wakefield Lodge estate. Wakefield belonged to the Duke of Grafton, who was himself involved in improving his house, grounds and home farm between 1747 and the 1770s.[33] Elizabeth seems to have viewed her work at Wicken as part of a self-consciously improving aesthetic: she certainly celebrated the completion of the first riding in Lilby Woods in July 1772 with a tea party for 50 guests, who were shown the new riding and entertained by her brothers' band.[34]

Moreover, Elizabeth's plans for improvements extended well beyond the park pale. Improvements to the agricultural estate had actually begun under Elizabeth's father-in-law in the mid-1750s. Like his wife's grandfather and predecessor on the estate, Charles Hosier, Thomas Prowse bought out large numbers of freeholders: whereas there had been at least 400 acres of freehold

---

29 NRO, 364p/70, 7 May 1776; 68, fo. 38; 69, fo. 40.

30 Prowse, 'Memoir', pp. 37 and 60.

31 NRO, 364/69, fos 66–7; GRO, D3549/15/1/1; Prowse, 'Memoir', p. 71; M. Andrews, *Search for the Picturesque, 1760–1800* (Aldershot, 1989), pp. 153–4 and 200; G. Clarke 'The moving temples of Stowe: aesthetics of change in an English landscape over four generations', *Huntingdon Library Q.* 55 (1992), pp. 479–509; J. Hunt and P. Willis, *The Genius of Place: The English Landscape Garden, 1620–1820* (London, 1975), pp. 26–9; S. Seymour, 'Eighteenth-Century Parkland Improvement on the Dukeries Estates of North Nottinghamshire' (unpublished PhD thesis, University of Nottingham, 1990), pp. 176–82, 204–10; *ODNB*, 'Aislabie, John (1670–1742)'; 'Aislabie, William (1699/1700–1781)'.

32 Prowse, 'Memoir', pp. 30, 68; T. Eyre and T. Jeffries, *Map of Northamptonshire* (1780), stored as NRO, Map 2647; A. Bryant, *Map of Northamptonshire* (1827), stored as NRO, Map 1118.

33 *VCH Northants* V, pp. 304, 312.

34 Prowse, 'Memoir', p. 42.

Drawn by J.P.Neale.
Engraved by R. Acon.
WICKEN PARK,
NORTHAMPTONSHIRE

Figure 9.1 Wicken Park House by J. P. Neale, 1818. Reproduced from an original print owned by the author

land in Wicken in 1717, 40 years later Prowse owned the whole parish, with the exception of the glebe and a handful of cottages.[35] These purchases were clearly undertaken with a view to enclosing the open fields. As a result of negotiations in 1756 by which he acquired one of the last remaining common rights, Prowse achieved unity of ownership and the final enclosure was completed the following year without recourse to an Act of Parliament.[36] It was most likely then that the land held by each farm was reorganized to produce the kind of rational layout later advocated by agricultural improvers like Nathaniel Kent and Arthur Young. This was certainly the case by 1796, when a rental demonstrates that the nine principal tenancies on the estate were each made up of consolidated blocks of land.[37]

Yet if the enclosure of the open fields was achieved by her father-in-law, Elizabeth nevertheless introduced a range of agricultural improvements and innovations to the newly enclosed estate. These included improvements to both the tenant farms and the home farm. By March 1768, less than a year after her husband's death, Elizabeth had settled with all but one of her tenants to replace their yearly tenancy agreements with new leases. She offered them favourable terms, including a rebate of half the first year's rent, as well as agreeing to contribute towards a range of improvements on the farms.[38] The farmer who quit his farm rather than take a lease was already thought to be 'taking advantage', and it may in part have been his attempts to profit at the expense of the long-term quality of the land that prompted Elizabeth to suggest leases to her tenants.[39]

The shift from yearly tenancies to longer-term leases was no doubt aimed at encouraging the farmers to invest in their farms. Unfortunately, none of Elizabeth's leases survive, so we do not know if they specified particular rotations or contained covenants aimed at encouraging tenants to adopt improved agricultural methods, although other Northamptonshire leases of the period certainly did.[40] However, there is good evidence for improvements being undertaken in partnership between Elizabeth and her tenants, many of which were agreed when the tenants took new leases. Thus there are entries in the ledgers for ditching, hedging, fencing and other improvements, as well as

---

35 NRO, H(W)65, 111 and 133; 364p/65. The figures for the freehold land are drawn from a copy of the 1717 terrier. The accompanying map gives slightly different figures.

36 NRO, H(W)62; 364p/14.

37 NRO, YZ 8944.

38 NRO, 364p/68, fo. 207.

39 Prowse, 'Memoir', p. 27.

40 See, for example, NRO, D2666, SS3838 and SS3866; S. Wade Martins and T. Williamson, 'The development of the lease and its role in agricultural improvement in East Anglia, 1660–1870', *Agricultural History Rev.* 46 (1998), pp. 127–41.

quantities of grass seed, all paid for by Elizabeth and agreed to as part of the negotiations over tenancies.[41]

Elizabeth also invested in repairs and improvements to the houses and outbuildings on her tenants' farms. Either Elizabeth or her father-in-law built a new farm called Little Hill on the former open fields in the south-west of the parish soon after enclosure, with work continuing on its outbuildings into the early 1770s.[42] Elizabeth also contributed towards repairs to barns and stables belonging to two other tenants in the late 1760s, as well as installing water pumps in at least four of the farms, in the yard and stable at Wicken Park and in some of the estate cottages in the 1770s.[43] This was followed by another programme of repairs in the early 1780s which affected all eight rented farms and included thatching and glazing, repairs to the pumps and work by a mason, carpenter and smith.[44] Moreover, when she organized insurance for Wicken Park House and the home farm, Elizabeth also paid the premiums on the tenant farms, a malting house and kiln and 51 estate cottages.[45] All this no doubt contributed towards the good relations between landlords and tenants advocated by Kent and other leading agricultural writers, and it is perhaps not surprising that Elizabeth's tenants should be hailed as 'the happiest set of peasants in England', as they were by one visitor in 1777.[46]

Alongside improvements to the eight tenant farms, Elizabeth undertook similar improvements on the ninth farm, which she kept in hand. For example, she invested considerable sums on improving the soil quality of parcels of land lying to the north, west and south of Wicken Park House which together made up the home farm. In the winter of 1772 she marled areas of the Dial Ground to the north of the House, presumably with the intention of putting the former parkland under new crop rotations.[47] Elsewhere, she drained, burned and eventually ploughed the Great Leys, and also spent £70 clearing the ground of anthills – a particular problem in Northamptonshire and one noted by the

41 NRO, 364p/67, fos. 120, 12, 123, 127 and 128; 68, fos. 189, 192 and 196.

42 Eyre and Jeffries, *Map of Northamptonshire*; *VCH Northants* V, p. 426; NRO, 364p/67, fos. 122, 127–8.

43 NRO, 364p/67, fos. 15, 40, 120–34; 68, fo. 197; and 364p/501.

44 NRO, 364p/69, fos. 185–205 *passim*.

45 NRO, 364p/501 and 67–9 *passim*.

46 N. Kent, *Hints to gentlemen of landed property* (London, 1775), pp. 158–70; GRO, D3549/12/1/4.

47 Prowse, 'Memoir' p. 40; T. Williamson, *The Transformation of Rural England: Farming and the Landscape, 1700–1870* (Exeter, 2002), pp. 67–8.

Board of Agriculture in their report of 1794.[48] Another problem on the heavy clays of Northamptonshire was poor drainage, a difficulty Elizabeth tackled by installing stone drains on part of the estate.[49]

Here and elsewhere Elizabeth seems to have attempted to run the estate along the lines proposed by the leading agricultural improvers of her day. Whilst we know little about any formal education she received as a child, Elizabeth's memoirs and ledgers provide strong evidence that she read widely throughout her adult life, taking regular newspapers and purchasing numerous books. These included religious literature, poetry and history, as well as a wide range of didactic material concerned with the practical management of the estate. Thus, for example, she paid 6*s*. for 'Mr Kent's Book' in 1775 – presumably *Hints to gentlemen of landed property* – and she later acquired other popular texts, including one of Arthur Young's *Tours* and Kent's *General view of the agriculture of the county of Norfolk*.[50] In both Kent and Young, Elizabeth found support for many of the improvements she had already put in place at Wicken, including the conversions of yearly tenancies to longer-term leases, consolidated farm layouts and good relations between landlords and tenants.[51]

Yet Elizabeth's improving contemporaries were by no means the only conduit through which she accessed ideas about landscape improvement and estate management. Instead both her husband's family and her own family played a key role in shaping her attitudes towards, and interest in, agricultural modernization and improvement. For example, it was a trip to her mother-in-law's property at Berkeley in June 1770 that seems to have inspired Elizabeth to experiment with the animal feeds used at Wicken. Whilst there, she noted the quantities of cheese, cream and butter produced by the dairy herd.[52] From 1772 onwards, Elizabeth was growing cabbages on the home farm which were fed to the milk cattle in an attempt to improve the milk and cheese at the same time as saving grass and hay. She carefully recorded the number and weight of the cabbages grown on the estate and appears to have been disappointed when she compared these figures to the yields at Berkeley.[53]

Another area for experimentation was with the agricultural machinery used on the estate. Elizabeth's brother, James Sharp, was a London ironmonger who

---

48 NRO, 364p/68, fos. 196, 199, 202; J. Donaldson, *A general view of the agriculture of the county of Northampton* (Edinburgh, 1796), p. 66.

49 NRO, 364p/68, fos. 190 and 191.

50 NRO, 364p/68, fo. 38; 69, fo. 5; Prowse, 'Memoir', p. 86.

51 P. Horn, 'An eighteenth-century land agent: the career of Nathaniel Kent (1737–1810)', *Agricultural History Rev*. 30 (1982), pp. 1–16.

52 Prowse, 'Memoir', pp. 34 and 46.

53 Ibid., pp. 43 and 46.

manufactured a wide range of agricultural implements – including Rotherham and Dutch ploughs, draining and trenching ploughs, seed-drills, harrows, hoes, wheelbarrows, winnowing-machines and horse-shovels for removing anthills.[54] As she carried out the improvements in the late 1760s and 1770s, Elizabeth used much of this technology, particularly the so-called 'rolling' carts and carriages (Figure 9.2). These had rollers instead of wheels and were designed to stop the roads becoming rutted by the passage of wheeled carts. James brought several of the carriages to Wicken in the winter of 1771–72, where they were used on the home farm in the construction of the new riding and stone drains, as well as for 'carting which is all towards the improvements of the estate'.[55]

As the estate ledgers make clear, the carts were operated at first by James's oxen and horses, which were fed and sheltered by Elizabeth at his expense.[56] In this sense, Wicken clearly functioned as an important test site for the rolling carriages; whilst James kept horses at his Southwark yard in order to demonstrate the utility of his ploughs, shovels and carts to interested parties, at Wicken he had access to a considerable estate on which he could experiment on a far greater scale than was possible in his London manufactory.[57] Thus it was only after a successful season at Wicken that the carts and carriages appeared more widely, at first fairly locally and later much further afield. In the winter of 1772–73, James gained a government contract to extract timber from Whittlewood Forest and transport it to Northampton using the rolling carts. As part of the venture, he took a house and yard at Old Stratford and used the carts to transport coal and timber from Northampton and Warwickshire which he sold locally.[58] The rolling carts were being used on the estate of Elizabeth's mother-in-law at Berkeley by January 1774, as well as for journeys into Warwickshire, Staffordshire and Bedfordshire.[59] There had even been talk in the previous year that the rolling carriages might be introduced into Holland.[60] The rolling carriages were said to be especially useful in heavy clay soils like those found in Northamptonshire and elsewhere in the Midlands, and James clearly saw his success at Wicken as critical in promoting wider adoption of the rolling carriages. In 1773 he placed several advertisements in the London newspapers and the *Gentleman's Magazine* inviting the public to view the rolling carriages at work in Northampton and

54 GRO, D3549/12/2/1.

55 NRO, 364p/68, fos. 190, 194 and 199; Prowse, 'Memoir', p. 40.

56 NRO, 364p/68, fos. 7–8, 190–91.

57 GRO, D3549/12/2/1.

58 Prowse, 'Memoir', p. 41.

59 Ibid., p. 46; GRO, D3549/12/2/1.

60 GRO, D3549/13/1/S13.

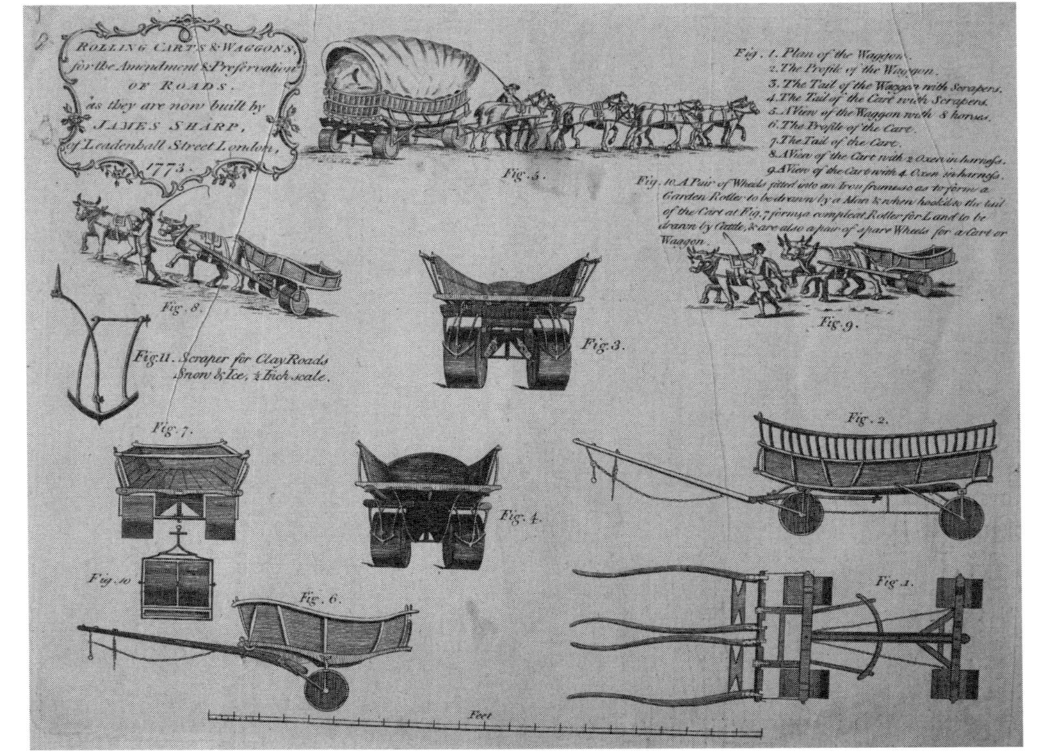

Figure 9.2 James Sharp's rolling carriages and wagons. Reproduced with permission from Gloucestershire Record Office, D1245/FF38/B1

Stony Stratford.[61] In these adverts, Northamptonshire was imagined as a site of successful experimentation, even if – for obvious reasons – Wicken was not explicitly mentioned. Elizabeth too saw the experiment with the rolling carts as a success.[62] Having initially paid her brother for his work on the home farm, she later invested in several of the carts for her own use on the estate, buying two double-shafted rolling carts from James at a cost of more than £40 in 1776.[63] Thus the use of the rolling carriages at Wicken proved to be a mutually beneficial experiment for both James and Elizabeth, as well as for the tenants, several of whom purchased rolling carts and carriages in the mid-1770s with the help of small subsidies from Elizabeth.[64]

III

As the preceding section has argued, Elizabeth Prowse was clearly committed to a programme of agricultural improvements at Wicken. This said, she was nevertheless sometimes uneasy about some of the things her predecessors had done in the name of progress. In the Grafton Park notebook, she records how her father-in-law had cut down an avenue of trees and drained – or as she put it, 'destroyed' – a pond.[65] Like Fanny Price in Austen's *Mansfield Park*, Elizabeth seems to have been above all upset by the loss of the avenue, noting how the trees had given the previous landowner particular pleasure. Elizabeth drew up the two estate notebooks in *c.*1801–03 and her disapproval at the destruction of the avenue was no doubt partially informed by concerns over timber availability during the Napoleonic Wars.[66]

Yet the reference to the avenue also hints at a much wider critique of improvement. The destruction of avenues was used by the picturesque theorists Uvedale Price and Richard Payne Knight as a device to criticize the landscapes of Lancelot 'Capability' Brown, and was later adopted by the anti-improvement movement more generally in its critique of both Brown and Humphry Repton.[67] Thus, for example, William Cowper censured the gentry and aristocracy for

---

61 GRO, D3549/12/2/1.

62 Prowse, 'Memoir', p. 40.

63 NRO, 364p/68, fos. 194–5; 70, 7 May 1776.

64 NRO, 364p/70, 7 May 1776. At least one tenant also bought, and later returned, one of James's American stoves (GRO, D3549/12/1/4).

65 NRO, 364p/61.

66 S. Daniels, 'The Political Iconography of Woodland in Later Georgian England', in D. Cosgrove and S. Daniels (eds), *The Iconography of Landscape* (Cambridge, 1989), pp. 43–82.

67 Ibid., pp. 62 and 65.

their bad management of estate woodlands and avenues in *The Task*, and by the time *Mansfield Park* was published in 1814, the destruction of an avenue had come to stand for all the very worst excesses of improvement.[68]

For many in the late eighteenth and early nineteenth centuries, these criticisms had a social as well as an aesthetic dimension. Robert Southey wrote of old tenants who had been 'cut down with as little remorse and as little discrimination as old timber, – and the moral scene is in consequence as lamentably injured as the landscape!'[69] Price and Knight both used trees – particularly oak and ash trees – as symbols of their paternalistic attitudes towards their tenants and the reciprocal obligations owed by landowners and the poor.[70] In Edmund Burke we see a dislike of excessive estate improvements, and a careful distinction between necessary improvements and destructive innovations which threatened the established social order.[71] This distinction was used by William Gilpin in his 1798 parable *Moral Contrasts*, which told the story of two young landowners and their contrasting attitudes to estate management and improvement. While Leigh borrows huge sums in order to drastically remodel his estate, felling woodland and engaging in huge earthmoving works 'in opposition to nature', his neighbour Willoughby carefully considers the cost and design of his improvements and carries them out slowly over seven years, employing labourers only in seasons they can be spared from the tenant farms. Leigh's tenants and steward steal from him, but Willoughby lives on easy terms with his, continuing his father's pensions and employing the tenants' children as servants. As his reward, he marries a woman whose aim in life is to be of 'service to her neighbours', while Leigh takes a spendthrift mistress with a violent temper and eventually loses both his fortune and his estate.[72]

Whilst Elizabeth was keen to rationalize and modernize the estate, she was – like Gilpin's Willoughby – also deeply concerned about the welfare of her tenants and labourers. Like many elite women, she involved herself in a range of charitable activities on her estate. The role of the landowner's wife as 'Lady Bountiful' had been established since at least the Middle Ages and typically

68 A. Duckworth, 'Mansfield Park and estate improvements: Jane Austen's grounds of being', *Nineteenth-century Fiction* 26 (1971), pp. 25–48, especially pp. 28–35; T. Fulford, 'Cowper, Wordsworth, Clare: the politics of trees', *John Clare Society J.* 14 (1995), pp. 47–59, available at http://www.johnclare.info (accessed 29 Sept. 2009).

69 Daniels, 'Political Iconography', p. 51; R. Southey, 'On the State of the Poor' (1816), in *Essays, moral and political* (London, 1832), p. 180.

70 Fulford, 'Politics of trees', online version not paginated.

71 Duckworth 'Estate improvements', p. 33.

72 Fulford, 'Politics of trees', online version not paginated; W. Gilpin, *Moral contrasts: or, the power of religion exemplified under different characters* (Lymington, 1798), pp. 29, 32.

included visits to the poor and sick as well as giving out doles of money, food and medicine.[73] Elizabeth was at times shocked by the conditions in which the less fortunate local residents lived: for example, she noted in her memoirs how the want of blankets and sheets available to the Wicken poor in the winter of 1774 was 'beyond beliefe'.[74] As a result, she spent nearly £12 on sheets and blankets for them, and her memoirs and account books provide good evidence of her involvement in a similar range of activities. Examples include providing five of her tenants with medicine after they were bitten by a rabid cat in 1776; helping one of her gardeners get sober and repay his debts; and finding apprenticeships and jobs for her coachman's seven children when he suddenly left after being discovered 'making money in what he had no right to do so'.[75] She also made small gifts of money and clothes to villagers, local children and unnamed paupers, all of which were recorded in her pocket expenses.[76] This said, the same accounts also included various presents to her servants and to her nieces and nephews, so that the line between gifts and charity – a term she does not use in this context – is not always clear.

Yet if some of this giving was irregular and ad hoc, Elizabeth was also involved in a number of philanthropic projects which aimed to improve living conditions and educational achievements amongst the poorest Wicken residents in a much more systematic way. Here Elizabeth's philanthropy was directed towards the most vulnerable on her estate. It was, moreover, clearly informed by an awareness that the social and economic costs of enclosure and estate improvement were often borne disproportionately by the poorest in society. In her memoirs, she quotes a section from Nathaniel Kent's *General View of the Agriculture of the County of Norfolk*, which draws attention to the high costs of feeding draught and coach horses compared to them, thereby demonstrating an explicit concern about the impact of agricultural improvement on them.[77] Like Kent – whom she may have met in Fulham in the winter of 1791 – Elizabeth seems to have recognized agricultural labourers as the very 'nerves and sinews' of rural society without whom 'the richest soil is not worth owning'.[78] Three brief examples will illustrate the point.

Firstly, soon after acquiring the estate Elizabeth embarked on a programme of repairs and improvements to the estate cottages. She paid for the cottages to

73 Gerard, 'Lady Bountiful', p. 186.

74 Prowse, 'Memoir', p. 49.

75 Ibid., pp. 54, 52 and 68.

76 NRO, 364p/67, fo. 75; 68, fos. 56–60; 69, fos. 65–8.

77 Prowse, 'Memoir', p. 86.

78 Kent, *Hints*, pp. 228, 230; McDonagh, 'Women, enclosure and estate improvement', p. 162, n.93.

be re-thatched and glazed, and may also have installed water pumps in some of the cottages, as she did in the tenant farms.[79] The greatest expenditure occurred in the late 1760s, reaching a peak in 1769 when more than £64 was spent on repairs.[80] This clearly represented a concerted effort on Elizabeth's part to raise living conditions amongst the estate's labourers, and by the mid-1770s much smaller annual sums were being spent on regular maintenance.[81]

Secondly, Elizabeth was paying for the cottagers' children to attend a school in the village from at least 1768. She may have founded the school and certainly contributed significant sums to the running costs: in the mid-1770s she spent more than £30 a year on the schoolmasters' wages, along with clothes and shoes for the children, which together accounted for between about a third and a half of all spending in the cottage accounts.[82] There were then at least 12 'charity boys' in attendance, as well as several girls who were taught to make lace and cloth, the sale of which both provided a return for Elizabeth and made a small contribution to the Overseer of the Poor's accounts.[83] Elizabeth was also involved in establishing an early Sunday school at Wicken, which was first held in the spring of 1788.[84] Moreover, she continued to support both the day and the Sunday schools *post-mortem* with the gift of a share in the Grand Junction Canal Company, which by the 1830s contributed about £10 a year to the running costs.[85]

Thirdly, Elizabeth was concerned to provide locally available and affordable foodstuffs to her tenants. Here she was probably influenced by Nathaniel Kent, who believed that labourers were disadvantaged by having to buy food at market rather than in small quantities and at lower prices in their home village.[86] Kent offered no solutions to the problem, but one approach was for landowners like Elizabeth to sell grain, milk and other key foodstuffs direct to local labourers. This was clearly the case at Wicken, where very little of the produce from the home farm was sold at market. Instead, most of it was used in the house or sold locally, either to the village butcher or direct to the tenant farmers and labourers. Moreover, as the account books demonstrate, Elizabeth sold meat and cheese to the poor at a subsidized price. For example in 1778, 15 cheeses made on the home farm were sold to the poor at a reduced rate of 2½*d.* per pound, rather

79 NRO, 364p/67, fos. 15–16; 68, fo. 19.

80 Ibid., fos. 15–17.

81 NRO, 364p/68, fos. 18–22.

82 Ibid.

83 *VCH Northants* V, p. 435; NRO, 364p/39; 67–9, *passim*.

84 Prowse, 'Memoir', p. 74; NRO, 364p/501.

85 NRO, 364p/48; GRO, D3549/13/2/13; *VCH Northants* V, p. 435.

86 Kent, *Hints*, pp. 263–5.

than the usual price of nearly 4*d*.[87] She sold a beef cow to the poor every winter at 2*d*. a pound and in 1783 gave them the meat for free, 'it having been a hard winter for them'.[88] She also sold firewood from the estate woodlands to the village poor, presumably again at a subsidized rate.[89] Much of this activity was focused in the winter months, when conditions were at their harshest. Importantly, this was also the season Elizabeth spent in London and it is clear that she sought to improve conditions for the poor even whilst in the capital – something unusual amongst country-house women, whose charitable hand-outs were not normally a year-round benefit to the rural poor.[90]

As well as being heavily involved in local charitable projects on her estate, Elizabeth also contributed to a number of the new subscription societies and charitable institutions which emerged in the second half of the eighteenth century.[91] For example, soon after acquiring the estate, Elizabeth and George gave £100 to the Northampton Infirmary, though they were recorded in the benefaction book as 'a Lady and Gentleman who desire their names may be concealed, paid by the Revd Mr Quartley of Wicken'.[92] That Elizabeth was mentioned before her husband may imply that she was the real donor, and we know that as a widow she continued to attend fundraising dinners and balls on behalf of the hospital, as well as contributing an annual sum of a guinea to a lying-in charity based at the Infirmary.[93] Elizabeth also subscribed to several London-based institutions, giving regular sums to the verger at St Paul's Cathedral and to the Clergy Orphan and Widow Corporation, a charity founded in 1678 for which Elizabeth's brother Granville acted as a trustee in the 1780s.[94] In 1779 she made a gift of a guinea to the Society for the Propagation of the Gospel, though her name does not appear in the various lists of ladies making annual

87 NRO, 364p/68, fos. 13, 15, 16.

88 Ibid., fos. 9, 11, 14, 94; 69, fo. 17; 70, 2 Apr. 1778, Mar. 1776, Dec. 1777; 68, fos. 11, 14.

89 NRO, 364p/66.

90 Gerard, 'Lady Bountiful', p. 192.

91 D. Andrew, *Philanthropy and Police: London Charity in the Eighteenth Century* (Princeton, 1989), especially pp. 49–57; D. W. Elliott, '"The care of the poor is her profession": Hannah More and women's philanthropic work', *Nineteenth-Century Contexts* 19 (1995), pp. 179–204.

92 NRO, Northampton General Hospital Benefactions Book, 1743–1814 (no MSS reference).

93 For subscriptions to the lying-in charity see, for example, NRO, 364p/68, fos. 58, 60; 69, fo. 67. For the balls, see Prowse, 'Memoir', p. 45.

94 NRO, 364p/67, fos. 26, 63, 129 and 133; 68, fos 56, 58, 60; 69, fo. 65; GRO, D3549/13/1/C10.

subscriptions to the charity either before or after 1779.[95] Her brother Granville first became a member of the society in 1785, and it is clear that her involvement with the charity – however brief – predated his.[96] Granville also supported numerous other metropolitan charities, including the Lambeth Refuge for the Destitute (founded in 1806) and the London Female Penitentiary (founded in 1807).[97] It seems likely Elizabeth contributed to some of these institutions, although evidence is lacking as a result of the loss of her later account books.

Both her choice of London institutions to support and her own charitable activities at Wicken were clearly informed by her deeply held religious beliefs. Elizabeth came from a staunchly Anglican family, many of whom held important ecclesiastical positions in north-east England. Her grandfather was archbishop of York, her father archdeacon of Northumberland and one of her uncles dean of Ripon. Two of her six adult brothers were Anglican clergymen, and the whole family shared a great love of devotional music.[98] Elizabeth too was a committed Anglican and at Wicken she sought to set the standard for religious observance. As well as supporting the day and Sunday schools – both of which undoubtedly aimed to train poor children to be hard-working, religious and content with their lot – she covered the cost of a monthly sacrament and had a bell fitted above the house which was rung as a signal for prayers.[99] She also attempted to stem the rise of nonconformity in the area, dismissing her dairymaid in 1801 for

---

95 NRO, 364p/69, fo. 65. For example, B. Shute, *A sermon preached before the Incorporated Society for the Propagation of the Gospel in Foreign Parts; at their anniversary meeting on Friday February 17, 1775. By Shute Lord Bishop of Landaff* (London, 1775); B. North, *A sermon preached before the Incorporated Society for the Propagation of the Gospel in Foreign Parts; at their anniversary meeting in the parish church of St. Mary-le-Bow, on Friday February 20, 1778. By Brownlow Lord Bishop of Worcester* (London, 1778); J. Thomas, *A sermon preached before the Incorporated Society for the Propagation of the Gospel in Foreign Parts; at their anniversary meeting ... on Friday February 18, 1780. By ... John Lord Bishop of Rochester* (London, 1780); J. Butler, *A sermon preached before the Incorporated Society for the Propagation of the Gospel in Foreign Parts; at their anniversary meeting in the parish church of St. Mary-le-Bow, on Friday February 20, 1784. By the Right Reverend John Lord Bishop of Oxford* (London, 1784).

96 B. Lewis, *A sermon preached before the Incorporated society for the propagation of the gospel in foreign parts; at their anniversary meeting in the parish church of St. Mary-le-Bow, on Friday February 19, 1790. By the Right Reverend Lewis Lord Bishop of Norwich* (London, 1790), p. 72.

97 GRO, D354913/1/D17.

98 Prowse, 'Memoir', pp. 2–3; B. Crosby, *Private Concerts on Land and Water: The Musical Activities of the Sharp Family, c.1750–c.1790* (Royal Musical Association Research Chronicle 34, 2002).

99 NRO, 364p/67 fo. 56; 68, fo. 208; 69, fo. 188; GRO, D3549/12/1/4. For more on the function of Sunday schools, see Gerard, 'Lady Bountiful', pp. 196–7; T. W. Laqueur, *Religion and Respectability: Sunday Schools and Working Class Culture, 1780–1850* (New Haven, 1976), pp. 6–7.

attending Methodist meetings at nearby Deanshanger and for encouraging the youth of the village to accompany her.[100]

The church at Wicken had itself been rebuilt in the late 1750s and 1760s. This was a project in which Elizabeth played a significant part. The building work was started by her father-in-law in 1753, and was one of the few examples in Northamptonshire of a church wholly rebuilt at the same time as a parish's open fields were enclosed.[101] Only the seventeenth-century tower was left untouched: the rest of the church was rebuilt from the foundations up entirely at Thomas Prowse's cost. Prowse was an amateur architect who also worked on buildings in Wiltshire, Somerset and Norfolk, and who drew up his own designs for the late thirteenth-century style nave and Perpendicular-period chancel.[102] The latter included an elaborate plaster fan vault probably modelled on the late medieval examples at Gloucester Cathedral and Bath Abbey, both in the vicinity of the Prowse family homes at Berkeley (Gloucestershire) and Axbridge (Somerset).

The church was unfinished at Prowse's death in 1767 and Elizabeth took control of the project along with the estate. She oversaw the installation of the new pews, altar furniture and paving in 1770, meeting with John Sanderson at Wicken in April and July in order to direct his work on the church interior. She also personally supervised the workmen as they dug a new drain around the church so 'that no offence should happen respecting the graves'.[103] The church was finished by October 1770, when Elizabeth's mother-in-law met the final costs of the project.[104] At the same time, Elizabeth donated a Bible, three prayer books, an altar cloth, fabric for cushions and a new salver, and also paid to clean the plate, at a total cost of more than £25.[105] She later paid for one of James's stoves to be installed in the church's north chapel, which was probably the space used for the Sunday school.[106]

As well as being staunch Anglicans, the Sharp family were both political radicals and committed philanthropists. Elizabeth referred to her brother James in her memoirs as a 'bill of rights man', whilst her youngest brother Granville

---

100 Prowse, 'Memoir', p. 98; *VCH Northants* V, p. 237.

101 NRO, 364p/28; *VCH Northants* V, p. 433; M. Cragoe, 'Landscape, Enclosure and Popular Culture in Northamptonshire, *c.*1750–1850', paper delivered at the Institute of Historical Research, 10 Mar. 2009.

102 H. Colvin, *A Biographical Dictionary of British Architects, 1600–1840* (New Haven, 2008), pp. 837–8. Prowse was also involved with drawing up plans for the Shire Hall in Warwick in 1754 (Warwickshire RO, CR125/34–6; CR125a/3).

103 NRO, 364p/30 and Prowse, 'Memoir', pp. 32, 34, 36.

104 Ibid., p. 36; NRO, 364p/30.

105 NRO, 346p/67, fo. 32.

106 NRO, 364p/69, fos. 194–6, 200.

was one of the founding members of the Society for the Abolition of the Slave Trade.[107] He was involved in a number of key legal battles concerned with the rights of slaves and their owners, including the court case following the Zong massacre.[108] Granville also campaigned for colonial rights in America, Ireland and later India – as well as drawing attention to national complacency about a range of injustices within the empire, including British settlers' actions in West Florida and the land grab initiated by British speculators in St Vincent.[109] Both James and another brother, William, were involved with Granville in the campaign against the slave trade, and Elizabeth closely followed their activities and successes.[110] Like them, she was aware of and concerned about events in the British Caribbean: thus, for example, she gave £7 to the 'sufferers at Jamaica and St Dominion' in 1781, presumably in response to the hurricanes which hit the islands in October 1780 and August 1781.[111] She also read many of Granville's pamphlets, noting their publication dates in her memoirs and eventually constructing a library at Wicken to house her brother's books.[112]

Yet if the Sharp family's involvement in the campaign against slavery arguably influenced both her world view and attitude towards the poor, the converse was also true: Elizabeth's experience caring for the poor at Wicken impacted on her brothers' attitudes and concerns. Despite suggestions to the contrary by several scholars, Granville was certainly not unconcerned with the plight of the poor in Britain.[113] He prepared a defence of gleaning as 'a clear right of the poor', using legal and religious proofs to support his argument as well as corresponding on a wide range of social issues, including food prices, imprisonment for debt and pressing.[114] He was also involved in various schemes to support the poor independently of parish assistances, and on his own small estate at Fairstead (Essex) Granville established a charity which let one-acre plots to labourers in

---

107 Prowse, 'Memoir', p. 37; *ODNB*, 'Sharp, Granville (1735–1813)'.

108 A. Rupprecht, '"A very uncommon case": representations of the Zong and the British campaign to abolish the slave trade', *J. Legal History* 28 (2007), pp. 329–46.

109 C. L. Brown, *Moral Capital: The Foundations of British Abolitionism* (Chapel Hill, 2006), pp. 161–2 and 170.

110 See, for example, Prowse, 'Memoir', p. 21 where Elizabeth recorded the date and circumstances of Granville's first meeting with the slave William Strong, and p. 38 where she noted his involvement in a trial to free another escaped slave.

111 NRO, 364p/69, fo. 67; M. Mulcahy, *Hurricanes and Society in the British Greater Caribbean, 1624–1783* (Baltimore, 2006), p. 198.

112 Prowse, 'Memoir', pp. 87; for her notes on the publication dates, see pp. 21, 40 and 71.

113 Brown, *Moral Capital*, p. 179 argues that Sharp did not associate the anti-slavery movement with philanthropy, whilst Ditchfield in *ODNB* argues that Sharp 'was more concerned with constitutional issues than with the social grievances of the poor in Britain'.

114 GRO, D3549/13/1/L14.

order that they could keep a cow or pig, and put the money from their rents towards schooling poor children.[115] Nathaniel Kent advocated a similar scheme in both his 1775 *Hints* and a pamphlet of 1797, and given Elizabeth's known interest in Kent it seems likely it was her who brought these texts to Granville's attention.[116] She certainly took an interest in the Essex estate, writing various memoranda about it in the notebooks which were later used to construct her memoirs.[117] Moreover, Granville's interest in the scheme post-dated Elizabeth's involvement in similar charitable projects on her estate by more than a quarter of a century, and it is tempting to suggest that her experience at Wicken fed into and helped shape his involvement in the cottage land project at Fairstead.

IV

As a widow, Elizabeth Prowse managed the estate at Wicken for more than four decades between her husband's death in 1767 and her own in 1810. Her ledgers and notebooks provide good evidence for her careful supervision of the estate finances. Importantly, Elizabeth herself kept the ledgers and personally audited her senior servants' accounts, rather than relying on an estate steward.[118] Together with her memoirs and other family papers, the ledgers also chart the broad range of agricultural innovations and social improvements she introduced to the Wicken property. In addition to extending the house and landscaping the gardens, park and estate woodlands, Elizabeth invested heavily in the newly enclosed estate. Much of the hedging and subdivision of the new allotments was achieved by her, and within months of her husband's death she had converted the existing annual tenancies to longer-term leases, presumably in the attempt to encourage her tenants to invest in improvements such as drainage and marling. She improved old pastures and extended arable cultivation on the home farm, where she also experimented with new feeds for the dairy cattle and new agricultural implements, some of which were later adopted by the local tenant farmers.

At the same time, Elizabeth was deeply concerned about the welfare of her tenants and clearly sought to combine agricultural modernization with material improvements to the living conditions amongst the poorest Wicken residents.

115 GRO, D3549/13/1/D17, L15 and S8.

116 Horn, 'Nathaniel Kent', p. 7.

117 Prowse, 'Memoir', p. 73.

118 D. Andrew, 'Noblesse Oblige: Female Charity in an Age of Sentiment', in J. Brewer and S. Staves (eds), *Early Modern Conceptions of Property* (London, 1995), pp. 275–300 notes that it was also usual for women to have secretaries to write letters.

Thus she paid for repairs and enhancements to both the farms and the labourers' cottages; sold foodstuffs and firewood to the poor at a subsidized rate; and invested large amounts of time and money in the local day school, Sunday school and village church. She was also aware of the destructive aspects of improvement – whether it was trees or the poor who suffered – and occasionally expressed herself in ways which verged on anti-improvement sentiments. It was perhaps as a result of this ambivalence about improvement that Elizabeth involved herself so deeply in charitable concerns. Her activities certainly reworked and extended the traditional role of landowners' wives as Lady Bountiful, not least because she financed her charitable activities from the profits of the estate rather than redistributing her 'pin money' as charitable gifts of food and medicine or relying on male relatives for the funds to invest in schools, hospitals and other charitable institutions.[119] Moreover, rather than being wholly personal and local – as Gerard has argued was the case for most country-house women – Elizabeth's philanthropy mingled charitable giving on her estate with subscriptions to societies based in Northampton, London and even overseas.[120]

As a corollary to this, the chapter has explored how propertied women accessed ideas about estate management and landscape improvement. In Elizabeth's case, we know she read widely, taking newspapers and buying the latest publications by leading agricultural improvers like Kent and Young. In these, she found support for many of the improvements she had put in place at Wicken as well as detailed information about developments on improving estates in East Anglia and elsewhere.[121] She also visited a number of newly landscaped and improved properties both in the Midlands and further afield, particularly during the northern tour she made with her brothers and sisters in 1785. That she showed a great interest in what had been achieved on these and other estates is evidenced by the notes she made on her mother-in-law's dairy herd at Berkeley. In other words, Elizabeth herself played a key role in bringing new ideas to Wicken, whilst her stewards – mostly local men who lived on the estate – probably played a more subsidiary role in the circulation of ideas, knowledge and expertise than was the case for properties managed by professional land agents.[122]

---

119 Elliott, 'Women's philanthropic work', p. 195; Gerard, 'Lady Bountiful', p. 191.

120 Ibid., pp. 184–5.

121 Kent, for example, detailed the drainage techniques in use in Essex and elsewhere, whilst Young included a lengthy discussion of Arbuthnot's experiments with mould-board shape and plough designs – something in which Elizabeth's brother James was also no doubt interested (Kent, *Hints*, pp. 19–24; A. Young, *The farmer's tour through the east of England* (4 vols, London, 1771), vol. 2, pp. 251–560).

122 Webster, 'Land agents', pp. 61–2.

Yet Elizabeth's improving contemporaries were certainly not the only influence on her attitude towards estate management and agricultural improvement, as the example of her charity work demonstrates. Instead her upbringing, her religious convictions and her brothers' ongoing political and social activities – including Granville's involvement in the anti-slavery campaign – provide an important context in which to understand her philanthropic activities at Wicken. At the same time, Elizabeth's brothers also provided her with more practical assistance on the estate. James helped her manage the accounts in the first year of her widowhood and later ordered books such as Young's *Tours* for her in London. Granville also sourced books for his sister, as well as occasionally undertaking tasks which might otherwise have been carried out by a solicitor or land agent.[123] Importantly, it was through James that Elizabeth accessed the latest domestic technology and agricultural machinery, including the coal-powered stoves used in the house and church, the rolling carts and carriages and probably also the trenching ploughs and horse shovels with which the drains were cut and anthills cleared. At the same time, James utilized the estate as a site to experiment with new agricultural technology, and here and elsewhere we see how Elizabeth's experience at Wicken fed into her brothers' activities, interests and successes. Crucially, Elizabeth was the only one of the Sharp children to control a sizeable landed property, and her life interest in Wicken provided her extended family with a range of opportunities they would not otherwise have had.

How representative was Elizabeth Prowse of other female landowners? Certain aspects of Elizabeth's story undoubtedly render her unusual amongst her contemporaries; not least that so much archival material relating to her survives today. We might also point to her relatively modest social background and her continued involvement in her brothers' business and professional interests, as well as to the fact that the Sharp family were probably far more radical in political terms than most middling provincial landowners. Nevertheless, there were also commonalities between Elizabeth's experience managing Wicken and those of the other propertied women managing Northamptonshire estates discussed briefly in the introduction.[124] Clearly elite women did not universally retire into the domestic sphere in the later eighteenth century, but rather made significant contributions to the myriad agricultural changes – and the accompanying discourses of improvement – which transformed the Midland landscape in the century after 1750.

---

[123] NRO, 346p/67, fo. 32. For example, Elizabeth paid Granville for checking information in the ecclesiastical registers at Peterborough and Lincoln in 1782 (69, fo. 195).

[124] For a more detailed discussion of other Northamptonshire women, see McDonagh 'Women, enclosure and estate improvement', pp. 149–52 and 156–7.

Chapter 10

Improvement on the Grant Estates in Strathspey in the Later Eighteenth Century: Theory, Practice, and Failure?

Alasdair Ross

> There is hardly that country to be nam'd in the world, where there is no room for improvement by industry and application. [...] Labour makes gain, and gain gives strength to labour.[1]

The sheer volume of literature published on the interlinked themes of enlightenment and improvement in Scotland post-1700 is quite forbidding. A number of authors have tackled different aspects of these phenomena, ranging from the written theory to the physical accomplishments in terms of designed landscapes, through to the social effects of these momentous changes.[2] Agricultural improvements, particularly those occurring during the eighteenth century, have also been discussed; yet few authors have paused to draw breath and question whether they were always positive in their outcome. Nor have they asked what social and economic costs were incurred both by an estate and its tenants whenever such improvements failed.

Failure, of course, is a subjective term and there were probably as many different degrees of failure as there were different reasons for failure, all dependent upon which perspective is chosen. This chapter will focus on a particularly stark example of agricultural improvement on the Grant estates in Strathspey after 1762 and discuss the theories that underpinned the improvement, the reactions of the tenantry to the changes and the scale of the social and economic costs involved. To all intents and purposes, the mass conversion of traditional shieling sites and their accompanying 'waste' into tenant-occupied farms with enclosed

---

1 Daniel Defoe, *A plan of the English commerce being a compleat prospect of the trade of this nation as well the home trade as the foreign* (2nd edn, 1730, repr. New York, 1967), pp. 33–5.

2 N. T. Phillipson and Rosalind Mitchison (eds), *Scotland in the Age of Improvement* (Edinburgh, 1970); T. M. Devine (ed.), *Improvement and Enlightenment* (Edinburgh, 1989); Charles W. J. Withers and Paul Wood (eds), *Science and Medicine in the Scottish Enlightenment* (East Linton, 2002).

field systems which took place here was the application of a model of planned improvement that had been successfully applied elsewhere. It could have worked in Strathspey, to the benefit of both estate and tenantry in the longer term, but unfortunately for both parties there were significant associated factors outwith the direct control of the estate that forced the landowner to alter his original plans, and which eventually resulted in huge social and economic costs.

I

At the end of the seventeenth century the core of the traditional Grant family estates in Strathspey was centred on Freuchie. The estate consisted of the four parishes of Cromdale, Abernethy, Inverallan and Duthil, with many outlying estates like Glen Urquhurt on Loch Ness. The Grants had first gained control of the core of these lands by marrying a local heiress before the 1430s and had thereafter gradually added to their property through small grants from the Scottish crown, particularly during the reign of King James VI and I, and from the Earls of Huntly and Moray.

The surviving evidence suggests that the pre-1762 economy of these Grant estates was largely focused on the profits to be made from transhumance, whereby shielings and their associated hill grazings were heavily utilized by tenants to fatten different animals at different times of the year. Importantly, these hill and mountain pastures could also be rented out to customers who normally either had no access to such an important resource or who needed to purchase extra grazing resources. Market forces seem to have decided whether and how much high grazing was rented out to customers at any one time. The best surviving evidence relating to this latter practice comes from the extensive Forest of Strathavon, which bordered on the Grants' Strathspey estates. There, between 800 and 1,200 horses, oxen and cattle (no sheep or goats) were grazed by different Lowland tenants each year between March and October, each having travelled between 20 and 70 miles with their herds to reach the high shielings of Strathavon amidst the Cairngorm mountains.[3] There is no evidence relating to this type and scale of transhumance after the 1760s, and the disappearance of this from the sources neatly coincides with the 'improvement' of most shielings into permanent farms by the Grant family.

By the eighteenth century, however, the Grants seem to have resided in Strathspey for no more than two months during the course of a year, preferring to

[3] GD 44/51/354/1–4.

live in London.[4] Like other estates with largely absentee lords, their estates were run by factors and chamberlains. One of the most important and influential of these in relation to the theory and practice of agricultural improvement was William Lorimer from Banffshire in north-east Scotland.

William Lorimer was born at Dytach (near Cullen) in 1717. His father, also called William, was factor for the Findlater and Seafield Ogilvie estates in Banffshire and his uncle John was clerk to the Regality of Cullen. Yet another brother, Patrick, was a factor on the Ogilvie estates.[5] William Lorimer graduated in the arts from Marischal College, Aberdeen, in 1737 and taught for the next 10 years at Deskford before his appointment as tutor to the future Sir James Grant (1738–1811), son of Sir Ludovick Grant (1707–73), in 1747.[6] His appointment ended in February 1756 when Grant officially began his studies at Cambridge and, shortly afterwards, Lorimer sailed to America, arriving there on 24 April 1758 before travelling onwards to Albany on the Hudson River in New York province.[7] Part of the reason for his journey was to deliver letters to Lieutenant-Colonel Francis Grant, Sir Ludovick's brother, who was serving as second-in-command of the 42nd Foot.[8] Lorimer stayed in America for less than two years and was back in Britain by February 1760.[9] There is every reason to believe that he continued to write to his former tutee during their period of separation (and *vice-versa*). Lorimer never relinquished his position as chief adviser before his death in January 1765.[10]

As a tutor to the future head of the Grant family, Lorimer occupied a unique position of influence. He seems to have provided much of the driving force behind the improvement of all the shielings on the Grant estates after 1762, when Sir Ludovick retired to Edinburgh and handed control of the family estates over to his son.[11] It is clear from Lorimer's surviving letters that he was

---

4 GD 248/49/2/16.

5 GD 502/1/8/1.

6 *Oxford Dictionary of National Biography* (*ODNB*), Grant, Sir James, of Grant (1738–1811). His mother was Margaret Ogilvie, daughter of the second Earl of Seafield. Peter John Anderson, *Fasti Academiae Mariscallanae Aberdonensis* (3 vols, Aberdeen, 1898), vol. 2, p. 309; George Dixon, 'William Lorimer on forestry in the central Highlands in the early 1760s', *Scottish Forestry* 29 (1975), pp. 191–210, GD 502/1/12.

7 GD 248/177/1/46.

8 Between 1756 and 1758 Francis had been writing increasingly irate letters home to his brother Sir Ludovick about the lack of personal contact between the two men, the last of which was sent from Fort Edward on 16 June 1758 as he was preparing to march to engage the French, GD 248/44/7/2/81.

9 GD 248/461/2/1. This letter is addressed to him in 'Angleterre'.

10 GD 248/177/1/93; Dixon, 'Lorimer', p. 192.

11 Ibid., 191.

both well read and well travelled. As a result, it is difficult to pinpoint the exact source of his ideas about improvement, although there were probably two main influences. First, there was what he had either heard about or personally seen on other British estates. Second, there was what he had witnessed on estates near the American frontier along the Hudson River and elsewhere. Given his education, it is also likely that Lorimer had read widely on the subject of improvement, though it is impossible to prove this from the surviving documents. James Grant's own enthusiasm for far-reaching agricultural improvement on his estates should not be overlooked, though this too may be a result of Lorimer's influence as tutor.

The earliest record relating to Lorimer researching improvement is found in one of Grant's commonplace day books. In this, he notes that whilst he and Lorimer were travelling south to Cambridge during 1755, they stopped off to examine the 'Norfolk Method' of farming. There, according to Grant, he learned how the farmers mixed marl, sand and soil to improve their fields, the benefits of turnips, new dunging regimes, the division of land into arable, grass and fallow and the benefits of using seaweed as manure. In the same passage Grant also refers to the improvements made by Lords Deskford and Findlater on their Banffshire estates, and how they sent young men to John Cockburn's Ormistoun estate and to other similar estates in southern Scotland to be educated in land improvement.[12] Presumably, given his family connections to these Banffshire estates, Lorimer would have been familiar with these developments. At this time Grant also read a number of books about improvement theory and was particularly impressed by the works of two authors, Tull and Hale.[13]

According to Lorimer's surviving correspondence, on his return to Britain in 1760 he began to write to improving landlords and visit improving estates, presumably on the instructions of James Grant. For example, both he and his tutee corresponded with Lord Kames, the famous Scottish advocate, judge, agricultural author and improver.[14] Kames was very impressed with Grant and obviously approved of the latter's plans for improvement:

> I could not wish my own son to show himself in a more advantageous light than you do in this letter. To find a young man newly imported from the splendour and dissipation of foreign courts, applying himself with ardour and even without

---

12 GD 248/472/8, p. 17. Also see James Colville (ed.), *Letters of John Cockburn of Ormistoun to his Gardener, 1727–44* (Edinburgh, 1904).

13 The exact titles were not specified but were probably editions of Jethro Tull, *The horse-hoeing husbandry* (London, 1733) and Thomas Hale, *A compleat body of husbandry* (London, 1756).

14 *ODNB*, Home, Henry, Lord Kames (1696–1782).

> drawing breath, to the improvement of his country and to make his people happy, is a rare example of good sense as well of benevolence. Puplick [sic] spirited men do not over-abound among us and the early marks you give of that spirit makes me fondly hope you will be a blissing to your country. [...] In dedicating some share of your time for the good of your country you cannot propose to yourself a better example than your uncle Lord Deskford who for publick spirit has justly acquired the esteem of all good men [...].[15]

In some instances Lorimer did not have very far to travel to visit improved estates. In his letters he specifically refers to the improvements initiated by Lord Elchies above Rothes in Lower Strathspey in 1725. These seem to have involved the conversion of some hill ground below 250m into arable, which allowed Elchies to increase his estate rental by £100 sterling per annum.[16] In turn, Elchies would have had access to a good role model: Sir Archibald Grant of Monymusk (1696–1778). Archibald Grant began improving his Monymusk estate in 1718–19 and his achievements were both well known and much discussed.[17] He certainly dispensed advice on improvement matters to several members of the Grants of Strathspey during his lifetime, particularly in relation to the maintenance of high population levels, and he also wrote a book about how to overcome the obstacles to improvement.[18]

The attention shown by both Lorimer and James Grant to the theory and practice of improvement should not, however, be regarded as unusual in Scottish terms. Grant of Monymusk was only one of a number of Scots who demonstrated an early interest in improvement. For example, a diary belonging to William Baird of Auchmedden, written between 1714 and 1756, refers both to seventeenth-century English literature on improvement and to the practice of improvement in such far-flung places as Flanders, Venice, Amsterdam, Caithness, Andalucia, New England, Carolina, Virginia, Mexico, Peru and India. There is

---

15 GD 248/49/2/8.

16 GD 248/37/4/3, p. 163. Unfortunately, due to the cumulative effects of two fires it appears impossible to verify Lorimer's statement from the Elchies muniments as no pre-1790 papers now seem to survive.

17 Henry Hamilton (ed.), *Selections from the Monymusk Papers, 1713–55* (Edinburgh, 1945), p. xlv; Hamilton, *Life and Labour on an Aberdeenshire Estate, 1735–1750, Being Selections from the Monymusk Papers* (Aberdeen, 1946).

18 GD 248/49/2/56; Sir Archibald Grant, *A dissertation on the chief obstacles to the improvement of land, and introducing better methods of agriculture throughout Scotland* (Aberdeen, 1760).

no indication that Baird had personally visited any of these places so it appears that he must have been an avid reader on the subject in an international context.[19]

With such a high degree of interest about improvement among Scots, it comes as no surprise to find that Elchies was not alone among the Strathspey Grants in experimenting with improvement on their estates before Lorimer returned from America in 1760. In fact, it is clear from Lorimer's letters that Sir Ludovick had granted a few improving tacks on his estates as early as 1735.[20] On the whole, these seem to have consisted of granting favourable 14- to 19-year leases to single tenants of small stretches of moorland 'waste' (and very occasionally shielings) which they were to convert into enclosed arable. The terms of the 19-year rentals were generally fixed at £2 per year for the first seven years, then £15 per annum for the next seven and £20 for the final five.[21] The difference between the pre- and post-1762 improvements on the Grant estates, however, was one of scale and planning.

During 1762 Lorimer visited estates further afield in Scotland that were going through the process of improvement or gathered information about them from third parties. That year he referred in his letters both to the successes of the Laird of Macleod – who had raised his rents by £800 per annum, but whose tenants continued to live in 'great ease' – and to Sir James MacDonald on Skye, who had just had his estate surveyed and was intending to raise his rental by over £1,000 per annum.[22] Lorimer was also intimately acquainted with the improvements that had been initiated by the Gordon family, particularly those in the lordship of Lochaber which had ended 'cattle raiding, idleness and inapplication' by encouraging the industry of cultivation.[23] These, however, were not the first occasions on which Lorimer had encountered ideas about social engineering in relation to improvement.

It seems clear both from his letters and diaries that Lorimer had read some of the works of Daniel Defoe, particularly *A plan of the English commerce: being a compleat prospect of the trade of the nation, as well the home trade as the foreign* (1728). In this book Defoe advocated the retention of people on estates (encouraging them to procreate), together with the improvement of waste grounds. The relevant passage is worth quoting at length:

---

19 National Library of Scotland, MS. Adv. 31.4.12. See also, T. M. Devine, *The Transformation of Rural Scotland* (Edinburgh, 1994), pp. 29–30, for further examples.

20 GD 248/84/3. This improvement was located in the *dabhach* of Delnabo in the lordship of Strathavon. The Grants held this *dabhach* as tenants of the Gordon family.

21 GD 248/250/2; 431/6; 500/1.

22 GD 248/49/2.

23 GD 248/37/4/3, p. 2.

> This keeping of the people together, is indeed the sum of the whole matter, for as they are kept together, they multiply together; and the numbers, which by the way is the wealth and strength of the nation, increase. As the numbers of people increase, the consumption of provisions increases; as the consumption increases, the rate or value will rise at market; and as the rate of provisions rises, the rents of land rise: so the gentlemen are with the first to feel the benefit of trade, by the addition to their estates. As the consumption of provisions increase, more lands are cultivated; waste grounds are inclosed, woods are grubb'd up, forests and common lands are till'd, and Improv'd; by this farmers are brought together, more farm-houses and cottages are built, and more trades are called upon to supply the necessary demands of husbandry: In a word, as land is employ'd, the people increase of course, and thus trade sets all the wheels of Improvement in motion. [...] I once saw a calculation of trade for the planting a new town on the south part of England, where, for the encouragement of people to come & settle, the Lords [...] agreed to give a certain quantity of lands to fifty farmers. To every such farmer, they allotted two hundred acres of good land, rent-free for twenty years [...] Here are fifty farmers, who with their servants make up three hundred and fifty people in all, but necessarily draw one thousand people more to them. Thus people make trade, trade builds towns and cities, and produces every thing that is good and great in a Nation.[24]

Many of these ideas appear in Lorimer's letters of advice to James Grant:

> Now if Sir Ludovick Grant has within these seven or eight years settled some 200 tenants on new grounds, thence in the space of 20 years will in all probability have produced to him not under 1000 people, who will cultivate more land and enable him to spare 1[00]–200 men for the army and navy, besides increasing his rent-roll by £2[00]–300 [per] annum so that an improver of new grounds in this way is one of the greatest patriots of the Kingdom. Numbers of people are the strength of a country.[25]

---

[24] Defoe, *Plan of the English commerce*, pp. 18–27. The editor of a recent edition of this work commented: 'Although it is logical to assume that Defoe was more than familiar with seventeenth-century economic theory, we cannot certainly pin down how closely he had studied and been influenced by the specific works of the more prominent English thinkers of the period.' John McVeagh (ed.), *Political and Economic Writings of Daniel Defoe* (8 vols, London, 2000), vol. 7, *Trade*, p. 17.

[25] GD 248/37/4/3/172.

> [...] the Master will have more rents and more tenants, and an increase in tenants will give opportunity to form a town and raise manufacture.[26]

Lorimer may also have encountered the practical application of some of these ideas along the frontier in America. Defoe had strongly advocated the settlement and improvement of America, which he portrayed as a new Eden, 'abounding in fish, fowl, flesh, wanting nothing but to be inhabited by Christians, and ally'd to the rest of the Christian world by commerce and navigation'.[27] Once Lorimer began travelling around New York province it is clear that he was impressed by the agricultural improvements he saw, particularly those undertaken and completed by Palatine colonists. The Palatines were a relatively large group of mostly Protestant settlers from the Rhineland. Initially offered freedom from religious persecution by Queen Anne, they travelled to England in increasing numbers in 1709. Defoe championed their cause and he devised various schemes to settle them in little colonies, though these plans were not implemented. Instead, a number of Palatines were shipped to Ireland as the lord lieutenant there, Lord Wharton, saw advantage in planting communities of Protestants among Roman Catholics. The government shipped an even greater number to America, where the English authorities intended to employ them in making pitch and felling timber for the navy on lands along the Hudson River, before they were eventually scattered throughout New York province and Pennsylvania.[28]

Judging by his approving comments, it seems likely that Lorimer had visited and seen the accomplishments of the Palatines in improving the American wilderness. For example, in a letter written at Tay Bridge dated 21 September 1761, Lorimer complained to James Grant, wishing 'that I could get a thousand persecuted Palatines to settle on your estate [Strathspey] — how rich it would make them and you too!'[29]

While he was in New York province, Lorimer must also have heard about a controversy concerning the size of private estates. Many colonial bureaucrats complained about the size of land grants, accusing the proprietors of deliberately keeping the province underpopulated by their refusal to create smallholdings that might attract potential colonists. Effectively, blame was placed on the

---

26 GD 248/38/1/20.

27 Defoe, *Plan of the English commerce*, pp. 366–8.

28 H. T. Dickinson, 'The poor Palatines and the parties', *English Historical Rev.* 82 (1967), pp. 464–85. The landscaping and improving achievements of the Palatines were also greatly admired by Anne Grant of Laggan. Mrs Anne Grant, *Memoirs of an American Lady with Sketches of Manners and Scenes in America as They Existed Previous to the Revolution* (2 vols, New York, 1901), vol. 1, pp. 191–3.

29 GD 248/49/2.

proprietors for the slow population growth within the province. Successive governors also seem to have complained that New York province was being drained of settlers by this selfishness and that the proprietors were obstructing improvement.[30] It has been argued, with good cause, that this was a biased viewpoint as the refusal to create smallholdings deprived the colonial officials of potential sources of revenue.[31]

In fact, it has also been shown that some of the great proprietors who possessed estates along the Hudson River between New York and Albany did believe that the settlement of land with numerous tenants was a good idea, as it would eventually boost the commercial value of their estate through an increasing supply of farm produce. To attract sufficient farmers to improve and exploit the great estates, the owners needed to offer smallholding leases at competitive rates. Incentives included an initial rent-free period of up to 10 years and the provision of basic farming implements, building materials and, occasionally, houses for the new tenants. As it has been demonstrated, the land improvements initiated by these estates were closely linked to the development of commercial activities.[32]

In this instance it is difficult to establish whether Lorimer either blindly followed colonial administrators in condemning the perceived lack of smallholdings or had instead visited some of the great estates which were trying to attract colonists to aid in the improving process. What is clear is that once he returned to Britain, Lorimer constantly nagged James Grant about the undesirability of a policy of farm enlargement as it led to depopulation. Lorimer referred to the economic successes occasioned by rapid population growth in America and argued that an estate in Scotland should also have numerous small tenants.[33] He had an ally in Sir Archibald Grant of Monymusk, who wholeheartedly agreed with these sentiments.[34]

It is also possible that colonial ideology underpinned the Strathspey exercise in improvement. Canny has shown that the arguments the English used to justify the colonization of Ireland were later employed to justify similar policies in North America. A succession of authors made comparisons between the lifestyles of the Irish Gaels and the Native Americans, and regarded both as pagans. In addition, since the native Irish Gaels practised transhumance, it was possible for the English settlers to compare them to the barbaric Tartars and

30 Sung Bok Kim, 'A new look at the great landlords of eighteenth-century New York', *William and Mary Q.*, 3rd ser., 27 (1970), pp. 581–82.

31 Ibid., p. 584.

32 Ibid., pp. 599–607.

33 GD 248/37/4/3/172; 38/1/20; 471/7.

34 GD 248/49/2/56.

Scythians, both of whom also wandered through the wilderness driving their flocks before them.[35] To the English colonists in America, 'such a vast and empty chaos was free for the taking because it was always lawful to take a land which none useth, and make use of it'.[36]

It is clear that Lorimer was familiar with some of these English colonial writings (or had seen them in practice) and was influenced by them. For example, he frequently compared the inhabitants of the Grant estates in Strathspey (together with all other Highlanders) to both the Native Americans and to Africans, both of whom were 'uncivilised peoples'.[37] Not content with this comparison he also described his master's tenants in the following uncompromising terms:

> Highlanders resembled the Scythians and Tartars in eating blood; they [the men] regard labour of any kind as the work of slaves in which they resemble the Germans, according to Tacitus.[38]

Such attitudes are virtually identical to colonial opinions about the native peoples of America.[39] Finally, it is also clear from his letters that Lorimer believed that the practice of transhumance encouraged barbaric thievery and idleness.[40]

These views may seem excessive given that Lorimer was born and brought up in an area less than 40 miles from Strathspey. There is, however, probably a subtext here as many men in Strathspey, including some from the Grant estates, had fought for the Jacobite cause during 1745–46.[41] Lorimer himself was clearly no lover of Jacobitism and frequently referred to the post-1746 governmental legislation that abolished heritable jurisdictions as the 'civilising acts'.[42] It may be that both Lorimer and James Grant calculated that attracting hundreds of non-Highland settlers into the Grant estates and encouraging them to both

---

35 Nicholas P. Canny, 'The ideology of English colonization: from Ireland to America', *William and Mary Q.*, 3rd ser., 30 (1973), pp. 575–98, at p. 587.

36 James Axtell, *The Invasion Within: The Contest of Culture in Colonial North America* (Oxford, 1985), p. 137.

37 GD 248/37/4/3, p. 3. Similar opinions regarding the Highlanders were also held in Scotland until *c.*1670 when Scottish antiquarians began to seriously question such views: Michael Lynch, 'A Nation Born Again? Scottish Identity in the Sixteenth And Seventeenth Centuries', in D. Broun, R. J. Finlay and Michael Lynch (eds), *Image and Identity: The Making and Re-Making Of Scotland through the Ages* (Edinburgh, 1998), pp. 82–104 at p. 93.

38 GD 248/37/4/3, p. 13.

39 Axtell, *Invasion Within*, pp. 152–3.

40 GD 248/37/4/3, p. 2.

41 Rev. Walter Macleod (ed.), *A list of persons concerned in the Rebellion* (Edinburgh, 1890), pp. 108–13.

42 GD 248/37/4/3, p. 8.

improve the land and breed successive generations of loyal patriotic settlers would dilute any lingering Jacobite sentiment across large areas of Moray.

II

Given Lorimer's attitudes to both Highlanders and transhumance, together with his influence over James Grant, it does not require a great deal of effort to predict the foci of improvement on the Grant estates after he returned from America in 1760. The surveying of shielings and their associated 'waste' was under way by early 1762 and all suitable areas for improvement were marked out. The first areas chosen to be improved were the core Strathspey parishes of the Grant estates: Abernethy, Duthil, Cromdale and Inverallan. Of these, Cromdale was the clear focus of the first wave of mass improvement, with 60 separate conversions of either shielings or 'waste' into arable in 1763. Inverallan parish had 21 improvements, Abernethy parish 19 and Duthil parish just two.[43] This initial disparity in the numbers of improvements between parishes may have occurred because Ballindalloch Castle and its demesne lands were located in Cromdale parish and James Grant and Lorimer were coincidentally landscaping its immediate environs. Many trees were planted around this time to screen off sections of unattractive landscape, such as peat bogs; and some of the watercourses around Ballindalloch were altered and straightened to improve the view from the castle.[44] In 1762 the Grant lands in Urquhart on the north side of Loch Ness were also surveyed so that all the shielings there might also be improved and enclosed.[45]

It seems these 1762 surveys had been carefully timed so the rearrangement of the landscape coincided with the granting of many new tacks on Whitsunday 1763. At that time, accumulated arrears on the Strathspey estate amounted to just over 20 per cent of the annual rental.[46] Lorimer later admitted that the estate carefully worded the new tacks of established tenancies so there was no specific mention of either grassings or shielings. This freed up large numbers of existing pendicles for improvement and enclosure.[47] It appears that some of the existing estate tenants did not notice until after they took possession of a tack that they no longer had access to these pendicles.[48] Of course, by this time

43 GD 248/242/3.

44 GD 248/1542.

45 GD 248/38/1/19.

46 GD 248/36/2/10.

47 GD 502/1/12/9.

48 GD 248/52/3/26.

it was too late for them to back out of their new tacks without penalty; and it seems obvious that the estate had taken advantage of the way in which tacks were awarded (tenants sent bids to the factor, often on the assumption that the tack would be unchanged) to hoodwink their existing tenants. In any event, it did not take long for the tenants to begin complaining to the estate about the new arrangements, though the estate brushed aside their concerns:

> I don't wonder that the present tenants complain of the improvements of the hills – this a new thing to them – they have not so much room for pasture – there present ideas are confined to feeding cattle – But in a few years when they are obliged to till more ground & to till it better – less ground will maintain their cattle – they could not use the whole bounds of their old commons and hills and therefore many of them were quite useless – Hereafter every part will be improved for corn or pasture and one acre in corn is worth more than 20 in pasture. Necessity will make them apply to the raising of corn and by degrees they'll find the advantages of it profitably to pasture & do it of choice. Hence it is probable the tenant will not be hurt … .[49]

These new 'improving' tacks all seem to have been for 19 years and most specified that all improvements had to be enclosed within three years and ploughed within nine years, under pain of forfeiture.[50]

Only a small minority of the new improving tacks of the 1760s mention houses and those that do all refer to traditionally built structures of faill (turf) and wood. By the early 1790s, however, the tacks specified that both old houses and faill dykes were to be replaced by new structures of stone and lime.[51] A few of the new tenants on the improvements were not required to pay rent for the first three years. Others just paid a couple of hens over the same period before a money rent was required.[52] In the majority of cases, however, the rent seems to have been set at £3 Scots for three years, £6 Scots for the next three, £9 Scots for the following three and £12 Scots for the final 10, in addition to two hens yearly. It is possible that these variations in rent among the new tacks can be explained by the estate taking account of the quality of the ground that was about to be improved. Alternatively, new palaeo-environmental evidence indicates that a little cereal cropping had been occurring at some shieling sites in parts of Strathspey since *c.*1650 and it may be that the higher initial rents in some of

---

49 GD 248/38/1/20.

50 GD 248/38/1/27.

51 GD 248/1020.

52 GD 248/38/1/12.

the new improving tacks took account of the fact that ground had already been tilled.[53]

Some of the pre-existing tenants attempted to circumvent the new economic realities by purchasing leases of their old shielings and grassings and running them as absentee landlords. The estate retaliated by both stipulating and reiterating that all improvers must reside on their new farm and that nobody was permitted to pasture *gall* (stranger) cattle in summer.[54] At this time, in 1763, the estate also chose to reintroduce the old customs and services, like carriage and harvest attached to each *dabhach*, which had been commuted into cash some 30 years before. At first there seems to be no obvious reason why this might be to the advantage of the estate other than that many of the new farmers had previously been either cottars or tradesmen – people who perhaps traditionally would not have been considered for tenancies with written leases – and may not have had any substantial cash reserves. It should be noted, however, that exactly this type of rental that mixed 'in kind' and cash payments over a fixed period had proved successful on the improving estates in New York province, and Lorimer may have decided to reintroduce this type of payment in Strathspey on the basis of what he had seen in America.

In any event, it looks as though the mass conversion of shielings and 'waste' into farms in Strathspey was staggered during the years immediately following 1762 because some of the pre-existing tenants appear to have thought that they still possessed a legal right to hill grazing as late as 1770.[55] By that time, however, these tenants were experiencing great difficulty in getting their livestock to pasture because the enclosed arable associated with the new farms invariably cut right across the traditional access routes to the upland grazings. Consequently, when attempts were made to either cross or circumvent the new enclosures, livestock belonging to the existing tenants were poinded (seized) by the new tenants and the herders assaulted.[56] These actions by the new tenants resulted in the widespread sabotage of the new enclosures by unnamed parties,

---

53 This research, conducted in Abernethy parish, was undertaken by my colleague, Dr Althea Lynn Davies, and has not yet been published. Her palaeo-ecological research in Glen Affric (A. L. Davies, 'Fine spatial resolution Holocene vegetation and land-use history in West Glen Affric and Kintail, Northern Scotland' (unpublished PhD thesis, University of Stirling, 1999)) strongly indicates the growing of cereal crops at shieling sites long before 1700. Victor Gaffney, *The Lordship of Strathavon* (Aberdeen, 1960), p. 29 also refers to pre-1700 cropping at shielings in the lordship of Strathavon, which bordered on Abernethy parish.

54 GD 248/38/1/27.

55 GD 248/44/4/5.

56 Ibid; GD 248/431/6; 523/1.

usually under cover of darkness.[57] It is interesting to note that it was neither Sir James Grant nor his factor who were directly targeted. Instead, it was the new improving tenants who both took the blame and bore the brunt of these clandestine Luddite activities for some 30 years.

It is impossible, however, to evaluate these mass improvements of shielings and 'waste' in isolation because they occurred just three years before the planned village of Grantown-on-Spey was laid out in 1766. In fact, the idea of erecting a planned village in Strathspey also seems to have been first mooted by Lorimer in 1763: '[...] the Master will have more rent and more tenants and an increase of tenants will give opportunity to form a town and raise manufacture'.[58] T. C. Smout has classified these new eighteenth-century villages into four main categories: agricultural villages, fishing villages, villages with small rural industry and, finally, the factory village. He argued that Grantown-on-Spey fell within the third group, villages with rural industry.[59] It is impossible to pin down where Lorimer got the idea for building Grantown-on-Spey. While he could have visited earlier examples of planned villages in Scotland, he could also have read about the theory of planting new towns in the work of Defoe or even seen the theory in practice along the Hudson River in America.[60] It may even be that all three sources and examples in some way contributed to Lorimer's decision to convince James Grant to establish Grantown-on-Spey. In any event, the creation of new villages was also a policy of the Commissioners of the Forfeited Estates after 1746 who wanted to use planned villages as a way of introducing Highlanders (and Jacobites) to industriousness and civilization.[61]

Perhaps the greatest puzzle in the creation of Grantown and all of these new permanently settled farms is what the estate intended to do with all the new cereal crops at a time when there was a consistent upward trend in the prices of wheat, bere and oats in Scotland, reflecting relative shortages in provision.[62] While the Grant family at that time owned significant amounts of property in burghs and towns the length of Britain, there seems to be no evidence of them trading in cereal in those same urban conurbations, even though there was an established trade in Grant-owned timber between Strathspey and London, via either Garmouth or Findhorn; and it is known that Grant brought in cheap grain

---

57 GD 248/44/4/15.

58 GD 248/38/1/20.

59 T. C. Smout, 'The Landowner and the Planned Village', in Phillipson and Mitchison (eds), *Scotland in the Age of Improvement*, pp. 89–95.

60 Defoe, *Plan of the English commerce*, p. 20; Sung Bok Kim, 'Great landlords', p. 602.

61 Smout, 'Planned Village', p. 79.

62 A. J. S. Gibson and T. C. Smout, *Prices, Food and Wages in Scotland, 1550–1780* (Cambridge, 1995), pp. 179–81.

from Maldon in Essex for his tenants through Findhorn in 1801–03.[63] Indeed, a plan by Sir James Grant to establish a corn and meal market in Inverness was only raised after 1796.[64] More tellingly, perhaps, there is also no indication in the records of any pressing need to improve the local road infrastructure to allow the efficient transportation of large amounts of grain to ports along the coast of Moray.

All of this would indicate that the two men were looking at local markets for all their grain. Perhaps they regarded the inhabitants of the new town of Grantown, together with other similar planned new towns in the Spey valley, as the primary consumers of all these new cereal crops. However, Lorimer and Grant never expressly state this in their personal correspondence; nor do they ever refer to the mass conversion of shielings into cereal-producing farms as a local solution to alleviate high grain prices. Instead, they might have expected their new tenants to sell their own cereal crops locally and been content to reap the anticipated rewards of the high prices that these crops would fetch in the form of higher rents.

All of these improvements add up to social, economic and landscape engineering on a massive scale. There can be no doubt, even with the benefit of hindsight, that James Grant was taking a huge risk in the reorganization of his Strathspey estates as much of his income depended on his tenants' ability to engage with and make a profit from the traditional cattle and droving trade. If their profit margins declined, so did their ability to pay rent on time and clear existing arrears. To begin with, the evidence indicates that many of the inhabitants of Strathspey who had not previously rented land (cottars and craftsmen), together with subtenants and anyone else without a lease, enthusiastically adopted the new economic and social polity. In fact, by the late 1760s they had seized the initiative and began to write letters to the estate to suggest further suitable areas of 'waste' that they considered ripe for improvement.[65] An additional economic and social effect from this phase of improvement was the increased demand for farm servants. With so much new land coming into cultivation, together with the associated building and dyking, there must have been at least a temporary shortage of labour; and it comes as no surprise to find complaints about increasingly high servant wages in the Grant muniments from the late-1760s onwards.[66]

Following this Strathspey 'land-rush', there are even some indications that the estate temporarily lost either track or control of the process of improvement.

63 GD248/168/3; 452/12.

64 GD248/85/1.

65 GD 248/523/1.

66 GD 248/27/4; 508/2/30. My thanks to Dr Andrew MacKillop for this latter reference.

During the period 1765–75 there are a number of letters of complaint from improving tenants asking the estate to send out birlaymen to perambulate and re-fix the boundaries of their new possessions. This was because their neighbours, who were also improving tenants, were encroaching upon, stealing and enclosing their newly improved lands and pasture.[67] There are also a small number of cases where the improving tenants cleared the ground, enclosed it and planted it, only to find that their new possession had previously been a pendicle belonging to a township whose tenants wanted their land back, probably because it was still named in their tack.[68]

III

The biggest gamble taken by Grant and Lorimer was their decision to interrupt the local cattle trade in favour of arable production. By granting so much of the 'waste' and virtually all shielings to improving tenants, they effectively destroyed a major part of the local economy because sitting tenants were now either completely unable, or found it increasingly difficult, to practise the transhumance which was central to pasturing livestock. Clearly, both men were willing to take this chance and, as we saw, they regarded one acre of improved ground as more valuable than 20 acres of 'waste'.[69]

Their tenants were certainly not convinced and many complained that the loss of their traditional grassings and shielings had resulted in financial hardship. Three such men were John Grant in Aird of Dalvey, David Stewart in Bellennalen and George Grant in Achinernach whose shielings had been granted as an improvement to John Murray, a weaver, between 1762 and 1766. Having lost their shielings, Stewart and the two Grants had been forced to send their cattle outwith Strathspey for summer grazing at considerable expense. These years saw the tenants trying to adjust to the new economic realities rather than giving up their traditional economy or moving on or emigrating to America. Essentially, all they wanted were their traditional shielings returned to them, for which they were prepared to pay extra money.[70] The evidence indicates that the estate refused all such requests and that the pace of improvement gathered momentum to at least *c.*1767.

It seems likely that Lorimer's death encouraged a degree of rethinking. There was a realization that the wholesale rapid improvement of shielings and

---

67 GD 248/523/1.

68 GD 248/431/6.

69 GD 248/38/1/20.

70 GD 248/431/6; 44/4/4 and /8; 533/3/100.

'waste' had been a mistake and the estate began to re-convert selected improved farms back into common grazing and evict their new sitting tenants.[71] This did not happen quickly (it was still continuing in 1803); nor were all of the new improvements converted back into pasture. In fact, there is a sense that the estate entered into the re-conversion process reluctantly and only did so under pressure from an irate, and increasingly desperate, tenantry. Indeed, it is likely that, having invested a lot of time and money in promoting improvement in the first instance, the estate was unwilling (or indeed financially unable) to re-convert all of the improved ground. Accordingly, it settled on trying to compromise between the needs of transhumance and improvement. One plus was that they did not have to compensate the sitting tenants who were evicted from their newly improved possessions as there was no clause regarding compensation in the improving leases of the 1760s. This relatively quick re-conversion of improved farms back to pasture would indicate that the increased costs experienced by the tenantry in relation to buying pasture outwith Strathspey for their cattle, together with increasing rentals and high servant wages, had a knock-on effect on estate finances, probably either through late or non-payment of rent.

As if the threat of eviction were not bad enough, many of the improving tenants had to cope with jealous neighbours who openly coveted the remaining newly improved farms for themselves.[72] To make matters even worse, there is evidence that in the early 1770s the estate began to subdivide these new farms, and there are a number of petitions from angry tenants complaining that their new possessions would be worthless if this occurred and asking for their leases to be terminated.[73] Clearly, by this time the hunger for land may have outstripped the remaining available resources. Upon being forced to re-convert at least some improvements back to pasture post-1766, it is likely that subdivision of the new improvements was the only possible response that the estate could have made to satisfy the demand for land. That said, it also seems that Grant moved away from the advice he had received from Lorimer in the 1760s and the consolidation of small farms was well under way by the 1790s.[74] Before the turn of the century, James Grant had clearly come to believe that large amalgamated farms were a superior form of improvement in comparison to smallholdings.

---

71 GD 248/431/6; 533/3/19; 366/15455/7. These re-conversions of improvement back to pasture were not confined to the upland Grant estates. They also occurred on their Lowland estates in the Laich of Moray and in Banffshire.

72 GD 248/533/3/19; 452/14.

73 GD 248/44/4/4/8. The subdivision of improvements can also be traced through the rentals, for example GD 248/1891.

74 Sir John Sinclair (ed.), *The statistical account of Scotland* (21 vols, Edinburgh, 1791–99), vol. 8, p. 255.

This development cannot be dated precisely so it is difficult to even speculate about what persuaded Grant to reverse estate policy.

In spite of all these complaints, there is every chance that the improvement of shielings and waste, together with the foundation of Grantown-on-Spey and its associated industries, could eventually have been a success story for the Grant estate. One factor they could not control, however, was the weather.

During the course of the eighteenth century, adverse but unspecified weather conditions had decimated the rent roll of the Grant estates in Strathspey on a number of occasions. For example, it is clear that during the years 1702–12 the estate was experiencing severe financial difficulties: rests (rent deferrals) were accumulating at the rate of over £2,000 Scots per annum and by 1710 the estate was forced to give rent reductions of £3,500 Scots from a total Strathspey rental of *c.*£14,000 Scots. To put this in context, one of the largest annual arrears accrued by the estate during the so-called 'seven ill years' of the 1690s was in the region of £790 Scots.[75] The difficulties experienced by the Grant estate between 1702 and 1712 were shared by other parts of Scotland, and a virtually identical picture of financial woe can be found on the Buccleuch estates in the Borders where we know it was caused by repeated flooding. These sums, however, were minuscule in comparison to the extent of the family debts by the 1780s, which amounted to £123,438 Scots in total. The Strathspey estate alone was responsible for over 41 per cent of that total debt.[76] Unfortunately, it now appears impossible to determine exactly what percentage of this total debt was incurred by the improvements of the 1760s and the accompanying disruption of the cattle trade, and what proportion was due to bad weather.

It is well known that parts of Britain experienced poor weather conditions during the years 1782–84, partly resulting from the sulphuric dust clouds ejected into the atmosphere by volcanic eruptions in Iceland. Scotland was no exception and the mean temperature in 1782 seems to have been 12 per cent below normal.[77] Unfortunately, no contemporary local historical source directly links the poor weather experienced in Strathspey post-1782 to the volcanic eruption in Iceland. Accordingly, care should be taken not to assume that this eruption was wholly responsible for the climatic downturn in Strathspey at that time, particularly since the estate had previously suffered from extreme weather

---

[75] GD 248/108/16; 113/7. It was claimed that the crops in Moray were unaffected by 'seven bad years' due to the nature of the soil: GD 248/472/8, p. 11.

[76] GD 248/657/1.

[77] I. G. Simmons, *An Environmental History of Great Britain from 10,000 Years Ago to the Present* (Edinburgh, 2001), p. 121.

events earlier in the century.[78] In any event, a variety of local sources, including the *Statistical Account*, give some indication of the seriousness of the problems, stating that severe frosts began in August 1782 and destroyed almost all crops.[79] Although Sir William Fraser rather blandly noted that the Strathspey factors had trouble collecting rent in the 1780s,[80] the primary unpublished sources can add much more detail. In 1787, for example, a Grant tenant in occupation of a Strathspey improvement asked to give up his tenancy because 'as the seasons are now so greatly altered and cold it [his crops] do not yield seed'.[81] This body of written evidence clearly suggests that climate change had become a major factor in estate indebtedness.

Of course, it might be objected that the latter petition could be construed as a cynical attempt to procure a reduced rental for the tenant in question. This was not the case. In Strathspey the increasingly desperate tenant petitions of the 1780s were the result of cumulative bad weather patterns that had begun back in the early 1770s when both flash and more prolonged flooding were major problems for at least four years. For example, tacksmen in the lordship of Strathavon, which bordered on Abernethy, wrote about the time of the 'great flood' of the 1770s that had entirely carried away three oxgates (perhaps as much as 78 acres) of arable land and the entire pasture of the *dabhach* of Delnabo.[82] In Strathspey itself a number of tenants were fined for cutting turf from high pasture for their buildings as the place where they regularly sourced this material had been 'under water for some time'. In Duthil parish the tenants who possessed lands along the Dulnain River complained that a flood in 1772 had carried away much of both the arable land and the trees, and that another two years of frequent spates had covered the remainder with sand and gravel. In fact, the inhabitants of Cromdale and Abernethy parishes made numerous identical complaints in relation to spates and flooding after 1772, as their 'arable lands and manure were carried off down the Spey'.[83] Although some remedial work

78 M. G. L. Baillie, 'Suck-in and smear: Two related chronological problems for the 90s', *J. Theoretical Archaeology* 2 (1991), pp. 12–16; Lisa Dumayne, Rob Stoneman, Keith Barker and Doug Harkness, 'Problems associated with correlating calibrated radiocarbon-dated pollen diagrams with historical events', *Holocene* 5 (1995), pp. 118–23; Althea L. Davies, 'Upland Agriculture and environmental risk: a new model of upland land-use based on high spatial-resolution palynological data from West Affric, NW Scotland', *J. Archaeological Science* 34 (2007), pp. 2053–63.

79 Sinclair (ed.), *Statistical account*, vol. 4, pp. 315.

80 W. Fraser, *The chiefs of Grant* (3 vols. Edinburgh, 1883), vol. 3, p. 449.

81 GD 248/245/7.

82 GD 248/523/1.

83 Ibid.

was undertaken to strengthen the banks of various rivers that ran into the Spey, it is clear that some of these, like the River Nethy in the parish of Abernethy, completely changed their courses during this period of prolonged flooding.[84] Previous research has demonstrated that Sir James Grant had lowered the rentals of his Strathspey estate by as much as 85 per cent by 1775, and the reason for this has been traditionally sought in a collapse in cattle prices in Scotland during 1772–73.[85] It seems likely, however, that within Strathspey severe flooding, together with the associated damage to arable land and wooded floodplains, not to mention loss of livestock, were also significant factors in rent reductions at this time.

IV

In contrast to the earlier part of the century, by the 1780s estate policy towards annually increasing debt had hardened. The mass removal of tenants in arrears was contemplated for Whitsunday 1785. This deadline passed without action and it is clear that the estate had anticipated an improvement in the situation, for all tenants charged to remove were allowed an additional two months to clear their arrears, in addition to a proportion of the costs the estate had incurred in obtaining the decreet of removal in the first instance.[86] The net result was that although a few tenants were cleared off the estate at this time, many must have managed to collect enough cash to either cancel or pay off most of their arrears, although a few unfortunates simply had their livestock confiscated and sold by the estate.[87] Unfortunately, this only proved to be a temporary solution and, although the estate had reduced its overall debt burden to £113,693 in the early 1790s, by that time it had also lost patience with tenants in arrears and initiated a policy of mass clearance.

The Strathspey evictions of the 1790s and onwards were planned well in advance: for example, 19-year leases that fell due for renewal on Whitsunday

84 GD 248/506/1. According to the available evidence, the floods of the 1770s seem to have caused more damage in Strathspey than the 'great' flood of 1829. GD 248/3392/2; William Forsyth, *In the Shadow of Cairngorm: Chronicles of the United Parishes of Abernethy and Kincardine* (new edn, Lynwilg, 1999), ch. 30.

85 Andrew MacKillop, 'Highland estate change and tenant emigration', in T. M. Devine and J. R. Young (eds), *Eighteenth-Century Scotland: New Perspectives* (East Linton, 1999), pp. 237–58, at p. 251; T. M. Devine, *Clanship to Crofters' War: The Social Transformation of the Scottish Highlands* (Manchester, 1994), p. 35.

86 GD 248/533/1/1.

87 GD 248/458/2.

1792 were renewed, but only for one year.[88] Rental surveys were also conducted during 1790 and 1791 to see who deserved to retain their tacks and the opportunity used by many to get rid of troublesome tenants or neighbours. There was resistance to these processes: for example, officers (presumably sheriff's officers) were deforced by Captain John Grant of Lurg in Abernethy in 1791.[89] Such protests were to no avail. In 1793 the Grant estate obtained decreets of removal against hundreds of its tenants, some of whom owed as much as 12 years' back-rent.[90] These mass removals were evenly spread across all of the parishes that formed part of the Strathspey estate and continued virtually every year until 1809. (Evictions continued after this date but not in such large numbers.) All of the legal work associated with these evictions over the 19-year period was undertaken by the procurator-fiscal for Moray, Thomas Sellar. For part of the time he was aided by his son Patrick, whose name is associated with the later Sutherland clearances.[91]

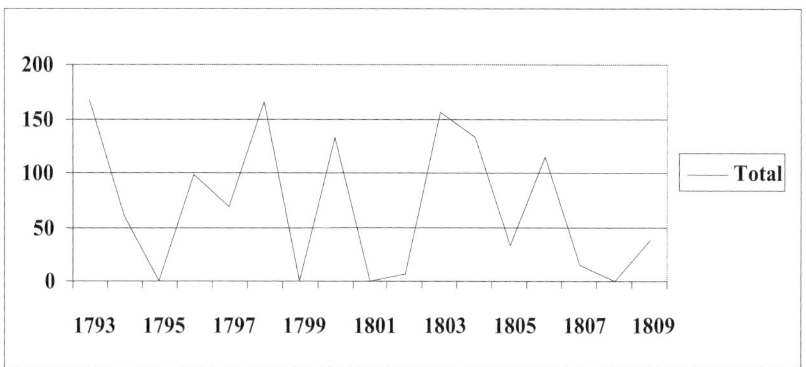

Figure 10.1 Approximate numbers of tenant evictions in Strathspey, 1793–1809

[88] GD 248/371/6.

[89] GD 248/456/18. To deforce is to resist with force an officer of the law when carrying out his duty.

[90] GD 248/533/5/37. By an Act of Sederunt of 1756 any heritor was allowed to remove a tenant who had not paid rent for two years. Though only one person was named in the order, it applied to everyone who lived on the holding. For more detail see T. M. Devine, *The Great Highland Famine* (Edinburgh, 1988), p. 156.

[91] Eric Richards, *Patrick Sellar and the Highland Clearances: Homicide, Eviction and the Price of Progress* (Edinburgh, 1999).

The exact number of people cleared off the Grant Strathspey estates between 1790 and 1810 will probably never be known as only the tenants were directly named in the eviction orders (see Figure 10.1).[92] There is no way of telling how many of these people were married, how many successfully challenged the orders or how many subtenants, cottars and servants were caught up in the evictions. Nor were the Strathspey evictions only confined to farmers: many of the inhabitants of Grantown-on-Spey were also ordered to remove during this period. Little is known about what happened to those cleared, although the population of some north-east parishes that contained substantial towns like Huntly or Mortlach increased by over 50 per cent during the same period of time.[93] Possibly some of those cleared from Strathspey ended up in such places. It is probable that the evictions also interfered with Sir James Grant's intention of recruiting a fencible regiment from Strathspey: the composition of his first battalion, raised in 1793, shows that just over 25 per cent of the men came from the Grant estates.[94]

What is noticeable, however, is that while a number of the older townships and farms remained unaffected by removal during the period of these evictions, virtually every one of the remaining 1760s improvements was cleared, some more than once. If those that were reconverted back into pasture are also taken into account, it means that almost all of the improvements created on the Grant Strathspey estates between 1762 and 1766 had, in some sense, failed before the turn of the century – either as a result of direct intervention or because they were not economically viable during prolonged periods of bad weather and climatic change.

In terms of general Highland history, these mass evictions seem to contradict the norm. The period over which they occurred, the Napoleonic Wars, was one of general British economic growth that saw massive price rises in large numbers of basic commodities. At this time, the majority of Highland estates seem to have done everything in their power to retain their tenantry, and many of these tenants were happy to bet their economic future on continuing rises in the prices of beef, mutton and wool.[95] Clearly, Sir James Grant and his factors

---

92 These figures should be regarded as the minimum numbers of people targeted for eviction because the data sets are not complete. For example, the figures for Cromdale parish evictions in 1794 are missing, as are those for Abernethy parish in 1805.

93 David Turnock, 'Stages of agricultural improvement in the uplands of Scotland's Grampian region', *J. Historical Geography* 3 (1977), pp. 327–47.

94 Andrew MacKillop, *'More Fruitful than the Soil': Army, Empire and the Scottish Highlands, 1715–1815* (East Linton, 2000), p. 115.

95 T. M. Devine, 'Landlordism and Highland Emigration', in Devine (ed.), *Scottish Emigration and Scottish Society* (Edinburgh, 1992), pp. 84–103; Bruce P. Lenman, 'From the

may have been acting out of desperation. The suspicion is that two factors forced them to evict tenants rather than try to retain them. The first of these was the continuing burden of debt owed by the Grant estate, a proportion of which was now owed to banks rather than to family members or friends. The second factor must have been the sheer scale of the arrears due by the existing tenants after the cyclical extreme weather events between 1770 and 1785. Although there is no proof of this, it is possible the estate simply decided that the existing tenants would never be able repay their debts due to lack of capital. Accordingly, the decision was taken to replace the majority of them with new tenants who did possess capital reserves.

As far as the future economic success of the estates was concerned, this appears to have been the right choice. It meant that not all of the Strathspey improvements failed completely since some of them carried on as farms with new tenants until the last few decades of the nineteenth century, when a proportion were either converted into deer forest or turned over to game shooting.[96] This somewhat limited 'success story', however, depends upon how failure is defined. In this instance, the initial re-conversion of many of the new arable improvements back into pasture after 1766, together with the eviction of the sitting tenants in most of the remainder between 1790 and 1809, is hardly typical of the perceived economic and social successes of improvement, but perhaps more typical than we realize.

Union of 1707 to the Franchise Reform of 1832', in R. A. Houston and W. W. J. Knox (eds), *The New Penguin History of Scotland* (London, 2001), pp. 285–93.

[96] GD 248/3363.

Index